WHAT YOU'LL LOSE
IF YOU DON'T OWN THIS BOOK:

The next time you want something from someone, will you get it? Or will you get nothing because you haven't mastered the techniques in this book?

"But I'm not selling anything."

If that's what you believe, that's why you aren't getting your way more often—why you aren't persuading more people to accept your opinion. That's why your advice isn't sought more often—why your influence doesn't reach further and cut deeper.

The truth is, you're constantly trying to sell quite a number of ideas, beliefs, and goals, aren't you? You want your point of view to win more often with members of your family, with friends, associates, and neighbors, and with the world in general, don't you? Are you pleased with how well you're doing all this? Would you like to improve your performance at the gentle, satisfying, and profitable art of selling?

Maybe you don't like the word *sell*. Let's say persuade and dissuade— better yet, talk into and talk out of. You also need to motivate, instruct, encourage, and reassure people from time to time. And you want to achieve your goals so that you can get what you want from life.

You care intensely about—what? A special person, your family, your religion? A political, social, or environmental cause? You're heavily involved with life in many ways; you have concerns, interests, problems, and opportunities galore—so many, in fact, that you have to ration your time, money, and energy among them. Have you ever considered what an enormous waste of time failure is? When there aren't enough hours in our days to savor all the successes we're capable of achieving, why should we give so much time to preventable failure? So much failure is avoidable when we know how. Preventing failure—any kind of failure in personal, business, or public life—starts with understanding *why I don't do what I know I should do,* which is the title of chapter 5.

But it isn't failure that hurts us most—*fear* of failure does the greatest damage. Failure is in the past; fear of failure can destroy our future. That's why this book puts so much emphasis on methods that beat down our fear of failure, on methods that banish our fear of rejection. Use this book to learn how to waste less of your time on failure and fear. When you're doing that, you'll automatically enjoy life more.

Every technique in this book has proven its value on the firing line of sales work. Almost every one of them can add new dimensions of effectiveness and excitement to your private life. They work when you work; they work when you play; they work when you cope with life. Use them to help make more good things and fewer bad things happen. Use them to oil the rough spots around the house; squire them in where your friendships are squeaking.

Every successful person is good at selling himself or herself. What does this mean? That successful people are successful because they sell their ideas, beliefs, and aims better than unsuccessful people do. Showing you how to do that is the business of this book.

Look over the contents a couple of pages further along; check the how-to's in the index at the back. Then decide. Can you afford to face tomorrow without all the aids this book gives you?

If you want more attention paid to your needs,
If you want to achieve more in your personal life,
If you want to enjoy people more,
If you want to have more impact on your community,
If you want to influence your family more,
If you want more people to value your ideals and beliefs,
If you want to sell more of your products and services,
If you want to make more money,

Take this book home with you tonight.

How to Master the Art of
SELLING

by TOM HOPKINS

SECOND EDITION

Edited by Warren Jamison

WARNER BOOKS

A Warner Communications Company

A Warner Communications Company

Printed in the United States of America
First Warner printing: October 1982
10 9 8 7 6 5 4 3 2

Library of Congress Cataloging in Publication Data

Hopkins, Tom.
   How to master the art of selling.

   Reprint. Originally published: Scottsdale, Ariz.:
Champion Press, c1980.
   Includes index.
   1. Selling. I. Title.
[HF5438.25.H66 1982]   658.8'5   82-7040
ISBN 0-446-37494-6 (U.S.A.)   AACR2
ISBN 0-446-37495-4 (Canada)

ACKNOWLEDGMENTS

This volume exists because thousands of the people who attended my sales seminars went on to become Champions of Selling. Their success after learning this material has convinced me that it should be published in book form.

Hundreds of people have contributed to my knowledge of selling. I'll be able to single out only a few here but my gratitude goes to them all. Tom G. Murphy has been my closest friend and counselor. The Edwards family, Doug, Jerry, and their son Jay, have been an unfailing source of encouragement and support. Danielle Kennedy, herself one of the nation's great sales trainers, proved to me that any price is worth paying to make your dreams come true. I am indebted to Art Mortell for much of the basis for chapters 5 and 6.

And for countless well-dones, my thanks go to every member of my staff. Their energy, competence, and loyalty have made our company's growth and this book possible.

CONTENTS

Contents

FOR MAXIMUM RESULTS
FROM THIS BOOK,
PLEASE READ

This book is written to make money for you. I encourage you to do more than just read this book. Take notes, use a hi-liter pen to mark the book in any manner you see fit or anything else that makes this book a more effective tool for increasing your income.

AUDIO TAPES

It is imperative that you try as rapidly as possible to get my techniques into your subconscious mind so they become part of you and come out automatically in your own words. In today's hectic world many of us don't have the time to read as often as we would like. Because of this many of the top salespeople we train absorb the material easier by listening to audio cassettes while doing other activities. If you have a time problem, I heartily suggest you consider using our audio training program, "How to Master the Art of Selling Anything." It's available from your local distributor or from our home office in Scottsdale, Arizona.

These tapes are the sound track to our video tape training program which we produced at a cost of over a quarter of a million dollars. This cassette tape album consists of twelve one-hour tapes along with a workbook. All of these topics are covered:

1. The Profession Called Selling
2. What is a Champion?
3. Control with Questions
4. Minor Reflexive Questions
5. Emotions, the Triggers of Selling
6. How to Handle Failure and Rejection I
7. How to Handle Failure and Rejection II
8. Referral Prospecting
9. Non-referral Prospecting
10. Telephone Techniques
11. Pre-planning your Sales Presentation
12. Contact
13. Qualification
14. The Visual Aid Presentation
15. Presentation Demonstration Tactics
16. Objections—Premise
17. Objections—Solution
18. Test Closing
19. Anatomy of a Close
20. Power Closes of a Champion I
21. Power Closes of a Champion II
22. Turning Little $ into BIG $
23. Time Planning Organization
24. Goal-setting

MOTIVE

My primary concern in telling you about these tapes is your success. I know personally how lonely and frustrating the life of a salesperson can be. When I started, I was as much a failure as anyone until I was able to get the proper training to insure my success. At that time, I swore if ever I could share my success with others, I would do it with high quality and at a price that anyone could afford. You may feel that I am trying to sell you something and that is true. We are in the business of selling just like you. However, if you know something is good, you have an obligation to offer it to your customer. You will make a small investment for these tapes and that constitutes one sale for us. However, it may mean hundreds of sales in your career and thousands of dollars for you and your family. In this way, I hope that my company can play some part in your continued success. Thank you,

Tom Hopkins

INTRODUCTION

James Buchanan Brady could borrow millions on the strength of his name. Before he was thirty, he was creating a legend. Brady hobnobbed with the leading industrialists and financiers of the day. Lillian Russell, the most glamorous actress of the Gay Nineties, was his great friend and frequent companion.

You know this man by his trademark. Diamond Jim walked around wearing more wealth than most banks held in their vaults. His cuff links, watch, cane, and every finger glittered with diamonds.

Why am I telling you about this man? Because Diamond Jim Brady was a salesman. He made more money selling railroad equipment than he could get rid of as Broadway's biggest spender. Brady was a super pro.

Selling itself goes far back beyond that. We now know that stone age men traveled great distances to trade for goods they couldn't get where they hunted and gathered food. There's reason to believe that barter is older than war, that we're all descended from peaceful traders—salespeople, because barter requires salesmanship—rather than from violent marauders who lived on plunder.

The next development in selling was the open air marketplace. But before history dawned, the exposed marketplace was obsolete. Merchants were moving inside and selling from permanent stores. Wandering traders were now carrying less merchandise on their backs and more on animals and ships. Then development stopped except for details, and this ancient system for distributing goods came over to the New World.

In the early 1800's, a revolutionary development took place and selling as we now know it was born. It happened very quietly. The owners of a small woolen mill in Massachusetts decided they wanted more business than the traders were giving them. With New England directness, they went straight to the heart of the matter. They hired a man to take their samples to shops in distant places and get orders for future delivery. This seems painfully obvious now, but it was a startling innovation in those days. It took intelligence to conceive that idea, courage to try it, and persistence to make it work. And work it did. Within a few years, the new system had spread to other mills and other industries, and the distribution of goods has never been the same.

During this period the first railroads were being built. The new way of getting around suited the new way of selling perfectly. Traveling salesmen with their bulky sample cases became a familiar sight wherever the rails ran.

But they weren't called salesmen yet. Everyone called them drummers after the old time peddlers who beat drums to attract an audience as they drove their wagons into small country towns.

The man who was to become the first super pro of sales was born in 1844. John H. Patterson was still a young man when the railroads connected our two coasts, but by that time his career had already been meteoric. Patterson created the first national sales force. He was the first man to organize sales training, the first man to have a fully organized sales staff with regional and district managers throughout the nation. He set the first sales quotas. And he was the first to guarantee exclusive territory to his salesmen. Before Patterson, many companies pitted two salesmen against each other in the same territory, and let them fight it out selling the same products to the same customers. This practice died out after Patterson revealed its folly.

In 1895, a young man joined Patterson's company. This man, Thomas J. Watson, was destined to become another super pro of sales. After working his way up to become one of Patterson's top assistants, they parted ways. Watson went on to become the driving force behind one of the most dynamic companies the world has ever seen.

Watson's finest contribution to the profession of selling was his concept that no one should ever be out of training. This is a very profound idea. You don't have to go to school today to continue your training, to keep on learning. There are books, cassettes, lectures, seminars, magazines, videotapes—the list of training and learning sources goes on and on. If you stop training and learning, you start sinking. Nobody can float: you're either rising or sinking. It's been this way for a thousand years. The only difference is that you can rise, or you'll sink, a whole lot faster now.

The next super pro was H. W. Dubiski. When he arrived in this country right after the turn of the century, Dubiski had just turned fourteen and he couldn't speak English. Four years later he was a chalk boy posting prices in the New York Stock Exchange. Only three years after that modest beginning, he opened his own securities firm. More than any other man except Watson, Dubiski understood the opportunities that Patterson had discovered. Feeding off Patterson's concepts of selling, Dubiski perfected mass training. He perfected the prepared sales talk. He perfected the inspirational sales meeting in an age when it worked. And he developed the original philosophy that securities could be sold during one call. Dubiski was the master of staging what we used to call — well, never mind what we called it—the Shot in the Enthusiasm meeting. Every morning his salesmen (they were all men in those days) got together for a session of chanting, cheering, and singing that, in a commercial way, had almost the fervor of a religious revival meeting. Nobody got a sales management job in that firm unless he could give the men a motivational shot every morning and lead them through the company songs and cheers. After Dubiski's salesmen were pumped up to the bursting point with enthusiasm and determination, the managers would turn them loose on an innocent world. Barely a dozen years after he reached this country, Dubiski sold out and retired with five million dollars in government bonds. In 1914 that was an awful lot of money to have earned by the ripe old age of twenty-six.

Twenty years later, I started looking for work. I went into sales because, in the bottom of the great depression, sales work was the only kind available. My first job was with a traveling sales crew. The system was easy to understand. If you didn't sell that day, you didn't eat that day. I mean that literally. We sold personal stationery to school teachers and secretaries. They were making about four dollars a week and our stationery was $3.75. That was a tough sell. We closed because it was the only way we could survive.

We were gypsies then. When we found something better, we changed. You name it, I've sold it. After the Second World War, I became the sales manager of an aircraft distributor. We sold 3,000 planes in one year, a record that's never been approached by anyone else. Then the bottom fell out of the aircraft business. Demand for airplanes vanished. The industry augered itself into the bottom of the earth.

I went into the information business with a very bright outfit that was advising business on taxes and regulation. I almost walked away from it when they wanted me to learn their canned sales talk. Fortunately, the man hit the right note with me. He asked if I knew everything I needed to know about sales and I had sense enough to admit that I didn't. So I got involved for the first time with a formal sales presentation in a situation that forced me to learn how to sell. In three months I was a marketing executive with that firm, and then I met the man who was to become my mentor. Bob Barber was a sales genius, a super pro, and I owe my foundation in the profession of selling to him.

Later, Barber, myself, and some other people formed a company to market the first magnetic wire dictation machine. That venture was very successful, and we soon sold out for a nice figure. Suddenly I had nothing to do.

For years I had been aware that there was a hole in the rapidly developing field of selling. Researchers and business consultants we had, but no sales consultants. I decided to create a new profession out of whole cloth. That's what I did, though it turned out to be a lot tougher job than I'd bargained for. The biggest problem was that, in spite of my sales skills, I couldn't go out and sell my services for the same reasons that doctors and lawyers can't go out and peddle theirs. So I started speaking to any group that would hear me. Slowly, from my audiences, I started building my professional sales consulting career. My first client paid me $25 a day, which was the smallest amount of money I'd made in many years.

My first real break came after I recruited and trained a sales force for the local agent of a major insurance company. When corporate headquarters saw the results, I acquired my first national account. At last, I was on my way.

In 1959 I released a recording entitled "Closing the Sale." That recording broke new ground. For the first time, the art of selling was broken down into specific tactics and techniques and made available to anyone who wanted to learn them. That recording became the best selling business recording ever produced, and at my speaking engagements people started introducing me as "the father of modern selling."

Around this time, I met Tom Hopkins. I remember the occasion well. At a training seminar in California, I noticed a young man sitting in the front row. I couldn't help noticing him because he was wearing a band uniform. Never in my life have I seen anyone take notes as fast and thoroughly as he did. He seemed to be trying to snatch the words before they got out of my mouth. I marked him as a man to watch.

The next time I saw him, he met me at the Los Angeles airport. I was there to consult with the firm he worked for. Tom was wearing a new suit and he was driving a new car. Back at their headquarters, the president told me that Tom had memorized my techniques, and then he had taken off like a rocket.

Tom went on to become the greatest real estate salesman that ever lived. Then he went into sales management for a few years. The next thing I knew, he was living next door to me and pursuing his goal with the kind of zeal that would have impressed all the sales greats of old. Tom adapted and refined and added to the material I gave him just as I had adapted and refined and added to the material that was given to me.

Since then, Tom Hopkins has spent years advancing the profession of selling with his seminars that teach and inspire, and with his cassettes and videotapes that carry his message where he can't be. And now comes this book, the culmination of a century of development in sales training, written by a true super pro, Tom Hopkins. Everyone who aspires to success must read it.

J. Douglas Edwards

Seeing's believing, but feeling's the truth.
— *Thomas Fuller*

All excellence is equally difficult.
— *Thornton Wilder*

That you may be strong be a craftsman in speech, for the strength of one is the tongue, and the speech of one is mightier than all fighting.
— *Written 5000 years ago by Ptahhotep.*

HOW TO MASTER THE ART OF SELLING

1

WHAT THE PROFESSION OF SELLING REALLY IS

I learned a long time ago that selling is the highest paid hard work—and the lowest paid easy work—that I could find. And I also found out another exciting thing about selling—the choice was mine, all mine. By myself, I could make it the highest paid hard work, or I could let it be the lowest paid easy work. I discovered that what I'd achieve in my selling career was entirely up to me, and that what anyone else wanted wasn't going to make much difference. What anyone else would or wouldn't give me wasn't going to make much difference, either. The only thing that really mattered was what I did for myself, and what I gave to myself.

Will you agree with me on that? I hope so, because the whole point of this book is that the skills, knowledge, and drive within you are what will make you great, and that these qualities can be expanded and intensified—if you're willing to invest time and effort and money in yourself. Is there any better investment than in yourself? Most of us know there isn't, but many of us don't act often enough, or decisively enough, on that belief.

You are your greatest asset. Put your time, effort, and money into training, grooming, and encouraging your greatest asset.

Let's talk about some of the advantages of selling.

The first advantage and the reason I love selling is its freedom of expression. Ours is one of the few professions left in which you can be yourself and can, in essence, do what you want to do. This freedom you've won for yourself by successfully competing where resourcefulness and perseverance are demanded and highly valued. No activity is more vital to the economy's health than selling; no activity is more dependent on individual initiative than selling.

The second advantage of selling is that you have the freedom to become as successful as you'd like to be. In our profession no one limits your income but you. There are no income ceilings.

You may question that statement. You may think the limit is the highest income anyone has yet made selling for your company. Does that mean it's not possible to earn more? Of course not. But it does mean that all the salespeople in your company who aren't earning the highest income aren't applying all the strategies and techniques of the Champion.

The third advantage of selling is that it's a daily challenge. You can go into almost any business and have no challenge. That's never the case in selling, where every day you're confronted with new challenges. Let that fact refresh you, not weary you. Glory in it. Our overregulated and highly organized society provides few lucrative work activities where the end of each day isn't known before that day dawns. You are privileged to be

1

involved in one of those precious few activities where freedom and challenge aren't rarities, they're constant companions. In sales, you never know
what opportunities the day will open up, what prizes will be offered that
you can win—what catastrophes may befall you. To the salesperson, every
day is an adventure. Working at this profession, we can go from the heights
of exhilaration to the depths of discouragement within forty-eight hours—
and climb back to the heights again the next day. Isn't that exciting?

Say yes.

Every morning, tell yourself that challenge is exciting, it's fun, and you
look forward to it. Tell yourself that—and mean it. Psyche yourself up to
enjoy challenge. Then go on the prowl for it, find it, and overcome it. If you
want to be better than average, do that. If you aspire to greatness, you won't
hesitate. The shortest route to high earnings goes straight through the
challenges you'll encounter.

The fourth advantage of selling is that it offers high potential returns
from a low capital investment. What does it cost to gain entry into this
profession that has no income ceiling? Compare whatever you think that
cost is to the investment required for one of the fast food franchises that have
been so successful. Typically, the owner of a new location invests $200,000
or more, works long hours, and pays himself a small salary. He does all this
in the hope of a $40,000 return on invested capital the second year. You can
launch yourself into a sales career for a tiny fraction of the franchiser's
investment and, by applying the systems in this book, have greater earning
power sooner. This enormous leverage on the small investment that getting
into selling requires has always fascinated me. What an exciting prospect!

The fifth advantage of selling is that it's fun. Do you know how many
people aren't having fun with what they're doing for income? My philosophy is that if it's not fun, it's not worth doing. Life was meant to be fun, and
there's no reason not to have some of it while you're earning a nice income
for your family.

The sixth advantage of the selling profession is that it's satisfying. You
feel good when your client walks out with your product. It's a thrill to know
you've helped people when you go home at night and can say, "I got
another family happily involved in what my company provides." When an
executive or official signs your purchase order, it's exciting and satisfying to
know you've helped that organization carry out its purposes. The people
you serve benefit in direct proportion to your ability and skills. The better
you are at sales, the more you benefit others—your clients, your family, and
the nation's economy.

No one limits your growth but you. If you want to earn more, learn
more. That means you'll work harder for awhile; that means you'll work
longer for awhile. But you'll be paid for your extra effort with enhanced
earnings down the road.

Most people in this world have jobs and professions—existences—that
can't fulfill their potential. The scope of their labor is confined to narrow
limits; their toil hinders rather than fosters their growth; they dislike everything about their employment except the sense of security its familiarity has
bred in them. So, instead of venturing into what they don't know and might

love, they allow themselves to be trapped by what they do know and don't like.

The professional salesperson recognizes no limits to his or her growth except those limits that are self imposed. They know that they can always reach out for more. They know they will grow in direct proportion to their competence. And they have little fear of the unknown in change because overcoming the unknown is their daily work. That's **the seventh advantage** of being a professional salesperson: it stimulates your personal growth.

To earn more, develop more competence. Study this book's sales skills. Study your product or service. Study your customers and your territory. Practice your growing skills at every opportunity. Do what you know you should do. Follow that program and you can't fail to push your earnings to a much higher level.

That's my purpose in life—to help you make more money. Please don't let me down—develop more competence, earn more money, get your share of life's good things. Developing competence is the only way. I know many salespeople making over a hundred thousand dollars a year, and some making over half a million dollars a year, and I'm always intrigued by the variety of their backgrounds, the diversity of their personalities, and the range of their interests. Yet they have many things in common, foremost of which is this quality: they are competent. They know exactly what they are doing. This book, like my seminars, is aimed at helping you learn how to become competent.

Please notice that I said *learn*.

There's an obstacle to learning how to become competent that we meet with here.

THE MYTH OF THE NATURAL BORN SALES WONDER

So many of us believe in this that we've come to look on it as an old friend. It's a tempting devil. It lets us avoid taking full responsibility for our own performance. This common fallacy is a destructive idea that I'd like to eliminate from your mind right now.

Having trained nearly a million salespeople in my national seminars, I've met a lot of strong individuals who are on the fast track. I've met with large numbers who haven't put their foot on the lowest rung of their potential yet. And, sadly, many of these people never will climb very high on their potential's ladder because they are firm believers in the myth of the natural born sales wonder.

The myth cuts two ways.

A few believe they're naturals. That's great for confidence but it's often the source of raging overconfidence. When that overconfidence persuades people that they don't have to bother learning to be competent like ordinary mortals, they trap themselves far below their potential.

Many more people believe they're not naturals, think it's hopeless to work at becoming competent—and trap themselves far below their potential.

"I'm just not a salesperson by nature. Wasn't born with the golden touch like Joe Whizzbeau over there. If I'd been born with his wit, charisma, and bear-hug personality, I could tear 'em up too. But I wasn't, so I'm never going to make it big in sales."

Don't be too quick to say you're free of this myth. I hear it far too often from my seminar audiences to take it lightly. In fact, I'm convinced that most salespeople who operate far below their potential suffer from it. Let's attack this dangerous idea now and get rid of it.

There never has been a great salesperson who was born great. Imagine a woman in the delivery room. Her newly born infant is saying, "Make yourselves comfortable, folks, and if you have any questions, please feel free to ask me." The little feller has a long way to go before he can even start learning how to walk, talk, and operate without diapers. He's got a lot to learn, and if he's going to be a great salesman, he's got it all to learn. Psychologists still argue whether it's instinct or learning that causes us to jump at a sudden loud noise, but they agree that everything about selling is learned.

So stop excusing yourself from the hard work of learning how to be competent in your sales career. It doesn't matter whether you think you're a wonder or a non-wonder, you still have to pay the learning price.

And you never stop learning and reviewing. Professionals work on the basics once every year. That's where we're going to start.

THE FIVE BASICS THAT'LL MAKE YOU AS GREAT AS YOU WANT TO BE

What so few of us are willing to accept is this fundamental truth: great salespeople, like great athletes, simply do the basics very well. Some of us would like to believe that there's a shortcut around the basics; that, if we could only find it, there's a secret formula out there somewhere for just sitting back and letting the money roll in. The sooner you get rid of that illusion, the sooner you can get on with reaching the heights you want to reach through effective use of the basics.

The first basic is **prospecting**. If you're like most of the people in my audiences, just hearing the word pushes you back a little. Don't think that way. If you don't like to prospect, it's because no one has taught you the professional way to do it. We're going to.

The second basic is making **contacts** the professional way.

The third basic is **qualification**. Many salespeople spend most of their time talking to the wrong people. If you do that, it doesn't matter how eloquently you present your service or product. Your earnings are still going to be low. We'll show you how the professional makes sure that he invests his time with the right people who can make *yes* decisions, instead of expending it on the wrong people who can only make *no* decisions.

The fourth basic method of developing your competence is to learn how to handle **objections** effectively. Possibly you never get any. In that case, you'll want to skip this one. But maybe you've had prospects who want to wait and think it over, prospects who already have one, prospects who've been doing business with your competitor for years. Have you ever heard any of these things? If so, read on. You'll find material that'll make you smile the next time you hear these objections. You'll smile, bore in—and close a delightful number of them. But there's a price to pay for that smile: you've got to learn the concept, adapt the idea to your offering, and learn the words that make it work.

The fifth and final basic is **closing**. Many average to good salespeople prospect, make contacts, qualify, and handle objections so well that they manage to get by without learning to close competently. And that, of course, is what keeps them from being great. Closing contains elements of both art and science, and all of those elements can be learned.

But many of us have forgotten how to learn, so let's quickly review the steps to learning that apply not only to everything in this book, but to anything you choose to study.

MONEY STUDY: THE LEARNING TO EARN FAST FIVESOME

Money study—I call it that to emphasize how vital it is to learn how to acquire new knowledge quickly and thoroughly. Knowing how to learn fast is the key to rapid personal growth and quick sales success. As adults, it's easy to fall into the habit of skimming over new knowledge, of avoiding any organized effort to grasp and hold new knowledge. That's no good at all. Superior earning ability grows out of the superior performance that superior learning makes easy. The place to start being superior is to acquire and use a superior learning system. Here it is:

One. *Impact.* You've noticed that the more you're interested in a subject, the more easily you remember details about it. To learn something with greater thoroughness and speed, first take a few moments to psyche yourself up. Dwell on how much that knowledge is going to help you; visualize the benefits you're going to get from possessing it. Form a clear and vivid picture in your mind as to why you're learning that material. Then, each time you start to study it, take just a second or two to recall that vivid picture of the benefits you're seeking. Do that and you'll intensify the impact of that material, and make it yours faster.

Two. *Repetition* is the mother of learning. Repeat anything often enough and it will start to become you. All the great salespeople I know started with statements they knew worked. They tailored those statements to their own operation and molded them into their own personalities. Having done that, they proceeded to repeat and review the statements until they controlled those words. Then they delivered them with conviction— and the results they wanted were there.

In four words, they used repetition effectively. What is effective repetition? It's far more than bleary-eyed singsong in the middle of the night. Effective repetition means your review is wide-awake and intensive. Effective repetition means you cut the material apart and sew it back together to fit you. Effective repetition means you write it, read it, speak it, and hear it. Effective repetition means you dramatize the material and make it dance in your head. Effective repetition means you pay a good price in effort to make good material yours.

Those first two steps are vital. They're the foundation and the floor. But don't stop when you've completed them—don't even slow down—because you can't live in a house with no walls. Push on immediately to the next step of learning.

I frequently return to cities where I've already given my sales seminar and, on these occasions, I always see dozens of Champions who are coming back through the program again. The ones who tell me they've doubled or quadrupled their incomes say that happened because they worked energetically through the next step.

Three. *Utilization.* The basic law of possession is USE IT OR LOSE IT. That law applies to all learning, and it applies with special force to sales skills. Use them or lose them.

There's a wonderful truth about skills and knowledge: they don't wear out with use. Quite the contrary. Knowledge takes on greater depth and meaning through hard use; skills become strong and tough through hard use.

And the hard use of sales skills and knowledge is the only road to high earnings. To travel that road, you must utilize your time efficiently to put yourself in the right places at the right times to give the right people the benefit of your powerful, perfected statements. Timing is more important in some sales activities than in others, but talking to the right people is vital to success in all sales work. Reaching the right people consistently demands a high degree of organization.

Perhaps by now you've seen where we're heading: Learning for the mere sake of learning is sterile. It's a form of play. For any kind of learning to have meaning, it must not only be capable of utilization, it must be used. Unused learning is fertilizer left in the sack.

We hear a lot about renewable resources these days. Can there be any more renewable resource than skill and knowledge used well? That doesn't happen by itself. You must make it happen. Bring out your skills and knowledge; spread them on the fertile soil of your territory. Let them bloom.

Discover the golden hours when your offering sells best.

Then organize.

Schedule yourself tightly. Utilize all your time efficiently so that you can make the best possible use of those golden hours and maximize your earnings.

That's utilization, as it applies to the sales skills you're learning.

Get in front of the executives considering corporate jets, computers, or whatever you're marketing. Meet with the families in need of your appliances. Get into the living rooms of the people now wasting the money they should be insuring the futures of their loved ones with. Now is the time to use the powerful sales statements you've organized for the benefit of others. You've turned yourself into a sales machine; now turn that machine on. Produce results.

The moment you get into high gear and start using your material efficiently, you'll glimpse your bright new destiny. Reader, Champion of the future, at that moment you'll be ready to break out above the average and join the ranks of the excellent. You'll be ready to fly higher and farther because of your newly-gained abilities. You'll be ready to take the fourth step toward learning and toward greatness.

Four. *Internalization.* This occurs when you've exploited impact, when you've molded the standard material to your needs and made it yours, when you've made your new skills strong through hard use. You've utilized them so efficiently that your first good results generate the energy to accelerate you into superperformance. All of a sudden these new concepts stopped churning within you, and a new reality is born: You and the concepts are one. They have literally become you. You have become them.

I've had Champions bring their spouses to my program to say hello. In a few minutes the spouse says, "My husband (or wife) sounds just like you."

But it really isn't that way. They aren't hearing their spouses imitate my words and manner of speaking, they're hearing their spouses express themselves with the language of achievement that's common to both of us. We, their spouse and I, have been using the same techniques. Now we voice the similar experiences of success that have grown out of the shared knowledge we've both internalized.

Internalization is the next-to-last step to completing any learning. When the day comes that you can truly say you've internalized all the concepts of this book, or have internalized all the concepts of any other body of learning you aspire to, then and only then are you capable of greatness with that learning. In the case of the learning we're primarily concerned with here, you'll be capable of going on to greatness in sales—and you'll also be in great danger of sliding back into average performance.

Five. *Reinforcement.* When you achieve the status of superprofessional salesperson, you'll be tempted to despise the very labors and methods that put you there. When you're still struggling upward, you'll find it easy to say, "Oh, no, not me. When I get there, I won't forget how I did it." But you will, and some of that is good. You don't want to dwell on past difficulties except to laugh about them. Still, the toughest task I have as a trainer always is with the superprofessionals who are slipping. They don't want to believe the explanation for their troubles is that they've stopped doing what made them superprofessional in the first place. Can there be any other reason for them to slip back into average performance? You might say, Maxie Kwotabuster's sales are down because of his three-martini lunches, his three-hour handball games during the golden hours, or because of the manner he's adopted since becoming successful. But when old Max was fighting his way clear of being average, his lunches were businesslike and left him refreshed for an effective afternoon; he guarded his golden hours jealously and used them effectively; he treated people cordially. And you can be sure that when Max was making his first run at success, he found the time necessary to effectively perform all the basic functions of sales work.

When you entered the profession of selling, you learned your product. You learned some sales techniques, you got out there amongst them and put your knowledge to work, and you started to make some money. Then, all of a sudden, you got smart. You quit doing what your company asks you to do. And then you started to slip.

Many of you reading these words will put this book down and in six months double your income. Then you'll stop doing what I've asked you to do. You'll stop doing the things that caused your income to double.

Don't stop.

Instead, do what professional athletes do. There's a lot of similarity between the professional athlete and a professional salesperson.

You know that high school teams practice. That doesn't surprise you—the kids have to learn the game. You know that college teams practice. Okay, they're still quite young. But, before every season starts, the pros are out there sweating it up. The first string is out there. The star quarterback is out there. He's making a chunk but he's running. He's perspiring. He's spending some of his time on new wrinkles, certainly, but most of the time he's drilling on fundamentals. Reviewing the basics. In fact, what's interesting is that the more professional and talented an athlete is, the more that athlete—man or woman—practices and trains. This comes back to that neat little thing called discipline, doesn't it? It calls into play that business of making yourself do what you know you should do.

Put a note in your tickler file to review this book a year from now. When the time comes, I know there's a good chance you'll say, "I'm not going through that stuff again. I know it. I've milked it for everything it's worth."

I hope you won't say that. I hope you won't limit the effectiveness of your learning. I hope you won't put a ceiling on your income-earning potential. I hope you won't decide to slip back into the quagmire of mediocrity. Reinforce your learning. Do it at least annually. Preserve your hard-won skills. Enhance your knowledge. Add to it.

Reinforce.

Keep your greatness.

Instead of letting your greatness wither, make it grow. You'll find this true of all learning that's important to you: every time you review the material in depth, you'll see things you never saw before and discover concepts you weren't ready to use before. Whenever you review effective knowledge, you reinforce your previous insights with richer insights.

YOUR PRIMARY TOOL

Let me ask you a question. If the professional golfer uses a club, the tennis player a racquet, and the carpenter a hammer, what do we professional salespeople use?

We use something that's gotten us in lots of trouble, don't we? But is there a pro on the golfing circuit who hasn't used his or her club to drive the ball into a sand trap? Is there a tennis player who hasn't used the racquet to feed an opponent a sure winner? Is there a carpenter out there who hasn't used a hammer to smack his thumb?

Is there a salesperson who's never used his primary tool to say something that lost an account?

Your primary tool—the opening in your faced called a mouth—must be used with confidence. But it can malfunction. The words you speak can destroy sales as well as create them. That's why you should think of your mouth as a sharp-edged tool that has to be used intelligently if it's going to do you more good than harm. But set reasonable goals. You can't reasonably expect to never say the wrong thing to prospects and clients.

Hitting the ball wrong in tennis is much like saying the wrong thing in sales. Every year at Wimbledon, the eventual winners use their racquets to feed a few easy shots to their opponents, and they lose the point every time they do. But, far more often, they use their racquets to hit winning shots themselves.

In both activities, you can learn to avoid making the common mistakes. But in the profession of sales, you're constantly involved in new and unique situations, which means that you're faced with a steady stream of opportunities to make new and unique mistakes—usually by saying the wrong thing.

The good news is that, if you learn enough right things to say, and if you concentrate on warmly saying them to your prospects and clients, there'll be very little time left for saying things that you'll regret. And there'll also be less chance that you'll lose any vital point if you do happen to let an unfortunate remark go. Work toward having the relaxed, cheerful, and confident manner that comes from dwelling on what you know you'll say right rather than worrying yourself into a tense, gloomy, and fearful attitude because you've occasionally blundered in your choice of words or topics. Accept the fact that what you say will sometimes come out badly. Then cultivate an honest respect for all people, make yourself the butt of your jokes rather than other people, and learn all the right statements to make. Do that and you'll never cut yourself with the sharp edge of your mouth.

Accentuate the positive through knowledge. That's our program for developing your primary tool into a reliable instrument for winning success in the profession of sales.

My life is working with people who have the desire but not the training to earn more. Usually I work from a seminar stage—just now I'm working in a quiet room on this book—but the object is the same: to deliver that needed training. After I've done that, it's up to you. I know that I can do my part because I've been fortunate enough to have had the opportunity to train thousands of the top salespeople in this country and abroad. They had the desire but not the training or the income. They came to the seminar. They learned the material. They used it daily. And then, all of a sudden, they not only had the desire and the training, they also had the income they wanted.

The highlight of my life comes when people take my training, go out with it and win whatever amount of success they need, and then tell me about it.

Now let me tell you about some of the Champions who've done that.

Here's a Champion whose action may startle you. Until he was eighteen, Robert Burns worked on his father's ranch. It was dependable work, but he wanted more from life than he could lift with a pitchfork, so he decided to enter the profession of selling. He took our training. Recently, when Robert celebrated his twenty-third birthday, his sales earnings were headed over the half-million mark for the year. I don't know any better word for it than excitement. It's exciting to know that if you learn the material and then go out and do what you know you should do, there's no ceiling on your income. People often tell me that they're too young for sales. Robert Burns wasn't too young.

And other people say they're too old. Let me tell you about Gertrude Nunn. I met her seven years ago, not too long after her former employer had said that she was getting too old for the job and should retire. She walked out, puttered around for a month, and decided that she wanted to be where the action is. Gertrude had no background in sales but, by happy accident, she heard about our training and took it. Now, seven years later, Gertrude Nunn is seventy-five-years young, she's earning over a hundred thousand dollars a year, and she's never enjoyed life more.

Jimmie Walker is another Champion. He started learning about professionally selling insurance when he was sixteen. Last year Jimmie sold twenty-five million dollars of ordinary life insurance, a feat comparable to running the mile in three minutes. How many people do you know at any age—let alone their early twenties—who've earned enough money to acquire a major professional sports team? Jimmie Walker did.

Our next Champion, David Bernstein, became one of the top four in luxury car leasing at a very young age. For years I've preached the importance of sending thank-you notes, but I've never seen anyone use this technique more effectively than David Bernstein does. Within a week after meeting him as a prospect, a member of my staff and I received four of these notes from Bernstein, all of them well-written, sincere, personal notes that made a solid impression. David Bernstein, a true Champion.

Aside from being graduates of the Champions Unlimited training, what do all four of these people have in common?

The twelve characteristics of a Champion is what they all have. In the next chapter we'll take a careful look at these marks of the Champion.

2

THE TWELVE SOURCES OF SENSATIONAL SELLING SUCCESS

They're interwoven. All twelve overlap. You can't improve in one of these characteristics without helping yourself improve in all the others; you can't ignore one of them without damaging your potential over the whole range.

ONE. You know the Champions when they walk in the door. Whether they're dressed conservatively, clad in clothes that are ahead of the latest fad, or they're wearing anything in between those extremes, they project the unmistakable stamp of strong personality with their attire and grooming. Just by looking at them, you know that you're in the presence of a powerful force. They reflect a sense of unique individuality and a solid consciousness of worth that's far more impressive than mere good looks. Whatever nature gave them and time has let them keep they've molded into a commanding, memorable *appearance*.

TWO. The Champions we've trained take tremendous pride in the profession of selling and in themselves as human beings. They base that pride on the serious way they've met their responsibilities and capitalized on their potential. And they do that without feeling any need to look down on anyone who is less effective than they are. No one is a Champion without achieving an honest *pride*.

THREE. Champions radiate confidence. If you're new in sales, you might ask, "How can I be confident when I don't know what I'm doing?"

I agree that you should be wary of feeling confident in any situation where you don't have a clear idea of exactly what you're doing. Overconfidence will float you down the river and over the falls nearly every time. If that's your problem, a few hard drops will quickly put you in step with your knowledge. And there'll be no harm done; you'll simply get some opportunities to develop your sense of humor.

Coming down with a permanent sense of underconfidence is a great danger. Every day, as you gain skill, you must practice being more and more confident. Remember that your clients and prospects look to you for only the very narrow area of expertise that thorough knowledge of your product or service represents. The people you come in contact with are moved by your belief, by the conviction and confidence you display in your offering. When you finish this training, you'll have every tool necessary to help people make the yes decision, you'll have faith in your worth, and you'll radiate *confidence*.

FOUR. Gertrude Nunn epitomizes one of the qualities I teach: she warmly and lovingly leads people. Am I saying that she's so warm and nice that she can't close people? Of course not. The top people close warmly.

You may find that confusing, especially if you have any tendency to regard the profession of selling as essentially being the business of unjustly separating money from unwilling people.

Let's talk about that idea because it's out there, and it has some reality to millions of people. It arises from the actions of the minority of salespeople who believe that selling is purely and simply aggression. Eventually all such vultures will be driven out of sales by the new breed of enlightened salespeople who qualify their prospects, care about their customers, and make sure their clients get benefits from their purchases that outweigh the prices paid. The change is already in the works. Trained salespeople, who neither want nor need to stoop to unfair practices, are gradually taking the place of the get-'em-for-all-you-can crowd. Admittedly, it's a slow process, and we'll wait a long time to see it completed. But it's happening. I'd like to enlist you in fighting the good fight for sales integrity.

We've all heard people say, "I used to sell, but I wasn't pushy enough." The ex-salespeople who say that don't realize they never learned how to prospect, contact, and qualify professionally. In fact, many of them never even learned the sales meaning of the word qualify. So, in desperation, they tried to close prospects they knew in their hearts shouldn't be closed on their particular product or service. That made these ex-salespeople feel like crooks. Because they are basically honest people, they had to escape the guilt; instead of getting into sales training, they got out of sales work.

Champions don't have that problem because they never close people they know shouldn't be closed. A Champion doesn't push people with warmth. His techniques are so strong that he leads people smoothly to the close that'll benefit them—with genuine concern and *warmth.*

FIVE. Most Champions look to only one person for their self assurance, and that one person is themselves. They realize that we live in a world where many people really don't care, and there's not as much involvement as there should be. People are apathetic even about their own welfare beyond immediate satisfactions. Champions know that they can't change the prevailing culture all by themselves. So they float through life without being overwhelmed by problems they can't solve. They concern themselves with helping their customers and their loved ones through the profession of selling. Many of them are active in other causes, but they're always careful to put their efforts into activities where they can be effective. In everything they do, they believe in themselves and act with *assurance.*

SIX. Champions want to get rich. That's right, rich. The Champion wants the high income that'll provide the capital for investments to make him or her independent. There's nothing wrong with getting rich as long as the people you serve along the way benefit. The true Champion shapes his values and organizes his lifestyle to achieve his object of *getting rich.*

SEVEN. A quality I can't measure, but I know it's always present in Champions, is the burning desire to achieve. For years, sales managers have thought, "If we could only measure how much desire each person has, we'd have the whole problem of selecting salespeople solved. We'd know who'll keep on working in spite of problems and disappointments, and who'll sit down and give up. No more sweating it out with capable-looking people who've got all the tools except desire, so in the end they fizzle out." Sales managers think it would be wonderful if they could, but there's no way to measure how much desire another person has. Only you can measure how much desire you have, and here's how you do it. Ask yourself, these questions:

How much pain can I handle before I quit?

How many problems can I put up with before I stop, go home, and lay down?

If you have the potential to be a great Champion, your answer will be that you don't quit no matter how much pain and how many problems you encounter, because those things are nothing compared to your *desire*.

EIGHT. We've discussed this point before, and we'll discuss it again because it's the very blood of success. Champions learn what their fears are, and often that's not easy since we're all so good at concealing them from ourselves. But the Champions persevere in this. They learn what they fear. Then they attack what they fear, and overcome their fear. Once they've done that, they radiate a confidence that only comes from *overcoming fear*.

NINE. A lot of salespeople are only up when everything else is. Their enthusiasm depends on other people and outside events. Are you that way? If you are, let me ask you to think deeply about why you allow yourself to be knocked this way and that by the fickle fumblings of fate. Why think of yourself as a mere passenger on your voyage through life? You can take the helm and steer any course you choose to any place you want to go.

Why should you only feel good when things are going well? That's what you do when you're determined to remain average. That's what the "salesperson" does whose idea of selling is to stand around until someone comes in and demands to buy. When you're with a Champion, you can't tell whether things have gone well for that person the previous hour, day, week, or even month. How can they hide their feelings that way? Well, in the first place, they aren't hiding their feelings. They are excited about life. They're confident. They know that they'll have problems—if not this week, next week. They know that over a five year period, some seasons will be better than others. They live very much in the present but they don't forget that tomorrow is coming right on schedule. They know that, no matter whether they're having good or bad luck today, it will change—but what won't change is their superior performance regardless of circumstances. They're happy. They bring their own sunshine. They don't let little things bother them. If they have an irate client, they handle it. They solve the problem. They forget it. What's done is done.

And Champions know that, no matter how good they get, they're still going to fail some of the time between their successes. So, while they're failing, they don't have to hide their true feelings because they're still filled with *enthusiasm*.

TEN. The top people we train get emotionally involved with the people they serve. Champions really care about their clients, and this true feeling comes through loud and clear to the people they're selling. That's why the Champion gets so many referrals. I don't think any salesperson ever made much money in a normal market without a rich flow of well-deserved referrals. We'll show you the techniques you have to use to get a lot of referrals because most people won't think of it by themselves, but the secret behind the technique is caring. When the buyer of your offering sees the cash register behind your eyes ringing up your earnings if he says yes, he'll automatically fight you. Instead of giving him a powerful emotional reason to want to do business with you (because he can see that you really care about his welfare) you've given him a powerful emotional reason for avoiding doing business with you.

I've met a few salespeople who hate other people. Out of the millions in sales, there are a few thousand who can't stand their fellow man. And some of them manage to make fairly good money. But I never knew one who wasn't always scrambling from job to job because people-haters make enemies faster than money. Champions, on the other hand, tend to stay with what they're doing for a long time. And they use some of the generous money they're making to build their clientele. It all comes about because they're experts not only in sales but also in *caring*.

ELEVEN. Do you take rejection personally? Maybe a client you're working with, someone you've made your entire presentation to, decides to talk to your competitor and says he'll call you next week. Not only does he fail to call you, he changes his phone number and firm name. When you get back to him the following week, he's already bought from the competitor. Or you meet someone who says, "I'm really interested," and when you arrive a week later for your appointment, they calmly inform you that they've been enjoying another brand of your product since the day after your meeting. Has something like this ever happened to you? If it hasn't yet, keep on plugging—it will.

That's sales. That's the business world.

You can't prevent situations of this kind, but you can train yourself to take them in stride. *Champions don't take rejection personally*.

TWELVE. This final characteristic of great sales people is also true of their companies. They all believe in *continuing education*. They study technique. They learn new skills. The company managements encourage their salespeople to go to seminars, to listen to cassettes, to watch videotapes, and to read books. You never have to push a Champion to invest in his mind. He or she knows that if you put better ideas into your brain, better performance will come out. Champions know that the place to start improving one's environment is inside one's own skull. Invest more time, money, and effort into your mind, and finer things will start gravitating to you. You'll take more enjoyable trips, live in a more comfortable and prestigious home, and have more of the goodies that money buys. I'm not giving you a new idea. Benjamin Franklin said, "Empty the coins in your purse into your mind, and your mind will fill your purse with gold."

WHY YOU CAN'T FAIL

Even though I've seen it happen over and over, I'm still amazed when I go back to the same city and, time after time, see the same people sitting there in front busily taking notes. I had a little fun with this a few months ago at one of my seminars where about fifteen-hundred people were in the audience. A gentleman sitting in the front row looked familiar. I said to myself, "I'll bet he's been here five years in a row."

I talked to him from the stage and found out that I was right. So I asked him, "Did you bring all your people?"

He said, "Tom, I'm the top salesperson in my company, so you'd think what I say would carry some weight. I told everybody about this seminar and talked it up, but only a few of our people are here—and they're all strong salespeople. It's the same every year; the people who need it most never go."

I said, "I hear that all the time. But suppose one of the struggling salespeople in your company, one of those who need this training most, goes home tonight and his spouse says, 'Our toilet's goofed up. It'll cost us $50 to fix it.' What'll they do? Believe me, they won't say, 'I won't go. I can't afford it.' They'll fix the toilet."

It's amazing what people choose to spend their money on before investing in themselves. I'm proud of you for investing in this book, but its cost is only a small fraction of the time-value you'll also have to put in if you're going to acquire its knowledge. Although you can get the money you spent for this book back thousands times over in your sales work, you still have to invest the time to extract its knowledge.

There's no way I can give you that time back. It isn't ever going to be today again. That's why I so deeply feel my obligation to make my message as powerful and effective as possible. That's my obligation, and it's a heavy one; yours is just as heavy. You have to provide the desire to succeed.

Since you're reading these words, you either already have all the desire you need to succeed, or you want to develop that desire. That's why you can't fail—you want to succeed badly enough to invest time, money, and effort in changing yourself to a more productive person.

But we live in a distracting culture, don't we? There's always something that demands our attention: Monday football, Tuesday TV, Wednesday bowling, Thursday poker, Friday TGIF party, Saturday night fever, Sunday brunch, game, and last fling at the weekend. How do you find time to study the knowledge and practice the skills of competence?

Desire takes the time. It cancels your reservations at the time-blasting spectator sports, and puts you on the field playing the most exciting sport of them all when you play it to win: the great game of your life.

Maybe you want to play that game, and play it hard, but you're afraid that you may be a bit deficient in the desire department. That's understandable. Desire is a learned response, but it's one of great and subtle complexity.

HOW TO DEVELOP DESIRE

Here are three methods of developing the burning desire to succeed that can't be denied. They work—if you want them to.

- The greatest obstacle to developing desire is our conviction that we'll never be able to satisfy it, so that safest course is to discourage the desire and avoid the frustration. John Galbraith calls this process "accommodating to poverty," and points out that people always choose the economic level they'll accept—it's never thrust on them. You are constantly in the process of schooling yourself to accept the level of prosperity that you have, or you are exerting extra effort to get more. If you've been coasting along on the idea that your ship will eventually get blown into port by itself, this can be scary stuff. A lot of us just aren't willing to face the fact that our ship ain't movin' until we climb aboard, sweat the sails up, and start steering. The Cubans who escaped Castro with nothing are now prosperous, the boat people and other Asians who practically swam the Pacific to get here are making it, so what's your excuse?

The fact is, there isn't any excuse for not achieving success in America today. There hasn't been since Peter Minuit swindled the Indians out of Manhattan. If you don't have a burning desire to better your life, you're cheating yourself and your loved ones with phony excuses. You're choosing a level of life that's poor compared to what you could have with the extra exertion you're capable of. It's all on your shoulders, and there's no way you can shift a bit of the responsibility to anyone else.

I know former migrant farm workers who've come out of the fields and made themselves wealthy. Do you think they did that without first believing they could succeed at something better paying that picking fruit? If your sunshine wants far outstrip your cold morning desire, have a talk with yourself. Then have a lot more talks with yourself. Convince number one that you can succeed—and you will succeed.

• Focus on the specific things you want. Make agreements with yourself: I do this, I get that. Don't try to make yourself work for nothing.

• Take it in steps. If you've never made more than the minimum wage, don't aim for half-a-million the first year. Always aim for the earnings level that excites you a lot and only scares you a little. The essential element is faith in yourself.

I hope you're as sincere as I am. You have a deep obligation to yourself and your loved ones. That obligation is to commit yourself to learning the material in this book. Make that commitment, complete it quickly, and then start operating at your full potential. Unless you do this, you won't achieve the quality of life that is within your reach.

S P R IS THE DIFFERENCE
BETWEEN HAVE AND HAVE NOT.

Right now, you're as good as your R's and no better. But your R's might not be very good because you haven't taken a good P yet. The thing is, it's almost impossible to take a good P unless someone gives you a good S.

My job in this book is to give you an eloquent S, and to give it to you with such excitement and enthusiasm that you'll take the P necessary to develop your own effective R's.

Let me explain.

What I just gave you is called the stimulus, pause, and response theory. If you walk into your den tonight and, failing to see your cat, step on its tail, you'll give your cat a stimulus. Your cat will have an immediate response. It won't pause and think, "All right, I'm going to get even later, but first I'd better make a noise and get out from under." The animal's instant reaction is S — R, Stimulus — Response.

Because of the power of our minds, we humans possess an enormously greater ability to respond to stimulus. We can receive a stimulus, pause to consider what our best response will be, and then respond. On a piece of paper write down the formula for our human reaction:

$$S — P — R$$

This stands for Stimulus — Pause — Response. Now draw an arrow from the P straight down, and write three words that can make the difference for you, three words that can make your pauses effective:

PRACTICE

DRILL

REHEARSE

At anything you choose to do, you'll be as good as the practice, drill, and rehearsal you went through before you actually perform the action. The toughest thing I have to do with new salespeople is to convince them that, if they don't know what they're going to say and do until they're in front of the customer, it's too late.

Salespeople like to wing it. That is to say, average salespeople like to wing it. Champions like to make money. So they don't wing it—they prepare. Intensively.

One of the reasons many new salespeople think they can wing it and win has to do with the faulty image they have of the sales interview. They think of selling situations as a slow-paced affair where there's plenty of time for telling jokes, chatting about sports and the weather, and for winging their way through any unexpected challenges. What these new salespeople don't realize is that, even in such a leisurely interview, the brass tack business part of it goes very, very fast.

And some purchasing agents are notorious for keeping the trivia going with any salesperson they don't know and favor in order to avoid hearing the presentation. Many buyers will do that. If you sell a product or service that's regularly bought by a purchasing agent—industrial supplies, for example—you can be sure that some of those agents have favorite salesmen. Unless you develop a unique, interest-catching plan to beat that game before you walk in the door, the favorite-players will finesse you every time.

Imagine what would happen to me if I went on the court with a tennis pro after saying I was going to beat him.

I'd plop my serve over and back it would come, headed wherever I'm not at. I see the ball coming and think, "Okay, hustle over there and hit it backhand." By that time, of course, the ball and the point are long gone. Considering the sorry state of my preparation, my response was quick, but it wasn't anywhere near quick enough. The difference, of course, is that the tennis pro has hit ten thousand balls for every one I've hit.

Not only that, you might think, but the tennis pro has a lot more natural ability for tennis playing than Tom Hopkins does. I'm not going to argue that point, but I am going to argue whether it matters—for a reason. If we could roll time back to the first day that tennis pro ever hit a tennis ball and end his tennis career right there—let's say he takes up swimming instead— and I go out for professional tennis. Never mind how well or badly I'd do on the pro circuit, I still hit ten thousand balls for every one the fellow who took swimming instead of tennis does. Then put us on the same court today. I've been engaged in tennis full time for many years, and he's been swimming all those years. He hardly knows a racquet from a banjo. What would happen? I'd blow him off the court, natural ability notwithstanding. The point is that through preparation, including psyching up and confidence-building, is the decisive factor in the overwhelming majority of cases. In sports, in sales, anywhere, superior preparation rarely tastes defeat.

What factor is common to all types of superior preparation?

Speed.

Superior preparation develops faster responses. When you respond faster, the quality of your response automatically improves. This happens not only because your responses always come quick enough to count; since you're not rushed, you have time to choose your best response and to deliver it smoothly. And, while you're doing that, you'll also have time to think about your next move. If you're trying to wing it, you simply can't keep up.

Champions collect objections. They like to hear them from other strong salespeople, read them in books, and think them up themselves. They enjoy finding new objections anytime—except when they're with customers. And, you can be sure, as fast as the Champions find new objections, they develop their best responses to them. But they don't stop there. They practice, drill, and rehearse their best response. Before they ever hear the new objection in a sales situation, they're ready to instantly fire their best answer at it. That's professionalism. That's the type of thinking and action that brings in the big money.

Along about now, you may be thinking "If it's that simple, how come every salesperson in the world hasn't already done that?"

The theory *is* simple, but its application is demanding, specialized for every product or service, and it's in a constant state of evolution. You don't just learn a few objections, memorize the answers, and then turn your mind off the subject of objection/response forever. Constant alertness for new objections and for better responses to old objections marks the Champion.

Could your prospects say any of these things about your product or service?

- "Three years ago we tried it (we had one of them), but we were disappointed at how it worked out."
- "You know, we're just not the type of people who jump into decisions like this. Your video recorder is beautiful; we love it; but we're going to look around."
- "Your price is too high."

Now you can look at those common objections and say to yourself, "Someday I'll make a study of how to respond to them, but for now, I'm getting by all right winging it. When I'm in front of the customer, the adrenalin's going, and sometimes I come up with some real good stuff."

Sure you do. That's why you're breaking all those sales records. Oh, you aren't breaking any sales records? Then possibly one reason you're not is that you're winging (improvising) your responses to objections instead of practicing, drilling, and rehearsing them. No one ever became great in sales without first becoming great at handling objections.

When you turn pro (which means that you decide to stop playing the game for free, and go for the prize money) you come up with an effective response to objections without pausing or thinking. You're like the cat whose tail gets stepped on. Your stimulus is the objection; your response is instant and effective.

In the chapter on objections, I'm going to give you proven responses to the basic objections that are common to a wide range of sales situations. Then, after you're through with practicing, drilling, and rehearsing your responses to those standard objections, you'll be familiar with the method. You'll be able to devise effective responses for the objections that are peculiar to your offering at this time in your territory.

Work these standard objection responses thoroughly. You hear most of them every day of your sales career. If you've never studied them, you don't realize that all successful sales interviews follow the pattern shown in this diagram:

THE PURCHASE PATH

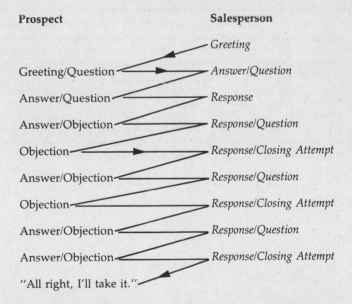

Prospect	Salesperson
	Greeting
Greeting/Question	Answer/Question
Answer/Question	Response
Answer/Objection	Response/Question
Objection	Response/Closing Attempt
Answer/Objection	Response/Question
Objection	Response/Closing Attempt
Answer/Objection	Response/Question
Answer/Objection	Response/Closing Attempt
"All right, I'll take it."	

Of course, the diagram is highly simplified. The greeting phase, for example, might include lengthy getting-acquainted small talk to establish rapport. Unless you're selling something over a counter, you'll have to ask more questions and respond well to many more objections than we've shown. But the essential elements are there, and it's the concept that's important. It expresses the simple essence of sales. The function of the professional salesperson is to know what a prospect might ask or object to, what information and responses will best meet the expected questions and objections, and what closes will guide the prospect toward approving the purchase. It boils down to them saying this, you answering that for a while, and then they walk out carrying the video recorder you just sold them. Why did that happen?

Because you learned exactly what they would say and what you should say.

And that takes us to the importance of practice, drill, and rehearsal. The techniques that have worked for many thousands of salespeople are in this book. The objections and responses. The closes. But you can't just read through them and expect to apply this mass of material smoothly when you're in front of a customer in his office with the phone ringing, or in your display room talking to a husband and wife while their kids are scuffling. Give this material a quick read and you won't be able to come up with more than a fraction of it during even the most relaxed and interrupted sales interview. You have to make the material yours. This means that you:

● Practice the precise words that you'll use until they're second nature.
● Drill yourself on delivering them with clarity and conviction.
● Rehearse delivering them in a life-like a situation as you can create, working in cooperation with other people.

When you've done that, when you've prepared professionally, you'll earn the high income that a professional commands because, when you're in front of a buyer and they give you a stimulus, you give back the immediate response that moves you toward closing the sale. You'd like to do that, wouldn't you?

Then do it. It's just that simple. Prepare professionally and you'll earn a professional's income. But don't delay. Make a strong start today.

These words sound familiar, don't they? They've been used over and over for many products and services to present benefits that will help people achieve their goals. You've bought my book, but now will you buy my concepts? Will you invest the time and effort that's required if you're to make them yours?

It's your life and your decision. I hope you'll make the right one.

3

QUESTION RIGHT AND SINK YOUR TEETH INTO SALES SUCCESS

When you work with a new prospect, don't you agree that you should try for several minor yeses before you go for the big yes that means they've bought? That makes sense, doesn't it?

Certainly.

Wouldn't it be helpful to have a reliable technique for starting a flow of minor yeses every time you work with possible buyers? That's what tie-downs do, don't they? And you're getting a little tired of all these questions, aren't you?

That's why it's so important not to overuse tie-downs. They're extremely effective but, unless used sparingly, they grate on people.

Tie-downs come in four styles: standard, inverted, internal, and tag-on. By mixing the four well, you can work this high performance technique quite heavily without it being noticed. We'll discuss all four types and suggest drills for making their use one of your most effective habits.

THE STANDARD TIE-DOWN

The tie-down is hung on the end of the sentence, as in:

"Fuel economy is very important today, *isn't it?*"

If what you said represents truth as the prospect sees it, won't that person respond by agreeing? And when they agree that some quality of your product or service meets their needs, they've moved closer to buying it, haven't they?

Here are eighteen standard tie-downs that you'll find useful:

Aren't they?	Don't we?	Isn't it?
Aren't you?	Shouldn't it?	Isn't that right?
Can't you?	Wouldn't it?	Didn't it?
Couldn't it?	Haven't they?	Wasn't it?
Doesn't it?	Hasn't he?	Won't they?
Don't you agree?	Hasn't she?	Won't you?

There are others, of course. Put them nicely on the ends of your sentences, and you'll gather thousands of minor yeses. Selling is the art of asking the right questions to get the minor yeses that allow you to lead your prospect to the major decision and the major yes. Selling is basically a simple function, and the final sale is nothing more than the sum total of all your yeses, isn't that right?

Now I want you to work with me. The professional athlete must do more than one thing at once. If the game is tennis or racquetball, the player must run, look at the ball, bring his arm back, and hit the ball at the right instant. A professional salesperson also does many things at once. While delivering his presentation, he's thinking about upcoming benefits and objections and watching what was said in the past to cover himself for the future. His mind is working like a computer, isn't it?

Start reading the sentences below and, as quickly as you can, write the appropriate tie-down on the blank line. Do this exercise before a mirror, checking from time to time to make sure that you're nodding sympathetically as you say the tie-downs. Professionals do more than one thing at a time, don't they?

Here are the tie-down exercise sentences:

"Many progressive companies are using computers today, _____?"

"It would be an advantage to have your own in-house telephone system, _____?"

"Family security is something we're all concerned with, _____?"

"They're fun, _____?"

"It just takes practice, _____?"

"They're coming out naturally, now, _____?"

"Quality is important, _____?"

"You'd like to retire and enjoy the delicacies of civilization someday, _____?"

"We've got to learn how to do several things at once, _____?"

"After you've practice a while, the tie-downs certainly pop out, _____?"

"That one just did, _____?"

"Over a period of time, you could develop hundreds of questions that will lead your clients toward the decision to enjoy the benefits of your product or service, _____?"

"At any time, Champions should be able to write fifteen tie-down questions for their offering, _____?"

"You're a Champion, _____?"

"She's chosen some lovely colors, _____?"

"This will add nicely to your investment portfolio, _____?"

"Safety is an important consideration for all of us, _____?"

"You're doing this exercise well, _____?"

That's the standard tie-down. Before we go on to the other types, be sure to take a solid grip on this idea:

Wait for the buyer's positive stimulus before using tie-downs.

If you tie them down without waiting for the positive stimulus, you could tie them down to a negative factor, couldn't you? For example, my product is office copiers and I have an appointment with the office manager of Makebux Corporation.

I've decided to sell one of my company's new SuperPow models to Makebux. Not only does the SuperPow make great copies fast, it also separates and collates fast. I want to sell this model because (a) it carries a bonus, (b) it gives me extra points in the sales contest, (c) there isn't a single SuperPow in that part of my territory, and I'm certain that getting one into Makebux will break the ice. All these reasons are excellent ones, but they're my reasons, not theirs.

When I drive into their parking lot after a long trip, the only copier I have in the back of my car is a SuperPow. I don't need any other because I'm going to sell them that model. I've already made the decision: they're going to buy it. Not only do I have the SuperPow strapped to an easy, roll-in transporter, I also have a beautifully typed presentation folder titled, "What SuperPow will do for the Makebux Corporation." I'm supercharged for SuperPow. I'm gonna do it.

As soon as the interview gets started, I say, "You want a copier that doesn't just make copies like all the rest, don't you? You'd like one that also separates and collates while it copies, wouldn't you?"

The office manager shakes her head. "No, we never collate anything in this building. Our subsidiary across the street has a complete printing plant that does everything like that for us. All we want here is a compact, trouble-free machine that just makes high-quality copies."

See how I've destroyed myself?

I didn't ask, I *told*. I didn't wait for the prospect's positive stimulus before committing myself totally to the one course that raced me straight for the trash heap. The professional closes on the buyer's positive stimulus, not on his own positive stimulus. As badly as I need to place a SuperPow in that part of my territory, as much as I want to win that sales contest, as fervently as I desire that bonus, Makebux isn't going to buy a SuperPow. In half the time I spent selling nothing, I could have closed them on our desk model SuperPup.

I could have done that had I ascertained their needs on the phone before the appointment. If that wasn't desirable or possible, I should have structured my presentation so that I could switch to whatever model did meet their needs.

THE INVERTED TIE-DOWN

For variety and for more warmth, put the tie-down at the beginning of the sentence. Before you decide that this is too simple to practice, consider that we're talking here about the habits of speech you'll make a career of using in the fast and demanding arena of the sales interview. A good mixture of the four tie-down types won't find their way into your sales interviews by accident. A Champion uses all four types smoothly, and without lessening any of his or her concentration of the client. Such a high level of skill demands rehearsal.

Use the tie-down exercise sentences for inverted form practice. Read through them quickly, recast each sentence as you go, and say them aloud in inverted form. Sometimes changing an extra word or two helps to smooth the sentence out. The first example is "Many progressive companies are using computers today, aren't they?" That inverts to "Aren't a lot of progressive companies using computers today?"

THE INTERNAL TIE-DOWN

The smoothest way to hide a tie-down is to drop it into the middle of a complex sentence. This is much easier than it sounds. Let's spread one example over three forms.

Standard form, the tie-down is last: "Once you get the feel of it, you can really control it well, can't you?"

Inverted form, the tie-down is first: "Can't you really control it great once you get the feel of it?"

Internal form, the tie-down is in the center: "Once you get the feel of it, can't you really control it well?"

Another variation of the internal form is more obviously a tie-down: "You really can control it well, can't you, once you get the feel of it?"

To change any simple tie-down sentence into the internal form, all you need do is to hang a phrase on the beginning or end of it. Take the shortest of the tie-down exercise sentences, "They're fun, aren't they?" Hook a phrase on the front and you've got a complex sentence and an internal tie-down:

"When you get used to them, aren't they fun?"

This isn't a difficult technique, and using it will keep your tie-downs hidden. Practice with the tie-down exercise sentences. Run through them, recast each one as a complex sentence with the tie-down coming in the middle, before or after the phrase you've added. Many of these phrases will bear some relation to time:

"Now that we've eliminated that problem, aren't you glad —"

"Next week when you take delivery, isn't your wife going to be delighted?"

"Once you have this new model in your home, can't you just see —"

"In these days of heavy inflation, aren't —"

"When you —"

"After we —"

"Since you're planning to keep your next _____ a long time, won't it be great that —"

Practice, drill, and rehearse fifteen tie-down questions of your own creation. Then go on to fifteen more. Keep a good mixture of all three types. You'll soon find that tie-downs have become an effortless speech habit that's lifting your sales, your spirits, and your bank account.

THE TAG-ON TIE-DOWN

Our last tie-down technique is used in a variety of ways. In its simplest form, you tag your tie-down onto any statement your prospect happens to make that's positive to the sale.

Prospect: "Quality is important."

You: "Isn't it?"

He said it, so it's true. Every time they say something helpful to the sale, if you tie it down you get a complete minor agreement. Don't you?

You caught that last tie-down, didn't you? That's great, isn't it, because it means that your reflexes are being built for consistent performance with tie-downs.

Don't you agree that the stimuli of sales opportunities are quick and varied? They are, aren't they?

That being true, shouldn't we build all the fast, sales-productive responses to those stimuli that we can?

Of course we should. That's our aim with all the material in this book. Not only can the use of all four tie-down techniques become reflex action with you, the techniques on all these pages can be learned so well that you'll instantly and automatically employ them in every situation where they can help you sell. If you'll learn this material that well, you can't fail to make more money. Can you?

And there's a good mix of the four tie-down techniques in the last five paragraphs, isn't there? You can use any of them as a springboard for tag-along questions that'll keep your prospect moving up the path to the big yes.

When you've trained yourself to recognize opportunities for tag-along questions before the prospect has them completely out of his mouth, when you can instantly and warmly use the proper tie-down and, as you're saying it, compose a tag-along question that'll both hold your prospect's interest and lead him closer to the big decision, you can truly say that you've acquired championship skill with this technique. And it's not that hard to do. Since you can increase your earning power so much so easily (and at no cost) by mastering this technique, will you be satisfied with anything less than championship skill?

Here's an example of tag-along questions working off tag-on tie-downs. When the prospect comes into your showroom, the matter of color immediately comes up.

Prospect: "I like green."

You: "Isn't green an emotional color? We're offering a choice of three new shades of green on our latest models. Which do you prefer, Bali Mist, Irish Sea, or Acapulco Spring?"

Prospect: "I go for Bali Mist. It looks like the most restful shade."

You: "Doesn't it?"

Continue with another tag-along question that'll lead your prospect closer to purchasing your product.

The tag-on technique is especially effective in tying down helpful points with strong-willed prospects who want to dominate the discussion. Ignore every statement they make that's negative to the sale unless you're forced to correct some misinformation they have. Concentrate on guiding the prospect into making positive statements that you can tag a tie-down on.

Prospect: "Your models are too boxy looking."

You: (Avoid agreeing with the negative statement.) "You've been looking at our standard line, sir. If you'll step over here, I'd like to get your opinion on our new Barrierbuster."

Prospect: "Now that's what I call style."

You: "Isn't that right? Tell me, do you get the same feeling I do seeing it sit there?"

Prospect: "Yeah, it looks like the speed of light just holding your floor down."

You: "Doesn't it? How do you think it would handle?"

Prospect: "Well, I don't know — but I'd like to find out."

How you proceed with the prospect from this point depends on whether you've already qualified him and on your policy regarding demonstrations. However, by skillfully using tie-downs to set up tag-along questions, you've been able to get three minor agreements and put yourself in scoring position. That's coming a long way fast.

Opportunities for tag-on tie-downs come and go quickly, so training yourself to snap them up is important. Fortunately, that's easy. Driving to work or to appointments, tune your radio to the news, or any other program where positive statements are constantly being made, and practice your tag-on tie-downs out loud.

Use any conversation to practice setting up tag-along questions. Casual talk is great for this purpose. And don't overlook the splendid opportunity to sharpen your techniques that you get every time you buy something for yourself.

For years I've called the next technique the Alternate of Choice, but I like my new name better because it drives home a pair of ideas: forward movement and choice. Under any name, it's one of my favorites because it's so effective and easy to use.

THE ALTERNATE ADVANCE

The Alternate Advance is a question that suggests two answers, both of which confirm that your prospect is going ahead.

If, instead of asking an alternate advance question, you ask one that suggests a yes or no answer, which will your prospect usually pick?

No.

We have something in common here — we all think it's easier and safer to say no than it is to say yes. That's why the professional uses the alternate advance method to avoid asking questions that put *no* into the prospect's mouth.

You can use this concept in minor situations and in the major closing sequence. In most kinds of sales work, it's almost impossible to make the sale without first making the appointment with the buyer. Generally speaking, more appointments mean more sales — will you agree with that?

So it's vital that you don't lose appointments unnecessarily, and get stopped before you can start. That's why the professional never asks, "Could I come by this afternoon?"

What answer does that suggest to most buyers? "No, I've really got a heavy schedule today. I'll call you when I have more time." Yes, he will. Sure.

A professional gives them two options: "Mr. Johnson, I'll be in your area this afternoon. Which would be more convenient, should I stop by around two o'clock, or would you prefer that I wait until about three?"

When he says, "About three would be better," you have the appointment. You got it by suggesting two yeses instead of a no that he would have jumped on.

These alternate advances are beautiful. "Mr. and Mrs. Johnson, we have to set up a delivery date. Which would best suit your plans, the first or the fifteenth?"

"Oh, we need it by the first." When they say that, they own it, don't they?

If your sales require some type of deposit, don't ask them how much of a deposit they'd like to give you. Put it in the form of an alternate advance. You have to design the question to fit your product and company policy. On a $3 million jet for example, before the sales representatives let people go out and fly the aircraft, they've qualified them, haven't they?

If you were selling jets, you could say, "What type of deposit would you like to give me?"

The old boy might show you a picture of Abe Lincoln and say, "Well, I've got a fast five bucks here. Gimmie the plane."

You have to structure all of this material to your product. You'd probably say, "As you know, we have a substantial purchase here. Which would you prefer, a five or a ten percent deposit?"

What are they going to leap on?

Five percent.

Hopefully, that's what you wanted. If not, re-write the question. So, the alternative advance is any question that gives your prospects two alternatives, but neither of them is no. Both alternates confirm that they are going ahead.

Suppose you provide one of the most fantastic services there is to sell: insurance. After all the publicity this product has had over the last century, it's astonishing that the average person doesn't know he needs insurance. The main reason he doesn't know is that he's never met a professional insurance salesperson.

If I was sitting in front of you (and had fully done everything you're learning in this course) and I smiled and said, "Mr. Johnson, will your wife be the beneficiary, or do you have a family trust?"

That's an alternate advance. If he says, "I want my wife to be the beneficiary," he now owns the insurance that he needs. The alternate advance — either way, they go ahead with the purchase of your product or service.

REFLEXIVE CLOSING QUESTIONS

A lot of things happened during my first six months in sales that seem funny to me today — but I didn't laugh much at the time. I did more squirming than laughing in those days. The whole problem was that I made only one sale during the entire half-year, and my income averaged forty-two dollars a month. I was nineteen. Box boys in supermarkets were making more in a week than I was in a month. Worse yet, I was aware that that made sense: the box boys knew what they were doing and, obviously, I didn't.

Do you think I was negative, depressed, and ready to give up selling? Either I had to learn what to do and start doing it, or I had to give up my dreams and take a job with an income ceiling and none of the benefits of the profession I'd chosen. It was decision time for me. In fact, if I didn't do something soon, money pressures would force the decision.

While staring out of the window at our office and worrying about my problems one day, I saw a sleek new sports car pull into the parking lot. I watched an impeccably-dressed young man get out of it and head for our door. He had an air of success about him that excited my curiosity. When we met at the front desk, I asked him what he did.

Radiating an aura of confidence that I'd never seen in a salesperson before, he told me that he was in sales.

"How're you doing?" I said.

"I'm doing well. I'll earn $25,000 this year." In those days that was a lot of money, wasn't it?

"How do you do it?" I said.

"I close," he replied. "Do you know how to close?"

"I don't have many clothes," I said, and went on to tell him that I was thinking of leaving sales work, that it wasn't for me.

He listened for a while and then said, "Have you ever heard of J. Douglas Edwards?"

"No."

"He's the master of closing."

"Great — but what's that to me?"

"He'll teach you what to say and what to do, and if you'll apply that knowledge, you can make it big in sales."

"That's what I need," I said. At the time, the company I worked for had a training program that went like this: "Hang in there." That was it.

The well-dressed young man then sat down with me and in the next half-hour closed me on going to the Edwards training program. It cost $150, and that was an awful lot of money to me then. But, luckily, he closed me on the benefits I needed, and I took the training.

After sitting in that classroom for an hour, I realized how little I knew about the profession of selling. It was an interesting seminar, much like the ones I now put on every month in different parts of Canada and the United States. We had to learn the closes word for word in order to graduate.

Like some of you, I fought learning them that way at first. Then some of what Mr. Edwards was saying got through and I thought, "Why shouldn't I learn them word for word? There's so little competition here, I could be one of the top students."

So I started studying all out, as though it was my life that was involved and not a test for the gold star in fifth grade. Two hours sleep a night for five nights. I learned the closes verbatim.

When I went back to selling, everything changed. I knew exactly what to say and that made all the difference. My sales took off, my income soared, I accepted myself, and all sorts of good things began to happen and build on themselves. All those closes are in this book; you can use them to cause wonderful things to happen in your life. But to use them you have to know them perfectly. A quick reading won't do it. We'll start with the minor closing questions.

THE PORCUPINE TECHNIQUE

Of the minor closes, this is the most potent. Imagine a little porcupine snuffling around in the brush with all its sharp long needles sticking out. If somebody put one in a sack and threw it at you, what would you do?

You'd throw it right back.

The porcupine is the technique of answering a prospect's question with a question of your own that maintains your control of the interview and allows you to lead into the next step of your selling sequence.

You may ask, "Won't prospects be annoyed unless I give them specific answers to their questions?"

Here's my porcupine answer: "Why are you so fearful of annoying prospects when your main concern should be to close them so that they can enjoy the benefits of your offering?"

In any type of sales work, you'll constantly encounter questions that you can answer yes or no—and have nothing. You'll also constantly be asked to give information that you can give—and have nothing. In both products and services, "When can we get it?" is a common question, one that's usually perfect for throwing the porcupine back to the buyer.

Prospect: "Could I take delivery by the first of the month?"

You can answer, "Oh, sure, that's no problem," and have nothing. What does the pro do when a prospect asks that question?

He smiles and says, "Does taking delivery by the first of the month best suit your needs?" The professional answers in this way because he knows that if the prospect says yes, he's bought it.

Believe it or not, some prospective buyers aren't looking for rapid delivery. Maybe they want to delay or spread out their investment and avoid the costs of warehousing or installing your product until the last possible moment. If so, the porcupine will smoke out their true feelings about delivery, won't it?

Let's look at two more porcupines:

Prospect: "Will this insurance policy have a cash value?"

You: "Is having cash value in the policy one of your concerns?"

Prospect: "Definitely not. I don't want to pay anything extra for cash value."

Isn't it vital to find out things like that? With this prospect, if you go on selling cash value as though he understands its worth, you're going to sell yourself down the river. Cash value isn't something that person will pay money for because he doesn't see it as a benefit. Sell him term, build your relationship, and upgrade his knowledge and his policy later. But, the prospect may say, "Cash value is a necessity as far as I'm concerned." Then you know how to shape the rest of your presentation, don't you?

Prospect: "Can we get this one in pink?"
You: "Would you like it in pink?"

The Champion understands how warmly the porcupine can be used, and how important it is to ask the porcupine questions with an air of friendly interest. The value of the porcupine is destroyed if it's overused, if it's thrown back at the prospect in a challenging put-up-or-shut-up tone. But, if you use the porcupine with discretion, it'll coin a lot of gold for you. The next technique is the powerful one that many professionals use to begin all their presentations.

THE INVOLVEMENT QUESTION

You may already be using this question regularly without realizing that this is an important technique with a name and a long history of success. If the involvement question came to you naturally, that's great. Let your previous success with it encourage you to work this winning method harder. Design involvement questions into all your sales interviews and you'll find yourself in more closing situations. What is an involvement question?

An involvement question is any positive question about the benefits of your product or service that buyers ask themselves after they own it.

In other words, an involvement question is an ownership question. When they ask an involvement question before they own your product or service, they confirm that they're going ahead. Let's try this on the owner of a business who is considering the purchase of a $3 million jet aircraft from you.

"Mr. Kirkham, do you think you'll be using the plane for your own employees only, or would you possibly consider leasing it out?"

That's an alternative advance, isn't it? But, on another level, it's an involvement question. Mr. Kirkham can reduce his cost of ownership considerably by chartering the aircraft out when it isn't needed for his own operations. You want him to be fully aware of that option before he makes his decision on the purchase, and you also want him to be thinking ownership thoughts.

Involvement questions can be created for every product and every service. You have both a challenge and an obligation to develop involvement questions for your offering — a challenge because not every product lends itself to this technique with equal ease, an obligation because you can't operate at your most effective level unless you create involvement questions to help your prospects own your product or service.

I can't write the involvement question for your product or service. That's fortunate. You'll be able to write more and better questions to get your clients happily involved in owning your offering than I could because you know it, you know yourself, and you know your market. Years ago, when I attended the J. Douglas Edwards sales seminar as a nineteen-year-old failure in sales, he told us, "If you want to turn pro, take my material and write your own material around your own product and personality. That's what the pro does, doesn't he?"

Your opportunity with the involvement question and all the other techniques in this book is to create something you can acquire wealth with. Put the stamp of your unique personality on your sales methods. Create, take your creations to the people—and grow rich.

I hope you'll allow me to stimulate your creative impulses. I know you're creative. We all have this gift in great measure—but some of us don't use it very often. I feel all this very intensely. **Creativity begins with imitation.** Michelangelo learned his techniques by imitating—that is, by studying—the methods of others before he began creating his own masterpieces. Shakespeare was an actor for many years before he was a playwright; he learned to write plays by acting in them. The imitation of this genius didn't stop there; many of his most popular works have plots that Shakespeare took from other playwrights and stamped with his own uniqueness.

When you read my words, my tie-downs, my involvement questions, my versions of the classic closes, don't sit there in your chair and tell yourself, "I couldn't say those lines. I couldn't use those words. They just aren't me."

That's great. That means you think there are better ways of saying more effective things, and stronger points to be made. If my words aren't your words, take any ideas and phrases that help you, discard the rest, and write your own words. Develop your own material. But don't worry about what's yours and what's mine in the words you use, concentrate on developing effective techniques that work and win new friends and sell new owners on your offering.

One of the great challenges in training salespeople—and perhaps in all education—is to provide an effective framework of techniques, theories, methods, and knowledge without stifling the creativity of those who learn. It's a challenge that's often not met, and the reason it isn't lies as much with the trainees as it does with the trainers. Most of us, when we approach a learning situation, want two incompatible things:

- We want to be shown exactly what's the right way, the best way, the only way, to do what we're studying.
- We don't want to have any rigid system forced on us just because we put ourselves in the learning mode.

Think about that. From this book you want to learn exactly how to master the art of selling what you sell, but you don't want to parrot someone else's words in sales situations where those words aren't natural to you.

At times, you might think it would be terrific if everything could be spelled out for you in sixty simple steps to sales success. But you know that if such a thing could be done, if people could read a book and become top-earning salespeople without deeply and intensely involving their own backgrounds and talents, and their own originality, drive, and enthusiasm, then anyone could do it. Effective sales work would become as poorly paid as stuffing fish in cans.

You don't want to be like me, to talk like me, or to sell like I do. You want to be you, talk like you, and sell like you. The power and the satisfaction of acquiring new knowledge and new skills lies in putting your own mark on them. That's my goal in writing this book, to have you tell yourself, "Now I've got the techniques and the concepts that'll allow me to become a professional. Now I'm going to write my own words for those techniques and make them mine."

If you're sincere about becoming an effective high-earner in sales, you'll create your own finished product of effective sales methods from the raw material that's in these pages.

The old prospectors said, "There's gold in them thar hills." So they piled their gear on a donkey, climbed the hills, and dug the gold ore out with pick and shovel. But they weren't done yet. They had to haul the ore out and sell it to someone who could refine it into gold.

There's gold ore in these pages, but you have to dig it out and refine it to get the glitter that'll make sales and win high earnings for you.

The process is simple. Learn my words, embed these concepts in your mind, and then develop that material into your own special systems for success. When you learn the material that's in these pages, you've made a good beginning at becoming a Champion. So you've got a challenge to go much further. Learning these minor closes is just the start of the process of making them your own.

MAKE TWO RIGHT TURNS TO SALES SUCCESS

Many salespeople who haven't reached the professional stage yet think professional selling is exactly the opposite of what it really is. When you entered the selling field, you may have thought, "Now my job is to talk and talk and talk."

So off you go. "Here it is, folks. Won't ravel, rust, or rip. Can't blister, break, or drip. Oh, you're going to love it. You better buy it right now."

The professional salesperson, the true Champion, realizes that people have two ears and one mouth, and each should be used equally. This means that, after talking ten seconds, you switch your mouth off, switch your ears on, and listen for twenty seconds. This means that, instead of overwhelming your prospects with words, you encourage them to talk. Let's compare the two methods:

Average salespersons speaking:

- "This is the best there is. Nothing on the market can touch it. We've got the best products because we're miles ahead of the competition. You better get it."
- "This insurance will do more for you than anything else you can find. You really better hurry and get it."
- "These items are on sale. Why waste your time shopping around? You can't get them for less."

When a "salesman" uses such methods, what's he doing?

He's pushing, isn't he?

He's arguing. He's telling people things they don't want to hear. He's trying to ram obviously self-serving statements down their throats. In effect he's saying, "I'm out to make you buy something. The only reason I'm doing that is to put money in my pocket, and I don't care whether what you buy helps you or not."

Such tactics quickly drive off everyone except the few who love to argue.

The professional salesperson, on the other hand, never gives anyone the impression that he's pushing them—for the simple reason that he never pushes. But he does lead.

By not talking all the time, by listening most of the time, by asking artful questions, the Champion leads his prospects from the initial contact to happy involvement in owning his product or service. In all this alert and pointed questioning, the true professional maintains a friendly attitude of interest and understanding that encourages the prospect to open up and give the desired information freely.

Have you ever bought something from a professional salesperson? You may never have had this experience because truly professional salespeople are in short supply—which is another reason why they earn large incomes. If you did buy something from a true professional (before you got into sales yourself), you may not have realized it. That salesperson was so smooth, relaxed, and skillful that you merely felt you were working with someone who was well-informed and friendly. But a Champion? That thought probably didn't occur to you.

Have you ever been surprised at how freely you've talked to certain salespeople before buying from them? They were alert and interested; you felt comfortable with them. Recalling those conversations, you may think that you were leading and the salesperson was following. Superficially, that was true—at first. In a deeper sense however, that professional salesperson was leading all the way and you were following all the way.

How did that happen?

Having a variety of products or services to offer you, the pro encourages you to start off. Once you set your direction, he or she gets smoothly in front and begins to lead you toward any of several open paths to purchase. When artful questioning reveals which of the several paths is best, the pro guides you smoothly and warmly to it. The halter goes over your head so softly that you never think about bucking. Instead, you buy.

USE BOTH BARRELS:

Discovery Questions and Leading Questions

Professional salespeople use two basic types of questions: (a) **discovery questions** (b) **leading questions.**

And, of course, these highly-skilled professionals often ask a single question that both leads their prospect and discovers more information. They can do that because they are fully aware of the dual role their questioning must play if the sales interview is to be successful.

Discovery questions are so simple and obvious that we tend to overlook their pitfalls.

"May I help you?"

"No, I'm just looking."

Many salespeople on the retail level ask that question and get that answer fifty times a day for years—and never stop asking it. That's why they're still selling pins and ribbons. The day they decide to stop asking that say-no question is the day they qualify themselves for a more advanced selling position.

> **You:** "Good morning. If you have any questions, just let me know. In the meantime, please feel free to look around all you'd like."
> **Prospect:** "Uh—I was wondering. Do you have—"

Sometimes the best discovery question in a given situation doesn't end with a question mark. It comes out like a statement but it gets the answer the salesperson wants more often than the bald question will. If you're in outside sales, you may never run into situations where you might be tempted to say, "May I help you," but you'll constantly be exposed to opportunities to ask say-no questions.

"May I quote on your next month's requirements for #10 Gunk?"

"No, we've got all we need for quite some time."

Instead of a say-no question, isn't it far better to ask a true discovery question?

"Do you use #10 or #12 Gunk?"

"Would you prefer that I quote on a monthly, quarterly, or annual basis?"

The first rule of discovery questioning is:

NEVER ASK A SAY-NO QUESTION.

This is an important concept, so I'm going to give it one more whack. What is a say-no question?

A say-no question is any question that can be answered by a yes or a no.

If you give them that choice, you stack the odds against yourself. People will pick *no* over *yes* between 51 and 99 percent of the time when they're given that choice by a salesperson.

HOW TO TAKE COMMAND WITH
LEADING QUESTIONS

Let's think about truth for a moment. What is it? That question has been debated for thousands of years and there's still no agreement. We're not going to try to solve this problem in a philosophical sense. All I want to do is emphasize that, in everyday matters, truth is what people believe it is. If you believe that Snortfire High Octane is the only gasoline that's fit to put in the sports car you love like a sweetheart, you'll go out of your way to get it. You'll be willing to pay more for it. The reality may be that a dozen other brands are better for your car; the truth is that you won't put anything in your tank except Snortfire—not if you can help it.

So let's agree that as a practical matter, truth is what we believe it is. I'm not being cynical; I'm simply being pragmatic. We may have the best product for our customer. Not only is it more durable and less costly, it has features no other make has. We know he needs our product's exclusive features. That's the reality. What's the truth? That he won't buy our better product unless he believes all these things.

How do we get him to believe what we know is true?

We can tell him. We can ram the facts down his throat whether he wants to listen or not. We can let him know how stupid we think he is because he won't admit the truth of our statements.

We can do all that and he's still not convinced. Why? Because we've told him. The professional salesperson operates on a different concept, one that's simple and effective. Here it is:

**If I say it, they can doubt me;
if they say it, it's true.**

That's the bedrock concept of professional selling. It's also the underlying concept for the successful use of leading questions. Salespeople who are guided by this concept never make their prospects think:

"You silver-tongued devil salesperson you, I know why you're telling me that—to make me buy your proposition. Well, I just don't have any faith in what you're saying because I know your kind. You'll say anything to make a sale."

When you're standing there pumping out the facts to prospects, and you're telling them how fantastic your product is, and you're laying it on about features and the warranties—have you ever noticed how they're pulling back? Have you seen their faces harden, their arms cross over their chests, their eyes start to dart this way and that?

When that happens, you're sending but they're not receiving. You've lost them—they just haven't vanished yet.

When the professional salesperson talks, his purpose is to encourage the prospect to say the things and ask the questions that will advance the sale. Let's try a few:

"You're interested in quality in the product you're looking for, aren't you?"

Now that, of course, is a yes or no question, but it's not a say-no because people don't reply, "No, don't give me quality. I'm looking for something that's a real piece of junk."

Here's another: "If you needed it, you'd like everything on the warranty to happen, wouldn't you?"

"Certainly." Is anyone going to say, "Oh no, we usually burn up warranties anyway. Who needs 'em? Just as long as it lasts till I get it home, I'll be happy."

"A reputation for professionalism is important, isn't it?"

How many prospects will disagree with that? "Oh, no, we don't want to do business with professionals. I'd rather buy from someone who doesn't know what he's doing."

"Working with suppliers who value their reputations for reliability and integrity is important, isn't it?"

"What? You have integrity? Get out of here." People aren't going to say that, are they?

That's why a professional doesn't tell people things, he asks questions.

But let's be careful. Don't drop this book, dash out, and start firing queries at every breathing thing you see that might be a prospect.

Control your enthusiasm long enough to read the rest of this chapter.

As a general rule, it's better to ask than to tell. But using questions powerfully is a bit more complicated than that.

Here's what's really effective and money-making-good:

(a) Ask the discovery questions that will reveal the benefits they'll buy so you'll know what specific products or services to close them on, and how to do it.

(b) Ask the leading questions that will cause them to affirm their belief in what you want them to believe about your offering. If you say it, they can doubt you; if they say it, it's true.

One more thing before you ask prospects questions: They must know the answer to every question you ask them.

How does someone feel when you ask them a question they don't know the answer to? How would you feel if someone came into your office for an appointment and said: "We have three types of machines: Our G Series with plotting and printing capability, our E Series that's plug-in programmable for over two hundred functions and operations, and our Super-Z Series that features microgrid difraction reduction and accepts snap-on modules for simultaneous QKD input. Which series are you interested in?"

Do you think the prospect will say, "Listen, I'm just kind of dumb. Give me whatever you think is best. And here's my checkbook. Fill one out and I'll sign it."

THE THREE PRINCIPLES OF QUESTION-ASKING POWER

PRINCIPLE NUMBER ONE: I always establish a bond before I go for control. How much time this will take will vary widely, but keep this point in mind: you'll stack the odds against making the sale if you instantly try to lead every prospect.

PRINCIPLE NUMBER TWO: I don't give them a chance to think, or the answer they come up with may not be the one I want. What does this take? Preparation. Practice, drill, and rehearse so that you can keep the excitement growing by keeping things moving fast. Also practice, drill, and rehearse how you'll recover from wrong answers the prospect may give you. Some of these answers you can ignore; others will force a change of course on you. Plan it all out in advance.

PRINCIPLE NUMBER THREE: I can't lead people to decisions until I make them. Do your clients know all your products? If you have several products or services to offer, how many of them will your average client usually select?

Just one.

Many salespeople have lines of fifty to five hundred products; one sample of each would fill several moving vans. Even those with much smaller lines can't carry everything they sell with them. The chances are that you can't either. You don't have to; you shouldn't want to even if you could.

Your job as a professional salesperson is to make decisions for clients. If you don't make decisions, why do they need you?

They don't. So they'll remain prospects to you and become clients to someone who can, and will, make decisions for them.

You may have difficulty with that one. I've been telling you to discover what benefits people want, and then to sell them something that will provide those benefits. So where does your decision-making come into play?

Let me illustrate the answer to that question. Suppose tomorrow morning you wake up with a high fever. You can hardly move and you know you're really sick. So you force yourself out of bed and stagger into the nearest doctor's office. He smiles at you and says, "Hi. Nice of you to come in. You look terrible. Any idea what you've got?"

"Not a hint."

"Well, no problem. There's a hundred books on the shelf behind you. Sit down, make yourself comfortable, and take a run at those books. I have to play some golf now and, hopefully, by the time I get back you'll have figured out what's wrong with you. If you can do that for me, I'm sure I can find a cure for what ails you right off." He's incompetent, isn't he? No matter how sick you are, you're going to crawl out of there and find yourself another doctor.

What would you do if your architect asked you to prepare the detail drawings for your new house? If your attorney asked you to outline your own case? You wouldn't use any of these people because they aren't professional. They aren't solving problems for you; they aren't making decisions for you; they aren't discovering opportunities for you.

Professionals have expertise that they use to solve problems and create opportunities for their clients. Doctors cure disease problems and create opportunities for people to be healthy and active; architects solve space problems and create opportunities for their clients to expand their life-styles; professional salespeople solve product or service problems and create opportunities for their clients to increase their productivity, enjoyment, security, income, and status, and to enjoy a host of other benefits.

In every case, the professional must have a larger fund of knowledge than any one client can use. This means that the professional must also have a means of discovering what part of that knowledge will best serve each client's needs. Professionals make this discovery through an organized, practiced consultation routine. A vital element in every professional's success is the ability to isolate, understand, and define the problems and opportunities that each client has. This is true of architects, attorneys, consultants, salespeople, and all kinds of professionals. To help them isolate, and then understand, their clients' problems and opportunities, some professionals have developed a consultation routine that's deceptively casual. It seems to have no structure. Why do they use this system? Because they've found that it's the most effective. They get more and better information from their clients with a relaxed, offhand manner than they do by direct grilling. Other professionals prefer — and have the skill to use successfully — a highly structured and very visible method.

Whether the method is subtle and indirect or briskly to the point, professionals control the consultation interview. They know what information they must learn from each client, and they proceed to get it. Basically, it's no different for the doctor, the lawyer, the salesperson, the management consultant — if they are competent they have more to offer than the client facing them at the moment can use. They control the interview to conserve their own and their client's time, and they make decisions for that client.

Take a moment and think about how many salespeople put themselves face to face with a possible buyer — either through referral or prospecting — and then let their prospective buyer control them throughout the consultation interview. If they manage to move on to the demonstration or presentation step, it's due more to luck and the buyer's determination to buy than any skill they've displayed. And then, when they present or demonstrate, they again allow the prospect to control the proceedings. The result is that their prospective buyers rarely obtain the benefits of their product or service. What a shame.

Such people tend to blame their troubles on their offering. "We're just not competitive in this market," they're inclined to say. But if anyone in their company is happily involving lots of people in that same offering and making lots of money doing it, how can it be the offering that's at fault? If anyone in the sales force can do it, everyone in the sales force can do it. Nothing will destroy your sales future faster than falling into the habit of blaming the product or service you sell for your own lack of professionalism.

An accountant must know taxes and business procedures; an architect must know construction and design; every professional must know his or her field—so what must you know?

You must know all these things in depth: your product or service; your professional systems for obtaining prospects; your professional procedures for diagnosing your prospects' situations and for isolating their problems and opportunities; and your professional techniques for surmounting objections, for demonstrating or presenting, and for closing.

It all starts with your intimate and detailed knowledge of what you're selling. You can't prospect with strength unless you know your offering; you can't demonstrate or present with strength unless you know your offering; and you can't close with strength unless you know your offering— which is the product or service that you're selling.

Take every opportunity to learn more about your offering. Go beyond that. Make opportunities to learn everything about the uses, benefits, and opportunities that your product or service provides, and also learn everything you can about its limitations and problems. Every product or service provides its benefits within narrow limits, and is ineffective outside those limits. Every product or service has problems; if you attempt to ignore them, your ignorance will quickly be exposed in circumstances you won't enjoy or profit from.

Your first priority must be to acquire a formidable bank of expertise about what you are offering. That knowledge will include an adequate understanding of the competition and a superior knowledge of what qualifications your buyers must have. Without such knowledge, how can you intelligently decide, both for yourself and the other person, whether any given prospect can—or should—become your client? It's impossible. From product knowledge springs the expertise to work with clients in the effective and professional manner that earns high income.

What does a doctor do when you come in sick? He starts by asking questions. Then he uses his diagnostic equipment to gather more information. Only when he has eliminated a multitude of illnesses, and zeroed in on one, does he decide on the treatment.

Isn't that what you should do? You start by asking your prospect questions. Then you use your diagnostic equipment—which may be a calculator and a pad of paper, a measuring tape, or simply your brain, and gather more information. Then you're ready to zero in on the exact product or service that will solve your new client's problem or open up a new opportunity for that person.

The transmission lines of your professionalism are the questions you ask. In the next section I'm going to give you all the steel and cable you need to erect a powerful array of your own transmission lines.

TWELVE POINTERS ON QUESTION TECHNIQUE

Here are the things you seek to accomplish when you ask questions of prospects or clients.

First, you ask questions to gain, and maintain, control.

Second, you ask questions to indicate the broad areas they are interested in where you might be of service, and then you ask more questions to isolate the narrow area that is your best opportunity to serve them, and then you ask more questions to pinpoint the exact item you can provide, or the specific service you can render.

Third, you ask questions to get the minor yeses that will start the stream of minor agreements that will swell into the major river of acceptance of your proposition.

Fourth, you ask questions to arouse and direct their emotions toward the purchase. A later chapter covers this in detail.

Fifth, you ask questions to isolate objections. Only in rare cases will a qualified and properly handled prospect voice all the standard objections to your offering; only a few objections will occur to, or be important to, any one client. By isolating the objections that are important to an individual client, and by handling those objections in a professional manner, the Champion knows that a qualified client won't continue to come up with objections until every one ever dreamed of has been voiced. There will almost always be some objections. Knowing that, the Champion seeks them out with eagerness instead of avoiding them with fear.

Sixth, you ask questions to answer objections. Unquestionably, the finest way to answer an objection is to porcupine a question that, when the client answers it, affirms that the objection is, in reality, of no consequence— or even is an advantage to the client.

Seventh, *You ask questions to determine the benefits that the prospect will buy.* Benefits. Yes, that's right, benefits. People don't really buy products and services, they buy the benefits they expect to receive by owning those products or services.

Eighth, you ask questions to acknowledge a fact. If you say it, they can doubt you; if they say it, it's true.

Ninth, you ask questions that will confirm that (a) they are going ahead, and (b) you should now go on to the next step in your selling sequence.

Tenth, you ask questions that involve them in ownership decisions and thoughts about your offering.

Eleventh, you ask questions to help your clients rationalize decisions that they want to make. You do that because you want them to make that decision too. Aren't we all looking for someone to tell us that we need that fancy new car, that we deserve the bigger house, that we'll benefit from and be complimented on that new $500 dress or suit? When we see that new electronic marvel, that glittering gadget, that sleek boat, aren't we hoping someone will come along and explain to us how necessary it is that we have it? Don't we all want someone to help us rationalize our desires, and work out the logic that will prove our desires are sound? When our emotions shout, "I WANT IT," don't we all crave support? Yes, ask questions to help your clients rationalize the decisions they want to make—and also make clear and firm statements to that effect.

Twelfth, you ask the questions that close them on the purchase. All the closes in chapter 15 depend on your question-asking ability for their potency. Don't make the mistake of concentrating solely on what you're going to tell them. Don't overlook the vital importance of asking the right questions, of varying your methods to fit their answers.

Now let's turn the page and explore how to create the conditions that are most favorable to sales.

4
CREATING THE SELLING CLIMATE

A Champion only sells the benefits and features that the prospect he's working with wants to buy. For years, I've watched this point, and I'm convinced that it's critical to success: *don't sell what you want, sell what they want.*

It's astonishing how many salespeople only talk about, explain, and try to sell the features of their offering that they like.

- "Oh, I just love the fact that it slices grapes," and the prospect doesn't give a hoot about what you love.
- "You know, I've got this same policy in my own investment portfolio," and the prospects don't see what that has to do with their investment decision because your circumstances are different than theirs.
- "When you pour the O.P.E.C. to this beast—look out. It's gonna ram you back in the seat. It's gonna peel rubber." And the prospect is a conservationist who worries about the high cost of fuel and wants an economy car.

The Champion doesn't sell benefits before finding out what benefits the prospect wants. The average salesperson plunges into selling benefits from the start and, inevitably, he soon has the prospect sitting there thinking, "None of this stuff I'm hearing is important to me." Keep that up for a little while and the prospect leaves if he's on your premises, or you do if you're on his. I'd like to be sure that we're together in this area. Who pays for your product or service, you or the buyers?

Then we should give them what they want. Doesn't that make sense? We should sell them the features that will do the things they want done.

How does this fit my teaching that you should make decisions for your clients?

Neatly. People want more than they can get. Money is only one of the great limitations that we all have. Time is another. People want their cars to be larger on the inside and smaller on the outside, their meals to be more delicious and less fattening, their investments to have higher return and lower risk. They want it all but you know they can't have it all, so you have to decide, among your many products and services and their many desires, what specific item will fly for them. In most cases, you can't afford to show them everything, and lead them step by step over every square foot of your knowledge to the one item they'll buy. That's not efficient, not professional, not money-making. The purpose of your consultation interview (which might be a few quick questions on the phone to a prospect, or a longer face-to-face interview in someone's office) is to diagnose their problem, and determine what their opportunities are. Following that interview, you decide how to proceed. This process requires that you decide not to discuss a

wide variety of possibilities with them that you have the professional expertise to know they won't buy anyway. Part of your service is to save their time
as well as your own. If you walked into a doctor's office with a broken arm,
you wouldn't want him to x-ray your leg.

SELL THE PEOPLE WHO CAN BUY

Many salespeople spend endless hours with people who can't say yes.
In commercial/industrial/government sales, this is an ever present problem.
Typically, you can't walk in and talk to the person who is in charge. In many
cases, you'll be told that no one individual will make the decision you seek,
that all such decisions are the sole prerogative of the board of directors,
trustees, or whatever. When you're told that, you'll almost always be given
to understand that every member of the decision-making group is away and
unavailable. In essence, they are an unreachable committee.

What you're hearing is the truth—it's just not all the truth. The committee exists. It meets regularly. It can make decisions. All important decisions
are approved by it. And its members are, for all practical purposes, unavailable to you. Under the law, or in the by-laws, all the power in that organization is given to this group.

However, such unreachable committees rarely exercise any power
that's important to you. They have it, but they don't use it because there's
too much complexity and too little time. Willingly or not, the directors,
trustees, and various boards of this and that have to rely on the nameless
gnomes in the backrooms for recommendations that they can only approve
or disapprove. Of course, the gnomes are nameless only in the sense that
they don't sign annual reports or get mentioned on cornerstones. *But their
signatures activate purchase orders.*

There are few situations in sales that are more complex and easier to
botch than the unreachable committee. In no other area will your sensitivity
to small clues and the subtle nuances of power be better rewarded.

Organizations have purchasing procedures that involve several people,
much time, more paperwork, and they all move through clearly defined and
tidy channels in complete conformity to law and the dictates of their gov-
erning bodies or owners. That's the face the organization shows to the
world, and it has the paperwork in its files to prove that everything has been
done according to their book.

In reality, though, very little is done according to their book, and the
real decisions are made outside the tidy channels. The paperwork to justify
those decisions is then created after the event.

The gnomes are smart. They use the unreachable committee dodge for
all it's worth. And they have other methods for frustrating and avoiding the
projects or people they don't favor.

Flexibility is vital in these situations. Rigidity is dangerous to your
success. Keep the ideas that follow in mind when you work with the
unreachable committee situation and they'll frequently help you find your
way—follow them blindly and they'll sometimes take you off the road and
over the cliff.

- The gnomes in the backroom are insecure, and jealous of the power they wield at the whim of the committee. *Make the gnome feel important.* Never let a gnome suspect that you're anything but delighted that you can work with him instead of whoever has the title and the official authority.
- You have faith in the value and importance of your offering to that organization. You need that faith, but don't let it blind you to the fact that most of the unreachable committee will be too involved with their own pet projects to care very much about yours. Never hint that you'll try an end run around the gnome to the committee until you're willing to accept the gnome's enmity. Unless you can somehow reach the unreachable committee and sell it on your proposition (and by definition that's impossible, or at least impractical), you probably need the cooperation of the gnome to close that organization. Keep that in mind from the first moment you think about selling to them.
- Make sure you're working with the right gnome, not some chair-warmer whose main job is getting rid of the salespeople the right gnome thinks he doesn't want to talk to.
- There are two kinds of gnomes: those who relish displaying their power by committing themselves, and those who'll never commit themselves. Never try to get an iron-bound commitment from a reluctant gnome—it can't be done. And the more you try, the worse you injure yourself.
- If you can't sell the gnome within a reasonable time, and if you think that organization is worth more of your time, try the end run. If you can't find a way to reach somebody on that unreachable committee through friends, political connections, or by direct and persistent pursuit, go over the gnome's head to anyone strong enough to push your proposition past him. You risk making an enemy of the gnome, but what do you have to lose? You've already lost—or failed to gain—his support. Now you have no way to go but up.

In chapter 12, I'll show you stratagems to overcome the problem of discovering the right person to work with. Bear in mind that difficulties in choosing the right person to sell aren't limited to organizational sales. The same problem plagues retail and family sales.

Let's suppose that you're working with married-couple buyers. You're getting along great with one of them—you're selling that person like crazy—but the reality is that the other half of the couple will give the real yes that makes the decision. Your job is to find out which one of the pair has the power to say yes on your particular sale and then to get that yes without inciting the second person to say no.

In retail sales, you'll frequently encounter three kinds of families:
Single parent.
Nuclear family (mother, father, and children).
Extended family (nuclear family plus relatives).

Unless you're a member of an extended family, or acquainted with one, you may not realize that their influence is still very much with us. The quiet oldster with the young couple may be the decision-maker.

DON'T SELL LOGIC — AROUSE EMOTIONS

Many of us try to sell our products through logic and only through logic. Highlight this:

Seldom do people buy logically

Some of us think that many things are bought and sold totally without emotion. For example, who gets excited about pork bellies, cocoa beans, and baled cotton? Speculators do; they're betting heavily that they can outguess the future. Producers do; they worry about oversupply and falling prices. Users do; they worry about undersupply and rising costs. Even in the most unglamorous products and services, fortunes and reputations are being made—and lost.

What about standard shelf items that meet established specifications?

A lack of difference between competitive offers means that the emotional factors are very likely to be magnified, not diminished. When awarding orders, the buyer can indulge in favoritism, score-settling, or just plain whimsy without fear of creating problems for himself. The role of salesmanship in these situations takes on a greater importance and a changed aspect.

CATCH THE CHANGE ON THE MOVE

What is the emotional process that leads to a purchase? It begins with a new development in the buyer's self-image. That is, the buyer sees herself or himself in a new way. If the projected purchase is small, that change need only be small, but if the purchase is a large one in relation to the buyer's income, the change in self-image that makes the purchase possible will be large. Such a change can come about very quickly. It can take place within a few minutes—or even within a few seconds. Champions are adept at spotting these changes in self-image as they occur during sales interviews. They are quick to reinforce the buyer's new idea that he or she can have and enjoy, will look good in and be complimented on, deserves, needs, and is worthy of, the marvelous new goodie they like. When you see that hangback eagerness—reinforce their self-image. Do that and they won't just like your product, they'll want it, need it, realize they can't get along without it—and then they'll buy it.

A few words of caution are in order here because this is selling's most common and most abused technique. It's automatic in the oriental bazaar, overused in the boutique, and heard too soon almost everywhere that apparel and accessories are sold at retail.

"It really looks good on you," they say — about everything you try on. Sometimes they'll say that without even glancing at you.

It's sad when a fine technique is beaten into a total turnoff by total insincerity and carelessness. Yet, when used right, this is a powerful technique. It requires attention; it requires discipline — but, given that, it delivers the results. Here's how to do it:

First, be genuinely interested in doing your best for the customer, and show this interest by asking questions that will tell you what they're seeking to accomplish. Rise above the limitations of your own taste and preferences. Recognize that what's right for you isn't right for everyone, and make an intense effort to see the world through your customer's eyes.

Second, use your expertise to guide the customer to the best solution for them that your inventory provides.

Third, wait for positive stimulus from the customer. When you get it, if you believe they've found something that helps them achieve whatever effect they want, reinforce their image about that purchase. Avoid the worn out phrases they've heard a thousand times; stay away from the words they stopped believing years ago. Concentrate on your customer. Say sincere and positive things that reflect your customer's uniqueness, and you'll not only make that sale, you'll create a client who'll send you referrals and buy from you again in the future. The key is to discipline yourself to wait for the customer's positive input. Unless you do that, you'll find yourself puffing something they don't like and, before you know it, you're caught in a web of obvious insincerity.

I had retail sales in mind when I wrote that, but the principles carry over to every kind of sales work because the one constant is that you're selling to people. Machines don't buy much.

If you stick to the facts, if you constantly work on your buyers with logic and avoid arousing their emotions positively, what will happen?

The mere fact that you're a salesperson will arouse their negative emotions and they'll start fighting you. Your prospects are either emotionally for you, or against you—and you can divide your chances of selling them by a hundred if they're against you.

At my seminars I ask my audiences to give me emotional reasons that cause people to buy. Things like this will usually be suggested first:

> "They can afford it."
> "It's the right size."
> "Prices are going up."
> "It meets their needs."

Most audiences will give me several logical reasons why people should buy before they'll give me a single emotion that will make people buy. This makes me believe that salespeople in general put too much emphasis on fact and too little on emotion. If we weren't the jangling bundle of emotions that we all are, everybody would buy everything based solely on logic—and then wouldn't the world be a dull place.

"They can afford it." They'll never think about whether they can afford it or not until you get them emotionally involved in wanting it.

"It's the right size." What does that matter if they don't want it?

"Prices are going up." Yes, they are, and that's a strong emotional reason for the buyer to hang onto his money and not buy anything he doesn't want.

"It meets their needs." It may meet what you think they need, but the fact remains that they're going to buy what they want.

Emotion. That's where it's at. Unless you're arousing positive emotions, they're raising negative emotions—and you've lost the sale. Again, I ask, what are the positive buying emotions?

At one of my seminars, a bright young woman who's going far as a salesperson said, "Style," and I jumped on it.

"We all have to wear clothes in our society, don't you agree? That's the logical reason for spending money on clothes. But do any of us buy the cheapest stuff that'll keep us warm, dry, and covered? Certainly not. We buy the style our self-image tells us to buy. We buy emotionally."

Another young lady said, "Color."

"Certainly color is one of the buying emotions. In clothing and home furnishings, it's commonplace for people to want their choice of color more than they want a particular product, and that attitude carries over to some degree on most purchases of things that will be seen. Colors make statements about the people who wear them, drive around in them, and sit among them in their homes and offices. We all have feelings about colors, and we buy the ones we want."

I asked for another buying emotion, and a man said, "Pride of ownership."

"Of course," I answered. "Human beings love to own things. Pride of ownership is, in reality, pride in oneself. This is not only a potent buying emotion, it's also an easy one to arouse. That's what the salesperson does who says, 'Your friends will know you've really arrived when they see you drive up in this car, won't they?' Plain transportation is all that we really need—on the surface. In the deeper senses, many of us need and want all the status that we can squeeze out of owning an automobile. And we buy what we want if we possibly can."

To get a thorough education in the emotions that sell, sit down with your children some Saturday morning and study the commercials on the programs they watch. You'll see advertising that grabs right at the emotions. It goes something like this:

Seven-year-old Stevie is sitting there when a commercial plays. On the tube, Johnny Powerful speaks directly to the boy. "You want to be like Johnny Powerful, don't you? Then have Mommy get Ookie-Gookies for you. You need Ookie-Gookies to be like Johnny Powerful," and he flexes his muscles. That happens over and over on every show.

Now here's little Stevie walking along a supermarket's aisle with his mother, and Stevie is looking around for something interesting. Suddenly he sees Ookie-Gookies. Stevie doesn't say, "Let's look at the ingredients listed on the box before we decide to buy it. All right, thiamin, riboflavin, niacin—hey, it's loaded with exactly the stuff we need more of."

Little Stevie doesn't do that, does he? He sees Ookie-Gookies and big Johnny Powerful flexing his muscles at the same time. So little Stevie yells, "Mom, I NEED OOKIE-GOOKIES!" Stevie was sold, not logically, but emotionally.

Logic in sales is a gun without a trigger. You can twirl it all you care to but you can't fire it. Emotion is another gun in sales and this one has a trigger. You can hit the target with it. Every time you generate another positive emotion, you're pulling the trigger on another accurate shot at closing the sale. Let's list the most widespread, effective, and powerful buying emotions.

Color and style	Peer pressure (keeping up with
Pride of ownership	the Joneses)
Vanity	Self-improvement
Security	Health
Prestige and status	Love of family
Ambition	Family getting larger
Employment change	Family getting smaller

No skill that you can acquire in sales will enhance your earning power more than learning how to arouse these emotions in your buyers in ways that are positive to the sale you're seeking. The exact words that you use will depend on your offering, your personality, your buyers, and market conditions. Study each of the selling emotions given above and develop a list of emotion-evoking questions you can ask your buyers. If you're selling luxury cars, you should be able to come up with several approaches for several of the buying emotions. But, if you sell plastic pipe to landscape contractors, you'll have difficulty coming up with useful emotion-evokers on anything except security.

You see that new bauble, that new neatarooney. There's no reason for you to have it other than the fact that all of a sudden you want it. Then you emotionally come up with reasons, urgent reasons, for getting it. But do those reasons explain why you want it? Certainly not. Their function is to *prove* that you *need* it—to your own satisfaction, at least. And it's amazing how fast you'll do this if the new goodie is good enough.

Put this item among your key notes, and review it often:

Positive emotions trigger sales; negative emotions destroy sales.

As you work at developing the skill to evoke emotions in your customers, always keep that concept in mind. You can destroy sales as rapidly as you can create them through the clumsy use of, or the lack of control over, the emotional setting. And also remember that your actions and manners, your words and how you say them, and your grooming and clothes are all things that trigger emotions in your prospects—whether you want them to or not. People will react emotionally to you. I'm not being facetious when I say that it's important not to have them react with fear, anger, or disgust. To see some salespeople approach prospects as though these potential buyers had just fallen off the garbage truck, you'd swear that they don't realize that prospects have feelings too. Prospects suffer the effects of fear when a salesperson comes on too strong; prospects get angry when a salesperson patronizes them; prospects feel disgust when a salesperson is nonprofessional in any way.

Let me give you an example. Picture yourself walking into a showroom with your spouse. The salesperson on duty meets you. "Hi. I'm Pat Swifty. Nice of you to come in, sir. Hello, nice of you to join in, ma'am. You are husband and wife? Goodlooking couple. How are you today?"

If a stranger opened up on you like that, would you feel a touch of fear, anger, and disgust? "Oh, oh—this crocodile is out to get us. What business of his is it whether or not we're married? And who needs his phoney compliments?"

Your sales interviews don't need any more fear. Your chances of success won't be improved by an injection of anger. Your prospects can't be closed if they're feeling contemptuous or disgusted.

I'm leading you through dangerous territory now. On the one hand, it's vital that you be keenly aware of how easily negative feelings can be aroused, and of how hazardous they are to your sales hopes. On the other hand, it's equally vital that you not become tense about it, or your tension will impact negatively on your prospects and destroy your chances of closing them. The solution to this problem is to understand it. With understanding, you can make the right moves, work with the odds always on your side, and close on positive feelings rather than be defeated by negative feelings that you've aroused yourself.

Everything you say to prospects creates images in their minds. That is, if you use words they understand, and if your prospects are listening and hear what you're saying—considerations that many of us aren't as concerned with as we should be—then your words will create images in their minds. Since life is complicated and varied, those images will be complicated and varied. Enormously so. But we're looking at this wide variety of images from the single viewpoint of closing the sale, and that makes matters simple: every image that our words create in the minds of our prospects either helps or hurts our chances of selling that person. By this standard, all images are either positive to the sale, or they are negative to it.

Let's explore the relative strength of negative and positive images. Are they very nearly equal in power? That is, will ten negative images balance out ten positive images and leave you still in there swinging? Or will a single positive image offset five or ten negative images?

The opposite is closer to the truth: one negative can wipe out many positives. If you're satisfied you can spray all the negatives on prospects that you care to because you're smarter than they are, and if you're sure you can always save the sale by pouring on more positives when the mood strikes you, think about the dry forest that's destroyed by a single lighted cigarette thrown from a car. The power of the negative is enormous. The Champion doesn't fool around with it. Making just one thoughtless comment to a prospect can destroy your chances of selling him. As I stated earlier, this is dangerous territory—but it's ground you have to cover every time you work with prospective buyers. We're not manufacturing problems here—we're just facing reality.

Understand the problem. When you're working with strangers, you can't know where their sensitive spots are, and if you try to guess, you'll guess wrong more often than you'll guess right.

So play the odds. Greet them with a pleasant but unforced smile and a soft attitude. Don't pay them compliments; don't ask them personal questions; don't welcome them with a bootlicking manner. Look again at the imaginary Pat Swifty's words a few paragraphs back. Did it shock you when I said that those words aroused fear, anger, and disgust?

Pat would claim he was just trying to be nice. Not honest maybe—just nice. But what did his words and manner convey to the couple who walked into his showroom?

Contempt, not niceness. His action told them very clearly that he thought they were suckers for a fawning compliment and a false smile. They were smart enough to instantly grasp how he really felt. Most people are that smart. They may not think it all out. They don't have to: logic plays no part in this and the emotions work fast. You lose all chance of selling a person by meeting them with negative images. Before you realize what you've done, that person is gone, and you won't ever get a chance to repair the damage. In fact, with most people in most sales situations, there's only a slim possibility that this kind of damage can be repaired once it's done even if the prospect stays for a while.

Play the odds. Always be professional when meeting new people. Do that and you'll close more sales. The Champion realizes that he must eliminate the fears his prospects brought with them without introducing new fears. He must arouse positive emotions without arousing negative emotions. Finally, he must provide the logic that will back up his buyers' emotional decision to buy from him. The Champion knows that he'll never get to that last phase unless he creates positive images that will triumph over the negatives.

One way to make that happen more often is to avoid the rejection words. Many of us don't realize how often we destroy sales by using certain words that ignite fear in the minds of our prospects. Let's study them now in the next section. Learn how to inspire confidence instead of anxiety when you talk to buyers.

REPLACE REJECTION WORDS WITH GO-AHEAD TERMS

Hundreds of thousands of salespeople don't know about rejection words or—and this is far worse—they know, but they keep on using them to drive dollars from their own pockets. Let's define what we're talking about:

A rejection word is any term that triggers fear, or reminds prospects that you are trying to sell them.

When prospects hear rejection words, their responses often run something like this: "Oh, no—I'm just looking. We're in no hurry. We're just killing time."

If you're deeper into the selling sequence when you let a rejection word slip out, your prospects will say things like, "We'll let you know. We'll sleep on it. We're just gathering information now. We'll call you when we're ready."

Rejection words really work well. They let you scare your prospects so much that most of them will reject you and your proposition. If you're using rejection words you don't need enemies—you've got yourself. Here's a horrible handful of these words:

COST OR PRICE. Every time one of your prospects hears you give value information in these ways:
  "The price is $99,000," or,
  "It costs eighty-five dollars,"
they know what's coming. You're going to put the pressure on, push them for a decision, try to sell them. That's why the pro calls it:

TOTAL INVESTMENT.

What do you do when you invest?

You put money to work in ways that will bring income or other benefits back to you, isn't that right?

What do you do when you pay a price or pick up a cost?

You spend money, don't you? You pay for dead horses and white elephants, incur expenses, run up bills, and shovel money out that you'll never see again.

The professional's favorite term here is total investment. But, like any other word or technique, it can be overused. Here are several alternatives that'll allow you to banish cost and price from your selling vocabulary forever:

VALUE, VALUED AT.
AVAILABLE FOR, AVAILABLE AT.
OFFERED FOR, OFFERED AT.
WORTH.

To avoid confusion and questions you don't want, use these alternatives with care. If you say, "This model is worth $975," your prospect may be inspired to reply, "Okay, but how much less can I buy it for?"

How you get around this depends on your selling procedures. If you quote prices from a printed list and your customer knows that your company has a one-price policy that eliminates bargaining, you can glance at the list and say any of these things:

"That model is worth $975."
"We show $975 for that model."
"That one is valued at $975."
"It's available for $975."
"We offer it at $975."

Write out exactly how you'll use these terms and role-play the situations you usually encounter when prices are discussed. If you think this is too much trouble, you think being professional is too much trouble. In that case, what are your chances of earning a professional income?

LIST PRICE, LISTED AT. These two terms are taboo except in resale situations where there's a retail list price and a lower wholesale price. To everyone else in our discount-happy society, if you say list price or listed at they'll think you're telling them to ask for a price cut. Talking about list price and saying listed at is even more destructive if you've made it clear that your prices are firm. In this case, every time you say these nasty words, you remind your listener that he'd better check your competition before ordering from you because they might give him a discount.

Use the same go-ahead terms to avoid list price and listed at that you use to avoid saying price and cost.

DOWN PAYMENT. If you're looking for a term that will strike fear into every prospect's heart, *down payment* is a splendid choice. But, if you'd rather reduce fear than increase it, talk like a professional. The correct term is:

INITIAL INVESTMENT.

MONTHLY PAYMENT. Here's another term that's extremely effective at doing exactly what you don't want to do, which is to magnify fear in your prospects. Most people are petrified of monthly payments. They have enough already. When you see those two words, what flashes through your mind?

All your bills.

You see yourself looking at the pile of paper that eats up your paycheck every month. "Dang it all, I'm sick and tired of that payment. I wish it was over with. Never should've bought the fool thing in the first place."

Monthly payment is a bookkeeper's term, and it's a favorite with bill collectors. Professional salespeople say,

MONTHLY INVESTMENT.

CONTRACT. When most people hear the word contract, what clicks in their minds? Lawsuits. Courtrooms. Judges deciding their fate. Attorneys sending them bills. Deep trouble.

The Champion doesn't call it a contract. He calls it:

THE AGREEMENT
or
THE PAPERWORK

Now let's look at another nasty word, and this one may surprise you. Rejection words aren't unusual terms that you might only use once a month or so, are they? I've been attacking your everyday vocabulary, haven't I? Now I'm going to take a shot at an even more basic word.

BUY. Please realize that no one wants to buy, they just want to own. Some salespeople plaster their presentations with sayings that go something like this:

> "Once you buy from us, we can sure get it to you fast."
> "When you buy our product, you'll be happy with it."
> "The people who buy from me get terrific service."

What does the prospect feel when those words hit him? "If I buy it, I'll have to spend money—and I don't want to spend any money. All I want to do is have it. What I'm looking for is more benefits and less trouble."

Professionals know that people want to own things, so they frequently talk about owning. Buying is the pain, owning is the pleasure. So eliminate buy and go with:

OWN.

Let's rewrite the three sentences quoted above to replace their buying pain with selling power:

"If you decide to own it, we can get it to you fast."

"When you own our product, you'll be happy with it."

"When you own one of our models through me, you also own a piece of me because I feel very strongly about giving top-notch service to my clients."

The desire to own is a deep-seated urge. It's a compelling buying force that's too important to let your use of it depend on what you'll snatch from the charged air of a sales interview by chance. The professional plans and practices exactly how he or she will tie the image of owning directly to every strong selling point that's available. This means that the Champion sits down and writes out the sentences that will accomplish this aim smoothly by repeating only the idea of ownership while varying all the other elements. What you don't want to singsong is:

"When you own our product, you'll be happy with its exclusive crossover feature. When you own our product, you'll be happy with our service. When you own our product, you'll be happy with its durability."

Design a set of ownership image-builders that will allow you to continually reinforce this potent buying force without continually reminding your prospects that your purpose is to sell them. It won't take long to write out the sentences that will keep your technique from being too obvious. In a few minutes, you can drill yourself on those selling sentences until they're second nature. But, however long it might take you, doing so will put more money in your bank account than bantering with the boys around the coffee urn. Here are seven more ownership image builders to add to the three recommended above as having selling power:

"This crossover feature is exclusive with our company, and it's built into all our models. So, when you pick the one *you want to own*, you can be sure that you'll be taking a crossover *home with you*."

"All of us here are proud of our company's reputation for service. It's as important to us as it is to our *owners* and, when you're one of them, I know that you'll be delighted with the way we carry out our concept of *total commitment to the service needs of our owners*."

"Since the profitability of your operation depends on one machine, durability is vital, isn't it? When you *own* one of our Banghards and are depending on it, durability is just one of its qualities that you're going to be very pleased with."

"I hope to show you a product today that will greatly enhance your opportunities when you *own* it." Before "when you own it," you can add, "for higher profits," or any other sales point that you want to emphasize with this wording.

"When you find the model *you'd like to own*—and I'm confident that we have it in stock here right now—you're going to be delighted at how low the initial investment is." Tailor it to your product or service: "When you find the model you'd like to own, you're going to be delighted with our warranty." If you sell a service, you might cast the sentence in this form: "When you choose the service you want to own, you'll be delighted with how much costly managerial time you'll free up for other, more important, duties."

Every worthwhile sales point that you can make about your offering can be welded to an image of owning. If you can't make the connection between the benefit and the joy of owning, either that point isn't important enough to mention, or you're not enthusiastic enough about your product or service. In some cases, of course, you'll have to connect in a negative way: "If you own our burglar alarm, you won't have to worry about—"

Maximize your selling power. Tie your strongest sales points to the basic and very human love of owning. Of course, you won't slam those sayings at them one right after another. You'll sprinkle your ownership image builders throughout each of your sales interviews, incorporating them smoothly into other aspects of your selling sequence. I'm reminding you again of the dangers that are involved when you overuse any technique and allow your prospects to notice it. Every time that happens, they're tempted to pit their sales resistance against your sales skill—and whenever it's fun for your prospects to fight you, you'll lose.

You can help camouflage the ownership image-building technique by reserving the strongest word—own—for your strongest sales points. For less important points, you can substitute one of the words or phrases given below in *italics*:

"When you find the design *you want to put in your living room*—and I'm positive we have it in our huge inventory right now—you're going to be impressed with our wide range of finishes."

"When *it belongs to you*, you're going to be tickled pink with the way it impresses people."

"When *you have this pattern on your walls*, you'll be delighted with the aura it imparts to your home."

"After *you've installed this model in your office*, you'll be very pleased with how much time it'll save you."

"If you *make this service yours*, you'll be very satisfied with the performance-improvement in your shipping department."

"If you choose our service, you'll find that you've *added an important asset to your company's net worth*."

"When you *put this beauty in your garage*, you'll —"

"As soon as you *take this model home*, you'll —"

"If you *acquire* this service, all your worries about breakdowns will be over."

"When *you've got our service on your side*, you can count on —"

"When *it's yours*, you'll know your problems with overload are a thing of the past."

"When you *have* our staff on your team—but not on your payroll—you'll be amazed at the costs you'll get the credit for saving your company." This selling method for fee-basis service is easily adapted to many products—just substitute the name of your cost-efficient machine for staff.

The last technique given above aims two separate emotional appeals at salaried people working for companies they obviously don't own. The second of the two is the most powerful because it speaks to the most important emotion driving the salaried person. This emotion is expressed by a question that's in their minds every hour they work: "How can I increase my prestige, security, and power?" Its name is ambition.

On the gut level, this comes out as, "What's in it for me?" I'm not speaking of bribery. Few buyers for organizations are on the take, and nothing is more disastrous than offering a bribe where none is wanted. You're on your own if you're willing to carry the bag because I'm convinced that no job is worth the ignominy of having to give bribes to hold it. There are some things in this life that you should never tamper with, and one of the foremost of these is your own integrity.

But most executives, officials, and other buyers, though honest, are driven by ambition, by this what's-in-it-for-me? emotion. Why should they approve the purchase of your product or service today instead of referring your proposal to a committee, taking it under advisement, or zapping the whole thing into file thirteen as soon as you're out of their door? Because there's something for them in your offering by way of company benefits they can gain some glory by ordering. Develop the ability to tie the purchase of your offering to your buyers' personal advancement, and you'll be amazed at how many more sales to organizations you'll close. All that's required is sensitivity, subtlety, and effort.

Important as this is, don't overlook the power of the other emotional appeal in the sentence last quoted. It's vital to remember that most buyers respond strongly to properly worded owner image-builders even though they don't own the company or organization they're buying for. This fact has its roots in a sort of tribal instinct. To some degree, everyone who works for an organization feels this pull of the group, this loyalty, this sense of it's-us-against-them. Us is everyone who works here, them is the rest of the world. There's the elementary force holding every group together that's going to survive for long, whether it's a family, a company, or any other organization. The higher in rank that people are, the stronger this feeling is. Since anyone who buys for an organization has some status, you can be sure that they'll respond to owner image-builders because they feel a strong loyalty to the group even though they may complain to you about their job.

SOLD AND SELL. It's not likely that anyone will fix a happy smile on you and say, "Wait till you see what a salesman sold me today." No, you'll never hear that spoken in earnest, though you frequently will hear, "Wait till you see what I bought today." On the emotional level, *bought* is much more than the past tense of *buy*—it's the present tense of *own*. Buying is dieting, owning is being slim. Describing what one just bought is a sneaky but safe way to boast of what one owns because, though bragging about possessions is frowned on, it's socially acceptable to get wildly enthusiastic over a new acquisition. And people love to do it. In fact, this is an important emotional need that buyers are always seeking to satisfy, though few of them realize it and even fewer would admit it. If your product or service is right for this technique (almost all are), do the homework that's necessary to fold this zinger into your selling sequence. It's a powerhouse.

When people talk about *what I bought today*, they're really saying "Wait till you see the new status-raiser that I own as of today." They've done something. Now they want everyone to admire their wisdom, style, and power—and they won't willingly share the glory with the salesperson who closed them. Why? Because they don't want to admit that anything entered into the choice except their own desires and decisions. Keep this firmly in mind whenever you speak with anyone known personally to one of your buyers. Avoid saying things like, "I sold it to him." When you say, *I sold*, you're the hotshot who pulled the buyer off the street and pushed him into signing on the line you had to check in red so the twit could find it. This is poaching on the buyer's territory. Take all your glory from the people on your end, and let the buyer have all the glory on his end.

Some salespeople will tell prospects, "You're probably wondering who else has our service. Well, I'd like you to know that last week I sold our service to the Martunian family right down the street."

What does that make them think? "You might've sold the Martunians, but you ain't selling me, buster." They're fighting you because they don't want you to do anything to them. If anything is done, they want to be the ones to do it.

Sell has a similar effect. The word throws an image of slick fellers in flashy shoes talking people out of their money. A professional never sells anyone anything. He gets people *happily involved*. The most frozen-faced accountant is put in a better mood by better products, so even on the corporate level the Champion is getting clients happily involved instead of selling them.

You can get different people happily involved all day long, but if you hit the same person with that phrase over and over, you'll raise welts. Eliminate sell and sold by playing variations on these themes:

HAPPILY INVOLVE,
ACQUIRED (BOUGHT, ORDERED,
PURCHASED) THROUGH ME.
HELP OBTAIN.
COUNSEL OR CONSULT.
WORKED WITH ME ON THE ARRANGEMENTS.
AID (OR ASSIST) THE BUYER BY
ELIMINATING DIFFICULTIES,
PROVIDING EXPERTISE, OR
SUPPLYING (VITAL, NECESSARY,

8

USEFUL) INFORMATION.
HAD THE HONOR (PRIVILEGE, PLEASURE,
CHALLENGE) OF ACTING AS AGENT,
REPRESENTATIVE, OR INTERMEDIARY.
DEVELOP THE OPPORTUNITY.
WORKED OUT THE DETAILS.

Avoid sounding pompous or flippant by matching what you say to what you've done. "I had the privilege of consulting on that acquisition," is laughable if you're selling unpainted furniture at the discount store, but not if you sold the store. If you say that you "helped with the details" on a multi-million dollar purchase, people may think you're a clerk.

Let's put a few of these phrases to work to highlight how they can smooth your daily performance:

"You're probably wondering if anyone nearby has our service. Do you know the Martunian family right down the street? Fine. All of them are happily involved with our Plan Six—I know because they worked with me on the arrangements. Would you like to give them a call right now and confirm how they're enjoying our service?"

To a new plant manager at one of your old accounts: "Mr. Klein, this is Frank Macy at Lift-Trucks-for-Less. Your company acquired a Gruntless Marvel through me two years ago. I'm calling to see if it's still doing a top job for you."

To a referral calling you for the first time: "Yes, I had the privilege of developing a fine opportunity for Mr. Raiche last year."

Compare those statements to, "Yeah, I sold it to him." Then practice the phrases that will make the most money for you because they build confidence rather than fear and antagonism.

PITCHES AND DEALS. The profession of selling has been my life for nearly two decades. I love it. But I don't love hearing about pitches and deals. Some people in our profession insist on projecting the worst stereotype ever hung on us: that of the cold smiler who thinks like a shark, talks like a carnival barker, and struts around making pitches and deals.

"Yeah, I gotta go out on another pitch tonight."
"Lemmie give you the pitch on this terrific little number."
"After you hear my pitch, you'll know I've got the best
deal in town."

When you choose to express yourself with down terms, you put yourself down. What you say decides how you feel about yourself.

Let's not make pitches. Be eager to have your people hear your presentation or watch your demonstration. And don't offer them deals. If you do, you'll focus their attention on price, and you'll raise expectations that you'll have to beat down later — if you can — to make the sale. Invite people to:

HEAR THE PRESENTATION I'VE DEVELOPED
FOR YOUR COMPANY.
PARTICIPATE IN THE DEMONSTRATION.
GET INVOLVED IN THE WONDERFUL
OPPORTUNITY WE HAVE FOR YOU.

If you don't believe that words create mental images, arouse emotions, and cause things to happen, sales is the wrong line of work for you. *Pitch* and *deal* are verbal garbage, and slinging them not only casts powerful images into the minds of those who hear you, it also reinforces old images, or creates new ones, precisely where they'll do the most damage — in your own mind.

If you're addicted to talking about pitches and deals, you have a beautiful opportunity to discover the power of the images, attitudes, and emotions that words create in the mind. Take this opportunity, act on my next suggestion, and I promise that your sales skills and earning power will increase dramatically. Before we get to the suggestion, let's dig at the roots of this problem.

There are deep emotional reasons why you want to talk about giving pitches and making deals instead of having a more positive attitude toward your profession. Face those reasons. Cope with them creatively. Do that and you'll break the chains that now prevent you from being a great salesperson. You may need to show that you're street smart and tough; you may need to show contempt for your work to ease your fear of failure; you may have other needs to feed pitch and deal garbage to. It's an expensive habit: On the practical level, those garbage needs set limits on how much you can earn and attain. They have that power because of three basic truths:

- How you feel about what you do determines much of how you feel about yourself.
- How you feel about yourself is the image that determines how effectively you will work.
- How effectively you work determines how much you will earn.

Stop talking about pitches and deals. Start asking people to hear your presentation, watch your demonstration, and consider the opportunity that you're offering. In other words, start showing respect instead of contempt for your work and the prospects you work with. Make that change and you'll make more money.

You'll find that it's a challenge to drive those two words completely out of your thoughts and speech. That's what it takes. Simply not saying them to your prospects won't change your underlying attitudes. To achieve change, you have to ban them from your thoughts, from all conversations no matter how casual, and especially from your talk with other salespeople. The last will be the hardest, but your new attitude will make clear to your associates that you're in the business of succeeding, not failing. That will push you toward the winners and away from the losers, something that's always a good move. Make no mistake about it, if you've had a need to garbage-mouth your problems away, it won't be easy to stop—unless you're determined to succeed. In that case, you'll find it easy, effective, and enjoyable.

Here's my suggestion. It's a simple one. The very blood of sales is the power that words have to create favorable mental images. Use that power. Take a few moments now to form three positive images in this manner: Relax, close your eyes, and picture yourself dressed and groomed to your business ideal. Then imagine that you're: (1) giving a smooth presentation; (2) conducting a well-organized demonstration; and (3) offering your wonderful opportunity to people who want, need, and can afford it. Make all these positive images bright and specific in your mind, and name them *presentation, demonstration,* and *opportunity.*

Whenever you hear or think (of course you'll never say) *pitch* or *deal,* immediately throw that image out of your mind and replace it with the proper positive image:

● Now I'm giving this terrifically effective presentation.
● Here's me laying on my polished demonstration.
● What a beautiful opportunity I have for these people.

This method can be applied to a wide variety of negatives. Take charge. Use the good to drive out the bad.

But it won't happen overnight. Give it a month. If you say one of the words, or even think of one without instantly replacing that negative image with a positive one, start over. Stick with it until you've controlled these images for thirty consecutive days. Then count how much money your deliberate use of positive images has made for you.

SIGN. Our last rejection word is the nastiest of all because it sinks your boat so near home you can smell the biscuits baking and hear your old dog snore. For the salespeople who constantly hit the cold water because of this word, the worst part is that they never figure out what keeps knocking their planks loose.

The trouble starts without warning when you've sailed right up to your big close and dropped anchor. You've covered everything. It's gone well. You've finished filling out the agreement your prospect must approve if the sale is to go through—and now you get excited. But you conceal your excitement, turn the agreement around, and slide it across the desk to him. "There we are. Now, just sign on that line and we'll get the wheels turning for you right away."

Suddenly your prospect's smile loses truth. He stares at the agreement for a moment. Then he clears his throat and mumbles, "Uh huh, yeah, well, ah—my Daddy always told me to read the fine print before signing anything."

The trouble is, that's exactly what his Daddy—and his grandmother, his attorney, and his wife—did tell him. So when you say *sign here,* you trigger an automatic defensive response that makes him think, "If I'm not careful, I'll nail my fanny to the barn door with a ballpoint pen. Well, that's not going to happen, because I'm not signing anybody's one-sided company contract before I scrutinize every dot in it."

And that's just what he proceeds to do. One of the first provisions reminds him of a tax angle to check out, and then he spots something he wants to talk to his attorney about—and all at once there's no chance he'll okay the paperwork during this meeting with you.

You follow it up energetically, of course. But things happen that you can't control. To begin with, his attorney is on vacation. The day she gets back, you're far away working the year's most important trade show. Before you're through explaining to and negotiating with his advisers, there's a new development. Something happens in the economy, your price goes up drastically, or a new trend shakes his industry—and now the emotional climate is wrong. Delay and change have robbed your opportunity for the buyer of all its freshness and excitement, and suddenly it doesn't look opportune to him anymore. Then it's time to say goodbye to the sale that would have been yours if you hadn't said *sign here* several weeks before.

Even if your sales agreement is a simple order form, *signing* is still a scare word. A Champion never even hints that his clients will be expected to sign anything. Instead, he asks them to:

OKAY THE PAPERWORK.
APPROVE THE FORM.
AUTHORIZE THE AGREEMENT.
ENDORSE THE FILE COPIES.

There's a small but important item to watch when you turn your sales agreement around, smile warmly at the client, and say, "If you'll please okay the paperwork for me, I'll get your order moving right away for you."

Make sure they write their name, not *okay*.

I hope you'll invest the time necessary to own this section because forming the habit of using terms that are truly positive in an emotional way will give you potent force in every sales situation.

THE TRIAD CONCEPT:
HOW TO MULTIPLY YOUR EFFECTIVENESS

Many of us have one sales message. Because it's successful with some of our prospects, we overlook the fact that our single message falls flat with most of them.

Let's suppose that your basic presentation takes about five minutes. Of course, you vary it slightly to fit each prospect's situation but, basically, you give the same presentation in the same way to everyone. The style that you always use might be described as brisk, businesslike, and pleasant.

Very good. You've chosen a style that's effective between thirty and sixty percent of the time. (Effective in the sense that it'll allow you to make the sale if everything else is right.) Now let's go after the other forty to seventy percent who are turned off by brisk, businesslike, and pleasant types with their shiny shoes and cheerful smiles.

"Wait a minute," you might be thinking at this point, "Wild-eyed funny folks don't buy my product. I work with substantial people only."

Maybe so, but some of those substantial people have been talking to brisk, businesslike, and pleasant types several hours a day for twenty years—and now they've got combat fatigue. They feel like shooting themselves in the foot to get away from the front lines every time another salesperson exuding the standard manner comes through their door. So they send distress signals—tell jokes or sad stories—and hope that their message is heard and understood.

It rarely is.

The average salesman has his signal-receiving antenna raised high every time he goes in for any kind of a sales interview, though he doesn't hear much besides static because he's thinking too intently about himself and what he's going to say. So he misses the message, plods doggedly ahead with his standard presentation, and soon is trudging away without the order. The Champion also has his antenna up. The message to him comes through loud and clear because he's giving all his attention to the prospect. He knows what he's there to say much too well to give any thought to it when he's face-to-face with opportunity. In fact, the Champion knows three versions of what he's there to say. Having his mind clear, the Champion easily gets the message, goes with the version of his presentation that best fits this prospect's attitude, and soon is flying away with the order safely tucked in his pocket.

Be a Champion. Use the triad concept. Design and practice three variations on every aspect of your selling sequence. You may be varying your approach to some degree now, but you'll enormously increase your ability to fit your words and actions to each prospect if you'll consciously work at creating triple-headed responses.

Let me explain further, because I'm not simply telling you to devise three answers to every objection (although that's certainly not a bad goal). I'm recommending that you practice three ways of phrasing every good answer that you have to each objection. One phrasing might be slangy or homespun, another might be lofty or long-worded, and one should be clearly stated in standard English.

The triad concept doesn't stop here. Each of those three phrasings of the single answer can be said fast, at medium speed, or slowly. You can speak softly, in normal tones, or loudly. Your attitude can be respectful, friendly, or aggressive. That's eighty-one variations on a single answer to an objection. $(3 \times 3 \times 3 \times 3 = 81)$ When you apply this idea to every aspect of your selling sequence, you'll quickly develop such a huge inventory of responses that finding the perfect fit for every prospect will be easy. (Perfect in the sense that if there's any way the sale can be made, you'll make it.)

Start with your basic presentation and devise three variations. Here's one set of possibilities:

(1) Casual, relaxed, and alert.
(2) Brisk, businesslike, and pleasant.
(3) Intense, candid, and personal for the large number of people who automatically fend off company parrots, and work only with fellow human beings on an intimate one-to-one basis that recognizes their individuality.

The above are variations of emotional focus. Now let's look at content. Again, it's easy to think in terms of three.

(1) Technical
This treatment puts heavy emphasis on the technological innovations

your product has. Explore tax aspects and cost effectiveness if these apply. Appeal to the emotions in very businesslike terms.

(2) Even Mix
A moderately technical approach that uses strong appeals to emotion made in standard English.

(3) Gut Level
A straight appeal to the emotions in down-to-earth language, with only a few pinches of technical detail to salt the meat.

The triad above applies to what you say. How you say it provides another great opportunity to gain sales power by being able to adapt to any situation instantly. To accomplish this, develop three moods of delivery:

(1) Light
You can be easy without being careless, and you can be funny without getting hooked on it. I've known salespeople who'd rather get a laugh than make a sale. Do some of your laughing on the way to the bank by using humor in sales situations to further sales, not to amuse yourself.
1   If humor isn't your forte now, don't worry — it'll come in time. Meanwhile, cultivate a relaxed approach that'll ease you into closing position with the more informal of your prospects who can't stand the all-business attitude.

(2) Medium
A cordial, alert, matter-of-fact stance gives you the safest start with old customers who have volatile temperaments and with new prospects you don't know yet.

(3) Heavy
Be prepared to talk fast and concisely in high pressure situations. Nothing works well here except bone and muscle delivered in short, crisp sentences. No jokes, no flowery phrases, no confusing technicalities. Practice this one hard and you'll be surprised how often you'll use it, and delighted how often you'll win with it.

That's the triad concept. It sounds complex but it isn't. All you have to do is train yourself to think in terms of three:
three routes to every treasure,
three solutions for every problem,
three chances at every opportunity.
Do this and you can't fail to multiply your effectiveness, reduce your frustrations, and expand your income.

THE SENSES THAT SELL THE EMOTIONS
How many senses do you have?
Sight. Hearing. Touch. Taste. Smell. Intuition. A Champion does his

best to get as many of his senses involved as possible. Now, if you're the kind of person who's just talk, talk, talk, TALK, how many senses are you involving?

One only, hearing, plus a little bit of sight. But after a while they get sick of looking at you too. That's why the Champion operates on this theory, and it's one you should highlight:

**The more senses you involve,
the better your odds of making the sale.**

Throughout this book, you'll find techniques to help you involve more of your prospects' senses in the service or product that you're offering. In this connection, let me tell you about one of the Champions I've had the privilege of training. This young man quickly became number one in residential resales in his state.

You're familiar with the real estate open house—flags and arrow signs on strategic corners to guide people to a house that's for sale. And, of course, a salesperson is there to help people get happily involved in that or another housing unit in the area.

As soon as he had committed himself to pushing his volume far above average performance, this young man decided to review his entire selling sequence, starting from the basics. So he asked himself, "What is the lowest common factor that's always been present in every sale I've made so far?"

At first he thought it was something like needing a house or having the money. But he was seeing lots of people who met those requirements at his open houses. They came, they saw—and they bought elsewhere. Searching further, he realized that the lowest common factor—the condition that drove them beyond looking for a home to the point where they actually bought one—was a certain happening.

They became excited about one specific house. First they locked onto that house emotionally, and then they worked out the necessary details—in their heads and on paper—so that they could buy it.

The more he thought about it, the more convinced he became that this happening always occurred before he was able to make a sale. Once he began looking for it, he soon learned to recognize this happening even with people who habitually conceal their feelings.

What was the fuel that fired their interest to the critical level of buying excitement?

Information. In the widest sense of the word.

And how did that information reach their minds?

It didn't take this young man long to discover that professional psychologists don't claim a complete understanding of all the subtle processes they know are at work among our senses, our emotions, and our minds. So he decided not to ignore any of the senses in planning how to market his product. He made this decision even though it ran against the accepted way of doing things, even though it required thought, planning, and effort, even though none of his colleagues or competition were doing it.

This young man had grasped the fact that a short straight wire runs between what our senses seek and what our minds decide. He acted on his realization. He began loading that short straight wire with all the messages it could carry.

He used very simple methods to achieve his purpose because simple methods are almost always best. Have you ever walked into an open house when it's 100 degrees outside and found a fire burning in the fireplace? Probably not. It sounds like a stupid idea.

But here's what happened when people in light summer clothing walked into his open house and found a small fire merrily blazing: a look of amazement would appear on their faces. That's when he'd warmly smile as if to agree with them and say, "Are you wondering why I have a fire going in this weather?"

Aren't the odds good that they'll answer—and break the ice?

Then he says, "Let me explain. I want to do my best to help everyone coming in here experience the emotions of all four seasons. My wife and I really enjoy a crackling warm fire in the fireplace on a cold winter night— don't you?"

Is that involvement? Will they remember that home? Will they remember him?

Yes on all three.

Of course he didn't charge into his open house an hour late carrying an armload of wet stinkwood and a quart of diesel sludge to make it burn. With a little research in his fireplace at home, he learned how to build small fires that keep going the whole afternoon with little attention and give off delightful woodsy aromas the entire time.

But he didn't stop there in his campaign to happily involve all of his prospects' senses. After selecting a few tapes of mood music, he acquired a portable player he could take to open houses. In their kitchens he always pulled the old vanilla trick (baked a few drops in the oven) to fill that part of the house with a pleasant scent that evokes images of warmth, shelter, and good home cooking. He paid attention to how each room could best be lighted. In every house he looked for unique ways to appeal to prospective buyers through all their senses.

What did he achieve by bringing that high level of personal involvement to his selling opportunities?

He immediately began connecting with a higher percentage of the people who came through his open houses because they saw that he was different, bright, and concerned. He didn't have to tell them that, they saw it for themselves. Outstanding performance on open houses brought him the surge of referral business that vaulted him to the top in his state in prestige, earning power, and personal satisfaction.

He did it by using all his clients' senses to eliminate that powerful emotion called fear, and to create instead a galaxy of positive emotions that would draw them into happy involvement through him rather than through another agent. What he did—and does—is the very essence of what the Champion salesperson does: he makes use of every constructive and warm feeling that he can to bring his clients along with him emotionally until they say, "I want it, I want it, I WANT IT."

5

WHY . . . ?

"Why don't I do what I know I should do?" Ask this question of yourself. Ask seriously because the answer controls your future. Until you start doing what you know you should do, you're living under a law against success that you've imposed on yourself.

Behind that question stands this problem: How can I cause myself to do what I know I should do? We'll soon tell you how but first, before you go for the how, take time to understand the why.

You've frequently asked yourself questions like the above two. Everyone in sales has, except the top producers (who are doing what they know they should do) and the defeated (who've trained themselves not to ask anymore). You're not a member of that last group for many important reasons I can't know about, and for one that I do: You're reading these words. This means that you've opened your mind to new and possibly disturbing ideas, that you're willing to change your way of doing things whenever you discover a change that'll help.

When you began your new selling career, what did you have a big supply of?

Enthusiasm.

Do you remember? Burning desire. Excitement. The feeling of "Watch out world, here I come. Now that I've got this terrific opportunity in sales, there's no limit to what I can do."

Yes, you had enthusiasm and desire then. Yes, you were eager and excited about what you were going to do. No problem getting out of bed in the morning: you were raring to go. Everything necessary for success you had except one item: knowledge. You simply didn't know what you were doing. But that was okay, your enthusiasm made up for it.

Then what happened?

Some months passed. You learned your product, your way around the territory, how accounts are found, what the problems are. But, while you gathered that knowledge, what happened to your enthusiasm?

It dwindled a bit, didn't it? But your product is still as fresh to new customers as it was the day you started—it's just not fresh to you anymore. You've had time not only to see the negatives that every industry, company, and product has, you've also had time to dwell on them, time to let these negatives dominate your action.

Your gain of knowledge merely matched your loss of enthusiasm, and balanced your performance out to about average—far below your potential. For, and make no mistake about it, under your skin a Champion is struggling to get out. A front-runner. A big earner. A high flyer.

So now you know what to do, but you aren't doing it. Why? In most organizations, lack of the specific product knowledge required for that sales position isn't the main problem among the salespeople who've been there for several months. It probably isn't for you, either. Motivating yourself to do what you already know you should do is the main problem.

Why is this true?

Because what you should do is not what you want to do. If it was, you'd be doing it.

Now we've come to the cutting edge:

Why don't you *want* to do what you know you should do?

The reason you don't is that you're in conflict with yourself. This conflict comes about because the push forward of your wants and needs can't overcome the push backward of your fears and anxieties.

A bit later, we're going to study these wants and needs of yours in detail. Wants and needs are motivators and everyone feels them. We're also going to take a close look at the de-motivators that everyone also feels. When you feel a de-motivator, you feel fear or anxiety—which is why de-motivators are so powerful. They can dry your mouth, make your knees bang together like loose shutters in the wind, and light a fire in your stomach—or they can work in soft and subtle ways to kill your action. They're powerful, all right. That's why we're going to study them soon.

Almost every success-seeking person has been torn by this conflict at some point in their careers, and most of us live with it all our active lives. Perhaps we can't eliminate this ongoing battle. But we can decide whether we'll lose every day, lose usually, win usually, or win every time. We can't, of course, win every sale. Forces beyond our control will cost us a sale now and then. That's okay. What isn't okay is to constantly lose out to our same old unresolved fears and anxieties.

Think about that. In the privacy of your own thoughts, consider whether this conflict isn't the chief obstacle to your being an outstanding success. Not lack of ability, not lack of product knowledge, but simply non-performance of what you know you should do.

Resolving those fears and anxieties is surprisingly easy when you know how to do it. The first requirement is to admit that you're like everyone else—you have them. They may not show. On most people they don't show. But the people around you have them, and you have them. Recognizing that fact is the first gate you have to go through. The next one is to decide that you're not going to let those beatable fears and anxieties stand between you and what you want in life.

When you've made that decision, read on. Explore how you get depressed. Study this enemy and find the weak point you'll strike to eliminate it. Learn about the motivators and how to use them, about the de-motivators and how to defeat them. Then you'll start doing what you know you should do. You'll do that naturally and without great strain because you want to.

HOW YOU GET DEPRESSED

Do you ever get down? Do you ever have times when you just can't get up and make yourself do what you know you should do? Days when you'd just as soon drive right by the office, not call in, hide? Ever have that feeling? Let me show you how you got that feeling.

It's a safe bet that you wouldn't be in the profession of selling if you weren't interested in making money. And it's an equally safe bet that you'll agree with this statement:

I don't make as much money when I'm depressed as I do when I'm enthusiastic.

If you accept that, I think you'll go along with this idea: *If I can decrease the time I'm depressed, and increase the time I'm enthusiastic, I'll make more money.*

Notice that I haven't said, "Increase your enthusiasm and you'll automatically decrease your depression." Thousands of sales meetings every month prove that the pep imparted from the stage is lost before the depressed salespeople in the group get out the door. On the rust of conflict-caused depression you can spray any amount of enthusiasm—and it always flakes off. But enthusiasm does stick to alertness, knowledge, and purpose. That's why I make this assertion in complete confidence, "Decrease your depression and you'll automatically increase your enthusiasm." Compare the two quotation-marked sentences in this paragraph. The difference between these deceptively similar statements is enormous: the second one works, the first doesn't. Following the first statement produces the slim pickings of failure; following the second produces the riches and satisfactions of success.

Certainly, build your enthusiasm by every reasonable means. But, before you throw yourself into that useful activity, make sure your enthusiasm will have a clean surface to stick on. Sandblast the rust of depression off your brain first.

To do that, you need to know exactly how you get depressed.

Let's take a close look at the conflict that starts a frustration that grows until it depresses you. I call this whole process "forging the chain of depression" because it is a series of events. As with any chain, to destroy its holding power you need break only one link. Here is the process by which you've been forging the chain of depression within yourself; here are the steps to getting down:

1. Conscious of your wants and needs, you motivate yourself—and move forward. Imagine yourself starting the engine of a high-powered sports car.

2. Conscious of your fears and anxieties, you de-motivate yourself—and are stopped. Your sports car is sitting in mud up to its hubcaps; the drive wheels are spinning but you aren't going anywhere.

3. Some of the sales people around you are moving ahead—but you aren't and your frustration mounts rapidly. You see what they are doing, you know what you should do, but the more you want to, the harder it is to make yourself do it. In the sports car you gun the engine and throw lots of mud. But you don't move. Instead, you dig yourself in deeper. Your frustration runs into the red, and you pound the wheel angrily.

4. Because you aren't able to close sales and move forward to satisfy your wants and needs, you lose faith in your product and company or—what's much worse—in yourself. When any of these things happen, the frustra-

tion eating at you turns into depression. It's as though you give up trying to gun your sports car out of the mud, shut off the engine, and step out into the muck to go it on foot.

5. Now you're too depressed to take any effective course of action on your own, and you'll remain in that immobile state until some outside force moves you out of it.

A sports car driver, confronted by the simple mechanical problem described, would immediately squish off through the mud in search of a tow. But we're slower to go looking for help when confounded by depression in sales work because the solution to our problem isn't obvious. In fact, we might not even recognize that we have a common problem, one that can readily be solved.

If you're depressed now about your sales performance, ever have been in the past, or think it's possible that you could be in the future, you need to review the sources of motivation.

THE MOTIVATORS

The first motivator of the great salesperson is money.

Why is money a motivator? It allows you to get the things you want and need. Money is good.

Repeat that out loud.

Money is good.
Money Is Good.
M O N E Y   I S   G O O D.

Money is good so long as what you earn is in direct proportion to the service you give. It's good, but money by itself won't make you happy. All that money can do is give you opportunities to explore what will make you happy. And, while you're searching, you'll be a lot happier with money than without it, don't you agree?

The second motivator is security.

Maslow's Theory of Accomplishments is the foundation of most motivational courses. This theory teaches that the average human being strives daily to supply physical needs, that is, to obtain security. In a primitive society, security might be a flock of goats; in our society, security is something bought with money. Without money, you can't buy clothes. If you ran around naked, would you agree that you'd feel somewhat insecure? If you aren't wearing the right quality and style of clothes for a given occasion, you also feel insecure. Money buys a wide variety of possessions that to some degree provide us with a feeling of security. So money is a tremendous motivator, both as a direct measure of success and as a provider of a sense of security.

Achievement is the third motivator.

Almost everyone wants to achieve, but almost no one wants to do what's necessary to achieve. I believe that people everywhere are broken into two groups: achievers and non-achievers.

Achievers make up only five percent of the world, and non-achievers account for the other ninety-five percent. This is explained by the fact that a non-achiever is achieving non-achievement, which is an achievement for the non-achiever. So the non-achiever finds it all too easy to accept his failure to achieve anything of real worth and meaning. People who have nothing are usually achieving what they think they deserve: nothing.

Many of us were raised in environments where our loved ones, mothers, fathers, brothers, sisters, were wonderful and upstanding people. They also might be non-achievers.

If so, that's okay — for them.

We're achievement oriented, but maybe we've learned from non-achievers in our own families, and adopted the characteristics of non-achievement. Let's not concern ourselves here with trying to rescue any of your loved ones who might be non-achievers — because it can't be done. The will to achieve is not something that can be imposed on anyone from the outside; that drive must come from within. You have that drive or you wouldn't be reading these words. Your example may inspire your loved ones. Your success may make it possible for you to open doors to knowledge and opportunity for them. But you can't force the will to achieve on them. You can't achieve anything of lasting worth by pushing a non-achiever through doors of knowledge and opportunity if that person isn't eager to stride through.

Are you ready to throw off being a non-achiever? Are you ready to join that elite five percent of the population who earn the right to enjoy the delicacies of society?

Through seminars, cassettes, videotapes, and now this book, we've been fortunate enough to train people who are tired of being average, people who are ready and willing to join the elite, people who want to reach out for more, people who are ready to pay the price in personal change and effort. I hope you've decided that it's time to quit messing around being average, time to stop wallowing in the quagmire of mediocrity, time to reach out for the greatness that's inherent in all human beings.

The fourth motivator is recognition.

This is an interesting motivator, one I often think is the most important to our breed of sales folk. People will do more for recognition than for anything else. Everyone needs recognition: husbands, wives, children—and even your boss. We all do. When you were young, why did you do cartwheels out in the backyard? What did you want to get?

Recognition. "Hey, Mommy and Daddy, look at me. I'm doing great!"

In our search for recognition as adults, we play far more complex games. The cars we drive, the clothes we wear, the restaurants we dine in, the places we travel to, and a host of other things are all devices that we use to seek recognition.

One can argue that most of these things are necessities. Perhaps. One can claim to enjoy these things for themselves. Certainly. But without the need for recognition, would we be so obsessed with style and personalization?

We all crave and require recognition. That's why this motivator has such awesome power when it's used at full throttle. Many sales managers boost their sales force's performance more with recognition than with any other motivator. Even more managers get scant benefit from it because they give too little too late and too carelessly. To be effective on a sales force, recognition must be real. It must be prompt. It must be given with sincerity and without favoritism. Its quality or value must be in line with what was achieved.

Acceptance by others is motivator number five, and this is a dangerous one.

Do you know how many people strive every day to be accepted by everyone else? With many people, including many in sales, that's their greatest motivation—and their greatest weakness. But we all want to be liked, don't we?

Now here's an interesting thing that happens to every new salesperson regardless of the product or service. When you're brand new to your company (and maybe you're also new to the profession of selling) and first go into your new sales job all loaded with enthusiasm, who's sitting there waiting to accept or reject you?

Is it the achievers or the non-achievers who're parked there? Is it the Five Percent or the Ninety-Five Percent?

Which group lives in the office? Which group is out running for more business?

The chances are good that someone will say, "Now let me tell you how things really stand around here." When that happens, you'd think there's one chance in twenty of that someone being an achiever, but you may not even see the achievers for weeks. They're busy doing the things that make them great. When you're finally introduced to one of the Five Percent, they'll say something like this and not much more: "Glad to have you with us. This is a terrific company, and you're going to do great here. Nice meeting you. See you later."

Some people in your company will tell you that this training won't help you. Without giving these concepts and techniques a fair trial, they'll say that. After merely skimming these pages looking for something to ridicule or twist, some of them will say that. Without even cracking this book open, a few will say that. These people are the losers, and they want you to join them. The last thing they want you to do is join the winners. To show why this is so important to them, let's get on the case of Jack Bumyears.

Jack's been in the sales department of your new firm for almost eleven years now—and he hasn't learned a new sales technique in 120 months. When you start, everyone from the company president on down wants you to succeed—except Jack and his friends. Every time someone new comes whistling in from nowhere and makes good, Jack is faced with a hard question: "This new jerk did it. Why can't I?"

Bumyears knows the answer to that question as well as anyone does: Jack is a non-achiever because Jack refuses to be effective. But that's the one answer Jack can't accept. To do so would be admitting to himself that his work habits and methods must be drastically changed before he can succeed. Too painful, too frightening, to think about. Far easier to blame the newcomer's success on favoritism, pure dumb luck, a lack of ethics— anything that will steer the guilt away from Jack's shoulders.

But, no matter how ingenious Jack's been about excuses, no matter how much time and effort he puts into keeping those excuses tight, the truth is always in there, gnawing to be free.

After this happens a time or two, Jack automatically develops anxiety whenever a newcomer shows promise. Alert, hardworking, eager-to-learn people have a nasty habit of quickly succeeding, Jack learns, and that always forces him into another agonizing search for an acceptable explanation. The pain reaches down into Jack's subconscious mind and demands relief. Then Jack begins to act on a sad and false belief: That the best way to cope with other people's success is not to have any of it around. Soon he's attained a high level of non-achievement by becoming skilled at stifling ambition among his peers. Every weakness detected in an eager person is deftly exploited. Peer pressure is subtly guided toward containing anyone who shows signs of drive. If these tactics seem to be failing, Bumyears and friends will suddenly turn cold, and reject the budding winner whenever they can. This is where the ambitious sales person who has a strong need to be accepted by his or her peers runs into danger, because the price of peer acceptance is to accept being average. Only the strong can resist this pressure; only the strong can pay this additional price of success.

Our profession of sales is one of the few that people can retire into. Normally, you retire to the pasture. If there's anyone who attacks the usefulness of this book, find out their income. If they're not making what you want to make, you've found a Jack Bumyears.

Surround yourself with people most like the person you want to become. Whether you realize it or not, what happens is that you become more like the people you associate with, and less like the people you don't associate with, as time passes. You unconsciously pick up little and large ways of achieving—or not achieving—from the people you rub elbows with every day. Unconsciously, you gather attitudes and ideas, and absorb everything from petty details to major concepts that'll spur you on to greater achievement—or sink you deeper into non-achievement.

Don't hang around with people whose financial and emotional thinking is on a lower level than yours. You need to grow. They don't. So they won't help you expand your horizons, and they can't inspire you. Choosing the right associates calls for hard choices. But we have to drift away from people more messed up than ourselves, or we'll continue to soak up their influence, advice, and failings. Family responsibilities are one thing; your choice of friends is another. Mix with people who are plusses. It's hard enough keeping yourself up so you can climb higher. Don't make it tougher on yourself—possibly too tough—by trying to drag a bunch of losers up with you.

Are you trying to get everyone to like you?

Are you holding back a little on your push for success because you don't want to anger certain people who've let you know they don't care for hard drivers?

Why? You can't afford to be popular with the losers.

Write down the names of the people you spend most of your time with. Go over that list carefully, and think about whether each person on it is an emotional plus for you. Put everyone who isn't a positive force in your life on a second list, and then consider finding new people to be around instead of the non-plussers on your second list. If you decide to replace any of your present associates who are negative with enthusiastic new friends, you'll be pleased at how effortless this process will be if you do it gradually. No open breaks. No frank discussions. Simply make yourself less available to the minus people, and fill the time saved with activities that'll bring you into contact with positive new people. Some of them will become your friends.

The sixth motivator is self-acceptance. I hope you get this one because you can't realize your fullest potential without this achievement.

We all hunger for it. Self-acceptance is calcium for the bones of our personalities. Many of us keep those bones weak by making our self-acceptance dependent on the approval of others. Weak bones make for a hard life. Confusing self-acceptance with acceptance by others makes for a hard life.

You may have trouble thinking about self-acceptance in any way that doesn't involve acceptance by others. Many of us simply aren't in the business of accepting ourselves, although few of us ever get out of the business of rejecting ourselves. Positive input depends on others, negative input we provide ourselves. This is a no-win system.

The harder we work at trying to succeed this way, the more vulnerable we make ourselves. People sense our need, play our weakness to their own advantage, and decide for themselves whether we fail or succeed. Watch carefully where you seek approval. If you drift into seeking it from someone who'd be threatened by your succeess, you're in heavy trouble.

Self-acceptance is the state of being your own person. You have arrived. Not where somebody else sent you, you have arrived exactly where you want to be. Self-acceptance marks the day when the opinions of other people don't control you anymore. It's the day you start making yourself heard when you don't agree. It's the night you suddenly jump a jet to Europe for a vacation; it's the morning you stay in bed because you want to. It's the hour when you're all through with the games you don't want to play, through with the roles you don't want to live. It's the minute you finally unlock your potential, become you, know that you've become you, and know that you are completely and gloriously your own person. Doesn't that sound exciting?

Very few people get there.

Why do so many of us fail to attain self-acceptance?

Because we don't limit the number of people that we must have approval from.

Because we demand more approval from the world than the world is willing to give us—and weaken our action in a vain attempt to get it.

Because we don't grasp how important it is to truly accept ourselves. Some of us dimly see what's lacking, and try to force self-acceptance on ourselves.

But those little voices inside our heads keep on cutting us down to size no matter how loud and aggressive and stubborn we act.

Yes, it is difficult to become yourself until you've learned to be comfortable with an attainable amount of acceptance from other people. Until you can stop worrying about this, you can't become you.

And you'll never reach self-acceptance, the state where you can function best and be happiest, until you get some recognition and enhance your self-image. You won't get recognition until you have some achievement. You'll never have achievement until you develop a feeling of security. And you won't have a feeling of security until you start making some money.

You can get money, security, achievement, recognition, acceptance of others—and still not have self-acceptance. You probably know successful people who have all these things except self-acceptance.

We've all read about entertainers who reach stardom and then commit suicide. They had money; they had security; stardom is defined as recognition and acceptance by others—but they failed to achieve self-acceptance. Everybody liked them. That is, everybody liked each of them except one person. That one person hated what they'd become to get what they thought they wanted. The most sincere form of self-criticism is suicide.

The next most sincere form is the living suicide that so many people inflict on themselves when their cravings for the satisfactions of the six motivators far outrun what they can attain. Those who feel they're entitled to these things as gifts react the same way when the world refuses to hand them all they desire. They retreat into destructive habits and attitudes, and rob their lives of productivity, joy, and meaning. Don't defeat yourself before you begin to fight: don't demand immediate satisfactions far greater than those you can immediately obtain.

Those are the six basic motivators—powerful, gut-level emotions that drive us all. Untamed, they drown us; harnessed, they supply unlimited energy. Study them.

They affect you in many ways: on the surface, in the shallows, and in the depths of your ego. You can't learn too much about them and about how you can control their enormous forces.

As a starting point, look at your past. Feel your past. Your past has determined where you are at this moment; your immediate future will soon be the past that will determine your more distant future. As we get further into these pages, please realize that I'm writing to you about your life. Time passes at the same speed for everyone — it just seems to pass more slowly in slums than in Monte Carlo. Where will you be in five years? Develop a plan, and then activate that plan to put yourself where you want to be in five years. And be sure to update your five-year-plan at least annually.

THE DE-MOTIVATORS

Now we're going to talk about why people don't get all the things they're motivated to seek. Open your mind up now because the first de-motivator is common to many of us. Do you know how many people are so afraid of losing the security they have that they won't give it up to get the greater security they crave?

But what exactly is security? Is it really possible to have it?

I believe that there is no such thing as security other than the security you build within yourself, that you are secure only to the extent of your ability to cope with the struggle called living, that you cannot be more secure than your capabilities for handling insecurity allow you to be.

This means that you have to give up what you've got to get what you want. Hanging onto everything you've got often means that that's all you're going to get. This applies to business matters and to personal matters: to possessions, responsibilities, opportunities, and relationships.

It means that you'll spend money to make money. This is true for all businesses. You may be a sales representative for a large firm, but you are in essence building your own clientele, your own business. And a professional knows, a Champion knows, that an investment is required—not only of time, but also of money. In a later chapter we'll discuss some of the methods of spending money to make more money: mailing pieces, for example. Few beginning sales people use the mails as effectively as they could and should. Why don't they? Primarily because they're unwilling to give up part of what they have to get what they want. They want to achieve the outstanding sales record that breeds a large income along with security, recognition, and acceptance. But they don't want to give up anything they have now to get what they want from the future.

Isn't that strange? It's as though they don't believe that the future will ever get here. Of that it doesn't need any room in their lives. If your future is to be better than your present, your future must have space. Your future must be built. And your future must be paid for. You may not need a mail campaign. But you do need to invest in your credibility, as expressed by your grooming and clothing. You do need to invest in building your sales knowledge and skills. Success looks the part. Success knows how to do the job. When you have all that going for you, is there any doubt that you'll do the job?

So the first de-motivator is fear of losing security, fear of losing what you already have.

To help combat this fear, give thought to the fact that all relationships, skills, and possessions require some degree of attention—or you lose them. Think clearly in this area. If you refuse to give up anything that you now have, where will the space, time, money, and energy come from for new achievements? A clean chin costs a beard.

The second de-motivator is fear of failure. Most people have a problem with this one. I did, early in my career.

Would you like to learn a method to guarantee that you'll never fail to make the appointment, never fail to make a strong presentation, never fail to close the sale? I can teach you that very quickly.

Here it is: never pick up the phone, never make a presentation, never try for a close.

You can avoid ever failing by just never trying. How many people in the profession of selling are hiding every day from the chance that they might fail?

Let me give you a personal example of this. The first time I ever stood in front of an audience was in a second grade school play. I'd been asked to play Prince Charming. I got to prance around, wave a rubber sword, and kiss the princess. Now this is exciting in the second grade. My Mom and Dad were there. My relatives and all my friends were there. I was excited to be the star. In the wings the night of the play, standing behind the curtains dressed in my purple pants and my purple cape, in my turned-up silver shoes and my glass-jeweled sword, I was ready for my performance. Keep in mind that I had never seen an audience's eyeballs.

Suddenly my cue line came. I walked out on stage.

I froze.

I could not move.

Finally, they came out and just led me off. Now you know that experience was traumatic. From that moment on I had a phobia about getting in front of a group. I simply would not do it.

Then, many years later, I was invited by a major firm to speak. They'd heard about my sales volume and wrote, "Will you come here and teach your methods to our sales staff?"

I shot a letter right back. "Pass. I don't talk to anyone."

Then a man very dear to my heart said, "Tommy, do what you fear most and you control fear."

Think about that. (We're not talking here about defying physical danger, about hazardous thrill-seeking.) Think of something you should do professionally, something that you aren't doing because of fear. Then picture yourself doing that feared thing with ease and skill and success. If you can make yourself believe that you're actually going to do that thing soon, you'll experience some symptoms of fear.

Or you may not be able to take all this very seriously—because your fear of actually doing what you fear may be too great. Sometimes we have to let ideas cook in our brains until we're ready to serve them up. But don't let this idea get lost. Write these words down and put them with your credit cards:

Do what you fear most and you control fear.

Read those words every chance you get. One day, when you're ready to act and eager to conquer your fear, those words will suddenly grab you. Then you'll be done with this sad truth: *If you don't control fear, fear controls you.* Then you'll prepare carefully, challenge your fear, and conquer that fear for all time. Looking back, it'll seem easy. And, every time you conquer one fear, you'll find it easier to take on and beat your next fear. But you don't always win the first time out. Be prepared for that. The important thing is to jump on that fear for the first time. After that, it's not an uphill road anymore.

But you have to get past that first time. After I thought about controlling fear by doing what I feared most, I had to agree that I was allowing a fear to control my life. So I called the company that had invited me to speak. I said I'd do it.

That was about a month before the date of my speech. I served those thirty days on death row, wishing every hour that I hadn't done it. The nearer the time for my speech came, the more panicky I got. "What am I going to say?" I kept asking myself. "Why did I do this to myself?"

At night, after writing out what I was going to say, I'd read what I'd written out loud. Then I'd tear it up and start over. Finally someone told me to put it all on 3 × 5 cards. So I wrote it all out on 3 × 5-inch cards.

The night before my first speech, I didn't sleep at all. The next morning I walked into a huge auditorium. Three thousand people were seated there. I stood off in the wings as they started my introduction. And what did I start re-living? My fiasco in the second grade. They introduced me. I walked out—

> By the way, if you're not a professional speaker, have them provide a podium. That gives you something to hang on to. And the audience can't see your knees banging together.

Well, I looked down at my notes and just let 'er rip. I never looked at the audience, I just kept on talking. I was scheduled to speak for forty-five minutes. In eight minutes I'd covered every point.

That first time was awful. The second time was terrible. The third time was yuk. The fourth time they clapped a little. The fifth time they stayed. Now, after speaking day after day after day with the finest group I know, salespeople, I wake in the morning with anticipation. Excitement. All this for overcoming the fear of failure in the beginning.

How many people do you know who won't try because they're afraid they may fail? Isn't it sad how many of us consign ourselves to the junkyard of mediocrity rather than accept the momentary rejections that success demands? If you take just one idea from this book, make this one yours and it'll repay your reading cost ten-thousand-fold: "I'm too proud of my future to beat myself out of it."

The third de-motivator is self-doubt. This one holds special interest for all of us in sales. Before you entered this field, you probably mentioned that you might to your friends and relatives. Then what did you hear?

"Selling? You're thinking about selling? For a living? Know what that means? Feast or famine. Chicken dinner one night, feathers the next. What are you, crazy?"

Listening to that refrain a few times can plant the seeds of self-doubt in your brain, and stain your enthusiasm with fear before you begin. That fear can spur you to greater effort—or it can cause you to look for a soft spot to fall. "Okay, I'll just give selling a try," you tell your friends and relatives. "I'll give it a chance. If I like it, fine. If not, big deal—I'll give something else a shot."

The trouble is, you hear your own words when you hedge your commitment to sales that way. Elsewhere in this book an effective method of convincing people is stated in these words: "If they say it, it's true." That method also works for us—for us or against us. You can't go into sales with a

give-it-a-whack, see-how-it-goes attitude without weakening your resolve
to do the difficult things (like facing rejection) that must be done if you are to
succeed.

Tell people you've decided on a career in sales. No ifs or buts. Commit
yourself to success in sales. Don't brag about all you're going to do, but don't
excuse yourself from all-out effort either. Don't predict your own failure and
then float out to prove how good you are at making predictions.

And don't set your sights on being average. If you do, that's what you'll
be. When you're new, with few or no sales yet, being average might seem
like a safe and successful place to be. It isn't. Here's why: In most companies, one-third of the salespeople do two-thirds of the business.
(Obviously, the exact figures will vary from year to year and from firm to
firm—though not by much.) That's neat for the top third, but the bottom
two-thirds of every sales force must live on the income generated by one-
third of that company's sales.

That's twice the people splitting half the money. Every time a bottom-
grouper gets one dollar, a top-grouper gets four dollars. Unless you're on
the right end of this split, it's tempting to blame company policy for this
huge difference. Resist that temptation. Yielding to it blinds you to three
truths that all great salespeople know: (1) management hates depending on
so few of its salespeople for so much of its sales; (2) management can't put
you into the top group, only you can put you into the top group; (3) if you're
only average, you're only making a fourth of what the top-groupers have
proved can be earned in your job.

You stop being average the day you decide to become a Champion,
because the average person won't make that decision. You stop being
average the day you commit to an all-out effort to win the level of success
you want, because the average person never makes that commitment. After
you've made that decision and that commitment, you'll start handling
rejection differently. When you fail to get the appointment, you don't ask
what the average sales person asks: "What did I do wrong?"

When people who refuse to talk to you come into your showroom or
display area and then walk out, you don't ask "What did I do WRONG?"

When you demonstrate or present with eloquence and verve until the
prospect warmly and with love throws you out the door, you don't ask
yourself "WHAT DID I DO WRONG?"

You don't ask that because doing so reinforces self-doubt. With enough
reinforcement, self-doubt becomes negative conviction.

When you're gripped by negative conviction, you believe that everything you do will be wrong; being wrong, everything you do will fail;
therefore, you will fail. That's negative conviction, and every sales position
provides ample opportunities to catch it if you expose yourself to the virus.
Negative conviction is especially dangerous to new people in sales. If they
take every opportunity to ask themselves what they did wrong, they'll
repeat that question an enormous number of times during their first few
months.

What does the Champion ask whenever he or she fails?

"What did I do RIGHT?"

The Champion keeps on doing what he did right, keeps his up-attitude, overcomes the rejection, keeps on trying, and starts to win. The wins pile up until they smother any sneaky self-doubt under a pyramid of positive conviction. Most people don't move because they are de-motivated by their self doubts, which they turn into negative convictions. From here on out, ask not, "What did I do wrong?" Dwell on "What did I do RIGHT?"

"Wait a minute," you say. "I'm standing by the showroom window, getting a face-tan and feeling good, when this non-buyer comes in, proceeds to give me a hard time, and then walks out. Until he came in, I was feeling good. Now I'm feeling rotten. Naturally I'm going to ask, 'What did I do wrong?' Any fool can see that."

Any fool can ask that question, but the Champion, the top-grouper, doesn't leave his or her self-esteem and up-attitude lying around where any stray hardnose can stomp on it.

The fourth de-motivator is the pain of change. This is the toughest and most challenging de-motivator for my seminar groups to learn how to cope with. It's also one of the most harmful de-motivators. I hope you'll make a special effort to conquer it.

Why does change always seem to involve pain? We resist change because it means that part of our old self must die, and that an unknown new self will be born. We grieve the loss of the familiar as we labor through the painful birth of the strange. It's all very primitive.

Some of us resist change because we've suffered sudden, painful events in the past, perhaps in childhood. In adulthood, this finds its echo in statements such as, "I don't like surprises," and the tendency to defend against disaster by striking at change.

And we resist change because we almost instinctively believe that changing and aging are somehow linked. "If we could just stop change, we could stay young," runs this desperate and touchingly human hope. You see this futile hope in people young and old who wear the styles of five or twenty-five years ago, who hold onto the manners and viewpoints of yesteryear, who stubbornly cling to methods that were effective in a time gone by. There's a place for nostalgia in our lives. It can be comforting and fun. But even antique dealers have to keep up with the times to stay in business.

Individuals aren't the only ones to fight change. Companies do it— nations do it. But the world changes anyway.

We've all heard this dull-witted comment many times, "That's how it is;" this pointless reason, "We've always done it that way;" this pure unreason, "I'm not changing." Meanwhile, the inevitable forces of change are modifying how it is by making that way unprofitable and phasing out the person who's not changing. We can fight the forces of change and win some temporary victories against it—but we can't win the war. In the end, we change or we lose.

Success avoids fights it can't win. Instead of fighting an unbeatable force, success uses it to win victories. Success adores change.

So don't fight change, make it work for you. That's easier said than done because we all tend to fight change with strong emotions, and to use change for less potent intellectual reasons. Here's how to break that pattern. Here's how to make change a powerful and positive force in your upward drive:

1. Face the issue squarely by thinking through your emotional fear of change. Then consciously separate your feelings about intensifying your work methods from your feelings about losing the familiar, about the passing years, and about coping with the strange and new.

2. Keep the best of the old in your life so that you'll have a strong emotional foundation on which to build helpful change.

3. Make a habit of trying new things when you don't have to.

4. Every day, tell someone that you're quick to adopt new ideas, that you like sampling new things, that you're always learning, changing, and growing. Keep saying that and you'll believe it, act on it, and make it true.

5. While there's an element of pain in all changes, those that are thrust on you by other people hurt far more than the change you put in motion yourself. Instead of sitting back and limply waiting for the next axe of change to fall on your life, be the cutting edge of positive change and improve your life.

My purpose isn't to ask you to change, it's to ask you to be happy. If you're unhappy, put up with the temporary pain that's involved in changing. However, if you won't put up with the necessary pain of change then just stay happy. Or, if you can't do that because your happiness is slipping away from you, recognize that you're starting to feel the pain of changes thrust on you by others. That situation is all too common in life. The best—and perhaps the only—way to beat it is to take command of your future and start changing things yourself.

There's going to be some pain involved in putting the ideas in these pages to work for you. Face it. I'm going to ask you to learn things you're not doing now. I'm going to ask you to do things you've never done before— such as ask for the order.

Do you know that there are salespeople everywhere who have never asked one of their prospects to buy? Never. Not one time. Don't look around in your next sales meeting for such a salesperson. Check your mirror first.

We all have certain ideas and values. We are us, and we're not going to change. Let me give you an example. Hypothetically, let's say that for health reasons it's a wise decision for you to lose weight at this time. Let's suppose that you're 50 pounds overweight. If you're happy being 50 pounds overweight, then you should just stay that way and never think about dieting. However, if you're unhappy with the extra weight, then you'd be wise to do something about it, don't you agree?

The day you commit to a diet, you're going to go through some pain. You're going to feel pain until you lose that 50 pounds. Then, as you slither down the street, and everyone asks how you did it, you'll smile and say, "Nothing to it."

Stop reading this book right now and copy on whatever notepad is handy:

The pain of every change is forgotten when the benefits of that change are realized.

This is true of all changes. Once you've done it, the pain is forgotten. A perfect example is the young woman giving birth for the first time. Quite often, while that's happening, she's making a firm commitment: NEVER AGAIN. And then the beautiful baby, who is the creation of her and her husband's love, is brought to the new mother. She holds it and nurses it to life. Sure enough, in two years she's back in that same delivery room. It's the same with all positive changes.

I remember when I was prospecting day and night. I didn't like prospecting any better than the next salesperson does—until after I'd done it and the money started pouring in.

The pain of change is forgotten once you do what you commit to do. And, besides that, there's such an excitement to taking command of your life in positive and effective ways. But now, watch this ever so carefully. Look how we begin our conflict. We all want the motivators, but we can't overcome the de-motivators.

"I want to make a lot of money so that I can have security, acquire a feeling of achievement, collect some recognition, and be accepted by the people I come in contact with. And when I have all that, I know I'll accept and feel good about myself. But I'm not giving up the security I have now. I don't feel good—but I'm not miserable. So I'm not going to call those people back —

— "If they don't want our stereo system in their home, that's tough."

— "If they can't see that our cars are the best on the road, that's their problem."

— "If they're incapable of grasping that our in-house telephone system will be more convenient and save them money, that's just too bad. They've got the problem, not me."

"And, if I don't call them back, they can't bang a *no* on my head."

So it's easier not to pick up the phone than to put up with the fear of failure, the fear of taking a *no* on the chin.

"So I better not call. Besides, I've told just about everyone I know that I shouldn't be doing this kind of work. My mother keeps asking me why I don't take it easier. And my father always says, 'Why do you work so hard? It's not expected of you.' Of course, he never amounted to anything, but he's happy—well, sort of. So I won't call them back just this one time."

When the next opportunity to follow up with a prospect comes along, this whole song is sung again. It always ends with "So I won't call them back just this one time."

"Anyway, the buyers we have to do business with in this company are impossible—a bunch of 6-volt minds trying to fake their way through 110-volt jobs. I've got twelve years of college and a doctorate, but this yo-yo I should call back right now can't grasp that I'm the whiz-kid with the expertise, and he's the dummy with the wool blanket for brains. He acts like he invented the silicon chip, but without his purchasing authority he'd be nothing. This is the kind of guy I'm supposed to change for? No way."

And who loses?

I do. Because of my inability to handle the pain that change involves, I lost not only this one order but a host of similar orders by cutting a pattern of self-imposed defeat. Every time I scratch myself from a race instead of running and risking that I won't win, I cut this defeat pattern deeper. When the opposition between the motivators and the de-motivators becomes a conflict in your mind, the result is the transitional stage called frustration.

"I'm so frustrated. I want to make more money, but I'm not leaving this place for anything."

"I'm so frustrated, but I'm not going through the files again. If they don't call me, that's their cold buns."

Once you get frustrated, the next stage is the interesting one called anxiety. That's a fancy name for emotional pain. Some people voice their anxiety with such words as "I just can't stand this pressure anymore." Others silently let the pain boil inside them.

The next stage you reach is your danger zone. Many of us go in and out of our danger zone every day.

When in your entire life were you the most comfortable?

In the womb.

Now that's security. Your own pool, all the food you could possibly want, and no taxes. Then all of a sudden comes the day when you enter this world. What are you greeted with after you come through the door? A nice slap—your first rejection.

Then they cut your umbilical cord.

Do you know how many people are walking around looking for a place to plug it back in? Think about that. If you can't handle the fear of insecurity by giving security up, if you can't overcome the possibility that they might reject you when you go for a close, if you can't cope with the fact that you have some of these doubts, if you won't change and develop your technique, then the chances are that you won't stay in your comfort zone very consistently. Let me give you an example.

I'm your sales manager. You and the rest of the sales staff at our branch are here for that always exciting extravaganza, our weekly meeting. I can handle *pain* and *anxiety* up to 700. On that scale, my P and A reading is 50 as I take a shower and think, "I'm all set to give those people a great meeting this morning. I'm really going to motivate 'em. Production isn't good—no one's making much money, but they're a really good group."

At the breakfast table I decide to check on my first flyer in the stock market. After being a little leery at first, I finally decided to give it a go. In the morning paper I locate the stock my broker assured me would keep my family cruising in the Caribbean for the rest of our lives. It's just dropped fifty percent. Suddenly my Pain and Anxiety meter is at 150. My wife figures that something's down, looks over my shoulder at the paper, and sees the report. She then proceeds to advise me in graphic terms as to just how good my stock-selecting ability is, and also that my brains are composed of a

single ingredient that has a short name. My P and A meter hits 300.
When I jump in the car, I know I'm running late. Heavy on the gas. A
policeman pulls me over. I'm so uptight that I don't use an assumptive close
on him.

> (The next time a policeman pulls you over, before he says a word look
> him right in the eye with a big smile and say, "Officer, please forgive me
> for bothering you just for a warning.")

But I'm too far gone even for that. So the traffic ticket pushes my P and
A level to 500. When I finally walk into that meeting twenty minutes late,
you're sitting there. The phone rings. You pick it up and tell me, "Tom, it's
for you."

"I'll take it in my office and be right back." It's the regional manager
calling to tell me how our office is doing and to give me a little motivational
inspiration. It goes like this:

"Hopkins, are you aware that your office's performance is the lowest in
our entire chain? Your people aren't working, your advertising budget's out
of whack, and in general you look incompetent. If you don't get those
people of yours moving fast, plan on looking for another job."

I hang up the phone. Through the glass wall of my office I see the sales
staff waiting for me to start our weekly meeting. I walk out there with my
Pain and Anxiety meter at 750, well into my danger zone. There's so much
adrenaline pounding through my head now that I'm down to just two
options: the ancient ones of run or fight. Since we usually don't literally do
either in business anymore, that leaves the modern equivalents: withdraw
or get hostile. I'm not leaving, so the meeting will now be different from the
one I planned this morning. It goes something like this:

"Good morning. Are you people aware that your production stinks?
We're the lowest in the chain. I warn every one of you—I talked to the
regional manager—hear me, and hear me good—if I'm bumped out, I'm
taking all of you with me."

Now, I suddenly feel great. I've knocked my P and A reading down to
50 by using hostility to get rid of my excess pain and anxiety. I got rid of
mine. Who'd I give it to? You and the other people on the sales staff. I've
driven all of you up to 750 and put all of you in your danger zones.

It's vital that you learn how to handle a situation like this. Make no
mistake. In every type of selling, you're going to have a load of pain dumped
on you every day, and you're going to have another load marked anxiety
dumped on you too. Every day.

The key to meeting and conquering this situation is to realize that all
you have to do is overcome the pain and the anxiety. Do that and you'll stay
in your comfort zone. Why? Because there really are only two zones: danger
and comfort. You have to be in one or the other. Pain and anxiety aren't real
until you make them hurt inside your head. If you refuse to do that, they
can't hurt you. Realize that every day there will be painful experiences.
These experiences will all have the potential to create anxiety in your
mind—if you decide to do that to yourself by concentrating on feeling pain

and anxiety and avoiding any further risk of failure. If you decide to concentrate on doing constructive things that'll turn your opportunities into reality, you'll stay in your comfort zone because your mind is on doing, not on suffering.

You've had people upset at you. You've had unhappy clients. Every active salesperson has experienced this many times. Let's not blink at the facts. As long as you stay in sales, you'll frequently have people get upset with you. No one who sails the seas of success can avoid this. It occurs outside of you and often is beyond your control. Anxiety occurs only within your own skin, and anxieties of this sort are within your control.

You've had customers that you've given your heart and soul to and they still aren't happy. They tell you about it bluntly, perhaps rudely. They may go beyond that with a nasty phone call or letter to your boss. That puts you in your danger zone, and many salespeople in this situation start withdrawing or become hostile.

In the next chapter, you'll find a step-by-step formula. Use it every time someone cancels an appointment, won't take a delivery date, says they wouldn't have your product around, every time someone tells you *no*. Apply this formula to every rejection you get and you'll start looking forward to rejection instead of hiding from it. That sounds hard to believe, doesn't it? Turn to the next chapter and see for yourself.

6
LEARN TO
LOVE NO

What was the first word your mother and father taught you?

The word no, wasn't it?

And how did they teach you the meaning of no? By inflicting pain on your bottom. Why did our parents do that to us? Was it because they didn't like us, or because they loved us?

They loved us, of course. And they knew that we'd hurt ourselves unless we were taught to avoid certain things. So, for our own goods, they imprinted the meaning of no on our minds the only way they could — by making us fear no.

Today, what's the only thing that stands between you and everything you want from your selling career?

The word no.

The problem afflicting most of us here is fundamental: we have the wrong attitude toward that most basic word. This attitude, held since earliest childhood, has long outlived its usefulness in our lives.

Don't make the mistake of viewing this problem lightly. Solving it will do more for your sales performance than learning a dozen new closes. This is true because you won't give yourself many chances to use those closes until you update your concept of no.

It's unlikely that you've ever thought about this subject. Few people have. Do that now by reading on in an active, questioning way. I'm going to prove to you that no is good, not bad. I'm going to show you why the fear-ridden response to no that you learned as a child has become your road to nowhere as an adult. I'm going to demonstrate how you can pave over that negative old response. I'm going to present your positive new attitude, an attitude that'll make no your highway to the everywhere of success.

Think back to when you were a child. Were there times when your mother and father got into their danger zones?

Sure there were. A slight difference of opinion between them became a little spat that grew into a mid-sized dispute that somehow flared into a full-blown shouting match. As we've said, when people reach their danger zone, they have only two options: withdraw or get hostile. If it was a workday morning when all this happened between your parents, your father probably left for work. That is, he withdrew.

Mom stays home, so she gets to become hostile. Mom has told you not to touch the saucepan. When she walks into the kitchen, there you are, you little rascal, straining to reach the saucepan. What happens next?

Our mother could've said, "Sweetheart, come here and sit on Mommy's lap. I love you, honey. Because I love you, I don't want you to hurt your body. If you reach up and pull the saucepan off, you'll scald yourself. Now, since I haven't been able to effectively communicate with you, darling, I'll inflict a degree of pain on your backside to help you understand. "I said *no*." Slap.

Time and patience being in short supply then as now, our parents usually left off that entire first paragraph and came in only for the "I said *no*" and slap part.

This happens hundreds of times to everyone. Without such protective discipline, few children would reach adulthood in our mechanized society. So, as we grow out of infancy, we get it pounded into us that no is rejection — and rejection is painful. No is bad.

Then we go to grammar school. We already know something about peer pressure, and in elementary school it gets fierce. All of us there want to be like everyone else. If everyone's cuffs are rolled under, we better roll ours under. If it's time to wear the thin belt, better wear the thin belt. If the group favors a certain brand of shoes, or a specific style of clothes, in grammar school you wear them to be accepted by your peers. Remember?

My mother, and I have a wonderful mother, had a fetish for lunch pails. At elementary school I might not have worn the best clothes, but I carried the best lunch pail. Since we moved a lot in those days, I started fifth grade at a new school. When I walked in there the first day swinging my zippy lunch pail, the kids pointed at me and yelled, "Look at the twit carrying the lunch pail. Ha ha ha." Pails were out. Brown bags were in.

Of course I wanted to be accepted by my peers, and I wanted to keep my mother happy too. So I'd leave home with my gorgeous lunch pail, hide it in an alley, and walk to school with my lunch in a bag. The scheme worked. No trouble at home and the kids accepted me. I was able to make everyone happy.

This is something we all want to do, isn't it? But in sales there are going to be times when you can't make everyone happy. And there are going to be times when your clients and prospects will use you to relieve their anxieties. Someone or something puts one of them in the danger zone before you walk through his door. He's staying, not leaving. So he gets hostile and dumps his anxieties on you. This is a side of sales work that we don't hear about very often. It provides opportunities, although the average salesperson doesn't see one of these situations as an opportunity at all. In fact, it throws the average salesperson right into his own danger zone. Once there, he can only withdraw—and lose the sale, or get hostile—and lose the sale. Either way, the average salesperson's attitude is destroyed for that day, or longer. Many otherwise capable people have left sales work because they couldn't meet repeated challenges of this kind.

When a prospect or client blows up over a trivial matter or gives you a rough time for no apparent reason, that person has been pushed into his danger zone—but not by you. He needs someone to stand in for the bad guy who isn't there.

Turn down the bad guy role, and grab the good guy role instead. You can win being a good guy. I'll tell you how in a moment.

Confronted by a prospect who has suddenly turned hostile, the average salesperson gets anxious about his own dignity. If it requires shouting before withdrawal, he shouts; if his dignity allows a silent stomp out, he silently stomps out—to oblivion with that particular prospect in either case. The Champion sees the situation in an entirely different light. He knows at once that his prospect is in pain, that countering the prospect's hostility with more hostility is non-productive, that his own dignity is beside the point. As a human being he wants to help relieve his prospect's pain; as a business person he wants to move that pain aside so he can get on with business.

Here's how the Champion wins by casting himself as the good guy: he keeps calm, listens carefully, and speaks to the heart of the matter at the first opportunity.

"Mr. Prospect, I'm getting the feeling that you're really more troubled by something that has nothing to do with me or my company than you are about what we've been discussing. (Don't pause.) I understand how these things work. Why don't you lay a little of that burden on my shoulders? I think that'll make it easier for both of us. Getting things like that off your chest is something you just have to do, and talking to someone not directly involved can be a great way to clarify your thinking about a problem. Would you like to tell me about it?"

Speak clearly as you say those words, and don't hurry them. The hostile prospect usually waffles at first—denies that he has a problem or pretends to ignore your statement. Then, if you've demonstrated genuine empathy, the chances are that he'll drift into talking about what's bothering him. Once he gets started, he'll probably use up the available time telling you all about it. Don't worry. He'll invite you back, or he'll say something like, "Enough of my personal problems. What're you here to sell me?"

You tell him.

"What would my cost be?"

You tell him.

"Let's skip the usual blarney. You know what our needs are. Can your machine handle them?"

You tell him it can. That's true, of course, or you wouldn't be there.

"All right, I'll give you a purchase order for it. Stop in and see me the next time you're out this way—I might have a lead for you."

A Champion knows when his most effective presentation is not to give one.

HOW TO REJECT THE NEGATIVE EFFECTS OF REJECTION

No one in sales will dispute that being able to overcome the ill effects of rejection is vital to success in our chosen field. What's needed is a system that'll allow us to do that all the time. Here it is. I call it The Champion Formula for Rejecting Rejection.

If you'll concentrate on this formula when you get rejected, you'll feel good instead of feeling bad. You may fight me on this one. All right, don't use my formula—if you're constantly out there risking rejection, if you're frequently finding it, overcoming it, and closing sales. Unless you're doing all these things, you need the formula. Don't fight it, use it. And use it wholeheartedly—it will ignite a rocket under your sales performance if you do.

Step One: As the first step to using this formula, you determine the cash value of each rejection that you receive. I can't give you that value because this book is written for all kinds of selling, and values change over time. But, to illustrate how it's done, let's just say that on the average you're paid $100 for every sale you close.

$$1 \text{ SALE} = \$100$$

Step Two: Champions operate on ratios. As a sales professional, you know your contacts to closings ratio, that is, you know how many people you have to contact to close one sale. Keeping track of this ratio takes hardly any effort and yields valuable information. For example, a drop in the ratio alerts you to the fact that there are problems in your routine before they get serious. We'll go into this further in a later chapter. For now, let's assume that you contact ten people to make one sale. This means that your contacts to closings ratio is ten to one.

Every Champion strives to improve his or her personal contacts to closings ratio, of course, but the 10:1 ratio we're using in this example is a reasonable average in many types of selling. Let's go with that. Here's how it works out:

$$1 \text{ sale} = \$100$$
$$10 \text{ contacts} = 1 \text{ sale}$$
$$\text{Therefore,}$$
$$1 \text{ contact} = \$10$$

You are not paid by the sale, you are paid by the contact.

This isn't a weird, twisted, nonsensical way of looking at sales activity—it's reality. You have to make ten contacts to close one sale. No contacts means no sales which means no earnings. Earnings are not started by sales, they are started by contacts. This being true, why should you convince yourself that you're paid $100 for a sale but nothing for a contact? That's not only self-defeating, it's untrue as well. But don't quibble. The difference between a Champion and the average salesperson lies in how they look at things like this.

So do as the Champions do: psyche yourself up with winning ideas. Use the above formula. Perhaps you average 12 contacts and $240 per sale: if so, for every genuine contact rejection that you get, you make $20. Find your own cash value and use that to psyche yourself up before each contact call, and after each contact rejection. The payoff is built into this fact: you'll make more contact calls because you'll suffer less pain doing so, and you'll make better calls because you're more relaxed. Then, a little later, you'll realize that you're enjoying it. Now you're really rolling. You're banging out five, ten, or twenty calls in the time you used to spend staring at the wall trying to think of reasons not to make calls. Your sales are booming. And you're having fun, because winning is fun.

Isn't this exciting?

Every time you hear no, you've earned a specific amount of money: the cash value to you of one rejection. This is when you realize that no is good, that no is where the money's at.

That's right, no is good. It's not a hard slap on baby's behind that carries over as a hard jerk on an adult's anxieties. Hearing lots of no means you're in orbit, you're making money, you're streaking for your goals. There'll come a time when you'll hear sweet music in the words of no.

Concentrate on the cash value of rejection and you'll start looking forward to being rejected. As I've said, Champions and average sales people differ primarily in how they react to basic things such as rejection. If you'll look at every rejection as $10 and handle it, some clients will give you two or three hundred dollars for just standing there. So what am I saying?

Start your climb to success by changing your attitude toward rejection. Now I know that some of us, because of our upbringing, are petrified of being rejected. What's the answer?

Do what you fear most and you control fear.

If you make yourself handle rejection—if you let yourself feel the rejection and then overcome it once, overcome it twice, overcome it three times, you'll begin to realize that it isn't so terrible after all. Keep going; you're developing the ability to cope with it. Then, suddenly, you'll find yourself handling rejection without pain—and you'll wonder why you ever allowed the fear of rejection to block you from your goals.

THE FIVE ATTITUDES TOWARD REJECTION

From all over Canada and the United States, Champions who've attended our sales seminars have written to me about these five attitudes. Their letters repeat this story over and over:

"Tommy, I took your advice and memorized the Five Attitudes Toward Rejection. Because of them, I've been able to handle more personal pain, more business pain, more emotional strife, more problems, more pressure—and still keep moving forward."

These attitudes will do the same for you *if you'll absorb these concepts*. Giving them a quick reading and then hurrying on won't have the slightest effect on you. To absorb these concepts, you must have the words in your mind. Then, when you need them—and when you're willing to use them— these concepts will be there, ready to revolutionize your attitudes toward rejection, able to plant the seeds of success in every pot of failure you can find.

Copy them on cards. Read them aloud. Commit them to memory. **THE FIVE ATTITUDES TOWARD REJECTION MUST BE LEARNED WORD FOR WORD.** To make it more emotional and powerful, I've given you three alternatives for each attitude. Select the version (A, B, or C) that you're most comfortable with. Then memorize your five custom-fitted new attitudes toward all results that are less than success. (Substitute *rejection* for *failure* whenever that word more closely expresses how you feel.)

FIRST ATTITUDE TOWARD REJECTION:

(A) I NEVER SEE FAILURE AS FAILURE, BUT ONLY AS A LEARNING EXPERIENCE.

(B) I NEVER SEE FAILURE IN NON-SUCCESS, I SEE A LEARNING EXPERIENCE.

(C) I ALWAYS SEE NON-SUCCESS AS A LEARNING EXPERIENCE.

SECOND ATTITUDE TOWARD REJECTION:

A) I NEVER SEE FAILURE AS FAILURE, BUT ONLY AS THE NEGATIVE FEEDBACK I NEED TO CHANGE COURSE IN MY DIRECTION.

(B) I NEVER SEE FAILURE IN NON-SUCCESS, I SEE INSTRUCTIONS FOR REACHING MY GOALS.

(C) I FIND COURSE-CORRECTING DATA IN EVERY NON-SUCCESS.

THIRD ATTITUDE TOWARD REJECTION:

(A) I NEVER SEE A FAILURE AS FAILURE, BUT ONLY AS THE OPPORTUNITY TO DEVELOP MY SENSE OF HUMOR.

(B) I NEVER SEE FAILURE IN NON-SUCCESS, I SEE THE OPPORTUNITY TO DEVELOP MY SENSE OF HUMOR.

(C) I'M ALWAYS QUICK TO SEE THE HUMOR IN MY NON-SUCCESSES.

FOURTH ATTITUDE TOWARD REJECTION:

(A) I NEVER SEE FAILURE AS FAILURE, BUT ONLY AS AN OPPORTUNITY TO PRACTICE MY TECHNIQUES AND PERFECT MY PERFORMANCE.

(B) I NEVER SEE FAILURE IN NON-SUCCESS, I SEE AN OPPORTUNITY TO PRACTICE MY TECHNIQUES AND PERFECT MY PERFORMANCE.

(C) I VALUE THE OPPORTUNITY TO PRACTICE MY TECHNIQUES AND PERFECT MY PERFORMANCE THAT EVERY NON-SUCCESS GIVES ME.

FIFTH ATTITUDE TOWARD REJECTION:

(A) I NEVER SEE FAILURE AS FAILURE, BUT ONLY AS THE GAME I MUST PLAY TO WIN.

(B) I NEVER SEE FAILURE IN NON-SUCCESS, I SEE PART OF THE GAME THAT I MUST PLAY TO WIN.

(C) I ALWAYS SEE NON-SUCCESS AS A NECESSARY PART OF THE GAME I'M PLAYING TO WIN.

Now let's take a hard look at these five attitudes toward rejection so that we can maximize our ability to reject failure.

1. When you go out prospecting and get rejected, when you present or demonstrate without making a sale, when you've already made the sale and then some small thing causes your order to be cancelled in a corporate decision, what have you been offered?

Something of great value: a lesson in practical salesmanship that's specific to when, where, and what you sell, that is, to this month's competitive and economic conditions, to your territory, and to your product or service. Don't refuse the lesson; you've already paid for it with the loss of a sale.

Sometimes you'll have to do some research to learn the lesson, and sometimes it'll be obvious. But you'll always have to think it through. In any case, spend your time and energy analyzing the facts and studying the lesson you paid a sale to learn, not on wringing your hands and crying, "What did I do wrong? Why did I lose that sale?"

The light bulb took a tremendous amount of mental and physical effort to invent. The main difficulty was to devise a filament that would burn for a reasonable period of time. Before he solved this problem, Thomas Edison conducted and wrote detailed notes on over a thousand experiments that didn't produce a practical light bulb. He kept on trying. Finally, Edison developed a filament that produced light for an hour, then a day, a week — and we were given the invention that has done more to improve our lives than any other.

People ask Edison "How did you feel when you failed over a thousand times?"

Here's what this man retorted: "I did *not* fail a thousand times; I learned a thousand ways that it wouldn't work." Isn't that amazing? It's all in the way you look at things. I find that our great Champions, the ones who earn huge incomes for themselves and their families, are people who have changed their attitudes and learned how to handle the same pressures and anxieties that defeat most people.

Everytime you're rejected in any way, tell yourself:

I never see failure as failure, but only as a learning experience.

2. If you're off course, it takes negative feedback to get you back on course. We've all had clients who fell in love with everything we show them:

"Oh, I like this one. And that's sensational. Look over here. Fantastic."
They never give you any objections or negative feedback, and it's almost
impossible to close them. You think they're going to buy everything on the
floor until they walk out empty handed.

Every morning we make a decision about our attitude that day toward
rejection. We can take it personally and have it destroy our day, or we can
slough it off and keep going. You decide this every day. I decide this every
day.

In my sales seminars, I use an analogy that I believe really drives this
point home. It's based on the modern-day target-seeking torpedo. When the
torpedo is fired from a submarine, a device in its nose homes in on the target
and guides the torpedo through whatever zigs and zags it must make to hit
that target.

Let's suppose that I'm the torpedo. There is the target. I'm fired from
the submarine and shoot out into the water. Right away, I'm getting off
course. The target-seeker kicks in and gives me a "No, thank you."

I turn a little too much and head off course again. The device gives me
another, "No, thank you." I turn again and again as I'm being rejected and
then, there it is: the target. I've reached my goal. Ka-blam. Terrific explosion. Goodbye target.

What would happen if the torpedo took rejection personally? What
would it do?

Go home.

Here's how that'll work. A torpedo is fired.

"You're off course, torpedo."

"I can't take it," says the torpedo. "I'm going back home."

Somebody on the submarine yells, "Oh, fud. Here comes one that
couldn't handle it." Ka-blam. Terrific explosion. Goodbye submarine.

In our studies of sales behavior, we've found many consistent patterns.
One of them crops up when outside salespeople get into their danger zones
because they can't handle the rejection that's part of their work. Where do
they start spending more and more time?

At home.

Too many sales people hide at home. Or go home early. Or take that
three-hour lunch hiding from the pain of rejection.

What else might the torpedo do if it couldn't handle the rejection?

It might explode in the submarine. People do that in sales. They can't
stand it anymore. So they blow up in their office or showroom. Ka-blam.
Terrific explosion. Goodbye job.

The torpedo might just decide to go in circles. Salespeople do that in
every industry. "I think I'll just kind of walk around today and settle my
nerves. I'm not going to talk to anybody, though. Oh, oh. Here comes that
hardnosed guy who's hot for our model 360. Ah, what luck, he's looking the
other way. I can duck into the restroom before he sees me."

Why would anyone in sales ever do a thing like that? Because the
possibility of having to take another rejection is more than that person can
handle.

Faced with the same client who emotionally destroys the average salesperson, the Champion becomes creative and takes this attitude: "Okay, Mr.
Hardnose, have at it. Sling your slop. That's nothing to me. But I'm going to
use your negative stimulus to find a positive way to overcome your objections, and *I will close*."

Doesn't it make sense to react that way rather than to crawl in a hole and
hide? Why let rejection shatter you? Why block out the negative feedback?
Be thankful for negative feedback. Take it, change course, and hit that target
— or a different one. It's fun.

It really is exciting when you know you won't let yourself be denied,
when you know you've taken charge of your career, when you know you'll
come up smiling after catching nine rejections in a row, saying:

**I never see failure as failure, but only as the negative feedback I
need to change course in my direction.**

3. This one is my favorite attitude toward rejection, and I think I've used
it more than any other. While I've been writing this book, I've also been
active on a new national seminar that my organization is developing. Because it has a lot to do with the mind and the emotions, Top Hopkins/
Champions Unlimited brought in a team of top-flight psychologists to
review that seminar's material. These professionals in the subject of emotions all said that this third attitude can do more to keep you moving forward
than any other concept.

Have you ever had a traumatic experience with clients that absolutely
wiped you out? After it happened, you felt so bad you simply couldn't call
them back. You were done. You didn't want to ever hear the names of those
people mentioned again.

But what are you doing three weeks later?

Getting laughs with your wipeout. You're telling people, "You should've
seen it. What a high dive into an empty pool. I went to see these clients, and
—"

Three weeks later it's hilarious. All the hurt vanishes the first time you
tell the story and laugh about your disaster. Unfortunately, until you can do
that, you're a disaster yourself: plowing the ground with your nose, the
wrong end of you up, enthusiasm gone, ability to handle your daily ration of
rejection down to nil. The weeks between disaster and laugh are wasted.

Life doesn't have to be that way. Laugh sooner. That's the key. Laughter softens anxiety's pain. Any humor helps, but the fun you poke at your
own bloopers, faults, and misadventures does the most marvelous job of
melting anxiety away.

All the great people I've met have a wonderful sense of humor. They
delight in looking at the world's reality, and they see an uncommon amount
of humor in it. Laughing is good. Laugh more. But don't laugh too soon.

If you take a call from a client who's just bought from you and the man
says "We're thinking of backing out," that's not the time to hoot and holler
and tell more funnies. First, you do everything possible to hold that sale
together. If it fractures anyway, then you look at the lighter side.

If you're new to the profession of selling and laugh every time something goes wrong, you're going to have a rollicking good time. As long as the laughs are directly related to the job and you're working effectively between them, why not? You'll be keeping your attitude up and learning fast. It's self-defeating to believe that unless it hurts, you're not working.

I gave you the key: laugh at your troubles sooner. In the beginning, you'll have to make an effort to laugh when you'd rather cry. But this too is a habit that's based on the attitude you've chosen. If you're willing to take charge of your life, you can develop the habits you want to live by. When success eludes you, always look for the lighter side by telling yourself:

I never see failure as failure, but only as an opportunity to develop my sense of humor.

4. Every time you demonstrate or present to clients but they don't buy, what have they given you instead of an order?

A chance to practice. Many of us don't realize the importance of this. People whose sales are below their potential have a tendency to sneer at practice, and that's one reason for their low sales. If their performance was perfect, could their sales be anything short of sensational?

A perfect performance is far more than a memorized sales spiel. No demonstration or presentation can be more than mediocre without including heavy participation by the clients, participation that's smoothly handled and guided by the salesperson. This demands practice and thorough knowledge of what you're selling. Whether you work with possible buyers in your showroom, their home, your display area, their office, or in some other location, every time you're with a client who says no, you've at least had a chance to walk out and say,

I never see failure as failure, but only as the opportunity to practice my techniques and perfect my performance.

After every rejection, dismiss the negatives, focus your thoughts on positive aspects, and move forward. Do that immediately, automatically, and firmly. This is one of the precious few habits that make success certain. It's a learnable habit. Make it yours.

5. Selling is a percentage game, a matter of numbers. Over the years, I've discovered that a single rule dominates every sales organization: Those who risk more failure by working with more people make more money; those who risk less failure make less.

If you risk failure frequently, you'll fail frequently. That's inevitable. It's built into the system. Also built in is the percentage effect: from a certain number of tries you get success. That being true, all you have to do is accept the fact that success demands its percentage of failure. So, when your efforts are crowned with non-success, tell yourself:

I never see failure as failure, but only as the game I must play to win.

If you know baseball, you know about Ty Cobb. During his best year he stole 94 bases in 144 attempts. Think about that. Two out of three times he was successful; sixty-six percent of the time he made it. On such records his enduring legend is built. On sixty-six percent.

Let's talk about another ballplayer. Max Carey was successful over ninety percent of the time; during his best year he stole 51 bases in 54 attempts. What a percentage. But today Max Carey is forgotten. In life, it's not the number of times you fail that counts, it's the number of times you keep on trying. Had old Max pushed his ego out of the way and tried more, he would have been number one.

THE CREED OF THE CHAMPION

Here is our basic philosophy at Tom Hopkins/Champions Unlimited. This is what we live by. It makes Champions of us; it makes Champions of the salespeople we're privileged to train.

I am not judged by the number of times I fail, but by the number of times I succeed, and the number of times I succeed is in direct proportion to the number of times I can fail and keep on trying.

Do more than just read the creed. Study it. Let it sink in. Let it change the way you look at any result that's not a success. I'd love for you to learn the creed word for word. Please set this book down, copy the creed on any handy piece of paper, and put it in your purse or wallet. Work with the creed and the five attitudes toward rejection; burn them deep into your mind and your performance and income will leap forward. From the bottom of my heart I believe that Champions are Champions because they've learned to fuel their drive by overcoming more failure.

Review the Five Attitudes Toward Rejection and Failure now, and use them every time you take a risk or make a move that results in less than a win.

1. I NEVER SEE FAILURE AS FAILURE (REJECTION AS REJECTION), BUT ONLY AS A LEARNING EXPERIENCE.

2. I NEVER SEE FAILURE AS FAILURE, BUT ONLY AS THE NEGATIVE FEEDBACK I NEED TO CHANGE COURSE IN MY DIRECTION.

3. I NEVER SEE REJECTION AS REJECTION (FAILURE AS FAILURE), BUT ONLY AS THE OPPORTUNITY TO DEVELOP MY SENSE OF HUMOR.

4. I NEVER SEE FAILURE AS FAILURE, BUT ONLY AS AN OPPORTUNITY TO PRACTICE MY TECHNIQUES AND PERFECT MY PERFORMANCE.

5. I NEVER SEE FAILURE AS FAILURE, BUT ONLY AS THE GAME I MUST PLAY TO WIN.

7

REFERRAL PROSPECTING
NON-REFERRAL PROSPECTING

How many of your organization's salespeople lie around the office like beached whales most of the time? I'm talking about the ones who ask things like:

> "Who should I call on?"
> "What do I do today?"
> "Oh, I hope some hot buyers walk in soon."
> "I wish the company would give me more leads."
> "Our advertising is a joke. How am I supposed to meet people if we don't do good advertising? Nobody calls us from our ads."
> "I don't know what to do."

It's sad, but the average salesperson doesn't really believe that people are the key to every door in selling. They say "It's all in who you know" without realizing that most people are knowable—if they'll just take the trouble to contact them.

Get on the phone. Get in your car and go out to the places where the people are who need your product or service. If you don't know the specific persons to call on, use your phone or your legs to find out from the people in the world outside your office.

Recently I gave a high-intensity selling workshop, a three-day affair. At the close I was emotionally and physically exhausted. As the last of the audience was leaving the auditorium, a gentleman in his mid-sixties came up and said that he'd been in sales nearly forty years. I had noticed him taking copious notes during the meetings, and I was impressed that anyone with his extensive background would be eager enough to learn new things to come to the training.

"I enjoyed your seminar very much, Mr. Hopkins. However, you could have shortened it."

"Was it too long?"

"Not at all. I learned a lot. But in two minutes flat you can give your next audience a secret that'll guarantee their success."

He spread his arms wide. "After pouring forty years into this business, I know the secret of selling success."

"Just a minute," I said. "You know *the* secret? Now look, my life is devoted to helping salespeople. Please—share this secret with me."

After looking at me for a moment, he said, "Tom, that's exactly what I'm going to do."

There was a charge of expectancy in the air—maybe even of reverence—when this great master of selling walked over to the board, picked up a felt pen, and drew this figure:

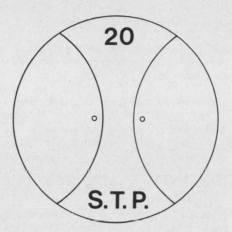

"There it is, Tom."

As I stared at his drawing, the charge of reverence leaked out of the room. Then I looked around, hoping I wasn't alone with this man. I was. Putting on a friendly smile, I said, "So that's the big secret, eh?"

"Exactly. Every month you talk to thousands of individuals who are struggling to make good in sales, don't you?"

"Yes, but a large percentage are already doing anywhere from good to great. They come to my seminars because they want to become even greater."

"Right—I'm in that category, and you've got a truckload of splendid techniques to help us. But the thing is, techniques count for nothing if they're not used. Tom, if you can get this one point across, you'll achieve your goal of helping everyone who hears you become successful in sales."

"Yes, but —"

He lifted a finger. "Tom, if you can motivate everyone to use my secret, they'll overcome every obstacle to earning big money." His hands flourished. "And the secret is:

"See Twenty People *belly to belly* every day."

Suddenly the air was charged again. He pounded his hands together and went on, "Get them to do that and they can't fail."

He's right. All my years in selling convince me of it. Never have I heard a formula for success that beats his for truth, simplicity, and practicality. Put your button near twenty other buttons a day and you'll soon be living on top of the hill. The key to making more money is to *see more people*.

It's a curious fact that, though few salespeople will deny anything in the previous section, many salespeople won't act on it. They know that they have to meet numbers of new people to be successful, and they want to be successful, but they don't get out and meet the people. Why not? It's the old fear of rejection that we talked about in the last chapter. By now, I'm sure that you've changed your attitude. Now you know that every time you get rejected, you've actually made money.

So you're ready to go out and meet some of those good folks who need your product or service. You're ready to pass through the next doorway to success that's called prospecting.

Selling is finding people to sell, and selling the people you find.

Easy, isn't it? That's what selling is, and that's all it is. The above idea is well worth highlighting, and so is the next one.

KNOW YOUR RATIOS, AND STRIVE TO IMPROVE THEM

All successful businesses use ratios. Your sales activity is a business. Therefore, you must use ratios to be successful. If all this gives you a pain in the inferiority complex you got by flunking math in high school, relax. Whether you can precisely define the word or not, you're already making frequent use of ratios. But you'll use them more effectively if you understand them better. Let me explain.

A ratio is just a fraction that measures something against something else. Let's suppose that you have two savings accounts. One of them pays 6 percent interest. This means that the interest your money earns has the same relationship to the total amount of money in your account that 6 has to 100. This relationship is a ratio. It can be written in several different ways without changing the relationship between the two numbers:

$$6 : 100$$
$$6/100$$
$$\frac{6}{100}$$
$$6 \text{ percent}$$
$$6\%$$
$$.06$$
$$.060$$

Business ratios are frequently expressed in percent because percentages are easy to understand and compare. Let's do it on both of your savings accounts:

Bank	Amount on Deposit	Interest Earned
A	$8979.80	$448.99
B	$ 332.00	$ 19.92

Few people can look at the figures above and immediately know which bank is paying the higher rate of interest. But if we compare two ratios, the answer is instantly obvious:

Bank	Interest Rate
A	5 percent
B	6 percent

You use ratios like these when you decide to buy the sports car rated at 30 miles per gallon instead of the station wagon that costs half as much but is rated at only 24 miles per gallon. Of course, you want the sports car; fortunately, logic practically forces you to buy it.

Ratios that will help you manage your selling business are serious stuff. Here are some that you should be keeping track of — and striving to improve:

Prospecting calls/per hour spent

Prospecting calls/appointments made

Appointments/sales

Hours worked/money earned

Prospecting calls made last month/income this month

Let's talk about each of these basic ratios in turn. When you're well into managing your selling business with this method, you may find other ratios that are more crucial to your particular operation than these. If so, great. Run with them. The point is this: Your activities can be expressed as ratios that, when studied, will show you how to best spend your time. If you're not keeping track you're not steering your ship.

PROSPECTING CALLS/PER HOUR SPENT. We can be astonishingly ingenious at finding ways not to prospect when we sit down to prospect by phone — or have the time blocked out to go out and do it. If you really want to succeed, you'll discipline yourself. This means you set reasonable performance levels and make yourself do them.

PROSPECTING CALLS/APPOINTMENTS MADE. As a very rough starting figure, the ratio for all kinds of selling is about 10 : 1. That is, make 10 prospecting calls: get one appointment. Don't ask about the ratio for your business around the office. The losers don't prospect because they're losers, and the winners don't prospect anymore because they're too busy with the referral business they built up through prospecting. Compile your own batting average. Start off with the assumption that 10 good prospecting calls will get you one good appointment, and take it from there.

APPOINTMENTS/SALES. Again, 10 : 1 is a rough average, but this ratio varies wildly from business to business. Salespeople working a route of established accounts may go for days getting an order at every stop; salespeople working airlines for aircraft manufacturers may go for years between sales. Most of us operate well away from routine order-taking at one extreme and salaried team selling at the other extreme. Once you've set your own ratio for this activity, study it together with the previous ratio. If you're getting lots of appointments but making few sales, you may be losing out before you walk in the door through not qualifying effectively. You can't make money trying to sell the wrong people.

HOURS WORKED/MONEY EARNED. At least twice a year you should run a check on exactly how much time you actually spend working, and compare that to how much you're making. It'll take a tight log to ferret out the facts, and no one can do it but you. If you're serious about making more money, take a cold reading on how much time you're productive as compared to how much time goes into nuzzling the dog. How you use your time determines how much you pay yourself. Take a hard look twice a year. You may want to make changes.

PROSPECTING CALLS MADE LAST MONTH/INCOME THIS MONTH. The idea here is to emphasize the direct bearing that the number of prospecting calls you make now has on how much you take home tomorrow. Using the right time lag is vital. Decide on how long it takes to work the average interested prospect all the way from initial contact to money in your pocket. This time delay may be three months or longer. Some salespeople fail because they don't gear their thinking to the time lag that's involved in their business.

Champions develop simple methods for keeping track of their personal performance ratios such as those given above, but they don't do it out of idle curiosity. They gather the necessary information for hardheaded reasons— so that they can recognize opportunities while they're fresh, and correct problems before they get out of hand.

Let's look at how this works out. Suppose you're fairly new in the business but you've acquired some skill at prospecting, qualifying, demonstrating, and closing. You're consistently making one sale for every ten prospects you meet. We're talking here about the people you find, not those who wander in off the street.

By making about one call a day, you're meeting about thirty people a month, so you're closing three sales a month. Now what's going to happen if you decide to make two calls a day?

Your sales go up to six a month, and your income doubles.

Suppose you elevate your performance level again, and start making four calls a day?

Your sales go to twelve a month and your income again doubles. So if you were making $1000 a month off three sales before, now you're making $4000 a month off twelve sales—and feeling very good about yourself.

When I drop these figures on people in my seminars, I can read messages like these on lots of faces:

"I can't make four calls a day."
"In my business, two calls a day is tops."

If you think that, I disagree with you. Every potential Champion has to fight that kind of negative thinking in the beginning. Here's how you do it. Sit down and work out a schedule that will allow you to double your sales. Next, throw that schedule away and work out one that adds one more call a day. Then work out the timeplanning and organizing that will allow you to meet this second schedule. You can do it. All it takes is desire, discipline, and determination.

You will close a certain percentage of the people you meet. Your goal should be to up that percentage. But let's be realistic. I'll tell you very honestly that I can't show you how to close 100 percent of the people you meet. In a free economy, it's impossible to close ten out of ten every time. So there does come a time when trying to raise the percentage of people you close is more frustrating than realistic, a time when you should be putting your effort into acquiring more prospects to apply that percentage to.

My goal as a trainer and writer isn't to have you close 99 percent. You can't. I want to up your percentages and increase your income—and you'll do that by making more calls.

Why not fewer and better calls?

Because more is better. If professional athletes only practiced twenty minutes a day, how long would their careers last?

There's another point I want you to remember—and act on. A Champion always makes one successful call after a rejection.

Why? Think about it. If you stop on rejection, what do you carry with you?

Rejection.

A Champion is determined to keep his winning attitude. If he hangs it up on a negative note, his winning attitude is damaged for the rest of the day.

While you're reading me, I'm reading you. You're thinking, "I might have to call four people or even more to get a good response."

Sure. Then call them. That's what a Champion does. That's what the Five-percenters, the great ones, the achievers do.

There's another time when you must call until you get a live prospect. Every time you make a sale to one of your existing customers or prospects, what do you have to do?

You have to replace that person.

After completing a sale, a Champion says to himself, "I must find two more good prospects to fill the space left by the person I just got happily involved in our wonderful opportunity."

Prospecting breaks into two parts, referral and non-referral. First we'll take up the Champion's favorite.

REFERRAL PROSPECTING

Ask yourself this question: Of these groups, which is the easiest to close?

The people who just walked in off the street.

The ones who called in from an ad.

The leads on little slips of paper that your company hands to you and says, "Go get 'em, Tiger."

Or is it the people referred to you by someone who knows them and is happy with your product or service?

The referred lead is the easiest to close. In fact, you'll spend half the time selling the referred, pre-qualified lead as you will selling the company-generated, non-qualified lead. That's an exciting fact. Highlight it.

A Champion closes referrals twice as fast as he closes non-referred prospects.

Even more exciting is the fact that Champions will close 40 to 60 percent of their qualified referrals. Compare this to the results they get working with their non-referred and unqualified leads. The Champion's success rate with referrals is 400 to 600 percent of what it is with non-referrals. That being the case, is it any wonder that Champions are champion referral-getters?

The fact that you're reading this book is a strong indication that one of your immediate goals is to double your income—or multiply it by an even greater factor. If you're going to make that happen, referrals will have to play a large part in your future, won't they? All right. Let's get to work and learn how to create a rich flow of these neat moneymakers. Have you ever asked your buyers something like this after you've closed them: "Do you know who might be interested in _____ (what they just bought)?"

You've done that, I'm sure. How many of them said yes?

Not too many, right? Most of them probably answered vaguely along these lines: "I can't think of anybody right now."

They are telling you the absolute truth. But, if you believe the old saying that birds of a feather fly together, you know they fly with people who wear the same feathers they do. That is, most of their friends have interests and incomes that are similar to theirs—which is why they are friends. Most of your buyers know people who would be interested in buying whatever they bought—but they "just can't think of anybody right now."

Why can't they? Because you've given them the entire world to look at with their mind's eye. No wonder they can't say, "Oh, yeah, Zack was telling me he wanted —" Most people have their mind's eye fixed on internal things right after buying something, and their excitement crowds out any possibility that they'll remember what Zack wanted.

Many companies tell their new salespeople, "Ask your buyers to refer someone else to you."

So you ask. "Do you know of anyone else I can give my product demonstration to?"

When about the fifth person says no, you come to a conclusion. "That doesn't work." So pretty soon you stop asking.

Let me show you what a Champion does. This is the backbone of their prospecting system. When you master this technique, you're going to walk out with qualified, referred leads after every sale. But you have to follow every step very carefully. There's another requirement: you have to use this

Prospecting

CARD REFERRAL SYSTEM

All you need is a few 3 × 5 inch cards of the kind sold in all office supply and most drug and variety stores. These cards allow you to get all the information you need to build a clientele. I'll give you the steps first, and then show you how to use them.

1. Isolate faces for them to see.
2. Write the referral's name on the card.
3. Ask qualifying questions.
4. Ask for the address.
5. If the address isn't known, get the phone book.
6. Ask them to call and set the appointment.
7. If they show nervousness or refuse to call, ask if you can use their name when you call the referral.

The roleplay that follows shows how the system functions. In it, John and Mary Harrison have just bought a new automobile from good old Tom. The Harrisons are ecstatic about their new car. They worked the figures out with me, of course, and they were shrewd and good. Believe me, I had to know my product and how to close. But it came out well. The Harrisons got the colors and options they were looking for; I got them emotionally involved, and I helped them rationalize the wisdom of their decision to own what they wanted. So they're happy.

Normally, the first time you can get a referral is right after you've completed the sale, and that's also the best time in many cases. But some Champions sell something that has a lengthy design, installation, or servicing period, and they prefer to work on referrals throughout that period. Different Champions select different times to gather referrals. Since this will be the key element in your expanding success, the vital thing is to have some specific event in the selling sequence that always triggers your drive for referrals. Never forget that every person who owns your product or service knows someone else who can own it too. All you need to get at that sale is the referral.

Read this roleplay and you'll see how it all happens.

The Harrisons are sitting across a table from me and my 3 × 5 cards and my ballpoint pen as I wrap up the sale of their new car.

Tom: "Well, John and Mary, I'm really happy for you both. I can really see your excitement with your new car. John, let me ask you, do you participate in any sport, hobby, or group activity? Do you do anything like that?"

John: "I like to bowl."

Tom: "You bowl! Great. Tell me, when you were bowling last week, was there anyone on your bowling team who either mentioned an interest in a car like your new one, or who you feel might be as excited with a new car as you and Mary seem to be?"

John: "Well, I know one guy who needs a new car."

Tom: "Oh, do you?"

John: "He might be interested, yeah. George Zack."

Tom: "George Zack. Hm. Mary, now I'd like to talk to you for just a second." (I don't write George Zack's name down when John first gives it to me. The reason I don't is that doing so triggers the "What are you doing?" set of fears. I've got George Zack hanging right here in my mind. Now I'm going for the referral from the wife.) "Mary, are you involved in organizations, or are you active with hobbies, play bridge, anything like that?"

Mary: "I play contract bridge."

Tom: "Do you. Well, when you were playing bridge last time, did any of your bridge players mention, or give you any hint, that they might be as delighted with a new car as you are?"

Mary: "I have a good friend, Lorna Tellis, who definitely needs one."

Tom: "Lorna Tellis, okay. John, tell me, what makes you feel that George Zack would be excited with a new car?"

John: "Well, for one thing, I took a ride with him. The way his car runs — whew. He's got about 140,000 miles on it."

Tom: "Wow. It's not a classic yet, is it?"

John: "No, definitely not. And never will be."

Tom: "Okay. Now, you're in a league that bowls every week, aren't you, so you know George pretty well?"

John: "I guess so."

Tom: (Here's a non-threatening question that'll help establish how well Mr. Harrison knows George Zack and also tell you a lot about Zack.) "How many children does George have?"

John: "Three. A couple of boys and a girl. They're all still pretty young."

Tom: "Then he has a medium size car now, doesn't he?"

John: "Yeah, and he probably needs at least that, or maybe a larger one next time."

Tom: "The youngest child's how old, do you think?"

John: "Oh, about seven, I'd guess."

Tom: "He might want a little larger car, then. Where does he work, do you know?"

John: "He's a soil engineer at Femmes and Loess."

Tom: "Hm. Well, fine. Mary, what makes you think Lorna would be excited about a car?"

Mary: "Well, her husband is so cheap, he won't buy her a car." (They all laugh.)

Tom: "In today's world, only having one car is a rarity. Do you know that the average family has two-and-a-half cars in this country? I wonder if he's aware of that?"

Mary: "Obviously not."

Tom: "I think she'd like to let him know, wouldn't she?"

Mary: "I'm sure she would."

Tom: "Do you know much about their family? How many children do they have?"

Mary: "She has two, and one on the way."

Tom: "Oh, one on the way. That'll be three soon, so they'll want a little larger car too. Being that he's cheap — of course we're being facetious, and I won't say that — do you think there'd be a possibility he'll be concerned with economy?"

Mary: "Oh, definitely."

Tom: "He would be. Excellent. I think I kind of know what she'll love and he'll go for. Do you know what I'd like you to do for me, John? Do you have some idea of the Zacks' address?"

John: "They live on Mainsail, I'm not sure of the number."

Tom: "That's M-A-I-N-S-A-I-L, isn't it? All right. And where does Lorna live?"

Mary: "They live over by Roosevelt High on Margrave."

Tom: "Okay. Would you like a nice fresh cup of coffee? Do you take it black or with cream and sugar?"

John: "Black for both of us."

Mary: "That's right."

Tom: "Black? Why don't we do this?" (Tom reaches for the phone book.) "I'm going to ask you a favor. While I'm getting all of us a cup of coffee, will you look up their addresses for me? Would you mind?"

Mary: "Oh, no."

Tom: "Here's one card." (Hands it to Mrs. Harrison.) "I use cards for this information so I'll always have it handy. There's the second card." (Gives it to Mr. Harrison.) "Now, I'm going to get the coffee. Be right back."

(A few moments pass.)

Tom: "Okay, here's your coffee. Ah, you've got their addresses. Good, good. When I have new owners who are happy with their new car call one of their friends and tell them about it, that friend often wants me to show them a car like it. Would you mind giving them a call? I'd like to think you'd do that for me."

John: "Okay."

Tom: "Wonderful. There's a phone on the desk over there. Why don't you give George a quick call while Mary and I just chat? Then we'll let Mary call Lorna. I'd really appreciate that."

Right here I'm going to change gears because you won't always hear good news like that. Instead of that ready agreement to make the calls, suppose the Harrisons look at each other and start backing off. They don't want to call. Let's pick it up from where I ask them to call.

Tom: "— I'd really love for you to give George a quick call and let him know I'm going to come by."

John: "Well, uh — I don't think I know him that well."

Tom: "I see."

John: "It would be a little uncomfortable."

Tom: "I understand entirely." (Notice that I get off this fast, and don't press them at all once they've indicated reluctance to call. By moving past the rejection fast, I'm very likely to get their approval of the next best thing. In actual speech, there'd be no pause between "I understand entirely" and what now follows.) "May I ask you this? Would you mind if I just used your name?"

John: "That's okay."

Tom: "You don't mind at all? — I think that's great. I'll call him. In fact, I promise you that I will. And I promise you too, Mary, that I won't forget Lorna either. And I'll let her know that I promised you I'd call her. May I?"

Mary: "Certainly."

Tom: "Well, again, I thank you so much, and I wish you happy days with your new car."

Realize that you must go through all seven of the steps (given before the roleplay) if you're going to be successful with the card referral system. And it only works if your buyers have a reasonable level of satisfaction with your product or service. Of course, it works best with buyers who are ecstatic, but some people aren't capable of ecstacy. Maybe they're simply satisfied, or just so darn glad to have the product that if you handle your referral request like this, they'll just get going with you.

As you read that role-play, how did it feel? Do you think the Harrisons wanted to help the salesman? I believe that most people on this continent, if you ask them properly, will help you do anything within reason. Do you agree? If you stop while you're out driving and ask people for directions, what'll they do? They'll start pointing. Many of them will come out to your car and, while you're trying to drive away, they'll hold on just trying to tell you. Millions of people will do that for strangers.

The people you know in selling situations will help you even more — if they like and trust you, if your product or service is what they're looking for — and if you'll let them.

Would you be afraid to do what I did in the role-play? I've done it hundreds of times in real selling situations, but I remember the first few times because I was fearful of trying the system too. It's natural to be afraid of what you've never done before, but it's not wise to let that stop you. Read the role-play aloud until you've memorized the entire pattern and can carry it off with the confident ease that people can't resist.

Prepare in depth and your success ratio with this powerful system will do wonders for your sales and income. Notice that I've asked you to memorize the pattern, not the words. Being able to repeat the words like a parrot won't help you much because every referral-gathering interview will be different, as dictated by your customers' different replies to your questions and statements. Memorize the role-play's pattern so you'll be able to instantly follow whatever direction your customers lead you in *and still get the information*. A thorough understanding of your objectives in this interview and how you should go about achieving them is vital to make this system work. Note how I jumped on every opportunity to make a small joke or go off on a brief tangent in order to avoid building tension. Note that my attitude was non-threatening throughout the interview, and yet I still maintained control of it. In this situation, a straight line is not the shortest route to where you want to go. There were jokes and asides, but we never strayed for long from the path I wanted to take.

Get the feel of the roleplay into your bones, and then write a script for a referral-gathering interview based on your own product or service. Decide what you'll say first, imagine what responses your customers might give, and write down the effective replies that you could then make to keep them moving toward your goal of collecting solid referrals.

I'll say it again: prepare in depth for the referral-gathering interview. It looks deceptively easy, but don't let that lull you into complacency. Time enough for that after you've mastered the technique and have all the referrals you can handle.

As you study the roleplay, notice how warmly I isolated a dozen faces for the Harrisons by pleasantly probing into the areas that would bring friends and referrals into their minds. How many names did John have to run through to cover his entire bowling team? And how many people does Mary play bridge with? In both cases, we're talking about very small numbers of people compared to all the people that John and Mary know. And don't people frequently talk about automobiles at social gatherings? But that's just an example. Forget autos and think about your own product or service.

Let's suppose that you sell to company executives. Do you think that the executive who just purchased a new computer system has lunch with executives from other companies?

Of course he does. And what does he do when he's having lunch right after approving the computer purchase?

He brags a little.

"I okayed the computer agreement this morning. It's knocking us back a quarter of a million, but it'll do a lot for us."

"Which one did you go for?"

"The Bytebarfer 2001. It's got some fantastic features."

"You know, we've got to get moving on a computer too."

We choose our friends from among those who share our status, preferences, and needs. When we like someone's product or service we're likely to brag about it. Our friends will be interested because they have the same interests that we do. And no one has the time to become expert at everything. So we have to rely on the people we know for much of the information that leads to our buying decisions.

This knowledge of the characteristics of buyers can easily be turned to great advantage in referral-gathering:

- If your procedure requires after-sale visits (so that you can make the delivery or give training, for example), ask the buyer which of his friends he's told about the purchase.
- If your procedure doesn't require after-sale visits, ask the buyer which of his friends he intends to tell about his purchase. (That is, brag about the purchase—but of course you never use the word *brag* to a buyer.)

In either case, the idea is to focus your buyer on those of his friends who are the best candidates for owning what he's just bought from you. Once those faces are in the front of his mind, you'll find that it isn't difficult to pull the information from him that you need for a solid referral.

What results can you expect from the card referral system?

The answer depends more on the level of competence in sales that you aspire to—and are willing to plan, practice, and work for—than on anything else. A single success with the card referral technique marks you as a comer who can go as far as he wishes in sales. When you're averaging one referral per sale, you've edged into the top half of the selling community. When you're averaging two referrals per sale, you're in the top 20 percent. When you're averaging three referrals per sale, you're in the top 10 percent. Four referrals per sale puts you into the charmed circle where the Five Percent make the really big money. Anything over that—five referrals or more per sale—proclaims that you're one of the great ones.

We've agreed that of course the referral is the finest type of prospect to work with. Referrals are people who have already accepted you. Now all you must do is get them involved with your product or service—something you know they need and can afford.

But you may be sitting there thinking, "I couldn't do the card referral thing. I just can't see myself pulling that off."

Now, before you give in to that emotion, examine your feelings carefully. See whether you really want to pay between $25,000 and $100,000 a year for catering to that kind of whim. Make no mistake about it—you can't pass up a powerful, basic technique like card referral gathering without paying a heavy penalty. I'm not stating that fact to make you feel bad—nor am I concealing it so you can feel good. You should know that accepting a lower level of competence in your chosen profession than you can achieve will cost you an enormous amount of money.

But there are situations where using the card referral system isn't realistic considering the level of your maturity and experience in relation to that of the customers you work with. (If this is the case, perhaps you should consider selling in a different field, one that you'll feel confident in. You can return to your present line after you've developed greater confidence and skills. Challenges that you rise to conquer give your career tremendous boosts; challenges that you can't conquer hold you back.)

If you're not going after referrals, you'll need to rely on the source of buyers that we'll discuss next.

NON-REFERRAL PROSPECTING

These are the leads you generate where there's no referral involved. Keep this in mind: they're not pre-qualified, so you'll only be closing ten percent of them. Therefore, we want to show you not only how to obtain leads through non-referral prospecting, but also how to pre-qualify them. Let's make sure we understand each other here. Please highlight what it means to pre-qualify the person or persons we call a lead:

A lead is pre-qualified when you know that the emotional and logical requirements for benefiting from your product or service are all present.

We've said it before: The sale depends on emotion backed by logic. The emotion comes first, and then the logic follows. It does not happen the other way around. You pre-qualify people by finding out whether the emotion that's necessary to carry the sale to completion exists or can be created. And you also have to find out whether the logic—which includes but is not limited to the ability to pay—exists or can be created.

Finding these things out is like catching a bird—if you go thrashing and pounding in a wild charge, the bird will fly away long before you can get anywhere near it. But if you softly work your way in close and then gently cast your net, you'll catch a lot of birds.

Here are a few things to talk about with prospects that are important qualification factors in selling many kinds of services and products:

1. Employment.
2. Marital status.
3. Number of children.
4. Product or service they now have.
   If you know what they've got now, in most cases that means you know what they'll get later—don't you agree?

Each general type of product or service has its own set of vital qualification factors. You probably know those that are important in selecting the people most likely to buy what you're selling. If you don't have a clear idea of who buys what you sell, one of your top priorities should be to research that question. A careful study at your company's files of completed sales should quickly tell you all you need to know on this score.

NON-REFERRAL PROSPECTING TECHNIQUE NUMBER ONE:
THE ITCH CYCLE

This is an exciting technique for prospecting, not a skin disease. It doesn't involve referrals, and I recommend it highly whether you're working referrals or not because it's a splendid way to acquire pre-qualified leads.

In real estate the average turnover is three to five years; that is, the average family moves every three to five years. So we can say that the average person gets an itch to move every five years. If you're in automobiles, you know that people get the itch to buy a new car about every thirty months. Office equipment salespeople know that their customers cycle their machines about every three years. These are the times when the itch is itchiest for most people, but can some people itch sooner?

Certainly. That's why a Champion keeps in touch with all his past buyers. Of course he does. Those buyers are an important group among the select few in the world who have favored him with their trust, and the Champion knows that he or she has a special bond with them. So he makes certain that he's there to scratch when the itch strikes his special people.

When should you start helping your past buyers get the itch to buy again?

Start your campaign to update your old buyers sixty days before the itchiest time.

If it's a home or something else on the five-year itch cycle, you really move in on them after four years and ten months; if it's an automobile, you really start driving to get that itch going after two years and four months; if your product is any kind of office equipment, you really start sitting on them after thirty-four months. As an alternative, or for longer itch cycles, try whetting their appetites after ninety-five percent of the itch cycle on their old item has run out. For example, you've determined that your average itch cycle is six years. Kickoff your itch campaign after five years and eight or nine months. The longer the itch cycle, the greater the variation. This means the longer itch cycles require a greater margin of safety to make sure that you're there before they start looking elsewhere.

And, of course, a Champion never kisses his buyers goodbye by letting years pass without renewing his acquaintance with them. Visits, phone calls, mail, lunches — these are some of the methods the Champion uses to maintain his contact with his clientele. If you don't maintain contact, you don't have a clientele; your ex-buyers are abandoned souls looking for a new home.

When I suggest letting ninety-five percent of the longer itch cycles go by, I'm merely suggesting a starting point. There's an ideal time to re-contact previous buyers of your offering that will give you the best chance to capture their replacement business. The exact ideal time — for your offering, area, and personality — can only be discovered by trial and error.

If what you sell involves weeks or months for design, custom manufacturing, recruitment, or whatever, you'll want to allow for that period; if your offering is a readily available shelf item, you may find that it's more effective to work closer to the itchiest time.

Be aware that the itch cycle for products differs from the itch cycle for services, and that all itch cycles vary from place to place for the same item. Many things influence this interval: seasonal factors, general economic conditions, the income level of the people you're working with, and especially the personalities of the individual buyers. But it's really quite easy to overcome these complexities if you go about it right. Here's the process:

First. Determine the basic itch cycle for your product with your customers in your area. I'll tell you how to do that soon, but for the moment, assume that you've discovered the basic itch cycle that you'll be working with.

Second. Consider the calendar factors. Some sales are affected by tax dates: year end, April 15, local date for assessing inventory tax. The sales of most products and services are affected anywhere from slightly to greatly by the changing seasons. And, of course, Christmas exerts a tremendous influence over discretionary buying, generally delaying every decision it doesn't accelerate. You simply look at each of these questions and then adjust your action accordingly. That is, you decide whether to speed up or slow down your re-contacting schedule to cope with these factors.

Suppose you have a basic itch cycle of thirty months and, on a particular group of buyers, you see that if you re-contact them to get the itch going after twenty-eight months, you'll come banging in during the holiday season. Since yours is not a Christmas gift item, you have a choice. (You should make this choice several months in advance.) Either you re-contact your soon-to-itch buyers after twenty-six months, in September or October, or you wait until January. What to do?

The answer is simple. If you wait until January, some of your former buyers will already be committed elsewhere. Make sure you're there, ready to scratch, when they start to itch: re-contact early, and then give them another contact in January.

Third. Every time you complete a sale, consider that buyer's personality in relation to your basic itch cycle. Impatient types (and people whose careers are moving rapidly upward) tend to itch sooner than average; low-keyed types (and people whose careers are on a fixed course) tend to itch later than average. Here's how you turn this awareness to your advantage:

At the time you close the first sale, decide whether that particular buyer is impatient, average, or conservative. (Put all doubtful cases in the average group.) When you tune your thinking on this wavelength, you'll find that about ten to twenty percent of your buyers will strike you as being jumpy types. Schedule them for early re-contact. About an equal number of your buyers will seem like noticeably steady people. Schedule them for late re-contact. (Classify your buyers in relation to each other, not to what you think is normal for the general population of the country.) The remaining sixty to eighty percent of your buyers are the average group that you should schedule for re-contact two months before your basic itch cycle has run its course.

"Sounds great," you may be thinking, "but how do I find out what the itch cycle is on my product? Nobody around my office has ever mentioned it."

HOW TO DETERMINE THE ITCH CYCLE
FOR YOUR PRODUCT OR SERVICE.

It'll take one full day. But while you're determining your product or service's itch cycle, you'll be picking up some tremendous qualified leads too.

Let's suppose that I just started at Champion Marine Sales. My product is boats. Since I'm new, one of the first things I want to discover is the itch cycle that I'll be working with at that boat dealership. You can do it for your product or service the same way that I use here.

Start by getting to the company files. Most companies today keep records on all their clients. Find out where the files are, sit down, and start making calls. I'll show you the method by giving the dialogue for one call.

If you'll spend just one day going at it as I do below, and call all the clients you can in that time, you not only will establish your product's itch cycle, you'll also strike some more exciting things that I'll tell you about. So come with me now as we go through the old buyer files at Champion Marine.

The first file looks interesting. It tells me that a gentleman named Max Polk bought a Spee-D-Ski boat eighteen months ago. Without wasting time, I call him.

Tom: "Good morning, Mr. Polk. My name is Tom Hopkins, and I'm with Champion Marine Sales. You've owned one of our Spee-D-Ski boats for approximately eighteen months now, and I wanted to call up and make sure that you're happy with it."

Mr. Polk: "Hey, that Spee-D-Ski is the best ski boat my family's ever had."

Tom: (Warmly.) "I'm happy to hear that. I'm in the process of conducting a little market survey to establish projections for the upcoming year. Would you be kind enough to help me by answering just a few questions?"

Mr. Polk: "I wouldn't mind. Go ahead."

Tom: "Prior to purchasing the Spee-D-Ski, did you have another boat?"

Mr. Polk: "I sure did—a Fastwater-16."

Tom: "Oh, really? How long have you been a boating enthusiast?"

Mr. Polk: "Well, Mr. Hopkins, ever since we moved into this area, about fifteen years ago."

Tom: "How many boats have you owned in the last fifteen years, Mr. Polk?"

Mr. Polk: "Let's see—well, about five, I guess, counting the Spee-D-Ski."

Tom: "About five boats. I also wanted to ask, are you familiar with Spee-D-Ski's new line?"

Mr. Polk: "They've already brought out a new line? What's wrong with the model I've got? It has everything anyone could possibly want."

Tom: "That's what we thought until we saw the Spee-D-Ski II. It's the work of the same design and engineering team, and they just aren't the kind of people who rest on their laurels."

Mr. Polk: "You mean they've changed the styling a little."

Tom:	"It's true that there's a wider choice of style features now, but the important changes aren't so obvious. They're in things like hull refinements that give you a smoother and safer high-speed turn in rough water. In fact, they've made a number of technical advances that only someone like you, who really knows the old Spee-D-Ski, can fully appreciate. And there are several exciting new options that we didn't have before. Would you mind if I send you a brochure?"
Mr. Polk:	"No, I wouldn't mind at all. I'd like to see the new models."
Tom:	"Fine. Let's see—you're still on Slalom Way?"
Mr. Polk:	"That's right, at 1218."
Tom:	"That's what I have here, 1218. Slalom Way runs into Flying Bridge Road, doesn't it?"
Mr. Polk:	"Sure does."
Tom:	"I'm going out to Flying Bridge this afternoon. Would you mind, while I'm in the neighborhood, if I stop by with the brochure and just take a minute to say hello? I'll be servicing your account from now on."
Mr. Polk:	"That's okay, but it'll have to be fast—I'm getting ready for a trip. But I would like to see your brochure on the new models."
Tom:	"Wonderful. I'll drop by around two, or would three o'clock be more convenient?"
Mr. Polk:	"Anytime before four."
Tom:	"I'm looking forward to meeting you, Mr. Polk. And thanks for all the help on my survey."
Mr. Polk:	"That's okay, Mr. Hopkins. I'm looking forward to seeing you too."

What is his itch cycle?

To get it, simply divide the time period involved (in Mr. Polk's case, fifteen years) by the number of times (five) that he bought the item in question. The answer is Mr. Polk's itch cycle — expressed in years — for that kind of boat.

What you're looking for is the same thing the Champion is looking for: the average itch cycle for a specific product when bought by a definable group of people. I'll explain what a definable group of people is in a moment, but first, let's discuss what you should count in the average that establishes the itch cycle you're looking for.

Suppose the first three people tell you that a Spee-D-Ski is the first boat they've ever bought. Not only that, they don't know when — if ever — they'll buy another one. How do you figure them in the average?

You don't. Leave them out. During the day you spend establishing itch cycles, you should talk to at least twenty people — and they'll all give you different answers. Do like the Champion does. Throw out all the offbeat answers and zero in on the average itch cycle for the involved, on-the-track owner of your product or service.

As you work through the day, you'll be learning what's important to your owners. And you may establish more than one average itch cycle. For example, perhaps the owners of Spee-D-Ski boats can be divided into two easily defined groups: active competitors (in boat racing and water-skiing) and non-competitors. The competitors might trade boats every two years, or even every season, while the non-competitors keep their boats for three years. Now that you've separated your owners into definable groups with different itch cycles, you know where to concentrate your efforts, don't you?

Mr. Polk is the perfect example of the itch cycle at work. Over a lengthy period, he's proven that he can't go more than about three years before the itch to have a newer and snazzier boat drives him down to the dock, checkbook in hand.

Did you notice the steps that I followed to acquire this vital information?

The first thing I told him was that I knew how long he'd had the product or service that prompted my call.

The second thing I told him was that I was calling to make sure he was happy with the product or service.

After those preliminaries, I moved in to qualify what product he had owned before his present one, and how many of them he had owned over a specific period of time.

Now you know how to establish the itch cycle for your offering. Before you set out to do that, let's cover the next technique.

NON-REFERRAL PROSPECTING TECHNIQUE NUMBER TWO:
ORPHAN ADOPTION

Orphan adoption? Before you decide that got mixed in here from another book, let me assure you that this technique is a gold mine if you're willing and able to use it. Please highlight this idea:

When I find orphans, I adopt them at once.

I'll explain. Every company has turnover in its sales force. When salespeople leave an organization, what do they leave behind?

Their clientele.

Now we know that many people fail in sales because they don't follow-up. Do you agree with that statement? But the salespeople who failed in your company did make some sales, and their abandoned clientele can become your goldmine clientele. Of course, if your company assigns specific territories, you'll have to be guided by that circumstance. If not, you'll find a lot of people like Mr. Polk in the files who need someone to serve them.

Here's a tip that'll take you straight to the richest tunnel in that goldmine. Your company's records may be filed by the customers' last names, by the cities they live in, by the item they bought, or in some other way that doesn't tie in with the itch cycle—but somewhere there's a record of when those people bought. Discover the itch cycle that applies to what you're doing, and then locate the record of who bought what—and when they did it. Take the clerk in the file room to dinner, butter up the chief accountant, sneak in—do what you have to do—but get a copy of that record. Once you have this information in your fist, you're on the fast track to the big money. Exercise your salvage rights. You haven't had to sweat it out for thirty months while those orphans were working up to the itchiest point on their itch cycle—they were doing that on their own time before you joined the firm. Zero in on them.

I've received letters from all over the country that tell me things like this: "Tom, as soon as I started going through the files of the salespeople who've left this firm, my income took off. I called these abandoned customers, re-established rapport, picked up pre-qualified leads, and closed a high percentage of them."

Why are these leads pre-qualified? Because you represent the product or service they're already happily involved with, and the files you have in your hands are jammed with details about them. You're in a perfect position to handle any little problems they might have; you're in a perfect position to advise them on maintenance; you have perfect reasons for re-contacting them.

But the exact way that you handle the re-contact is critical. Let me clarify that statement. If you're in commercial, industrial, or any other type of sales that involves big ticket items or large scale transactions, you're working with busy people, aren't you? Every day you talk to corporate executives, professional people, or independent businessmen who aren't careless with their time. The people sitting on the park bench watching the world go by generally aren't the sort of folks who make the decisions about purchasing in-house printing plants, installing new computers, or replacing corporate jets, are they?

Will you agree that the kind of person who buys what you sell gets a large amount of mail? What does the corporate executive—the busy doctor, engineer, or investor, the harried businessman—do with a letter from someone who's just writing to introduce himself as the new representative of a company that person has bought from in the past?

Zip into file thirteen. About 99.9 percent of the time, that piece of paper is on its way to oblivion as soon as the receiver recognizes what it is. The easiest thing to get rid of is a letter. The people you're selling have to get rid of a mass of paper every day or they'll be buried in it.

And what does this busy type of person say when the new representative calls them during their hectic work hours?

"Thanksforcallingoodbye." Click.

That happens eighty percent of the time when the new representative has nothing more in mind than to report his or her existence to the previous buyer. Why? Because the second easiest thing to get rid of is a phone call.

What's the hardest thing to get rid of?

A body.

That's why you should deliver the body when you re-contact these former clients of former salespeople. These busy people—unlike any other group of prospects you're likely to encounter—have already proven that they need, want, benefit from, and can afford your offering. And, if you pick the ones who've reached the right stage on the cycle, you know that most of them are starting to itch to do it all over again. So deliver the body. Your body. Go see these orphans in person.

If necessary, phone the executive's secretary for an appointment—but be sure that you have a strong answer ready for the secretary's inevitable question: "What is this concerning?" Because if you say, "I just want to introduce myself," you're not going to get the appointment, and that executive's secretary isn't going to let you at him to ask market-survey questions either.

That's why the Champion goes to see them. A surprisingly large percentage of people are more easily seen simply by going to where they are rather than by going through the routine of lining up an appointment. But first, you have to sift through the files.

Let's suppose that your company is fairly typical in this regard. You've determined that the itch cycle is three years; the files hold a large number of orphans; you can readily pull them out by the date they bought your product or service. Not only that, you're embarrassed by riches: the files are bulging with records of buyers who haven't been recontacted for up to ten years. Where to start? Hadn't you better start working on those old files of people who bought nine years ago before any more time passes?

Forget them. They aren't orphans any longer. If your offering really has a three-year itch cycle, those people have long ago made a connection to satisfy their urge to update your product or service.

Start right on the three-year mark, and work forward through the people who are just starting to itch until you've seen every orphan who bought up to two years and ten months ago. Only then should you start on the buyers who bought more than three years ago. Start with the buyers from thirty-seven months ago and work back until the returns no longer justify the effort. With most products, this won't take long if you've accurately determined the itch cycle.

In order to speed up the process of seeing the orphans who are itching to re-order your product or service because they bought it two years, ten months ago—and they're tickled pink with it—make discreet phone calls to determine whether they're still breathing and blinking at the same old stand. Some of them will have moved on. In personal sales, that's usually a dead end. In commercial and industrial sales, it simply means that Mrs. Newhouse is now making the decisions that Mrs. Oldbarn used to make. When the old copier Mrs. Oldbarn bought from your company starts to creak, Mrs. Newhouse will start itching to get the latest model on the same schedule that would have ruled Mrs. Oldbarn had she not retired.

Perhaps you're thinking, "Suppose they don't get the itch?"

The Champion believes that it's his or her obligation to help busy people become aware that they have a bad case of the itch. The Champion starts seeing them and calling them and doing all sorts of things to excite their interest and make them realize why they should cure that itch by re-ordering or replacing his product or service.

To be a Champion, you must know — and passionately believe in — compelling reasons why they should:

- Replace those old welding machines with the latest models that run beads twenty percent faster and save X dollars of labor cost . . .

- Trade in their old motor home for a new one that delivers more mileage and greater comfort . . .
- Get rid of the outdated system that, though it was a marvel three years ago, simply can't match the system you're able to help them enjoy today.

Find the reasons that make the product or service you're offering today so much better than the best available three long years ago. Make the effort and you'll find the reasons. Three years ago they bought the best—but what's best today is the latest. You want them to have the best, don't you? Then do your job. Show these people—who've already demonstrated their faith in your company by owning part of its output for three years—that your brand new state-of-the-art performance leader will deliver greater benefits to them than their old model does. You can do that, can't you?

Certainly you can—because you're a professional. The next time you walk in your office, go straight to the records and start looking for people who bought your offering from salespeople no longer with your company. Adopt those people. Make them your clients. Make them wish they'd bought from you. Then get them happily involved in a repeat performance with your offering.

NON-REFERRAL PROSPECTING TECHNIQUE NUMBER THREE:
TECHNICAL ADVANCEMENT

Of course you use the lure of technical advancement when you're talking to people who've made their itch cycle's full circle. But now we're talking about technical advancement as a specific prospecting technique in its own right.

Do you know that almost every product is already obsolete in the minds of its creators the moment it's scheduled for production?

Already they're looking to the future. They're thinking, "How can we make it better?" They know that if they don't, someone else will. And, of course, all those engineers, designers, and inventors aren't ready to fold their tents and silently steal away. They want to hang in there and keep on inventing, designing, and engineering tomorrow's surprises.

Many finished products quickly become obsolete, and few last long before they're outdated. Rarely do finished products wear out to the point where they can't be kept in service. Far more often, their original owners are used to the best, and they dispose of the product when it starts requiring frequent service, or when something better comes along. This applies to all finished products from calculators to supertankers. The people who could afford the best when the previous model of your product came out can still afford the best. In fact, very often they can't afford anything but the best. Sometimes this means that a blue-collar worker drives an old car so he can afford the latest dirt bike because racing them is his hobby. He can't afford to have anything but the best dirt bike for exactly the same reason the major airlines can't afford to have anything but the latest jet aircraft — they're both competing.

In this country—in fact, in the entire free world—we all want the best, latest, shiniest, newest, fastest, highest performance. I need it—isn't that how everyone feels?

I'm with you on this. We all feel the same way. A prime example of this technique could have been run off on me had any salesperson been alert enough to cash in on the opportunity that I represented. But no one was thinking along these lines, and I had to stumble on the technical advancement myself—as millions of people do every week because we salespeople aren't doing our job as well as we should. Here's how it happened.

I'm a football fan. A few years ago, while walking through a shopping mall doing a little looking, I saw something that stopped me cold. There it was! Football players seven feet tall on a television screen. I said to myself, "It's so realistic I almost feel like I'm getting bruised too." (Keep in mind this was two weeks before the Superbowl.)

Then I went on talking to myself. Why? Because I wanted it and, logically, I knew that I didn't need it. I'm not home much, and there wasn't any sensible reason why I should want anything more than my twenty-one incher. But I wanted it. I WANTED IT. I had a vision: all my friends over for the Superbowl, all of them mesmerized by that gigantic screen.

So I said, "I NEED IT." And then I went in and bought it. In my mind at the time was a hazy notion about how I logically needed that projection TV. Not until later did I realize what a perfect example of emotion dictating a "logical" reason for buying that was—and I'm the first to admit that my reason for buying was the phoniest kind of logic. But it ran through my head long enough for me to make the purchase and—you know what—I'm not sorry I did it because it gave me that much pleasure.

That was an expensive TV set. It generated a substantial sum to the salesperson involved, I'm sure. The point is, why did the television store where I bought my twenty-one incher let me stumble on projection TV in someone else's shop?

This was technical advancement to a massive degree. Why didn't the salesperson who got me involved in my old twenty-one incher—and that person knew my status—get me happily involved in projection TV? No attempt was made before or after I bought my big-screen set. As far as I know, no one in the entire area jumped on this sensational technical advancement. No one got on the phone with all the substantial people in the area who might be delighted to pay for the benefits of a fantastic development. Everyone just sat back and waited for the people who could afford this innovation to wander in on their own. While they were waiting, they weren't selling. And by waiting they lost the chance to sell everyone who wandered into some other store.

Someone should have called me and said, "I know where you're going to be in three weeks—you're going to be screwed into the floor in front of a TV watching the Superbowl, right?"

"Right, but —"

"How'd you like to be watching the game on a screen so big it makes the players look seven feet tall—and all this right in your own home?"

I would have said, "Get over here and tell me more."

When you have a new product—or an old product in a new style or with a new feature—call everyone who already has your product. Of course, use some discretion. If you used to sell them in packages of twelve, and now you have them in packages of a dozen, don't call everyone and tell them you have a fantastic development.

And use some flair. When you work with people, take a few minutes to find out a little about their interests and values. Jot that information down on 3 × 5 inch cards. Then when the exciting new development comes out next year—the one you haven't even thought about now—you can go through your card files, call the people, and say, "I know where you're going to be in three weeks—and wait till you hear about the exciting development I'm calling you about."

Of course, you call your own old customers first. Then sit yourself down and figure out a way to reach people you've never spoken to with that fantastic new innovation. Had I been a TV salesman when projection TV came out, I would have called every doctor, lawyer, and dentist in my area along with every other person I thought could afford it.

But it's late if you wait until the new innovation is in your showroom before you start to think about how to exploit it. If you sell for a company that's coming up with new developments all the time, start now on compiling a list of people to call when you have an especially important break-through to push.

Technical advancement. What an exciting and profitable way to collar new business.

NON-REFERRAL PROSPECTING TECHNIQUE NUMBER FOUR:
YOUR LOCAL NEWSPAPERS

A Champion does not dwell on the doom, destruction, and despair that crowd the front page. A Champion reads his or her local newspaper to generate business. And he reads the newspaper with pen in hand because dozens of people are advertising a message of great importance to every Champion in every issue. That message is, "I need help." But, of course, it's never written in those exact words.

Let me give you an example. Newspapers carry lots of little items about people who have been promoted because that's one of the ways newspapers build their own clienteles. You can count on a steady flow of these notices. Skim each article and send the person who was promoted a short note of congratulations. Do you think they'll appreciate that?

They'll not only appreciate the note, they'll probably be very receptive if you pick up the phone a day after you know they've received it and call to see how you can help them.

A story I heard from J. Douglas Edwards shows how this approach can be turned into substantial earnings by salespeople for a wide variety of products and services. One of Doug's close friends is a professional baseball player who received one of the largest salaries ever paid a ballplayer for going to a new club. In the city he was going to, the newspapers ran half-page articles telling about his coming, and that he was going to establish a second home for his family there.

Now, what did that well-paid professional athlete need in the new city? A home. If you're in real estate, here's a live one for the best neighborhood you serve.

Furniture and furnishings for that home. If you're selling an interior designer's services, furniture, carpeting, or any of a host of things for the home, here's a hot lead.

What about the grounds? A tennis court, a swimming pool, patios, landscaping—this man needs all sorts of products and services for his new home.

What else does he need? Money always burns a hole in our pockets, and this man has a bundle of bonus money. He's not going to be without wheels in either his new city or at the house he's keeping in his old hometown. So he needs a car. And, since athletes like to watch themselves on TV, he's going to need a video recorder. Of course, he doesn't want to miss detail, so he's a prime candidate for a projection TV.

With a new home and car, what's he going to need in the way of services? Not only the landscaping and interior design that I've already mentioned, but he's also going to need insurance for the house and car and his possessions, and for the liability risks he'll be exposed to in the new city. And he's moved up several brackets on the income scale. Now he's batting in a new league of tax and investment opportunities—so he might need new tax and investment counselors. And his wife needs charge accounts at the finest stores, along with a number of other products and services to go along with her new station in life.

You know, we Champions could help him spend all his bonus money, couldn't we? And while we're doing that, we'll be making sure that he and his family get the maximum benefit from it, won't we?

Here's the cruncher. The ballplayer moved into that new city several weeks after the story ran in all the local papers. Later, Doug asked if a swarm of salespeople had overwhelmed him with attention. The ballplayer said, as far as he could tell, not one salesperson had contacted him as a result of the newspaper stories. He and his wife arrived in that new city and set about satisfying their needs exactly like anyone else might: by asking people they knew for recommendations, by driving around and spotting things, and by checking the yellow pages.

Where were all of us when they came to town?

Just sitting in our showrooms, waiting for somebody—anybody—to wander in.

Very often it's the small, local publications that have the most leads for the alert salesperson. The Champion isn't looking for news about the latest catastrophe in Kabul, Karachi, and Kimpo when skimming through these papers. The Champion is looking for news about his or her sales territory or trading area. Who's been transferred in, who's been promoted, who's won an award, who's developing a new project? That's what the Champion wants to know.

Check out the little local papers that you've been finding on your doorstep and throwing away without looking at. Some of these papers are bulging with local news. And also check out the specialized business newspapers that cover certain industries or certain areas. These can be rich sources of leads. Obviously, if you're active in the yacht business, you'll already be reading the local boating newspaper—but what if you're selling insurance, fine furniture, art, luxury automobiles? People who can afford yachts don't buy their clothes at the Goodwill, and the dentist who's winning all the yacht races around there is almost certainly a heavy consumer in other areas of life. The chances are that he needs your product or service—and he'll appreciate a note of congratulations on his latest victory.

But what about the people who came in second, third—or just entered the race? They're heavy hitters too, and they'll be even more appreciative that someone noticed they competed.

More leads than you can possibly handle are being printed every day in your area—and your best source for them may be in publications that you've never thought of reading. If you're in any form of personal sales, expand your thinking. Search out new printed sources of leads.

NON-REFERRAL PROSPECTING TECHNIQUE NUMBER FIVE:
CLAIM-STAKING

After reading the last story about Doug's ballplaying friend, you may be thinking, "If I wait until someone new arrives at a club (or any local organization) it'll be harder to make a connection there in time to get the business. Maybe I should start working some clubs right now—before the new people who'll get publicity arrive. Then, when they show up, I'll be an insider and get first crack at them."

That's what the claim-staking technique is all about. You make yourself known, learn the ropes, get acquainted with carefully selected organizations where you feel comfortable and are meeting people who are pre-qualified—by income and interests—for buying your offering. This is one of the best techniques I've ever encountered because you can stake out as many claims as you can handle. Every one of them will be a gold mine of contacts and solid pre-qualified leads. Yes, there's no limit to how many organizations you can claim-stake, but don't be like some of the old time prospectors who wandered the canyons with a donkey and a slouch hat. Don't stake out more claims than you can work properly and lose out on all of them.

Bear in mind that with this technique, it usually takes a little time before you can start bringing the ore out of the ground. So start work right away. Put a few hours each week into developing this approach. Invest enough time to keep your presence and influence growing in the clubs or organizations you've selected for this technique, but don't allow this medium range project to prevent you from working your ready-to-buy-now prospects for all they're worth.

How many organizations should I claim stake? And how do I work them?

Check out as many organizations as you can before deciding on your answer to that question. Keep looking until you find an organization that offers you both encouragement and opportunity. Having one without the other is useless. When you locate such a group, the best way to work with it will suggest itself to you. Be as active as possible. If it's a country or social club, join it and volunteer for committee work — there's no better way to make your presence felt. If it's an organization that you can't or don't want to join, start taking its people to lunch, write thank-you notes, do favors, run errands, make yourself useful. If you're right for that group, you'll know the right song to sing there. If you don't, move on to another organization. One club may offer more contacts than you can possibly work with, or you may enjoy and profit from working with several. If you decide to claim stake companies — by getting acquainted with their personnel directors, for example — you may find that you can effectively work with twenty or thirty. The only rule about how many to claim stake is to do what's most effective for you.

What kind of organization is best for claim staking?

That depends on your offering, your preferences, your personality. The range of organizations that you can effectively bore into is almost limitless: private companies, business associations, charities, church groups, country and social clubs, amateur and professional sports organizations, special interest groups, service clubs, political parties, hobby clubs, and cultural societies. To determine the best group for you, compare the time, money, and energy cost of establishing yourself in any organization that interests you with the benefits that you can expect in the way of contacts and leads from doing so. Your analysis will develop the right answer.

NON-REFERRAL PROSPECTING TECHNIQUE NUMBER SIX:
SWAP MEET

The biggest waste of space in many American cities used to be the drive-in theatre. Though they were surrounded by thousands of homes, these paved acres did nothing but accrue taxes during the day. Then a very creative person had an idea, and today's swap meet was born.

The roots of the idea are lost in time. There may have been here-today-gone-tomorrow market fairs before there were cities to hold them in. People love the color and diversity and excitement of buying, selling, and trading in the open air for handcrafted goods and unexpected bargains.

Do you know that you can easily create a source for some of your best leads by setting up your own swap meet? You do it on a small scale; it costs you nothing beyond a little effort.

The idea is to meet regularly to swap leads with carefully selected salespeople who sell in non-competing fields. Four to six people is the ideal number; more than that gets out of hand.

Here's how to organize this fantastic fountain of new business:

Select four, five, or six strong salespeople in beneficial fields to join your swap meet, and agree with them on a time and place. That's all there is to it.

"Not so fast," you may think, "What do you mean by 'beneficial fields'? How do I select strong salespeople? And exactly how does the swap meet work?"

BENEFICIAL FIELDS

The best fields for you to draw your swap meet people from are those that involve the same kinds of customers that you sell to. As long as they're non-competing, the members of your swap meet can be selling in fields that are closely allied to yours, or they can be operating in entirely different industries. The important thing is that their customers have the same general interests, needs, and capabilities your customers have. If you sell home appliances at retail, you won't get much from—or be able to give much to—someone who sells word processing machines to large offices. But you will be able to swap lots of leads with salespeople in floor coverings, furniture, and residential real estate.

SELECTING STRONG SALESPEOPLE FOR YOUR SWAP MEET.

Here's the technique for picking the people you'll really enjoy and profit from. Suppose that most of my customers are executives who generally drive luxury cars, although that's not my line. I can assume that many of these executives lease their cars for tax and other reasons. So one of the people I'd want in my swap meet would be a top producer in the luxury car leasing field. Why? Because I can help him—and if I can help him, I know he can help me.

All right, now I know one of the fields that I want represented—but how do I contact a top producer?

Call the sales managers of leasing companies until you hit pay dirt. The chances are that you'll do that the first call you make. Tell the sales manager what you want to do, and ask him who you should get to go to your swap meet from his company. That sales manager is going to put you in touch with someone he or she knows will follow up on leads from your swap meet—which means you're going to get a top producer.

For top recommendations for your swap meet, go to the top. If you've called a sales manager worthy of the title, that person is going to be excited by the fact that you're creative enough to start a swap meet, and he'll want his firm to benefit from it by having a strong person there.

HOW THE SWAP MEET WORKS.

1. Meet every week. Unless you do, it won't become habit.

2. Meet at the same time and place. Otherwise the time consumed by making arrangements will kill the whole thing.

3. Meet the first thing in the morning. You'll never be able to get together on a consistent basis at any other time. Drop anybody who can't get up in time. Your swap meet is for people who mean business only.

4. Meeting for breakfast at a centrally-located coffee shop is the most convenient plan for sales lead swap meets. Don't burn anyone with the entire check—everyone pays his own.

5. Don't dawdle. This is not an excuse for killing time. Unless your swap meet is brief, upbeat, and useful, it'll wither away.

6. Everyone who attends commits to the goal of bringing two good leads to each swap meet. But sometimes people won't have two. Agree that they are welcome anyway; it's better to come with one lead than not to come at all. That person should then feel an obligation to bring three leads to one of the next swap meets.

7. At the meet, the leads are exchanged. As a group, you try to make sure that the person who can help any given lead soonest is the one to work on it first.

8. The strongest commitment must be made by all to follow up promptly and thoroughly with every lead they take. The swap meet won't last unless its members get solid benefit from it.

9. Nothing destroys a swap meet faster than letting it divide into takers and givers. If you see that start to happen, talk to the takers privately. Persuade them to change their ways or eliminate them from the group.

10. And no swap meet can survive being the dump for the group's gloom. Don't tolerate pessimism and put downs. Make it clear that the swap meet is to be the springboard for a day of effective selling and money-making, and that no one who's forgotten his enthusiasm is welcome.

I've been in swap meets as a salesperson and know I've been a lead at someone else's swap meet. Of course, I didn't figure that out until much later. So from both ends I know they work.

But you may think that swap meets only work for products. Not so. Let me tell you how they work for services. I have an attorney, an investment counselor, and a financial adviser. I know they're in a swap meet because not long after I started working with one, I found myself working with the other two—and they all happily involved me in opportunities.

The swap meet is exciting. It's fun. And it's a business-boomer. After you get your first swap meet running smoothly and making money for you every Monday morning—who knows? Maybe you'll want to start a second swap meet on Thursday mornings.

NON-REFERRAL PROSPECTING TECHNIQUE NUMBER SEVEN:
SERVICE YOUR SERVICE DEPARTMENT

If you sell any kind of mechanical or electronic product, your company probably has a service department. This means that the owners of your product call them when the old model they've got starts creaking and groaning. Now what happens when a machine's maintenance cost goes up? Its productivity goes down—and its owner starts to itch for a new one.

Check with the service department and find out who's calling in to get their existing equipment worked on. Service calls give you the perfect opportunity to go over and get these people happily involved in the new model that'll do a better job for them with no downtime.

This can be a tremendous source of business for the alert salesperson. An example of this happened to me not long ago. I take a portable stereo along on my travels because I love music. Since I travel so much, things get banged up. When a small but necessary flange on my stereo broke off, I could see that I wouldn't get any more music out of my portable until it was fixed. So I took it back to the store where I'd bought it.

After I told them what I wanted, the salesperson said, "This set shows a lot of wear and tear. Maybe you should get a new one."

"No one sees it," I said, "I don't care how it looks as long as it plays okay."

The salesperson shrugged his shoulders and wrote up the repair slip. I left the store.

Two days later I got a call from another salesperson in that same store. He said, "I know you, Mr. Hopkins. You're the gentleman who flies around training salespeople."

"That's me."

"Do you want to wait until you come back to town, or would you like to take a new stereo on your next trip? One that really sounds terrific compared to your present set."

"I'd love to have a new stereo, but I can't see what I'd do with the old one."

He said, "I have an idea for you. Your office, I notice, is just up the street from our store."

"That's right."

"If you can give me five minutes, I'll be right up to see you with something I think you'll be excited about."

Guess what I flew off with the next day. That's right, a new stereo. Not only because it looked better, but mainly because the sound was so much better. I didn't really want it—but all of a sudden I had to have it. He didn't get me involved logically, he got me involved emotionally by letting me hear the sound and see the set. Before I knew it, I was carrying my new stereo on a plane.

But what about that first salesperson, the man who wrote up the repair slip on my old set? He had a clear shot at me first—and he didn't pull the trigger. I was standing there in his store not ten feet from one of the new ones I bought two days later from the competent salesperson who came to see me.

The same system will work for you if you make a habit of going through the service orders. If you have a service department, service it every day and it'll service your bank account for you.

FIVE WAYS TO HOVER UNTIL
YOU'RE READY TO FLY

Those are my techniques for non-referral prospecting—seven powerful methods that can launch you into high production fast. But what if you don't have the confidence for any of them. What if you're satisfied to play that you're just a lazy character? (Notice that I didn't say "if you are lazy" because no one is lazy in the same sense of *is* that applies when we say that someone is deaf.) Laziness is a mood or a pose. It's like a coat—you can take it off whenever you decide to. If your game is playing that you have an infirmity called laziness, please stick with it, stupid. The longer you plow mud with your nose, the easier you make it for the rest of us who are eager to do a day's work every day. By the way, if I say anything that offends you but it's true—tough. I tell it like it is.

Let's suppose that, for whatever reason, you're not ready and willing to put on a strong prospecting drive of any kind right now. If you're in a situation where no business at all is coming at you, you're dead. You either have to change your attitude or change your job, because you're not going to make a dime at what you're doing.

But you may be in a situation or a territory where there's a flow of business that comes at you without any prospecting on your part; company-supplied leads, repeat business from established customers, things of that sort. The following methods will allow you to hold that business, and even build it up, while you're also building confidence and learning your product or service. Work hard at studying and practicing the techniques in this book in private and there'll come a day—it may surprise you how soon this will occur—when you can't stop yourself from putting them all to work. When that happens, you'll suddenly find yourself racing along the road to high income. Prepare vigorously, have faith, and success will be yours.

Here's how to hold things together until you're ready to make your drive for the big money:

1. **Send every client a thank-you note.** We'll cover thank-you notes thoroughly in chapter sixteen's System 8.

2. **Handle problems fast.** If someone has a problem with your product or service, take care of it right now.

3. **Call people back immediately.** One of the biggest problems most salespeople have is that they don't want to pick up messages and call people back. Return calls now. It's the only way you can build up a clientele.

4. **Keep every promise made.** To make the sale some salespeople will promise everything.
   "Oh, yes, I'll take care of that adjustment."
   "I'll make sure that item is included."
   "You can count on me."
   And then they don't do one thing they promised to do if they can avoid it. You'll never get a referral that way.

5. **Keep in touch.** Call or see your clients regularly. Letters and mailing pieces can't carry the full load because there's no feedback from the

disgruntled, or from those being wooed by a competitor. Phone them. Listen for their itch cycles.

Most of my top Champions send out some kind of mailing piece at least once every ninety days. Many top producers in the automobile business have a new company brochure going out in the mail to their list of clients and prospects between four and eight times a year. Almost every large company regularly produces literature that's designed to be mailed out by their salespeople.

Divide any sales force into low, average, and high producers. If you study what they really do with that mail, you'll discover that only the high producers actually get the mailers to their clients. All the others run out of gas before the mailers reach the post office. There's just too much detail for these unbusy people to handle.

One of the top insurance salespeople we've trained—and we've trained thousands—sends out a newsletter every month. He writes it himself. The newsletter is aimed right at his clientele and it's strictly business. He doesn't draw cartoons. Instead, he gives them a little review of insurance basics in each issue and a lot of new tax ideas and advantages that he's turned up from his own on-going research. (He's a professional, so he makes sure that he knows more about his service than his customers do.) And he tells them about the latest developments in pension plans. If you're in this field, you know how important pension plans are to insurance sales. This man gets a steady flow of referrals, as well as new business from old clients, while his newsletter is keeping his name before those of his clients who aren't thinking of making changes in their insurance and pension arrangements now. But they will—when they take a full turn on the itch cycle.

The monthly newsletter is backed up by a phone call every six months and a visit once a year. That's the program until he sniffs change, and then he swings into action. His clients are loyal and their numbers are growing rapidly. That's keeping in touch. Without the newsletter, he'd have to increase his phone calls and visits to inactive clients—at an enormous cost in time, which is money.

There are only three ways you can keep in touch: send them things, phone them, see them. The best mix of these operations depends on your circumstances, but it's a rare sales situation that won't benefit from a combination of all three approaches.

Your company may provide you with fancy new four-color brochures once or several times a year. Several outside firms will supply you with printed newsletters or magazines that can be imprinted with your name and mailed out. Many of these firms will even do the mailing for you. But these prepared mailers are often too slick, too institutionalized, too impersonal, and too general to be used alone. What you need is a steady mail program that zeros in on your customers and the opportunities and problems that are special to your trading area. Bridge the gap between your company's special concerns with a newsletter that you write yourself. Or you can write one personal letter that tells about a new technical advance every ninety days, and have an automatic typewriter service personalize it to your entire list of itchers.

This doesn't have to be one more thing you feel bad about not doing because you don't have both the time and the skill to create your own mailers. Instead of ignoring the problem, solve it. Organize a group of salespeople in your office—or in non-competing firms—to share the benefits and expense of having one newsletter written for all of you, a newsletter that's personalized to your general geographic area and to the general level of your several clienteles. The cost to you will be a fraction of the income you're missing by not using the mails effectively.

All of these mail systems can pay large rewards for small efforts. But they don't take the place of keeping in touch by phone and visit. Use mail to maintain contact and keep your image fresh with them; use the phone and visits to get the vital feedback you must have to be in time to put balm on their itch and your pocketbook.

If I were marketing corporate jets and VIP aircraft, here's how I'd operate. Every time I got a line on someone moving in the same circles as one of our owners, I'd go into orbit. I guarantee that I'd be in touch with that person. They'd get the brochure but that would only be the beginning. I'd fly them somewhere exotic for lunch. I'd flatter their egos. I'd let them know how much they crave the prestige of owning a personal or corporate jet.

The thing is, these people just don't realize that they need it—that their position demands it. So I'm going to make sure that they know. Isn't that my job?

The same procedure holds true for a great variety of products and services. The time and money you spend, of course, will have to be in line with the return you can expect from closing the sale.

I hope you feel the intensity that I'm trying to project into prospecting, because it's the lifeblood of sales. You have people in your sales force who've never generated a single lead on their own. You have people there who won't pick up a phone to prospect. You have people who won't leave the office to prospect—they simply won't leave the place unless someone calls them out. They're hoping the company will somehow do it all for them.

"Gimmie more leads. Gimmie more. Gimmie."

If you're Champion material, you'll build your business yourself because you know that's the only way it'll get built. You'll build it on happy clients, on itchers and service calls, with the card referral system, orphan finding, technical advancement, local newspapers, claim staking, swapping, and, most of all, by fulfilling your responsibilities to your clients so well that you richly deserve referrals and the success that attends them.

Relying on yourself instead of relying on the company is the only realistic way of building your own personal stature, don't you agree?

8

HOW TO FIND FORTUNE AND FELICITY WITH THE PHONE

It's amazing how few people in any sales office really understand the function of the telephone. Once they get the hang of dialing or punching the buttons—usually at the age of about three—they turn off their brains and just let their mouths run on automatic when they pick up this unique instrument.

You'll really need to open your mind in this chapter because it's impossible for me to take all the phone techniques I have for you and tailor them to your product or service. You'll have to stretch and twist and hammer them to fit your needs. All I can do is give you the basic concepts, and pass on an increased understanding of how you can present yourself more professionally and effectively over this potent audio-medium that sets on all our desks. The telephone is your second most important selling tool—the first being your mouth. Yet, for reasons that escape me, few salespeople really study the technique of the telephone. Only the extra ambitious—the potential Champions—do so. The average salesperson, who desperately needs greater skill with the telephone, won't bother studying such a fundamental thing. However, more than knowledge of technique is needed. To use the telephone with greatest effect, you must also have a keen understanding of its limitations. The worst misconception the average salesperson has about the telephone is the idea that a telephone call can substitute for a face-to-face meeting with the prospect. The Champion is convinced that no strange voice coming over a wire can ever match in-the-flesh presence for effectiveness. Here's the first of several ideas that we'll isolate so you can highlight them:

I MUST MEET ALL QUALIFIED, INTERESTED CALLERS IN PERSON.

That must be your goal in every conversation with people calling in who show interest in your offering and give an indication that they are qualified to buy it.

Companies invest huge sums in programs aimed at creating this kind of call: mass media and directory advertising, publicity, signs, direct mail, trade show and other promotions. All that money is wasted, and all those ads aimed at making the telephone ring are for nothing if, when the telephone does ring and you answer it, you fail to arrange a meeting with the caller.

Some salespeople think it's no skin off their noses when some of their company's advertising budget is wasted. They couldn't be more wrong. It's impossible to turn every call into a sale, but if you fail to do your utmost to make every call that reaches you pay off for your company and for yourself, you weaken both. Nothing stays the same in our dynamic world. Every day all things continue to grow—or they start to die. If you spend months or years of your life helping a company die instead of fly, you're doing the same thing to an irreplaceable part of yourself. You can't even get last week back again—much less re-run the last five years. Make your time count while you can—and the only time you can do that is right now and in the future.

More and more, ads are written to generate calls for more information as a first step to purchase. If you know how to handle the phone, such calls can easily become sales for you.

Let's take the process from the beginning.

1. What is the right time to answer the phone?

You may laugh, but there is a correct time to answer the phone. If you snatch it up before the first ring is fully rung, you'll frighten some people and make others think you're too anxious. If you let it ring six to sixteen times, they'll decide you aren't attending to business. The perfect time, the professional time, to answer the phone is on the third ring.

2. What kind of image does your voice create?

When you answer the phone with a tone and manner that suggests you're suffering from a terminal illness, they won't want to meet you. This is why the Champion answers the phone with some excitement, some happy notes in his voice, some enthusiasm. No matter what catastrophes you're involved with at the moment, every time you pick up the phone at the office you may be talking with someone who wants to be helped by your offering. If you're mature, if you're controlled, if you're competent, you'll be able to put your immediate concerns to one side while you speak cheerfully with the caller.

That's one of the reasons why you answer on the third ring. With the first ring, stop what you're doing, clear your mind, and pump yourself up. It's a simple trick. All it takes is a little practice and knowledge. Select a mental image that pleases you—a happy hope, a specific goal, a solid achievement you're proud of—or even just a good feeling that you can vividly recall. Make your choice and then, whenever you hear the phone ring, block out what you're doing at the moment and flash that mental image across your mind for an instant. Use it to shift gears so you can speak with a fresh and alert tone that declares you handle the finest product or service available and you're eager to meet anyone who's interested. With a little practice, you'll find that your inspiring mental image need be in your mind only for a split second to do its wonderful work.

3. Acknowledge the other person's interest.

Let your caller tell you why he's calling. He or she may refer to an ad or ask about some specific item. You might respond along these lines:

"Yes sir, we've had a lot of calls about our new Whippledipper. We're really excited about it."

Then you continue on to the next step.

4. Put them on hold so that you can obtain information for them.

But do this only if you can fit it in smoothly. The professional looks for an opportunity to put them on hold so he can gather his thoughts as though saying to himself, "All right, I've got a live one on the line—now what's my best strategy?"

So you put them on hold once, if you can, early in the conversation. Be sure to take careful note of this: never keep them on hold longer than seventeen seconds.

What happens when you leave them on hold for a minute or longer? When you come back on the line, they simply aren't the same human being who called in. If they're still on the line, they don't even sound the same. The roar of rage you hear isn't the opening movement of a beautiful symphony of sales achievement. Long holds equal lost sales.

5. Close for the name.

A Champion does his or her best to get the name of the person calling for several reasons, one of which is that it's very helpful in creating rapport with the caller if you can call them by name. The best way to get the name is simple, and the exact words are important. Here they are:

When you come off the hold, say, "Thank you for waiting." Always acknowledge their courtesy with courtesy.

Then say, "This is _____," giving your name. (Of course, you wouldn't do that if they asked for you by name when first calling.)

Pause an instant. Your caller may respond by giving you his name. But don't try to force it by waiting—just give him a chance to say his name if that's the natural thing for him to do at this point. If not, come right out with it in a warm and confident tone:

"May I ask who's calling, please?"

You'll almost always get the name this way if they're really interested in considering you and your firm for the purchase in question—provided that you've been cordial.

6. Answer most questions with a question and lead them to the appointment.

The appointment you seek might require you to go to their home if it's a personal or family sale; it might mean that they'll come in to your showroom or display area to see what your company has advertised; it may involve your going to the caller's office if it's a corporate situation. You might even meet in a public place. Whatever the case, you must always be moving for the appointment. Now, answering questions with a question means that you use what technique?

The porcupine.

For example, when a man calls and says, "Do you still have the special price on that copying equipment? — Is it still available?"

A Champion would not answer yes or no to that question. Instead, he'd say, "Is that copying equipment the type you were hoping to find?"

"Yes, it is."

"Fine. I'd be available today or tomorrow to talk further with you. Would you like to come to our display room, or shall I come to you?"

That's a Porcupine, but it's also an Alternate Advance, isn't it? That's double power.

7. When making the appointment, reconfirm all details.

I have to warn you about something. Studies have proven that only a small percentage of people will follow a set of instructions if they're only given to them once. Would you agree? When you set appointments, what happens many times? They either forget the whole thing, or they may not realize exactly where your location is. They may forget the time of the appointment, and they may not remember your name. That's why a professional reconfirms everything. Make a note to ask them to write down the pertinent details.

Here's what the Champion says:

> "Do you have a pencil handy? I'd like you to write down some pertinent details."

Guess what the pertinent details are. They include the salesperson's name, his office location, the address, the time, and anything the caller needs to get back in touch with you.

8. The Champion drops a second anchor after the appointment is set and confirmed.

This final step is especially important if you're going to be waiting for them in your showroom or in a mutually convenient coffee shop. Another ten percent of people will keep the appointment if they know you can call them up if they don't show. And, of course, it's always possible that something could happen that would make it impossible for you to keep the appointment. So, after confirming all details, you say:

> "If something very unusual happens and I have to ask you to change the time of our appointment, where could I call you?"

Whether you market a product or a service, there's at least a fifty-fifty chance that you'll have to call out to get leads. In fact, the true Champion, regardless of what he sells, knows that the telephone can enormously increase his sales volume. So he's always on the phone every moment he can squeeze from other needs, calling new people.

So now, let's discuss that kind of call.

OUTGOING CALLS

Almost everyone will answer the phone when it rings. Even salespeople afraid to make outgoing calls will take incoming ones. In fact, they're often so eager for someone to call that it's pathetic.

Why will salespeople cringe at the thought of prospecting by phone, but jump at the chance to talk with the same sort of person when they're receiving instead of initiating the call? When you stop to think about it, there's something really strange going on here. That something gets even more strange the more you dig into it.

After all, these salespeople are there to make money. They know they'll make money by finding more buyers. They also know that they'll find more buyers by using the phone to hunt them down. Prospecting is simply this: You get on the phone and call possible buyers until you locate one worth seeing in person. Then you go see that person and arrange for him or her to pay your company money. A portion of that money is then paid to you. That's the essence of sales work, don't you agree? It all starts with prospecting.

Yet there are salespeople who don't want to prospect. They can't be afraid of the telephone because they grew up with one, and another sits within arm's length on their desk. They've gotten used to it. They know it won't bite, explode, or cause a bad smell. But the thing does have this irritating habit of making a loud noise. Who can doze comfortably in an office chair with that annoying sound banging one's ears? Worse yet, if you don't pick it up and find out why somebody's bothering you, you're sure to be the target of angry looks and muttered insults from those nearby. That's if you're lucky. If you're not, you'll hear rude shouts. On the other hand, there's always a good chance that the incoming call isn't work or trouble at all—it may be misdirected and easily disposed of, or a friend wanting to chat. Most of us have worked it out long ago. On the whole, it's better to talk to the thing when it rings.

Calling out is different. No sense pretending that it isn't. In the first place, you are the intruder when you make the call, not the intrudee. It doesn't work to say, "Why are you bothering me?" when you're the caller.

You may think that's the reason you're not prospecting by phone. It isn't. Oh, sure, there's that vague unease that we all feel about telephone prospecting at first. It's uphill work, not a downhill slide; a movement out, not a withdrawal in. But that's the way mountains are climbed and fortunes are made.

Don't beat yourself with these nightmares at noon about not having the thick-skinned aggressiveness necessary to prospect by phone. That isn't what you lack, and it really doesn't take much in the way of courage and aggressiveness to be an outstandingly effective telephone prospector. It takes knowledge. If you're afraid to prospect, it's because you don't know how to prospect.

The first thing to remember is this: you can always say, "I'm sorry I disturbed you. Goodbye." Make sure that ends the matter in your own mind. After all, you've just called them; you haven't ruined their life.

The second thing to remember is that you must always have a success goal, not a performance goal, when you prospect. Let me explain. If you write down this as a goal: "I will make fifteen prospecting calls starting at nine tomorrow morning," you can make all fifteen of those calls and have nothing.

Set success goals: "Tomorrow at nine I will start telephone prospecting, and I will continue prospecting until I have three appointments to demonstrate my product to people I believe can and should buy it." Set a reasonable success goal and then do it. Stop for meals, go home nights, but keep prospecting until you achieve your success goal.

The third thing to remember is that, before you start calling, you must have an effective call formula and a good list of names and phone numbers. Your chances of success are no better than your formula and your list. If you're not getting encouragement after ten calls, pause, look at your list and formula, and consider making changes. By encouragement I mean making appointments, being asked to call back later, or being given names of people to call who might be interested. Don't let a few profitless calls discourage you. That is, don't let a few strangers—grouches you don't even want to know—cause you to walk away from success. Accept that you'll reach a few people who'll be less than delighted to hear from you. Be professional when you prospect—which means that you (1) have a legitimate offer that you're knowledgeable about, (2) call only during reasonable hours, (3) are unfailingly polite, (4) bring any unfavorable call to a quick and courteous close, and (5) put any unproductive conversation out of your mind and immediately make another call.

The last point is vital. In organizing your prospecting routine, set yourself up to chop off the negatives fast. Don't allow time for them to nag your enthusiasm away. Instead of singing sad songs for a spell after a washout call, give your head just one quick shake and immediately dial another prospect's number. Do that and you'll be delighted at how easily and effectively you'll prospect, and at how fast your prospecting sessions will go.

I have a little challenge for you here that's really an exciting opportunity. You get to write your own market survey now. Perhaps it'll go faster, and you'll wind up with a better survey, if you team up with two or three like-minded people in your sales organization and write a market survey together that you'll all use as a prospecting formula. Start with the basic format that follows and tailor it to fit your product or service, your trading area, and your company's strengths and selling methods. As you develop your survey, give careful thought to the order in which you'll ask the questions. After the third step, some other sequence may suit your offering better than the one I've given here.

1. Use the person's name immediately.

This is crucial. Using their name soon and often causes them to listen more closely to your message.

"Good morning. Is Mr. Hammersmith there?"

2. Introduce yourself and your company.

As soon as you have the right person on the line, identify yourself in warm and friendly tones.

"This is Tom Hopkins with Champions Unlimited."

Then move immediately into your market survey approach.

3. State your purpose and ask the first survey question.

Do that without pause between purpose and question. Use a pleasant tone that invites a conversational reply. Your first survey question should get right at whether or not they're interested in what you're marketing.

"I'm making a market survey—it'll only take a moment. Do you mind telling me whether you presently own a boat?"

4. If they say no.

With many products and services, getting a *no* at this point is great; with others, it means that you should pleasantly end the call and go on to the next one. If you're looking for a *no* here, carefully rehearse how you'll handle it. Frame your next questions to invite conversational replies that give you critical information and help to establish rapport.

"Would you like to own a boat sometime in the future, and if so, would you prefer a powerboat or a sailboat?"

Any time you have a friendly conversation with someone who turns out not to be an emotional and logical candidate for your offering, ask them for a referral. If you're working a good list, they're very likely to have a friend or two who is precisely the kind of prospect you're looking for. Use the card referral system's principle of helping people isolate a few faces from the multitude they're familiar with. For example, if the list you're prospecting from is a club roster, ask them if any of their friends at the club might be interested in having a brochure mailed to them on whatever you're marketing.

5. If they say yes.

("Yes, we own a boat.")
"Oh, fine. May I ask what type and make it is?"

After this step, your prospecting call can go off in any of several different directions, and how our boat salesman would handle them all need not concern us here. What's important is to outline the answers you're likely to get, and rehearse how you'll handle each one of them. Organize your response to each answer so that you continue to work toward an appointment to see the people, toward getting permission to send them a brochure, or to the realization they aren't a good prospect for your offering, so you should say a cordial goodbye.

6. Ask how long they've owned (used) it.

Find out where they are on the average itch cycle. The importance of this step speaks for itself.

7. Discover what they like about their present one.

Here are some of the questions you might ask if they own a product or use a service similar to what you're selling:

"Are you happy with the accuracy and promptness of your payroll computing service?"
"Is your intercom system doing everything you want it to?"
"What do you like most about your present deburring machine?"

Find out how people feel about what they presently own—what they like, and what they'd like to change. When you know that, you know how good your chances are of happily involving them in your company's latest version of that necessity. And you can see exactly how to go about involving them because you know what's important to them.

It's important to ask the question in positive terms: "What do you like most about. . . ."

Why is it important to be positive here? For three reasons: (1) people feel less threatened when you ask what they like, as opposed to asking what they don't like; (2) they're more likely to talk easily and tell you what they don't like if you don't ask them directly; and (3) you must be very careful about exciting their brand loyalty—unless, of course, you're selling the brand they're loyal to. More about this later.

You're looking for qualities and standards at which your product or service can outperform whatever they have now. If they like speed and your latest model is faster than the old one they own, you've found a strong emotional urge toward buying. When you strike one of those urges in a prospecting call, don't scare the rabbit away by shooting too soon. Go for an appointment to demonstrate. Don't talk to them about buying it, talk to them about experiencing its speed—or whatever their urge is. You want them to see, feel, touch, and operate it. That's all you want at this point. Not until they've sniffed the leather and heard the engine purr can you safely mention *owning* it.

8. Carefully uncover their negative feelings.

Unless they have some, you're running into heavy brand loyalty that requires careful handling. Never work yourself into a situation where you're knocking what they presently own because that's knocking their judgment. There's no quicker way to chill your chances than to let your prospect know you think he's a dummy for owning the product, or using the service, that he's already invested in. Ask for the vital negative information in a positive way that relieves the prospect of any need to defend his previous decisions:

"What would you like to see changed in your company's health insurance program?"
"Are there any features your present conveyor system doesn't have that would be helpful to you?"
"What improvements would make your present machine more efficient in your operation?"

With the market survey, you're searching for unsatisfied needs. You're trying to find something about their present product or service that your item can do better. They have to want more where you can give them more, of course.

Now, if you can give them more of what they want, this ability of your product is (1) something added or improved since they bought their present product, or (2) something in which your product or service was superior to what they bought all along. They just didn't know about it, or they didn't value that factor highly enough when making the decision to buy from the competition.

In the first case—something added or improved—you're bringing them good news. You can now solve a problem for them that you couldn't solve when they bought their present item. You can praise what they have now as being an excellent buy for its time—which has now passed. In the second case—your product or service was better all along—you have to cope with a situation that at best is delicate and at worst is explosive. There's no place for smugness or careless comment here. Every year, thousands of these situations blow up in the faces of overconfident salespeople who have logic on their side so they forget emotion. Then they can't close. Usually they don't know why. The reason is simple: the prospect won't accept the emotional distress involved in admitting a mistake. People can be extraordinarily sensitive on this subject—and equally obstinate. In many cases, the only way to replace the competitive product or service with your own is to make a convincing statement along these lines: You think the prospect made a wise decision when he bought what he now has. Given all the circumstances in force at the time, he did the right thing then, but in the changed circumstances that now prevail, the right thing today is to upgrade to your offering.

Surprisingly, there are many salespeople who prefer losing sales to helping their prospects save face. But it's more fun to concede the point and win the sale.

9. Introduce the strong points of your offering.

We all love to sell a basic competitive advantage—if we have one—but some of the most challenging and rewarding sales positions involve products or services that don't have any simple and easily-described superiority over their competition. If you do have a basic competitive advantage, drop it on the prospect at about this point in your survey:

> "Do your delivery trucks get thirty-five miles to the gallon?"
> "Is your present supplier giving you next morning delivery?"

10. The Windup Appointment Close.

As you conclude the telephone market survey with a prospect, thank them for their help. Then ask, "Could I mail you a brochure on our latest model? (On our latest schedule of services)?"

If they say yes, they of course have to give you their address, if you don't have it, or confirm that the address you do have is their current one. With the qualifying you've already done, you may decide that this contact is too good to let its momentum be lost in the mail shuffle. Use fast delivery of the brochure as your entree to meeting the prospect.

"After talking with you, Mr. Hammersmith, I feel that you have a need to know more about this new development that I'm excited about. With your permission, rather than wait for the mail, I'll drop the brochure by this afternoon so you can take a quick look at it and—because I know your time is valuable—if you have any questions, I'll be right there to answer them. Would around two—or three o'clock—be the best time for you?"

When you meet him, you may be able to go right into your standard presentation or demonstration and lead him emotionally to the close.

FINDING GOOD LISTS

Where do you get good lists of people to prospect with? Let me list a few of the sources:

1. Reverse Directories.

Also called the *by street* or *criss-cross* directory, this publication lists telephones by street and house number, and then gives you the name and phone number. This allows you to direct your prospecting efforts into the specific neighborhoods you believe will be most productive for you. An obvious use of the reverse directory is to pinpoint people in the right economic bracket for your offering. There are other uses. More and more, we are congregating by age and interest group rather than by ethnic background.

2. Club and company rosters.

Some of the best will be the hardest to get. But copying machines are everywhere. With a little persistence and ingenuity—and perhaps a lunch or box of candy in the right place—you can be the proud possessor of the list you want.

3. Libraries.

There are an astonishing number of directories published on this continent today. They cover every important industry and activity. Find a public library that has an outstanding business section. People with unlisted numbers in the local telephone book are often listed in the national directory that covers their specialty. Since most of these directories are organized by state and city, you can go through quite a few of them in a single evening at your library. See chapter 10 for details on some of the more widely known directories.

4. Mailing List Houses

Hundreds of companies are involved in selling mailing lists. If you can't find the list you want in a published directory, research the direct mail industry at your library. Some mail houses will develop special lists for you, but use this approach as the last resort because you'll probably have to look up the telephone numbers yourself.

TELEPHONE SCORING SYSTEMS

Let me give you some basic tips on using the telephone to generate money, not trouble.

1. Always be courteous.

No matter how badly you feel, you owe it to your sense of dignity and self respect, and you owe it to your company, to be courteous. You also owe that to the rest of us in the profession of selling—we all owe it to each other not to mess up our profession's reputation.

If you make people angry at you, they're angry at your organization too. Your employer not only has the right to your loyalty, he also has the right to have you enhance, not damage, the company's image. Treat clients with respect. That's an important way of treating yourself with respect too. Never lose your temper—that's what losers do. A Champion refuses to let someone else control his temper.

2. Do anything to meet them.

Some people call in and don't want to give you any information; all they want is answers. They can get pretty tough about it, but if you give them all the answers over the phone, why do they need to meet you? If you don't meet them, you won't sell them. It's that simple. I know it can be frustrating talking to people who want all the facts and figures although their attitude is, "Keep away from me, salesperson."

But, you know something? The people who try the hardest to keep from meeting you often are the easiest ones to close, once you break through to see them. That's why your goal has to be to meet face to face with callers.

When I was just getting up to cruise speed in my real estate sales career, we had a contest for a prize and a huge trophy. It was a large company situation with plenty of competition. Coming down to the wire, I was within striking distance of winning—but I needed one more transaction.

I took a call. The man wouldn't give me a name or number. I was getting desperate. "Please," I said, "Can't I come by for a few minutes and just meet you?"

"No way."

"Can I call you back, sir?"

He said, "What for? I'm in a phone booth."

"Oh, sir, I'm sorry. I didn't realize that. Do you have the streets where your phone booth is?" I was grabbing at anything.

"Let's see, I guess I'm at the corner of Chance and Main, yeah, that's where I am."

I said, "Would you hold one moment, please?"

Chance and Main was only two blocks from our office. I ran out, jumped in my car, zoomed over there, screeched to a halt by the phone booth, and there he stood, waiting patiently. I walked up, knocked on the glass and pantomimed, "It's me."

He walked out of that booth and said "I don't believe you."

But he soon started believing me because I knew what I was doing. So I got him happily involved in the magnificent opportunity called *owning your own home* in time to win the contest. Reader, do anything that's fair and legitimate to meet anyone calling to inquire about your service or product. They've already decided that they want and need what you're offering. If you can meet them, you can sell them.

3. Take good messages for others.

It's the only way you can get them to take good messages for you.

This is a pet peeve of mine. In hundreds of offices, few salespeople take good messages for each other—and this hurts everyone there. Get the name right, get the number right—double check these things with the caller—and put down the time of the call. Be professional.

I used to come back to the office and find scraps of paper with half a name on them and, if I was lucky, the whole phone number. So I'd call and try to fake it. "Hello there, Mr. Rawrupuhh—How are you today?"

And then there are the messages with only five numbers—and you're not sure whether they're the first or the last five. That's slow burn time.

If you're working out of an office that isn't able to control this problem, use an answering service. Print their number on your cards and give it to all your prospects and clients.

9

A SPECTATOR SPORT
BUYING IS NOT

Operating their mouths at high speed, some salespeople put on amazing demonstrations. They flip levers, punch buttons, zip stuff around. And out of the machines they're demonstrating come a flood of perfect parts, data, copies, or whatever. But they don't sell much with these superb performances.

Why not?

Because apathy rushes in where involvement fails to tread. Buying is action. It can't take place unless there are decisions, and decisions require a switched-on mind. *Watching* instead of *doing* is a switch-off. The longer your prospects are switched off, the harder it'll be to switch them back on again when you want the paperwork approved at the end of your demonstration.

The Champion avoids the long switch-off's low sales, and demonstrates by encouraging the client to enter the data, thread the needle, or feed the parts. Of course, the client won't do these things as well or as fast as a practiced salesperson can, but if he's doing them instead of watching, he's thinking about your product instead of wondering why his gums hurt and his horse ran last. In fact, he's doing more than merely thinking about your product—he's experiencing it. That means he's emotionally involved with what you're selling.

However great or small this emotional involvement may be, it's certainly going to be far greater than if your prospect just sits there while you sing your number. Owning is a very intimate form of involvement, don't you agree? Then doesn't it follow that the buying necessary for owning won't take place unless there's prior involvement?

If you accept that, you'll want to find as many reasonable and positive ways as you can to involve your prospects in your product. One of the best methods I know of is the client-participation technique that we've been discussing. If you've been switching your prospects off with I'm-the-star performances, you'll need to completely overhaul your demonstration to successfully convert it—and yourself—to the client-participation method. And you'll find that giving up I'm-the-star technique is like giving up smoking: you can't do it unless you really want to. Understand yourself here. Many of us—and I'm in this group—place a high value on applause, on appreciation, on being in the limelight. That's good—unless it leads you into making bad business decisions like sticking with I'm-the-star demonstrations when you're not selling.

But the truth is that you're the star twice when you master the client-participation demonstration: first when you have your prospects happily involved in your demonstration and product, second when you walk out with the endorsed file copies of an order.

The difference is small but vital. You win your oh's and ah's by showing your prospects how to do amazing things on your demonstrator, not by doing amazing things on it yourself. To fan their interest into a fire hot enough to melt their built-in sales resistance, you get them to chip rust, solve problems, or boil water with your device. That's always more fun than watching you run the game. With good products, familiarity breeds confidence and scatters fear.

And fun sells better than frustration. Remember that your prospects aren't used to your machine's peculiarities; keep your steps simple and your attitude encouraging.

Here's how to develop the client-participation demonstration technique into a powerful selling tool:

(1) List all the steps the uninitiated must go through to understand how badly they need your device's capabilities. Then figure out as simple an exercise as you can to demonstrate each capability. Make each exercise distinctive, and give it a name that's easy to remember. Use as much color as possible.

(2) List every question and objection that you're likely to encounter during a demonstration.

(3) Arrange the capability demonstration and the question/objection answering into a smooth-flowing sequence.

(4) Practice your new technique on anyone you can pull off the street. Check and re-check your lines: discard those that don't work well, and add new ones that do. The successful client-participation demonstration is organized so that each step is simple and leads smoothly to the next, yet the prospect feels a constant challenge and a growing sense of excitement. Keep the pace fast. Brush over minor details. And encourage, encourage, encourage:

"Terrific. You're catching on unusually fast."

"She's a whiz on this machine, Mrs. Lopez."

"You're learning the keyboard in about half the time it took me, Mr. Leach."

"It only seems tough because it's new, but you'll be delighted at how easy this machine is to operate when you know it."

"You're a quick learner, Miss Ellison—it must have taken me nine tries before I got that move down as well as you already have it."

"No—really—you're doing great. Everybody has a bit of a problem here at first."

"That's right—keep moving. We're just taking a fast overview now. Later we'll smooth out every detail."

"Everybody does that at first. Don't worry about it. This is a rugged little machine we've got here."

"Okay now—before you switch it on—I want you to promise to make lots of mistakes. If you don't, I'm going to feel very dumb because I sure goofed up a lot the first time I sat down with this machine."

Take the frustration and pressure out, put the fun and relaxation in, and you'll be successful with client-participation demonstration. When you're confident of your new technique, go out and happily involve two, three, or four times as many people in owning your product as you ever did before. Do that and two more benefits will automatically come your way:

(1) you'll spend less time making each sale because you will have solved the problem of involving people in your offering,

(2) you'll get more referrals because you will be developing greater rapport with your clients.

But what if you don't have a product to demonstrate? Perhaps you sell something that's built to order, or a service. Can you still use this advanced demonstration technique? And will it increase your sales?

You can, and it will. In fact, the more intangible your offering is, the more you need your clients actively participating in learning how it will benefit them—and the more you need your imagination working to make that happen.

Here's a golden opportunity for you people who sell things that can't be seen or touched. It poses a worthy challenge to your determination and willingness to grow. Overcome that challenge and you'll reap the rewards that go only to those who rise above the competition.

Of course, I can't tell you exactly how to do this with your offering because I don't have your expert knowledge of it. But the principle is simple and can readily be adapted to selling anything—services or products. One example will indicate the direction you should take.

Let's suppose that you sell life insurance and annuities to self-employed people by helping them set up Keogh retirement plans to fund the insurance and other investments. When you call on a prospect, you could sit there and blow tax and insurance technicalities at him until his eyes glaze over and he's desperate to be rid of you. You could load his desk down with charts and visual selling aids that you flip, point at, and are generally active with while he sits there watching. (As long as this approach isn't your main thrust, it's effective. I urge you to incorporate all the visual aids you can to support, but not make, your main arguments). You could do either of those two things, or you could show him how to calculate the advantages that you're offering. When he does that, he's actively learning why he should invest in your plan and your insurance. You'll lose control if you try to do this by talking while he's supposed to work it all out on a blank pad of paper. (If you're working on large transactions, prepare a prospectus for each client that clarifies all the formulas and simplifies all questions.) In the repetitive sales situations that most of us work with, have a packet of forms typed and run off on a copying machine. Keep them simple. Triple-spaced. Wide margins all around. Limit yourself to ten lines of information on each page, with no more than three blank spaces for the prospect to fill in.

Don't slow the process down with details. You can get things like social security numbers during the close or after the sale is made. For now, stick to the bare essentials, and urge the prospect to use the estimates and round numbers.

While your prospect is working his way through this benefit calculation folder of yours, have another copy in front of you so that you can guide him every inch of the way. Where do you wind up at? The close. And your prospect is ready to make a favorable decision because he understands what he'll be getting for his money, and he's grateful to you for making him feel smart and Keogh seem simple.

Earlier in this chapter we talked about salespeople who try to overwhelm their prospects with amazing demonstrations—and succeed only in boring them. You may not worry about that because you're troubled by the opposite problem: the prospects you demonstrate to aren't amazed at the show you put on, and they're too active, not too passive. They elbow you aside to get at the machine, pester you with questions, and demand instant answers. Your demonstrations remind you of a flock of seagulls scrapping over one fish. If you can hold your temper, you can make enough sales to keep going.

If that's a rough description of your usual demonstration, rejoice: you're only a few easy jumps from perfecting a very successful mode of demonstrating. All you need do is organize the steps so that you keep control and they keep the machine you're selling. In the next section I'll tell you how to do that.

THREE FORMATS FOR SELLING INTERVIEWS

Selling is two-way communication. It's not a transmitter sending to a receiver, not a preacher exhorting the sinner, not a politician stumping for votes. Selling is a tennis match, with one of the players—the salesperson—trying to hit the ball to the other player—the buyer—instead of away from him. This viewpoint is lost in the first of the three most common formats for selling interviews that follow. As we discuss these methods, bear in mind that nearly everything I say about demonstrating a product applies equally well to presenting a service.

MONOLOGUE

The plan here is to dominate the prospect with fast talk. Back in the days of the traveling salesman, when city slickers rode the train from one hick town to another, fast monologue worked pretty well. It doesn't anymore. We're running out of rubes.

TANGENT-CHASING

This system is popularly called "playing it by ear." In reality, it's simply *no preparation*. You go in there with your ears open and a bright smile clamped on your face. The first thing you do is hand control to the prospect by making it clear that you have no plan for the interview. Whatever tangent he takes off on, you follow—If he talks about the dancing bear he saw on TV last night, you talk about the dancing bears you've seen.

If he's slow to get the point that he is in charge of making the interview work, let him know you haven't had time to familiarize yourself with your company's latest catalog, price list, or policy—the one issued five weeks ago. If this doesn't convince your prospect that he'll have to open a book to learn anything while you're in his office, hit him again: say that the new product your company is making such a big thing about is a bummer. They may be claiming it's the breakthrough of the decade, but you kind of like the old gommie it replaces that he bought nine years ago from your company. About that tried, true—and out-of-production—model, you can tell him anything he wants to know.

Of course, many of the salespeople who rely on tangent-chasing know their product or service very well—but they don't know their customers well enough to lead them to the exact item they should buy. Which is to say, their prospecting and qualifying techniques are a drag on their product knowledge that prevents them from using that knowledge as often and as effectively as they could—and must if they're going to earn high incomes.

Since it doesn't require planning, preparation, and thought, tangent-chasing (playing it by ear) is a favorite with salespeople who intend to remain average. It's a method that sells no one and allows only the determined buyers to buy, so it minimizes the potential of your territory, your offering, and your abilities—but it sure is easy. Now let's talk about the format that does require planning, preparation, and thought—and, in return, is a sensational selling technique.

THE ORGANIZED INVOLVEMENT INTERVIEW.
Begin with a brief statement along these lines:
"To get the most out of the time you can give me this morning, I've planned my demonstration to answer the questions I'm most often asked about this machine in a natural sequence. If I don't cover something that interests you, the chances are I'll get to it in a moment.

"I've found that if I give a quick overview of the complete process first, and then come back to the detailed questions later, a lot of my customer's valuable time is saved. Okay? — now, Mr. Marzano, if you'll be good enough to feed another blank in here like I'm doing —"

Involve them all the way. Show them how it's done, then have them do it. Do it with great tact and courtesy because they aren't familiar with your machine, so they may be a little awkward and unsure of themselves. Ever notice how you have to concentrate when you first get in to drive a make of automobile that's new to you? All the little things you do automatically in your own car take thought, and maybe you don't do them smoothly at first. But if you're a passenger in that same strange car, you just flop into the seat and think about something else while the driver is doing what has to be done to get moving. Let your prospects drive instead of making them be just passengers during your demonstration.

Your opening statement conveys the idea that you know what you're doing, and that your prospect's time is not going to be wasted. No sooner do you get that across than you have him plugging the machine in, turning dials—whatever—as long as it's necessary and useful physical action.

You're in effective selling control, leading your prospect smoothly through your planned sequence, not trying to dominate him until he rebels.

You keep that control in a very simple way: by alternating selling statements and questions with involvement demonstration so that your prospect is almost continuously busy with your machine and with becoming its owner.

Of course, you watch very closely for signs of boredom if the tasks done on your machine are repetitious and the person making the purchase decision is a few rungs above those who'll operate it. Be on the alert for ways to keep your customers thinking and mentally active during your demonstration as well as physically involved. Use your ingenuity to devise involvement strategems to suit the varied personalities and positions of your clients. For example: you're demonstrating a revolutionary new sandblasting system to the owner-operator of a small rust-removing shop. Your involvement technique has him using the equipment himself on some of the jobs that are in his shop to be processed. But if you're demonstrating that same sandblasting system to an executive with a larger firm, your plan takes the difference into account. Hand the executive a stopwatch. Have him time his plant's regular sandblasting workers, and let him measure for himself how much faster your system is than his present method. This example is an extreme one. With your product, the graduations are probably more subtle—but they're still vital. The best involvement strategem in any given situation harmonizes the buyer's attitude and circumstance with the product's qualities.

The first step in preparing the organized involvement interview is to go over your present demonstration sequence and list everything that you can reasonably have the client do while it's going on. Remember that the more your prospective owner handles your product and the more things he does with it—that is, the more impact it has on his present consciousness—the more likely it is that your product will become part of his immediate future.

Next, list the questions you're usually asked in a sales interview.

Third, list all of your product's strong sales features.

Fourth, sit down with these three lists and outline a demonstration sequence that will cover all these points in a smooth flow from start to finish.

Fifth, go through that outline with this book in hand, and work in as many of the selling techniques given on these pages as possible. As you do this, always keep in mind that your attitude must always be courteously flexible when you demonstrate. Prepare yourself to speed up for the impatient, to slow down for the detail-minded—and to cope with the flitter-brained—without losing control of your selling sequence.

Sixth, practice your new selling sequence until you have a mental lock on it that can't be broken.

Seventh, go out and make a lot of money with it.

10

PUT CHAMPION SELLING POWER IN YOUR PRESENTATIONS AND DEMONSTRATIONS

Now we're getting into the area you probably enjoy most: working face to face with buyers. Unless I miss on two guesses, you're good at this—and you spend too much of your time doing it.

Let me explain. Our research indicates that most salespeople put in eighty to ninety percent of their time presenting and demonstrating, leaving only ten to twenty percent for other things. The Champion, on the other hand, spends only forty percent of his time presenting or demonstrating; not more than ten percent prospecting (some Champions spend no time at all prospecting because referrals keep them busy); and about fifty percent of their time goes into the vital areas of qualifying and planning. These percentages apply to net selling time, that is, to the total amount of working time remaining after the trade shows and company meetings are attended, the routine paperwork is done, and the old accounts are serviced.

When we at Champions Unlimited say that someone is a Champion, we mean that they are in the top ten percent in their sales force in terms of income and production, and also that they've made our training and techniques an important part of their success.

Let's look at the figures given above one more time. The Champion spends half as much time demonstrating or presenting as the average salesperson does, yet the Champion still manages to turn in at least twice the volume. Actually, most Champions do far better than that: they bring in between four and ten times as much business as the average salesperson will. It's not uncommon for a single Champion to outsell the entire bottom half of the sales force, and keep on doing it month after month, year after year. This drives sales managers crazy. If they could only get each of the people in the bottom half to sell a third of what the Champion does, their total volume would boom off the chart.

Obviously, the Champion closes a far higher percentage of the people he presents to than the non-Champion is able to close.

Not more than a fourth of this difference is accounted for by the Champion's greater skill and confidence in presenting or demonstrating. By far the greatest part of the difference between the Champion and the average salesperson lies in the Champion's attention to and ability at planning sales, at selecting and qualifying the right people to sell to, at overcoming objections and closing, and at deserving and obtaining referrals.

Techniques for becoming more effective in these areas are discussed in other chapters. All are vital—you must be competent in all major areas of selling before you can realize your full potential and become a Champion. So, as we discuss the techniques of presenting and demonstrating, keep in mind that, important as this part of selling is (and it's very important), if you do it with the wrong people because you didn't qualify properly, it's all for nothing. If you're working with the right people, but you let their objections beat you because you haven't prepared properly, it's all for nothing. And if you have no capability in closing, you're working for nothing. If you can't close, many sales you could and should make will go to the next competitor who comes along because you built the structure for the sale but couldn't close the door before he got there. You have to be a strong presenter or demonstrator to sell strongly. You also have to qualify strongly, handle objections strongly, and close strongly.

Before discussing how a Champion presents or demonstrates, let's draw an analogy to illustrate the basic concept. If you want to make a half-hour speech, you really should write a ten-minute speech. Here's why. If you're going to get your points across to your audience, you have to follow these steps:

1. **Tell them what you're going to tell them.**
   This is your introduction.

2. **Tell them what you're there to tell them.**
   This is your presentation.

3. **Tell them what you just told them.**
   This is your summary.

That's the outline of all successful speeches, presentations, and demonstrations. In other words, we use repetition. We don't say exactly the same thing three times, of course. In the first ten minutes, we're introducing our new ideas. In the second ten minutes, we're covering our points in depth and relating them to our listeners' interests and needs. In the last ten minutes, we're drawing conclusions from our points and indicating the direction that things should take.

Repetition is the mother of learning, yet the average salesperson doesn't like repetition. For one thing, he has used his material so many times that it's stale to him. In many cases, he's begun to think that anyone who doesn't get what he's saying the first time he says it is stupid. All too often, the non-Champion has gone worse than stale on his presentation and feels it would be better off buried. The Champion, on the other hand, never tires of phrases that work, ploys that sell, and ideas that make sense to his buyers and money for him. The Champion discards things in his presentation when they stop working, and not before. And the Champion never forgets that he's working with people who don't know his specialty as well as he does: he's always courteous and deferential about his superior knowledge in the narrow area of his expertise. So the Champion works happily with lines he's said ten thousand times. He is forever finding slight variations of phrasing and timing that enhance their effectiveness. He revels in the fact that he knows his lines so well that he doesn't have to think about them, but can concentrate wholly on his customers and the unique aspects of the situation he's working with at the moment. There's no question about it, one of the keys to the Champion's greater skill at presenting or demonstrating lies in his ability and willingness to use repetition effectively to reinforce every point. He doesn't mind repeating the sales points because he knows it leads to repeated sales to the same type of clientele.

So think in terms of tell, tell, tell. Please highlight this statement:

Repetition is the seed of selling.

When you prepare to make a presentation or give a demonstration, there's one point that should be foremost in your mind. I suggest that you also highlight this concept:

THE PRESENTATION (DEMONSTRATION) IS NOTHING MORE THAN THE PREPARATION FOR THE CLOSE.

Giving a powerful presentation or a deft demonstration should never be your purpose in and of itself—you're not there to win an award, you're there to close the sale. The only purpose for presenting or demonstrating is to get the prospect ready to approve the purchase. Except for its value as a training exercise, there's absolutely no point in giving a splendid presentation unless it results in a sale.

There's no essential difference between a presentation and a demonstration. Both are processes by which you prove the reality of the benefits that the prospects are seeking. In the presentation, you do it with graphs, numbers, and words; in the demonstration, you do it with tests, samples, and performances. The result should be the same: the implanting in their minds of the conviction that you are their best source for the benefits they want.

Let's go through the tactics or methodology of presentation and demonstration:

1. You control them constantly with questions.

We've discussed these techniques in detail in chapter 3.

2. You don't lose to objections, you win by handling objections.

On almost every product or service, any active salesperson will discover most of the built-in objections within the first month. A built-in objection is one that the prospect will give you nearly every time. After a few months in the business, the salespeople will say, "I always get hit with that objection."

If you think that, why not also say to yourself, "I'm lucky because I know in advance what objections I'm going to be hit with, so I can prepare to handle them before I go into my presentation."

One of our Champions told me a story that's a perfect example of what we're talking about. Scott Sparks was a high flyer in real estate sales at the time this happened. A builder he knew was having no luck at all closing out the last few houses in a large subdivision. All the other homes had sold so quickly—some even before they were built—that the developer hadn't worried much about the eighteen houses that backed up on the railroad tracks until several weeks passed without action on any of them. Then the builder discovered that he couldn't give those houses away. He ran ads. He lowered the total investment and cut the initial investment, and then he threw in some extra landscaping. Nothing worked. People walked in, looked at the tracks, and walked out. Of course it didn't help that there were several other new subdivisions selling against him in the area.

Scott Sparks heard about these eighteen houses that wouldn't sell and drove over to take a look at them. Then he went to see the builder and said, "If you'd like to market those houses in thirty days, give me an exclusive and I'll do it for you."

"I can't drop the price any lower," the builder said. "I'm already losing money on them."

"Don't lower the price," Scotty said. "Raise it enough to include a color TV and I'll move them right out for you."

The builder didn't really believe him. But Scott was the first agent in weeks who'd been willing to say he could sell the houses, so he decided very quickly to give him the go-ahead. The next day, up went a sign in front of the models that read, "Shown only at 2, 4, and 6 P.M." Why? Because that's when the trains came by.

Before each showing, Scott Sparks would get all the prospects together and tell them, "These homes have an advantage that few homes have, and I'd like to show it to you right now." He'd lead them into the living room, turn the TV on, and say, "All eighteen of these homes come with this beautiful color TV set. You know why? Because we want this TV set to overcome something that might be a problem for you. I'd like you all to take a look out that back window."

The people would look and see the railroad tracks. Then Scotty would go on, "Your children will get the opportunity to see the famous iron horse up close. Aren't they going to love it? But some of you may be irritated by the sound, so I'd like you all to do me a small favor. Let's be real quiet and listen, because a train's coming through in a few minutes."

Scott Sparks would time this so that there'd be four or five minutes before the train would come. The TV, of course, would be playing—not too loud, but loud enough to be heard. Pretty soon the people would be watching it, not saying much, and the train could be heard coming.

So it would come and go, and most of the people would glance at it and keep on watching the TV. Then Scotty would say, "You see? Thirty-eight seconds of sound, and that's it. We wanted you to hear it so you'd know what you'd have to put up with for the color TV. What do you think—is it worth it?"

Scott Sparks sold those homes in thirty days. Do you see why? He didn't hide the objection and hope they wouldn't see the railroad tracks—he bragged about the problem.

Another of our Champions is always on the lookout for problem things that no one else can market. I won't use his name because some of his clients might not be happy to realize that they bought something from him that practically no one else could sell. This man finds items that inspire objections, and then he figures out ways to brag about those objections.

I don't know about you, but that's too rough for me. Yet it's just a question of degree, because there isn't a product or a service on the market that doesn't have some built-in objections and at least a few minor problems. You believe in your product or service. Then believe in its minor problems and built-in objections too. Brag about them. If you do that, you'll find that it's never as bad as your prospects will think it'll be if they discover the difficulties themselves. In many cases, you'll be able to turn problems and objections into advantages if you'll just take the trouble to find crisp ways to accent them.

I'm not suggesting that you should set your potential clients down and, in an undertaker's voice, tell them, "This is why you're going to have big trouble with our product." Scotty Sparks didn't do that. He pointed out the problem, demonstrated that it wasn't all that much of a problem — and then went on to show that the advantage offered outweighed the disadvantage involved. Usually, if you plan how to bring up the major objection before your prospect hits you with it, you'll be able to settle that objection quickly.

3. You say it in words they want to hear.
All of us come equipped with a filtering device — we all have the ability to filter out unwanted sound. This device is indispensable; it allows us to mull over our inner thoughts in peace whenever people are pounding our ears with anything less interesting than our own brain waves.

Everyone you'll ever try to sell has an effective filter of this kind that can be switched on instantaneously because we all develop it in childhood. This means that you have to learn how to prevent the filter from being switched on. Otherwise, you'll make most of your terrific sales arguments to switched off, unhearing minds behind deaf ears. Let's face it — you can't make any money talking to yourself.

The basic problem here is that most salespeople sound exactly alike. Same ideas. Even the same words. And they're all tired, overused, and boring words.

In this, as in all things relating to sales, the Champion is different. The Champion has a view of the world that's new with every dawn, and he expresses his newly born ideas with phrases that have verve. He understands and respects the value of words, and is keenly aware of and interested in them. He constantly develops his ear for the beauty, power, and endless variety of the English language. He is forever trying new phrases, allusions, and words to expand the effective range of his vocabulary. He takes delight in spoken wit and sensitive expression.

GLAMOUR WORDS
The Champion sees himself as an artist who casts exquisite crystals of thought from the common sand and lead of language. To do that, he avoids the worn-out words, the commonplace expressions, and the dull descriptions that afflict the average salesperson's presentation with the monotony

of mediocrity. Instead, he enlivens his speech with glamorous words that conjure up exciting new visions for his buyers. They can't help listening to him because he captivates their attention.

What makes a word glamorous? It has a freshness that sticks in the mind, yet it's common enough to be understood by your listeners. The last part is vital. If you dust off some of the fancy words that only the aficionados of esoteric utterances will understand, your listeners will switch their filtering devices on again.

But it's better to make them stretch a little than to err on the side of boring them. People are flattered by being challenged a little bit—and they resent being talked down to even more than they resent being bored.

Never forget that most people can look at you and nod at the right times and have their mind forty miles away. They're thinking about a problem totally unrelated to you, or about something they need to do after you leave. If you drone on and on, you're not going to sell them, you're going to separate from them—empty-handed, permanently, and soon.

Seek out the bright words that we all understand but rarely hear used. The Champion does everything in his power to keep his prospects and clients emotionally and physically involved and listening when he wants to be persuasive.

I'm not going to give you a list of glamour words because what's glamorous in one situation is gross in another. Look for words that are charming, eloquent, picturesque, exciting, creative. Add sparkle to your speech by using common words in unexpected new ways.

WORDS TO REPLACE

From now on, when you have to listen to a tiresome speaker, listen attentively for the words, the phrases, and the manners of speaking that make him tiresome. Whenever you spot one, make a mental note to eliminate it from your vocabulary. But be aware that you have to replace it with another word that's more interesting. You may have to think a little to come up with one. If you've never deliberately worked on your vocabulary in this manner, it may seem difficult at first. But it won't when you get used to it. And there's a trick to this that takes all the strain out. Simply make a list of the words you want to get rid of on a piece of paper and go over it once a day. That will focus your mind on improving your vocabulary, and you'll find yourself spotting new words you want to use to brighten your speech as you read, listen to other people, and watch TV.

Slang is fresh and funny at first but it usually wears out quickly. Most of us use it too long. Jargon can also be fresh and funny, but more often it's lost on the outsider. The federal bureaucracy and the computer industry have spawned great clouds of words good only for hiding truth and blocking communication. You can't get decisions that way. Cultivate an appreciation for the short, strong words that have come down to us from the Anglo-Saxon roots of our language. Use lots of short, punchy words in your speech. The more shorts you use, the more effect a few less common longs will have by contrast.

Be bold in your choice of language. Take risks with words. Say a few striking things that will seize your listeners' attention. You'll occasionally have to restate an idea in different language, but if they ask, they're listening. When they're doing that, you can win. When they're not listening, you can't win.

LEARN MANY DIFFERENT LINGOES.

Do you know that the great Champions speak many different languages? I'm not referring to French, Spanish, and Navajo, but to the different languages of his clients. A Champion speaks to a plumber in plumbers' language and to a doctor in doctors' language. This doesn't require a tremendous training program. Your object isn't to make the plumber think you're a contractor and the doctor think you're a physician; your object is to make them both feel that you understand their problems, viewpoints, and opportunities. Every job and hobby has its own jargon, its own special language.

The Champion learns to speak many of these special languages because it's the most efficient way to establish rapport with many different groups of people. Rapport flourishes on common ground, but fails to sprout on the barren rock of difference. We identify with people who share things with us; we instinctively feel less fear and more trust with them. You can't change the school you went to or the state you were born in to suit every client. But you can learn to understand and use some of his jargon—if not of his specialty, at least of his general occupation. If you know a bit of construction jargon, you can talk more convincingly with carpenters, roofers, and craftsmen in a host of other specialties; if you understand an assembly line worker's special phrases, you'll be able to talk more convincingly with any factory worker.

For this very reason, the winners among salespeople often choose a certain group of people to concentrate their sales efforts on, even though they sell something like insurance that a wide variety of people buy. Since their chosen groups like and trust them—because they talk the same special language—they sell often and easily.

Many salesmen who never rise above the average spend an hour a day keeping up with sports, and justify it by claiming they need things to talk to their prospects about. Unless what they sell is tied directly to sports, this is a fallacy. Lengthy discussion of anything unrelated to the business at hand wastes time; rapport can be built without wasting time by talking the prospect's language during the presentation. And those special languages can be learned with the hours saved by skipping the sports page.

But how do you learn them?

Specialized magazines are one of the best sources for specialized language. Today there's a magazine devoted to almost every specialty you can imagine. Pay special attention to editorials, letters to the editors, and such things because they'll give you authentic viewpoints held by people involved with that special interest. Read these trade magazines with a pad and pencil. Make notes of any new words and viewpoints that you don't grasp, and then ask someone who's active in that field to explain them to you.

The best way to learn any language is the way children do it—by trial and error and constant use. You'll enormously expand your knowledge of specialized languages simply by taking every opportunity to do so. At counters when you have lunch, while you wait to have your car serviced— anywhere you can talk to people—find out what they do and then explore their special words and viewpoints. Your business is people; jump at every chance you get to learn more about them.

KEEP THE CLIENT MENTALLY INVOLVED.

How? By asking involvement questions that will keep him thinking about how he'll use your offering once he owns it. Pay attention to the answers; nothing destroys rapport like asking the same question twice.

KEEP THE CLIENT PHYSICALLY INVOLVED.

Give him simple things to do. Let him figure something out or run the machine you're demonstrating. Have your client take something from you. Don't ask, "Would you please hold this?" because the client may say he doesn't want to. Say just one word: "Here." The client's automatic reflex will cause him to take whatever you hand him, and then he's involved. Once you gain confidence in this reflex, you can have a lot of fun with it while you're establishing control. Don't overdo it, of course, or they'll get irritated and balk at the worst time. But if you smile warmly and say that one word, it's amazing what they'll accept. Your order pad, for example. I've had people take it and approve the order because I picked the right moment to smile warmly and say, "Here."

Once they have it (the remote control for the machine you're demonstrating, a copy of your proposal, the owner's manual, whatever will help you most) the process of emotional involvement in your offering is well started through their actual physical involvement with it.

HANDLE INTERRUPTIONS CALMLY.

You can be sure that your finest presentations or demonstrations will be interrupted. The phone will ring. Some emergency will demand an executive's (or a parent's) attention. Doors will open unexpectedly, and unknown heads will stick in. Dogs will bark, sirens will screech, and kids will cry.

Sit through it all patiently. No matter how often you're interrupted, don't let any irritation show. Use the time to review where you've been and where you're headed, and make sure that you haven't overlooked any clue to closing them that your questions may have uncovered.

If the interruption lasts more than a moment, do a brief benefit summary of the points your prospect has already accepted. This is urgent. Remember that any physical interruption causes a degree of emotional interruption. That is, if someone else comes into the room, if your prospect leaves the room or takes a phone call, his emotions are changed. He doesn't have to get red in the face or yell at somebody; if he's interrupted, his emotions change. So, before proceeding, you must bring him back to the emotional and mental attitude he had before the interruption.

GIVE THE ENTIRE BODY OF YOUR PRESENTATION IN LESS THAN SEVENTEEN MINUTES.

You may smile with disbelief, but hear me out. Suppose you're selling executive aircraft, and it takes your prospect an hour to get to the airfield. You've organized things carefully so that it only takes five minutes from the moment he arrives until you're ready to ask the tower for permission to move the aircraft, and another five minutes pass before you're in the air. None of this counts. Your prospect is excited: this time zips by for him.

But when you're back in his office two hours later presenting the case for buying that beautiful airplane, keep it under seventeen minutes or the fine cutting edge of his decision making ability will be dulled.

Regardless of what your product or service is, when you get to the gritty, cut through it in less than that limit. You can do it if you'll rigorously chop off unnecessary detail, if you'll streamline what you have to say, if you'll eliminate anything you're not positive is contributing to the close.

To become a Champion, you have to polish your performance and practice it against the clock until you can do an effective presentation or demonstration within the seventeen minute limit of maximum client concentration. It may be a stiff challenge, but meeting it will do wonders for your closing ability.

THE POWER OF PLANNED PRESENTATIONS

The most convincing way I can describe this amazingly effective technique is to tell you about one of our Champions, Robert Burns, who uses it to the ultimate degree of perfection. I've often talked about this young man in my seminars, and I get letters from all over the country asking how any twenty-three-year-old can earn half a million dollars a year in sales.

I can give you a personal example of how Robert does it, an example that will illustrate all the concepts we're going to discuss in this chapter. But first, let me go back to when I first met him. Robert took our training with the intention of applying it to real estate sales. When he completed the course, he came up to me and made a firm commitment. "I've set my goals to surpass anyone you've ever trained in the real estate profession," he said.

I smiled at him. "That's wonderful, but have you put your goals in writing?"

He said, "I thought you'd ask that. Yes, I have. Here."

I looked at the paper he handed me and whistled. "Well, you certainly haven't laid a soft job out for yourself. Robert, I'm really happy that you've taken the training to heart. Not many people will commit themselves to written goals, so you've already done something special. But the commitment is only the necessary first step, and living up to your commitment is the journey. Go our there and do it, and I'll be very proud of you."

Robert kept me informed of his progress. Soon he was winning awards and, in an amazingly short time, he achieved his goal of surpassing anyone we'd yet trained in his field. One of the primary reasons why he's reached the very pinnacle of sales success is that he plans every word and stratagem prior to presenting it.

The way he sold me a real estate investment is the most vivid example of the power of planned presentations that I ever expect to experience. He came in one day when I wasn't even thinking about making an investment in property, and in a few hours closed me on a $240,000 purchase. That's right—as far as I was concerned, it was all over in a few hours—but of course he had done a great deal of work beforehand. Our meeting was an astonishing display of selling skill and power—and there's no reason why you can't use the methods he used.

Robert came into my office right before Christmas one year—dressed beautifully in a custom-made suit—carrying two thick leather binders and a map case. He set them on the floor beside my desk, smiled, and said, "I'm glad I caught you in, Tom—I've been trying to see you for a month. How are you?"

"I'm fine, Robert. How are things going with you?"

"Unbelievable. Fantastic things are happening. And Tom, I'm so excited about the opportunity I have for you."

I caught my breath and just looked at him for a moment. Bear in mind that I knew he'd been doing what he'd told me he was going to do: surpass anyone we'd ever trained in real estate sales. So I braced myself and started thinking of ways out because I knew now that he wasn't there to talk over old times. He was there for big bucks.

Robert watched my eyes for a moment and then went on, "I've been waiting three years to find the plum —"

"What are you talking about, Robert?"

"Tom, may I ask you this: are you satisfied that you've sheltered all the income that can be sheltered from tax this year?"

I felt relieved—and sorry for him. "Robert, we tried but we couldn't quite shelter all of it. And, of course, it's too late now because I'm on the calendar year—there's only eleven days left. What with the holidays —" I shrugged to show that it was impossible for anything to be done.

He said, "Don't worry. I'll handle it."

I blinked at him. "Excuse me, but what are you talking about?"

He reached down, picked up the leather binders, and handed one to me. "Let me show you something, Tom." I looked at the binder and saw stamped in gold letters:

PROPERTY ANALYSIS
PREPARED ESPECIALLY FOR
MR. TOM HOPKINS

I stared at it for an instant and then mumbled, "Robert, this is a prospectus for an investment."

"Yes, it is, Tom. And it's one that I've waited a long time to find for you. But don't say a word—just let me show you something."

I'm just like you—I never want to be sold anything—but I was more than a bit curious. By now, it didn't matter that I'd known Robert when he was a student, before he had any track record in sales. Now I knew that he was a competent professional driving with full power for a large sale. So I was willing to look—but a little voice inside my head was telling me, "You'll have to find a way out of this."

He went to the wall, unrolled a huge aerial photograph, and fixed it on the wall with plastic stick-ons. "There it is, Tom."

"There's what?"

"Everything you need to make a wise decision today is on this aerial photo or in your binder."

The binder was about two inches thick. I wasn't about to open it right then. But I was intrigued by the fact that he had the audacity to come in cold and try to sell me a $240,000 investment. "Tell me more."

He did. Comparables of every piece of land around the thirty-acre property he had in mind for me were color-coded on the aerial.

After giving me some highlights, he said, "You probably don't just want to look at the photo, so if you'll turn to page eleven in the prospectus, you'll find all the comparable price information summarized there."

While I did that, he opened his copy and we went through the sale and listing information that justified the value of the parcel in question.

Finally I said, "It does look good, Robert. But, you know, I think I'm more concerned with the tax benefits of the purchase right now than just seeing that it's worth what I'd have to invest."

"I knew you'd feel that way, Tom. Turn to page sixteen."

I did. A table of information there showed the tax effect, based on my bracket, of all the depreciable items involved in the property: the wells, irrigation ditches, and buildings. I studied it for a few minutes and then said, "You've done a lot of work on this."

"Yes. Six months worth." What he meant, of course, was that he'd kept the project moving for six months—gathering information, getting the aerial photo taken, having people put the package together in its highly organized form. I'm sure he did every bit of this kind of work himself at first. I'm equally sure that now he has clerical and technical help which allows him to spend adequate time in front of the right clients and also on planning his next moves.

I was impressed, but I still felt compelled to say, "Robert, I'll be frank and tell you that I don't see how this can fit in with my plans right now, but maybe you can show me. The tax benefits are good, but let's face it: they're not enough to justify the investment all on their own. What would I do with it if I owned it? I wouldn't want to hold it forever, and I'm not looking for things to take up any more of my time."

"I know, Tom. Turn to page thirty-three."

We both did. On that page I found a brief statement of his plan for breaking the property up into three parcels, selling off the frontage, and ending up with a free and clear twenty-acre parcel.

I thought for a moment and realized that I wasn't feeling sorry for him about coming in too late anymore—I was feeling a bit sorry for myself. "Robert, I'm on the calendar year. We can't possibly close this transaction before December 31. So I'd rather not get involved with it at this time because I've got some other things in the works for next year."

He smiled and said, "I understand what you're saying, Tom. If you could take advantage of it this year, you'd be interested, wouldn't you?''

I thought, he can't possibly do it—there's too much paperwork to push through. So I said, "Sure, Robert—if you were a miracle worker, I'd be interested." I laughed. "But there's no way. Not in eleven days at this time of the year."

He said, "Tommy, it's all done. All I need is your approval."

That stopped me. There was a silence in the room for several seconds. Then I said, rather weakly. "What do you mean, it's all done."

"Tom, years ago you taught me that if it's good for the buyers, if they qualify and they need it, I must help them have it. And you need it, don't you?"

I squirmed in my chair. "Without even seeing it?"

"No, I understand that. I've cleared it with your secretary and I have a plane standing by. We can fly there and be back in the time it takes for lunch—and I know how excited you're going to be about this investment when you see it."

What could I do? I went, I saw, I bought. And today, of course, it's proven to be a tremendous investment. Robert hadn't done all that work for nothing—he was able to close it in time so I got the tax advantages I was looking for that year. And on January third—I'll never forget it—this great young man, this true Champion, knocked on my door at home. "Tommy, for letting me serve you, I've brought you this," and he gave me a beautiful silver tea set. Keep in mind that he earned $24,000 for helping me—and I think that's exciting.

"Thank you, Robert." A lot of thoughts were running through my head, not the least of them pride that I'd had a part in developing him to his present height of success.

He went on, "I got myself a little something for serving you. Take a look outside." There in the drive was his new automobile, one of the most beautiful silver gray Rolls-Royces I've ever seen. When you're making over half a million a year, you're forced to have that kind of tool—and toy—aren't you? Of course, his brokerage on my investment didn't pay the entire cost of the Rolls-Royce, but it helped, don't you agree?

That's what planning does for you in sales. Successful selling is the least aimless activity I know of. Successful salespeople aren't sitting around hoping that someone will come in or call up and buy something. The successful salesmen and saleswomen, the professionals, the Champions, aren't waiting for it to happen, they're making it happen. They are successful because they plan their prospecting, presenting, closing, and follow-through. In four words, they plan their success. Highlight this basic, vital idea:

A CHAMPION PLANS EVERY PRESENTATION IN WRITING.

You're backing off, aren't you? Telling yourself, "Plan every presentation in writing? Tom is kidding me. Nobody does that. I wouldn't know how to begin."

Don't worry—I'm going to show you how to plan every move and anticipate every problem. Of course, it will take some time—more time in the beginning while you're learning the technique. After it becomes second nature, you'll spend less time planning your presentations than the average wheel-spinning salesperson kills before going to see each prospect. You'll walk into every demonstration or presentation knowing exactly what they'll listen to, what they'll say yes to, what they'll agree with, and what they need. Read on and you'll find the steps and an aid for planning presentations, two of the finest tools that have come into the profession of selling in many years. Adapt them to your offering, put them to use, and you'll be amazed at how much planned presentations will boost your earnings.

HOW TO PREPLAN YOUR PRESENTATION IN WRITING

First, let's talk about where you get the information necessary to preplan your presentation on paper.

COMMERCIAL AND INDUSTRIAL SALES:

Published directories will give you an enormous amount of information. A few of these directories are available only on subscription, but many are in the reference section of public libraries. You'll generally find the best libraries for your purpose in the more business-oriented and affluent communities. Check with such a library before ruling out this source; some of them have surprisingly valuable material. The following are only a sample of the directories in the better public libraries:

Dun & Bradstreet Million Dollar Directory Lists most companies with a net worth over a million dollars in one well-indexed volume, and those with a net worth between one-half and one million in a second volume. Gives names of top officers.

Thomas Register of American Manufacturers This massive work lists large and small firms under alphabetically arranged product headings. A capital rating gives a useful idea of size.

Standard & Poor's Directory Lists thousands of small, medium, and large corporations with names of key people. A second volume lists hundreds of thousands of corporate officers, directors and principals, often giving college and residence data. A third volume has six indexes.

Who's Who Gives brief biographies of thousands of individuals in many walks of life. Included are schools attended, honors and awards won, positions held, and so on.

Gathering information in one directory and then researching that information further in another directory is often the most effective way to use them. For example, you discover how to apply your service to ball bearing manufacturers. In Thomas, you find several such firms listed in the area you work; in Standard & Poor's, you then find the names of their corporate officers, together with some personal details about each of them. With this combined data in hand, you develop your marketing plan.

- The directories listed above are revised every year. Look for books that may be helpful to you in the Directory of Directories. If you find one that's very helpful, having your own copy will save you valuable time.

If you're working an established territory, or adopting orphans, your office's sales records will have detailed and valuable information. Few salespeople use Dun and Bradstreet as effectively as they could. While the D & B Directory gives only brief coded information and a credit rating, the full credit report for each company has a wealth of detail about the officers, operation, and history of the firm. These reports must be ordered separately for each company.

GOVERNMENTAL SALES:

Products and services designed for commercial and industrial use often have many applications in governmental activities. A large number of companies recognize this by assigning salespeople exclusively to governmental sales. Other companies leave this market to their local outlets and sales managers. The agencies most often overlooked are called "special districts." These bureaus cope with flood control, mosquito abatement, bridge operation, and a multitude of other problems that most of us rarely think about. All of them have offices and operations with needs. Where do you find the special districts? Ask at the information office of every county you serve. For starters, look on your property tax bill. In many states you'll find the local special districts listed there.

EDUCATIONAL SALES:

Schools and colleges buy enormous amounts of equipment, supplies, and services. State and county school superintendents publish directories, as do some religious and private organizations. If you're unfamiliar with the school market but feel that you have opportunities there, call on a few schools and ask them what directories they're listed in. Also ask what conferences (these usually have trade shows) they attend. The educational field is well organized and easily reached.

INDIVIDUAL AND FAMILY SALES:

If it's a referred lead, get all the information you can from the client giving you the referral. Your office's sales records may have valuable data if you're working with an orphan customer. If the person seems to be a high achiever, he or she may be listed in Who's Who at your public library.

With most prospects in personal sales, the best source of information is the person involved. After you've made the appointment, lead into a few questions by saying, "So that I can save your time during our meeting and serve you better, could I ask —"

After a few questions it helps to remark, "Please don't think I'm being nosy, but it really will save us both time if I have an approximate idea of your situation."

WORKING WITH THE PRE-PLANNING FORM

One version is designed for retail sales of products and services to individuals or families. The second version of the pre-planner assists you in preparing for successful sales interviews with decision-makers at all kinds of organizations: corporations and other companies in commerce and industry, governmental agencies, and the groups serving the religious, educational, and cultural needs of the nation.

Some salespeople climb the highest peaks exclusively with sales to individuals and families. Other salespeople stay in that field, or work only the mom and pop kind of business sales, because they're convinced that organizational selling is too big-time for them. Yet it's basically the same: you're still dealing with people. I began my career selling shoes in a retail store at the age of sixteen. I soon went on to other things and other kinds of selling before I began marketing products and services to corporations. The basic principles are the same. You simply roll forward all your experience with people—and start doing more careful preparation and planning.

On both these forms, keep track of the sources from which you obtained your information. Knowing the source enables you to make a better guess as to its dependability, and it also helps you discard unreliable sources.

How you fill out most of the form is obvious. What they have now, and how long they've had it, tells you where they are on the itch cycle. What their choice was last time tells you much about what their next choice will be.

After listing the names of the family, be sure to put an asterisk (*) after the person you think will be the decision maker. That is the person you must convince and close—without making the other family members fight you.

If you're selling a large item the entire family will use and help pay for—a yacht, for example—the children may be of an age to have income that's important to the transaction. If so, note down their approximate ages and the sources and amounts of their incomes.

Find out where the husband and wife work, and what they do. If you know these facts, you know a great deal more about them, don't you? Will you agree that a presentation to someone who makes his living treating concrete with a jackhammer should be different than a presentation to someone who makes his living treating people with pills and bills?

The purpose of getting all this information is to move you closer to what they want and can afford.

Benefits Referrer Accepted: This is important. You'll often find yourself going in for an appointment with a prospect without having heard from his own mouth what benefits he's really interested in. If you can get this information when you arrange the appointment, fine. But never forget that many prospects won't tell you the truth about what they really want because they have a conflict. Someone in their family, or logic, or "what people will think" tells them to buy what they don't want. In other words, they can't square their wants with their needs. If you come in contact with them before they resolve this conflict, their problem becomes your problem—and your opportunity. Solve it and you sell them. Fail to solve it and you lose them. These opportunities arise constantly, whether you're prospecting on the phone or working with walk-ins.

PERSONAL SALES PRE-PLANNER

Name of Individual/Family _____

INFORMATION GAINED   SOURCE

Names Involved: (*Primary Decision Maker)

If Individual Only _____

If Family

Father _____

Mother _____

Children _____

_____

_____

Sources of Income & Amounts, Approx.

Man - Employed By _____

Position _____

Income Est. _____

Woman - Employed By _____

Position _____

Income Est. _____

Other _____

Type of Comparable Product or Service They Now Have _____

_____

How Long _____

Benefits Referrer Accepted _____

_____

_____

_____

_____

Other Benefits They May Accept _____

_____

_____

Other Information — Home - Furnishings Car - Hobbies - Group
Affiliations - Etc. _____

_____

_____

_____

SEQUENCE PLAN

Benefits to be Used to Gain Telephone Appointment _____
_____

Benefits to be Used in Qualification Questions _____
_____
_____

Benefits Planned For Presentation/Demonstration _____
_____
_____
_____
_____
_____

Anticipated Primary Objection _____

Planned Comparative Question to Eliminate Primary Objection. Isn't It True That _____

Demonstration and Presentation Equipment and Materials to be Used _____
_____
_____
_____

Similar Situation Stories to be Used (Name of Story Only) If on Cassette — Indicate with * _____
_____
_____

Physical Involvement to be Created _____
_____
_____

The Items Regarding Competitors — Current Market Position to be Referred to in Order to Underline Need or Desire
_____
_____

CORPORATE SALES PRE-PLANNER

Name of Company _____

Individual & Title _____

Is This Person Decision Maker? _____

If Not — Name Individual Who Is - With Title _____

Type of Company _____

Product or Service _____

Approximate Gross Sales _____

INFORMATION GAINED   **SOURCE**

Individuals Involved - With Titles _____

_____

_____

_____

_____

_____

Which One Greatest Problem. Why? _____

_____

_____

D & B or Other Financial Rating _____

_____

Benefits Referrer Accepted _____

_____

_____

_____

_____

Other Benefits They May Accept _____

_____

_____

Other Information — Competitors - Current Market Position -
Organizations Belonged To - Etc. _____

_____

_____

_____

_____

_____

Ask Alvin Gotmorkids what he's looking for and he'll say, "I need a small, stripped-down station wagon that'll go a zillion miles on one drink of gas." But when Alvin looks at small, stripped-down station wagons in auto showrooms, he grunts and swallows and walks out without buying. Finally Alvin stumbles into Ron Realist. Ron listens to Alvin's words, and hears the music he's playing too. So Ron takes Alvin over to the latest low-slung, tiger-under-the-hood, loaded-with-options model.

Alvin gets pale. Objections pour out of him. But he doesn't walk away. Then Ron suggests a trial spin. They put the tiger through all five gears around tight curves. Then Ron explains how logical it is for Alvin to own that car before he gets any older, and shows him how he can own it. Alvin buys.

If Ron Realist had been guided by what Alvin said about small practical station wagons, he would have been another auto salesperson that Alvin Gotmorkids did not buy from. Be careful about believing what the prospect says he wants.

With many prospects, the benefits that the referrer has already accepted and bought are a much firmer set of facts. They represent genuine emotions that were backed by action, not loose talk that may only express fashionable logic. People are heavily influenced by their friends, and they are much like their friends in the ways that are important to you. For these reasons, the benefits the referrer has paid for are often the most reliable guide to what the prospect will pay for. If there's any way to get this information from the referrer—and this will often be no trouble at all—don't go into a presentation without it.

Benefits to be used to gain telephone appointment: What are you going to tell them on the phone to generate the emotions that will make them want to see you?

Remember that all you want at this point is the appointment to see them. If you run off every bit of your good stuff to get the appointment, the actual face-to-face meeting may be an anti-climax. So use the lightest guns that'll get you the appointment, and save your heavy artillery for when you're with them going for the close.

Benefits to be used in the qualification questions: Use the qualifying steps given in chapter 12.

Benefits planned for presentation/demonstration: Note here all the benefits you believe they'll accept as having value to them. This is where you fire your big stuff. But never lose sight of the probability that what makes a heavy hit on some buyers will only be a light tap on others. And never assume that the feature you value most in your offering will be the feature your next prospect will value most.

Anticipated primary objection: Handling this area like a Champion is what brought Robert Burns success in selling me the real estate investment. At this point in his planning he said something like this to himself: "I know what Tom Hopkins does. I have an approximate idea of his income. I can make some good guesses at his concerns, and I know he's going to hit me with some objections. As a way out, he's probably going to say, 'I'm primarily interested in how to get rid of the property after I've taken the tax advantages I need.' So if I'm going to get him involved in this investment, I've first got to figure how to get him out of it with a profit."

After I made that investment, Robert told me he uses a form much like the one we're showing here to plan all his presentations. He said, "By using this form, I almost know everything they're going to say before I get there."

Wouldn't you like to know what they're going to say before you push the copier in through their revolving door, before you fly in to detail a new production facility, before you walk in to present your custom-tailored service?

If you spend all your time making layouts in four colors to solve the prospect's problem — giving no time to anticipating his objections — you're going to lose a lot of sales you could otherwise make. Fitting your service to their situation, demonstrating how the machine whizzes the stuff out, or explaining how the cog fits the track are all necessary to logic. Objections have their logical base too, but they are mainly emotion — which means that they control the purchase decision more than the logic of your presentation does. Make sure that you give adequate time and energy to anticipating objections and planning how to overcome them. One of the ways you do that is with:

Planned Comparative Questions to Eliminate the Primary Objection: A comparative question melts the primary objection down by focusing the prospect's attention on answering a minor issue. I begin all my Comparative Questions with the words: **"Isn't it true that —"**

An example from insurance sales will illustrate the concept of the Comparative Question:

The primary objection I anticipate here is money—the size of the premium. When it comes up, I say, **"Isn't it true that** the size of the premium is less important than your children's education?"

What are they going to say? One of the most important things to the average person is the education and welfare of his or her children.

When the entire picture is considered, the primary objection that most people raise in most sales interviews is not, in reality, the point of primary importance to them. It's our business as salespeople to put that primary objection into proper perspective, and smother its negativism with positive emotions.

Demonstration and Presentation Equipment and Materials to be used: Once you have the Comparative Questions written, list the tools you think will be most effective on that particular call. Most Champions don't take everything in to every prospect; they have a bigger bag of tools than they can get through the door with. And there are practical difficulties with time and space that must be considered. Again, speed is important. You want to make your basic presentation within seventeen minutes and then shift into your closing sequences. You may need to hand them a detailed prospectus, but limit your remarks to pounding the pith of the matter.

Similar Situation Stories to be used: We go into this detail in chapter 15. Being prepared to tell your prospects similar situation stories is an effective presentation technique; putting written Similar Situation Stories in your presentation binder is a better technique; having the words and voices of happy clients on cassettes is the best technique.

The last two items on the personal sales sequence plan need little comment. Can you get them physically involved by having them use your calculator or run the machine you're demonstrating? Devise some form of physical involvement for every presentation or demonstration.

Every salesperson will understand the need to create common ground through some item of mutual interest — but what some of us do with this item is wing it — we don't think about it until we're walking into the person's office. But how do you plan something of mutual interest to talk about when you don't know the person?

If it's a referred lead, the referrer will usually be able to fill you in on the prospect's interests. If your prospects are corporate officers or directors, there's a good chance they'll be listed in Standard & Poor's Volume II, or in Who's Who. If not, ask about their interests at the time you make an appointment.

THE CORPORATE SALES PRE-PLANNER

At the bottom of this form, you'll notice a change from the personal sales version as we raise the question of where the prospect's company stands in its own competitive race.

Here's how you use this information:

Let's suppose that you've just found a new market for your product or service by selling an air conditioning contractor for the first time. The person you sold claimed that their company is the largest of its kind in the city. Don't ask who number two is and upset him. Instead, go back to your office, pick up the yellow pages, and make a list of the air conditioning contractors who have the largest ads. By checking that list against the Dun and Bradstreet directory in your company's credit department, you quickly rank them by size, and discover that your new client really is number one in the city.

Start calling those air conditioning contractors. Number seven wants to move up to be number six, number six would like to move up to be number five, and so on. Most of them as their ultimate goal want to be number one. And in every one of those companies there's a corporate eagle who's watching how his company is doing. He's also watching the competition because the last thing he wants to do is slip down a notch or two. You can bet that they'll all be interested in what number one is doing — which is using your product or service. They'll all be wondering: Is what you've supplied number one giving that firm a further edge on them? They better catch up. That's why the Champion wants to know where each prospect ranks competitively.

WHEN DO YOU PLAN?

The night before your appointment. Be sure to fill out the front of the form right after making the appointment. Then you won't have forgotten a lot of vital details when you sit down to review the form, write your questions out, and plan your selling sequence the night before your appointment. This, by the way, is the habit of the pro.

Every Champion I know plans everything he's going to do on his next day's appointments the night before. And he does it in writing because then he knows he's done it; he knows he's impressed it on his mind; and he knows he can give it a quick review before walking in for each appointment. Please, let's stop winging it. Please stop going over to an appointment not knowing what you're going to say or do. If you walk in without having a plan laid out, you're going to cut your effectiveness in three pieces—and you'll have to eat off the smallest piece.

Why? Because inertia is always against you in sales. The easiest thing for the buyer to do is nothing. Maybe a better offer will come in tomorrow. The challenge of sales is to make something happen when something doesn't have to happen. Getting positive action requires positive planning. So please highlight this idea:

I pre-plan every presentation in writing.

If you'll make—and carry out—that commitment to yourself, to your family, and to your company, the benefits will astound you. As you get more into pre-planning in writing, as you catch the excitement that the power of this method creates, you'll find yourself seeing with greater clarity the pitfalls and opportunities that wait for you in each presentation. You'll find yourself driven to prepare even more carefully so that you can approach each presentation with even greater confidence—and your success ratio will soar.

Yes. Pre-plan in writing. The results will raise your sales performance to new heights.

VISUAL AIDS

If you sell for a large company, the chances are good that (a) they supply you with a variety of costly and colorful visual selling aids and, (b) you don't use those aids much.

Here again we find that the people who make the greatest use of company-supplied visual aids are the top producers. The ones who make the least use of them are the sellers in the cellar, the bottom boys, the ones who never make a quota and change jobs most often.

If you're in the category that doesn't use visual aids and isn't ranked in the top third of your sales force, don't feel guilty. It's a common failing. But you're reading this book to stop being common, aren't you? Then start using the tools of success. Some of those tools are called visual aids.

The top Champions we've trained realize a basic truth: people just can't sit and look at your face and listen to your mouth all evening. That's one reason why the top producers are always looking for new methods, and improving old methods, to involve more than their prospects' ears in their presentations.

In counseling with major companies on ways to increase the standard of performance in their sales forces, we've conducted many surveys aimed at discovering specific things. Over and over we relearn a basic fact: the top producers have only two basic tricks up their sleeves, and they're simple ones: (1) they use their time effectively, (2) they concentrate on what has to be done and ignore the non-essentials.

Winging it is not effective. Sure, it can save an hour of preparation time on a call that takes you an hour to get there, an hour to present, and an hour to get back. Winging it without visual aids and without adequate preparation almost guarantees failure. You can't be effective if you waste three hours to avoid working one.

Here's another fact we've discovered: Visual aids cut down preparation time.

And one more: If you think of future applications as you plan each presentation, you'll find yourself spending less and less time preparing as the months go by, and you'll prepare better.

One of the best examples of this is the prospectus type of presentation binder where you organize a mass of facts for your clients. The first time you do it, the task will seem overwhelming. But if you work with an eye to creating a format that you can use over and over, the second prospectus won't take half as long to prepare as the first, and each succeeding one will go faster.

Your contents page may not have to change at all. You'll find that many pages can be common to several presentations. Think ahead like the Champions do. Make everything standard that can be standard. Then concentrate on the pages presenting information that's unique to each presentation. Robert Burns did that before he came into my office and overwhelmed me with data on the real estate investment I literally had to buy when he was done. Three-fourths of the pages in the massive binder he put on my desk were material he had used over and over — necessary stuff — but he was organized so he didn't have to write the whole thing before every presentation.

If you're selling the same products or services over and over, so much the better. You can develop your skills to great heights by relying on visual aids and organized presentations that make use of reusable material.

SEVENTEEN MINUTES ARE ALL YOU'VE GOT

After seventeen minutes people start to lose interest. Boredom sets in; they remember other things they could or should be doing; they stop listening attentively. When you start losing their attention, you start losing your chance to make the sale.

The answer is to pack more punch into that seventeen minute period when you have the best chance to score a knockout. How do you do that? Not by talking faster, but by presenting better. This means using the visual aids.

Why is it that visual aids are so important, and so widely ignored by the very people who can profit most from them? I think that ego comes into it. We like to talk, and we like to think that we're persuasive. And we are—especially with ourselves. So we talk ourselves into the idea that if we just go in there and wing it—after all, we know our stuff—they'll just sit there and listen while we tell them the entire story about our offering. We want to hear our own words, not use what someone else has created. That's how we feel if we're not Champions. The Champion doesn't care who created it—if he can legitimately use it to make money, he does so. The Champion takes his pride in closed sales. If he wanted to be an artist, he'd buy an easel, rent a loft, and go to it.

Your company relied on a huge variety of talents to create the visual aids they've made available to you. Use what you're given. Exercise your creativity by finding new and more effective ways to make sales with your company's visual aids.

HOW TO MAKE VISUAL AIDS PAY OFF FOR YOU

They give you control and speed. Without control, you can't achieve speed, and without speed, you can't maintain control. You can slow down or repeat if you're going too fast, but if you're too slow, there's no way you can speed up enough to catch prospects you've already lost to impatience.

If you aren't in control, you can't sell—you can only take orders from the very few who are determined to buy no matter what. Right at the beginning of appointments, many salespeople lose control—and from then on they never have a chance. How do they lose control?

By not getting the seating right.

If you think that seating is too simple to bother about, compare it to putting gas in your car. That's simple too. But if you don't do it, you stop moving. If you don't control the seating in sales, you also stop moving.

Take the sales situation where appointments are made to go into homes and give presentations or demonstrations. Every time the salesman sits on a chair in the living room, he's killed that sale. That position forces him to swivel his head back and forth between the two of them while he's talking and trying to make notes on his knee. The process is painfully slow. Before long, the couple is exchanging those eloquent glances that married couples develop. Without a word being spoken between them about it, they agree to get rid of that salesperson as soon as possible.

Visual aids allow you to deliver more information in less time, but an even greater value lies in their ability to get you seated across from them at a table.

Why is this so important? Because it allows you to put yourself in the position of sales power. This occurs when:

a. You are able to maintain eye contact with both of them simply by shifting your gaze—without having to take the time to crank your head around. This is vital because it's fast.

b. You can see both of them at once.

c. You can make notes while they're watching the visual aid. This is necessary since their attention will wander if they have to wait while you scribble.

d. You can work quickly enough to complete your presentation within the first seventeen minutes—the crucial period that's usually the only time you have their full attention on your presentation.

You must know every page of your visual aid completely. But, even though you know what's on the page by heart, you still have to look at it. Why? Because of a common response that we all have. If I look at you, you'll look back at me—almost in self defense. Don't set your visual aid presentation up so that they're supposed to be looking at it while they feel your eyes on them. If that happens, they'll either stop looking at the visual aid and stare back at you, or they'll feel threatened and have trouble concentrating on anything.

Eliminate this by arranging your presentation so that you look at the visual aid, make a point or two, and then look up to regain eye contact with them for an instant. As you repeat this process, pause slightly after finishing a point to signal that you're going to look at them. Unconsciously, they'll slip into a comfortable, reassuring rhythm of shifting their gaze from the visual aid to your eyes and back again.

Maybe you're wondering, "What if I can't remember everything?"

Write notes in pencil on the back of each page of your visual aid. A flip chart or binder type of visual aid makes it easy to give your presentation the most effective sequence. You start at (a) work your way steadily and smoothly through (b) and (c), and then on to all the other steps. You cover everything in the sequence you find flows best. Nothing important is forgotten.

Let me warn you about something. Some salespeople have beat up old binders that they use for every presentation. Instead of working smoothly, they spend half their time flipping over pages and muttering dark things like:

● "You aren't interested in that."

● "We don't have that model anymore because it was a maintenance nightmare."

● "Doggone it, where's that side view I wanted to show you?"

Meanwhile, the prospect is getting more and more irritated. And he's losing faith in you and your company fast. What's in some of those pages you're flipping over so rapidly? Something he ought to know that might discourage him from buying what you're selling? At best you look disorganized and inefficient, at worst you look like a con artist.

You may say, "But I have so many products, I have to use the same binder for all of my presentations."

Baloney.

You can have a visual aid for each important product or service—or you can pull just the pages you need for each presentation from a master file and put them in a separate binder.

If you're selling, as opposed to merely order taking from a catalog you carry around, you can organize yourself to have a crisp presentation that you make from a binder that's free of dead pages. Look at the salesbooks or presentation binders the slowest selling half of any sales force carries and you'll see binders that are bulging with outdated, dogeared material that is anything but an invitation to buy. This sorry stuff is only there because the salesman it belongs to would rather read the sports page than purge his binder when he stops for a cup of coffee he doesn't need.

One of the top insurance salespeople we've trained—a multi-million dollar producer—has a visual aid for term insurance, for whole life, for income protection, for keyman insurance, for Keogh, for IRA — you name it. If it's any form of life insurance, he has a visual aid presentation binder for it that covers every aspect of the subject without skipping pages or having to grumble about things left out.

With a reasonable amount of thought and planning, you can have a visual aid to cover every separate major line or item you sell. And you can also have a format for quickly developing the unique details that apply to — and will appeal most to — each individual you work with. For maximum impact in some types of selling, you have to develop the unique details before you meet with the people; in other kinds of selling, you have to develop those details from information you can only obtain during the presentation. In either case, what's essential is to have a highly organized, fast-moving method of covering all the points the prospects must know about before making their decision.

Good visual aids employ psychological methods to convince prospects on both the emotional and logical levels that they should buy from you and your company. They do this by working on three vital areas:

1. **Visual aids tell them who you and your company are.** Many people feel that all companies are about the same. A strong visual aid gives you a chance to blow your company's horn without seeming to brag. You should be proud of your great company, and here's the time to let it show.

2. **Visual aids tell them what you've done.** People often base their decisions about the future on what's happened in the past because they have few more reliable guides than the past. If you haven't done much yet, tell them more about what your company has done.

3. **Visual aids tell them what you're going to do for them.** The visual aid, specifically and graphically, shows them what benefits they'll receive

after they own your product or service. A picture is worth a thousand words when it comes to conveying emotional impact.

PROOF LETTERS.

Letters from happy clients you've served are a powerful means of building trust in prospects. These letters take effort to acquire. First, you have to service your clients so well that they feel almost an obligation to give you something good back. Then you have to cope with the fact that not many people will sit down all by themselves and write a proof letter to you. They'll tell you on the phone how much they appreciate your extra efforts, how much they've profited from your expertise, but in the daily scramble, they just won't get around to writing that enthusiastic letter.

Carl Slane sells high technology machinery, and he's one of our top Champions. When Carl first started to do well in sales, he realized that proof letters would be a tremendous help to him but, although many of his clients said they were delighted with his product and service, he wasn't getting many letters. His clients were just too busy. Then Carl hit on a simple way to get those letters, and in a short time he built up a very impressive display of them. Here's how he did it:

When a happy client was on the phone, Carl would make notes of the conversation and, as soon as it was over, he'd draft a letter to himself that related in the client's own words what the client had said. Carl was careful not to add comments or praise the client hadn't given, and he was equally careful to leave out any knocking of the competition that might not look wise on paper. He'd have the draft typed, and then he'd make a luncheon appointment with the client.

Before leaving with the client to have lunch, Carl would show him the draft and say, "I put what you were kind enough to tell me on the phone the other day in letter form. If you still feel that way, would you mind having your secretary type this up on your company letterhead while we're at lunch? It would help me a lot." They always said yes. Clients are glad to help salespeople who've done an outstanding job for them.

HOW TO USE PRINTED LITERATURE

Use brochures and catalogs like you use visual aids. Hold the brochure in your hand, look at it as you talk, and frequently look up at your prospects to regain eye contact. Circle the important points that you talk about on the brochure; when you leave it with them, they'll review that brochure and remember what you said.

MODELS

Models are powerful visual aids, especially the kind that have moving parts and aren't too costly to leave with likely buyers. Some of our Champions who sell expensive industrial equipment have found that when someone is really keen on the model, they almost always buy the real thing. The prospect will take the model home to show his wife and kids how it works. All the time he's doing that, he's getting more involved with the whole idea, and he's convincing himself emotionally that his company should own the full-sized version.

VIDEO EQUIPMENT.

If used right, film or video presentations can be very effective. Keep in mind that these are still visual aids—sophisticated ones, it's true—but the same rules apply. Set up the screen so you can exercise control. If it's a silent film, be careful not to jabber all the time. If there's a sound track, it's even more important that you keep quiet while it's on. It's annoying when a salesman takes over a narration the client thinks is more interesting and informative. If you need to say something, stop the film; but if your projector doesn't lend itself to pauses, keep silent until the show is over.

Far better than talking is to sit where you can unobtrusively watch the prospects' reactions. From their facial expressions and movements, you'll discover what does and what doesn't interest them. One spouse will nudge the other at significant times. A member of the committee will whisper agreement or disagreement. Everybody will make small but revealing comments in body language with such things as nods, headshakes, and grimaces. Make mental notes of these emotional markers and they'll guide you to the sale.

If your projector has a pause button, use it—sparingly—to stop the film when great interest is shown in a particular scene and there are details you can add or point out. If your machine has the capability, replay any parts of the show that cause oohs and ahs.

The smaller showcase devices (with projector and screen all in one) can allow you to do all these things, and they're often more practical to use. Sit off to the side and control your showcase remotely so you can watch your prospects more than you watch the screen. You know your film too well, so guard against allowing boredom to show. A Champion doesn't have this problem. Instead of fighting boredom, he's busily noting how his prospects are reacting and planning his next move—how he'll maintain control and start his closing sequence when the film is over.

Here are some simple but vital tips on working with projectors and showcases.

1. Bring a long extension cord so you can set the equipment up in the best location for selling, not the only location the cord will reach.

2. Bring a heavy pad with you. Instead of plopping your projector down on their beautiful coffee table or polished desk, protect it with a soft pad or tablecloth.

3. Always get permission before starting to set up the equipment. You'll get it more readily if you bring in the protective pad first.

4. Accept offers to help set up. Our Champions tell us that prospects who help organize the showing watch it with greater interest. Many salesmen make a mistake here that few saleswomen do. Men often insist on doing all of the set up themselves, leaving the prospects sitting there fidgeting. Women welcome the help, start their presentations faster, and show them to prospects who are already involved because they helped plug it all in.

5. NEVER TAKE YOUR SCREEN OR OTHER VISUAL AIDS DOWN UN-
   TIL YOU'VE COMPLETED THE ENTIRE PRESENTATION AND TRIED
   ALL YOUR CLOSING SEQUENCES.
         This is vital. If you start folding your screen and rolling up your
extension cord, the prospect is thinking, "Okay, out. That's over. On to
other things. Let's see—who do I have to call?"
      You simply can't pack up and then sit down and go into your closing
sequence. The whole mood has changed by that time; the impact has blown
away. Even if your prospect takes a phone call, wait. You're not saving five
minutes by packing up then, you're losing all the time it took to get there and
play your whole number.

      One last point: TAKE CARE OF YOUR EQUIPMENT AND MATE-
RIALS. Use only clean, new looking visual aids, brochures, and catalogs. If
your visual aids are beat-up, dirty, wrinkled, and scratched, what will they
think? That if you're sloppy with your own materials, you'll be sloppy with
how and what you supply them. Organize your car to protect your selling
materials and visual aids, and once a month inspect all of it to make sure that
everything is clean, crisp, and ready to go.

11
FINESSING THE FIRST MEETING

Here's a scene that's repeated thousands of times every business day in the stores and showrooms of this country: A married couple goes in where merchandise is on display. Instantly, a salesperson takes off from his perch and swoops down on them like a vulture who's seen a rabbit go stiff. He tears in.

"Hi folks, I'm Bob Bountiful at your service. Thanks for coming in—it's nice of you to stop by. I'm happy to tell you folks that you've come to the right place. We beat every price in town, and we've got specials and sales you won't believe."

"We're just looking," the wife says.

"Right, and I know what you're looking for—a good deal. Well, you've come to the right place and the right man. Old Bob Bountiful will make sure you're treated right."

"Let's get out of here," the husband says—and out they go. Good old Bob Bountiful just shrugs his shoulders and mutters something like, "Some people just don't want good service that saves them money. What dummies. Oh well, there are more fish in the sea."

What happened? Why is old Bob standing there gasping for air? He didn't ignore the people. He came up, smiling, and introduced himself. He thanked them for coming in. He offered to be of help. He was so nice—and they practically ran out of the store. Why? Because he was practically shouting, "I'm going to sell you turkeys something."

That jerked up a tremendous psychological wall between Bob Bountiful and his prospects. They knew right away that no matter how they handled it, he was going to be puffing in their ears and working up a sweat trying to sell, sell, sell. And they didn't want to be sold. But, they did want to own something in that store or they wouldn't have gone in. The store never got a chance to take hold because good old Bob ran them off before they'd been inside ten seconds.

The original impression can ruin everything so easily. That's why this chapter is devoted to clarifying how you should handle the original contact with any kind of possible buyer.

The first principle of approaching prospects is to come on softly so that you relax them enough to allow their emotion of desire for your product to overcome their emotion of fear. You want them to be thinking about how much they want it, not thinking, "Watch out. This guy is really out to sell me." So they say, "We're only looking." If you make them say it as a defense, you'll almost always cause them to make that statement true by walking out empty handed.

This also happens on an appointment in their home or office. The only difference is that, when you do the vulture swoop on their turf, you encounter hostility instead of withdrawal. In both cases, they do the easiest thing: walk out of your store or brush you out of their place.

So how do we avoid making them fight or run? We understand and act on this idea:

OUR MAIN GOAL WHEN FIRST MEETING A PROSPECT IS TO REMOVE FEAR AND ALLOW THEM TO RELAX.

If the dominant mood in their minds is fear—that you'll push them, that you'll try to sell them, that you'll succeed in selling them—they simply aren't capable of making the kind of positive decision you're looking for. They won't even agree to one of your minor closes when they're dominated by fear. So your first aim with a new prospect always is to get that person to relax.

At times my schedule keeps me flying so much I feel like I'm living on jets. There's a lot more to my job than talking on a stage; I often have to work as I fly. I love people, of course, and I like to exchange stories and views when I have time. But if someone sitting next to me wants to chitchat when I need to work, I just wait. Pretty soon they ask, "What do you do for a living?"

Then I smile and say, "I sell for a living, and I can't thank you enough for sitting right here beside me."

Guess what happens next? They excuse themselves, go to the rest room, and never return.

We all have a natural fear of being sold. This is why it's so important in the original contact to create confidence, not fear.

Let's analyze the steps involved in meeting a prospect correctly.

1. Smile almost to the point of grinning.

Some people have forgotten how to smile because they don't do it much. Salespeople should practice smiling. Exercise your smiling muscles every time you throw the latch on the office rest room. You have everything you need there: a mirror, privacy, and your face. I'm serious. A Champion leaves no stone unturned in developing his skills. Certainly the ability to smile pleasantly—whether you really feel like it or not—is an important sales skill.

A smile radiates warmth. To come on warmly, smile almost to a grin when meeting people. Of course, it can be overdone in some situations, but a nice warm smile is almost always a necessary first step to a sale.

Some people have trouble putting on a smile when it's needed for another reason: they don't shut off old problems and feelings before greeting new prospects. You can be sure of two things: your new prospect isn't responsible for or interested in your troubles; and you won't help your problems by driving him off with a sulky attitude. Resolve now to give your problems and negative feelings an intermission every time you see a new prospect or a different client. Then, if you have to, go back to your troubles later—after you've given yourself a boost by handling the prospect well.

2. Look in their eyes.

Why do you think I feel it's necessary to make such an obvious point? Because many salespeople destroy all chance of making the sale by avoiding eye contact when meeting someone new. They look down or past the other person. Both habits are unnerving. Shifty-eyed people cause us to question whether they have both oars in the water and honesty in their hearts.

3. Greet them properly.

Give some thought to your standard greeting. If you're using only one, the odds are that it jars many of the prospects you say it to. Practice at least three different greetings. For starters, you may need a formal, respectful greeting; a friendly greeting; and a happy-go-lucky greeting. Later, you may want to work up even more variations. Study each person for an instant and then select the greeting you think best suits their personality. This is a great way to focus your attention on their individuality and get yourself thinking of the best way to work with that unique person.

4. To shake, or not to shake, that is the question.

Many average salespeople desire to press the prospect's flesh. They have a subconscious conviction that if they can just get the other person to shake their hand, they've got him sold. It's almost a superstition with these salespeople. The fallacy of this is that the salesperson is thinking of his own feelings, not about those of the prospect. Many prospects don't want to be touched by strangers. And what happens? Because these salespeople are anxious to shake hands with prospects who don't want to, they get rejected frequently and this rejection makes them even more anxious to shake hands. So they start getting more and more tense about shaking hands. The added tension is communicated to the prospects, who then become even more reluctant to shake hands with this overanxious, sweating salesperson. It's become a vicious circle.

I'm not exaggerating. A friend of mine owns a chain of drycleaning establishments. He said, "Tommy, I can always tell which of my customers are in sales. There's always this telltale mark where they keep rubbing the perspiration off their palms before shaking hands."

For the average salesperson, that quick rub to get rid of the cold sweat becomes a fixed habit along with, "Hi, there. I'm —"

In today's competitive selling, we have one bedrock goal in meeting and working with people. I've probably said this to more people than anyone else has because I work it into nearly all my seminars and speeches: Our main goal in meeting people is to have them like and trust us. That's why a Champion thinks when he's meeting someone: "This person is going to like and trust me, because I'm a very likeable and trustworthy individual."

Isn't that a good thing to be telling yourself all the time? "He's going to like me —" Don't keep telling yourself, "I've got to make this person like and trust me or I'll lose out." Every time you tell yourself, "I've got to do it," you make yourself feel anxious, perhaps even a little desperate. If you're relaxed and confident, you communicate relaxation and confidence to the prospect; if you're tense and worried, you radiate fear, and the prospect will pick that up too.

I have a very cleancut way to help ease this problem: if you're greeting a non-referred prospect (usually this will be the person who walks into your office, store, or showroom) don't expect to shake hands. Of course, if the prospect puts out his hand, you'll take it, but this rarely happens. If it's a recontact or a referred lead, you may shake hands or you may not — simply let them determine it. The important thing is to get rid of the idea that you have to touch them.

Now let's go over the two basic meeting situations in detail.

THE REFERRED LEAD.

Let's suppose that I'm meeting a married couple for the first time under circumstances where I know their names. We have an appointment to meet at my office, for example, and I see them coming in. As I walk toward them with my hand swinging easily at my side, I begin to smile because I'm genuinely looking forward to meeting them.

I'm going to introduce myself. This makes sense because they've never seen me before and I want to relax them by letting them know they're in the right place at the right time talking to the right person. So I say, "Good afternoon, Mr. and Mrs. Meisner. Tom Hopkins with Champions Unlimited." As I say *Mr. Meisner*, I look him in the eyes; then I flick my gaze to Mrs. Meisner's eyes as I say her name, returning to Mr. Meisner as I introduce myself. If I were a woman, I would probably be looking at the wife as I state my name.

It's important that I don't look down at their hands to see if one of them is moving toward me. I don't have to in order to see that movement because we're blessed with something called peripheral vision. This means that we can see things we're not looking directly at. Many people use their peripheral vision only to spot things to look directly at. But peripheral vision has another important function: it can feed information to you while you're looking elsewhere. To illustrate this, stand about fifty feet from a tree when there's a slight breeze blowing. Stare at the trunk where it goes into the ground and, without moving your gaze from that point of the tree trunk, notice how much movement you can see in the leaves and branches. You can do the same thing looking at the door of a multi-story building; while you're looking at the door, you can see windows on the second floor. Practice gathering information about the windows, walls, and roof of that building without taking your eyes off the door. It's amazing how much you can see that you're not looking at. This is something you can practice anywhere at odd moments to expand your consciousness in many ways. Not the least of those ways is catching a movement of shoulder or hand that shows the other person intends to shake hands with you. You see that movement without looking down, while you're maintaining the eye-to-eye contact that builds trust and confidence.

Practice your peripheral vision. Convince yourself that you don't need to touch your prospects. Then you'll stop wiping your right palm because you won't be sweating anymore. You'll be truly relaxed because you've taken the strain off the meeting situation, and more people will like and trust you because you're radiating warmth and confidence instead of tension.

As you walked up to Mr. and Mrs. Meisner, you were smiling easily and your right hand was swinging naturally at your side. If there's a movement and Mr. Meisner's hand comes out, you take it easily, give it a firm shake, disconnect promptly, and let your hand swing down as you turn slightly toward Mrs. Meisner. If you've shaken hands with the husband, there's more chance that the wife will make the same gesture. As you look into her eyes, be aware whether she's making any move to shake hands too. If not, your slight turn toward her and the dropping of your hand can work smoothly into a slight bow or nod to her.

NON-REFERRED SITUATION.

A couple walks into your store or display area. You don't know their names. At this stage it's just plain pushy for you to tell them yours. All chance of building the necessary relaxed feeling is often lost in the first moments by overanxious salespeople who stick out their hands and introduce themselves. The prospects are startled and embarrassed because they weren't ready for that kind of attention and commitment.

This situation often turns into a minor calamity. The salesman realizes that he's gone too far and drops his hand just as the prospect unwillingly raises his. Then the prospect quickly pulls his hand back, but not before the salesman starts his up in time to catch a second rebuff. By now everyone is embarrassed, and the prospects are silently vowing to get out of there as soon as possible and never come back.

Here's how to avoid the possibility of this happening. A couple walks in. You don't know their names and have no reason to believe they want to make your acquaintance. When you walk toward them, stop several feet away to avoid invading their space, and say something along these lines:

- "Hi. Nice of you to come in. Why don't you just make yourselves at home and look around. If you have any questions, let me know."
- "Hello. Thanks for coming in. Please feel free to look around all you want. If I can give you any information, please don't hesitate to ask."
- "Good afternoon, sir—madam. Welcome to _____ (name your store). I hope you'll both enjoy our display. If you have any questions, I'm at your service."

When you've spoken your version of one of those greetings, walk away.

That's right, walk away.

Don't whirl and run, of course. Turn away slowly. If you're where you should be, they can easily ask you a question if they care to.

It's curious how many people will head for the door when you crowd them, but will ask for the product or service they came in for when you speak courteously to them and then start turning away. By showing that you respect their privacy, you assure them that they'll be safe in asking for what they want.

Often they won't say much—especially in places where big ticket items are sold. Move off. You've done all you can do until those people make the next move.

Many of them will cruise around your showroom without stopping anywhere for more than a few seconds and then leave. These people almost always are killing time, are out of their price class, or really are just looking in advance of real need or willingness to buy. If so, you gain a great deal by letting them browse and go. They are far more likely to come back when they're ready to buy if they haven't been pressured the first time they came in. And, by lettting them go, you haven't burned up your energy and enthusiasm on hopeless cases.

If they don't ask a question or leave, they'll do what you should be hoping they'll do.

5. Let them settle.

If you leave them alone after greeting them, and if they have any genuine interest in your product or service and the ability to buy it, they'll home in on that item. All you have to do is let them settle.

If your product line is appliances and your store handles several types including television sets, watch without staring. Using peripheral vision, you can be looking at something in the dishwasher section when they light on a particular TV set. If they stay there for a full minute, they've settled. Now it's time for you to stroll over and casually move into the next step.

6. Ask an opening involvement question.

An involvement question, of course, is any positive question they'd ask themselves about the benefits you're selling after they own them. An *opening* involvement question will often be structured along the lines you could use on a couple who've been looking at the same TV set for a minute or two now. You don't know their names yet, of course, and it's too soon to ask.

Walk up and say, "Would the television replace your old one, or is it going to be an additional set for your home?"

With slight changes in wording, you can adapt this opening involvement question to almost any product or service. Once you get them talking about why they want what you're selling, you know how to go into your qualification and minor closing sequences, how to eventually lead them into happy involvement in a purchase.

12

QUALIFICATION IS THE
KEY TO QUOTA-BUSTING

Many salespeople never qualify before presenting or demonstrating. They simply never do it. Some of them don't know how, and others aren't organized well enough. Some are afraid to face facts. Whatever explanation there may be for failing to qualify prospects before giving a full presentation, the salespeople who don't do it are often depressed because they aren't making enough sales. They decide they couldn't close an Eskimo on a hot lunch when actually they are fairly good closers. Their problem is that they try to close the wrong people too often and too hard.

In other words, they don't fail to close, they fail to qualify. I really believe that most full time salespeople have a major problem in the area of qualifying prospects before running off their complete selling sequence.

It's often been said that sales work is largely a matter of using time effectively. For some reason, many average salespeople think that the only important thing is to demonstrate the product or present the service with a lot of slick phrases and gimmicks. If they do that, if they tell the prospects everything about it, they'll hear, "Yes, we'll take it."

Champions know better. They know that qualification is the key to high production. And, since they understand the need for and the methods of qualifying, they also appreciate the value of pre-qualifying techniques such as referral card system, swap meet, and orphan finding.

If you use those techniques, your leads are pre-qualified before you meet them. You're assured that they have the needs and resources to buy what you're selling—so you'll close fifty percent of them. You'll close one for every one that gets away. With unqualified leads, nine will get away while you're closing one. As a general rule, it takes as much time to see ten non-qualified leads as it does to see ten qualified leads. The primary difference is that your sales are 500 percent greater with qualified leads than they are with the non-qualified type. That's a figure that should give you pause if you aren't effectively qualifying your leads. Any system that can increase your sales five-fold fairly screams for your attention, doesn't it?

Will you also agree that, no matter what it takes to develop this skill, you must do it if you possibly can? Certainly you must. Fortunately, the process isn't difficult. When you're through reading the next few paragraphs, you'll have a superb qualification strategy. This strategy allows you qualify each prospect as you meet them. In many cases you'll be able to qualify over the phone before you meet them; if they don't qualify, you politely avoid wasting time seeing them. How often have you committed an hour or half a day going, demonstrating, and coming back, only to discover that they can't afford your offering, can't make the decision to buy it, or can't use its features? The most valuable thing a salesperson has is time. Time wasted demonstrating to non-buyers is time that could have been spent demonstrating to and closing buyers—or prospecting for them. Qualifying means that you work hard with people who will buy your offering instead of working equally hard with people who won't buy your offering. It's that simple.

Here are the qualifying steps that can increase your sales potential by 500 percent:

1. Find out what they have now.

When I know how they are presently handling their need for the benefits that I can supply, I know the kind of person they've been. Knowing what they've been tells me a lot about what they want to become. When I know where they're headed, I know how to sell them what they need to get there. Sometimes people will be eager to tell you what they have now. With other products and services, they may be less than eager to give you this information. In that case, you'll need to develop indirect lines of questioning that are capable of digging out the facts you need. Give this as much thought and practice as it needs. Qualifying is too important to allow some difficulty here to stop you.

2. Find out what they like most about the product or service they now have.

This is urgent. Knowing how they feel about what they have points you straight at how to make the sale—or, equally important, alerts you to the fact that you'll be wasting your time trying to sell that particular prospect. Every product and service has its limitations; trying to sell outside those limitations is a total waste of irreplaceable time.

Let's illustrate this point by going back to Champion Marine Sales. I'm on the phone with Mr. Ivey, who has the itch to replace the custom boat he's owned for three years.

"Tom, why don't you take a run out here and give me your opinion as to how much I could get for my boat on today's resale market. You could make the round trip in a couple of hours."

"I'd like to do that, Mr. Ivey. Tell me, what do you enjoy most about your boat?"

"Well, I guess that would be its seaworthiness. It's kind of a slow old tub, but I wouldn't be afraid to ride out a hurricane in it."

"A fast boat can put you back in a snug harbor before the weather gets really bad."

"Yeah—if your engine doesn't quit. My boat's almost a motorsailer—it's got a steadying sail that could get me home in a blow if the mill stops grinding."

Now I've found out what I wanted to know before making that two-hour round trip. Champion Marine sells the finest high-speed boats made—and no other kind. In other words, the boats we market are precisely the type that Mr. Ivey would never buy. After spending a few moments asking astute questions, I've eliminated Mr. Ivey as a prospect for me. He may be an avid yachtsman, he may be loaded with money, but Mr. Ivey isn't going to buy one of my Spee-D-Ski boats.

"Mr. Ivey, I really appreciate you're calling me, but we're not the right people to serve you. A good friend of mine is this area's leading expert on displacement boats. Let me give you his number."

All I need do now is place a quick call to somebody who sells the kind of boat Mr. Ivey likes so that yacht broker will feel obligated to send me people wanting what I have that he doesn't handle.

Notice that I don't ask Mr. Ivey to tell my friend that I sent him because there's not one chance in ten he'll remember to do that. Instead, I take it on myself to build my relationship with this non-competing member of my industry. Sure, it takes three minutes—but those three minutes can bring back qualified buyers.

With the time saved by not driving out to see Mr. Ivey's boat, I continue taking and making calls. An hour later, I'm talking to Max Schnell.

"What do you like most about your present boat, Mr. Schnell?"

"It's a goer, Tom. It gets me out to where the fish are fast."

"Your boat turns up about thirty knots, does it?"

"Thirty knots? No way. But it's good for a solid twenty-two right through a three-foot chop."

"The Spee-D-Ski II will take you through that same chop at a solid thirty knots. And that's cruising speed—not flat out."

"Wow. We've got to talk business, Tom. When can we do that?"

"At your convenience, Max. I'd like you to take a demonstration ride with me. Could you be here by three? Or would five be a better time for you today?"

"Hey, great. I'll see you at five."

If I'd rushed out to see Mr. Ivey's "slow old tub" I would've missed Mr. Schnell's call. Someone else around the office would have given him a trial run—and chalked up the sale. Don't waste your time working with people who want what you don't have. If you spend your time that way, you'll have the "bad luck" to be out every time the business comes in.

But if you follow these steps and concentrate on working with the people you can help enjoy the benefits they want, you'll be working with buyers who've pre-committed themselves to what you have. They'll literally be sold before you even demonstrate. Your demonstration will, in fact, simply be a confirmation that they've got to have it. Can you feel how excited and fulfilled you'll be closing in these kinds of situations? The right way to sell not only is the moneymaking way—it's also the easy way once you learn how to organize yourself to do it.

3. "What would you like to see altered or improved in your new (name the product or service)?"

A Champion uses the answers to that question to find out which qualities he must emphasize to close the sale.

Now I'm selling factory machinery. Paul Flinn answers this question by saying:

"I'd like to see some method of cutting down the setup time. The production rate is okay on our present machine, but we lose too much time changing over from job to job on it. You don't get many long runs in this business."

I'm going to file that vital bit of information in the front of my brain. When I'm doing my demonstration a few days later, I'm going to say something like this:

"Mr. Flinn, one thing we're very conscious of at Champion Machinery is the high cost of setup time. Not only is setup labor very expensive, but slow setup time eats profits by keeping the equipment out of production longer. So our company has invested huge sums in engineering faster takedown and setup. Here's what we've done to keep our new machine pumping out parts —"

Build your demonstration or presentation around the things they want altered or changed in what they have now. Feed back what they've told you they want, and they have to agree that you're making sense.

4. "Who in addition to yourself will make the final decision?"

It's understandable why people who can't make decisions want to give the impression that they can until the last minute—it makes them feel important. So you have to handle this carefully. Again, you'll have to structure your response to this problem around your own offering. The more time-consuming your demonstration or presentation is, the more important it is to have all the decision makers present. There's nothing more discouraging that putting on demolition derby for someone and then having them tell you, "That was great. But I really can't give you the go-ahead until I talk to Mr. Snodgrass. Gee, you sure went to a lot of trouble. I wish he'd seen it. Can you come back next week and do it again?"

5. "If we were fortunate enough today to find the right (name your product or service), would you be in a position to proceed?"

I didn't blurt out, "Look, I'm not about to sweat through the whole demonstration unless I know you're really going to buy the durn thing if it does the job for you."

When you say, "If we're fortunate enough today," shrug as though that's not very likely. This reduces the pressure on them because you've indicated that you don't think you're going to hit the right note today anyway—so they're more likely to own up to the truth about whether they can or can't go ahead today.

"Oh, no. Before we go any further, our board of directors has to meet and approve it."

I didn't really want to hear that, of course, but I know that negative reality doesn't self-destruct merely because it's ignored. I've discovered that going into the full closing sequence is useless until I get in front of the right people, so now I know how to move that particular sale forward.

The next two techniques are delightful to work with, and they're highly effective.

6. Bracket-in on Product or Service: Give them a Triplicate of Choice.

I'm going to give you an example of how you'd do this if your product is office copying machines, but of course you'll have to structure this method to your own offering.

Complete knowledge of your product line is the first essential. Let's say that your line includes eight different copying machines. Instead of trying to go from eight possibles to the one machine any given prospect will buy, frame them into the most likely three first, and then in a second step isolate the one that's best for that particular application.

"Mary, we have three basic functions with our copiers: copying, separating, and collating. Of these three, which is the most important to you?"

"Collating. We've got to have that feature on our next machine."

Because I know my product line, I instantly know that we've eliminated three machines. That leaves five for Mary to choose from.

Color and size often are important purchase considerations. What I must now determine is whether she's prepared to devote as much office space to copying as our largest, fastest, and most versatile machine requires. If not, we have a medium and also a small size. I explain the options in terms of size and ask her which best suits her needs.

"The medium size," Mary says. I'm not surprised. Most of the time, they go for the medium choice.

"Our machines all come in three colors: light beige, which would go nicely with your paneling. We also have a glossy black that looks very distinguished, and this unique shade of red. Which of these do you think will provide the right touch?"

"Definitely the beige," Mary tells me.

Now we're down to a medium size machine, beige in color, that copies, separates, and collates. Now the problem is not selecting the machine, it's determining if Mary's company is prepared to spend what that machine costs. My next step is designed to maximize the chances that she'll decide it is.

7. Bracket-up for money.

This is a beautiful strategy for overcoming what in many cases is the most tricky question of all. The average salesperson often stumbles here because he has no system for easing past this tight place. So he baldly states the price, frequently in a manner that shows he thinks it's outrageously high. That's not the way to close.

Instead of going in cold on price, use this powerful strategy. Stick as close to the exact wording as you can when adapting this technique to your offering because all the elements are important. Here's how it works:

"Most people interested in acquiring this machine with all its features are prepared to invest $12,000. A fortunate few can invest between $15,000 and $20,000. And then there are those on a limited or fixed budget who—with the high cost of everything today—can't go higher than $10,000. May I ask, which of these categories does your company fit into most comfortably, Mary?"

"We were thinking of spending about $12,000."

Why did she say that? In actual fact, Mary possibly didn't have an exact amount in mind. She doesn't want to be in the bottom category, so Mary opted for the middle figure.

I've structured the figures to allow me to say at this point, "What I'm excited about is this: the machine that meets all your requirements involves an investment of only $10,000—substantially under the amount you're prepared to spend." Where can Mary go now except to her desk for a purchase order?

I'd still be okay if Mary had assigned her company to the lowest category. You see how it works. Structure this technique so that you come up a winner no matter what figure they pick.

Here's the BUFM Formula, the Triplicate of Choice technique that allows you to bracket up for money:

(a) Begin by stating a figure that is twenty percent above your price. ("Most people . . . are prepared to invest $12,000. . . .")

(b) Continue by giving a range from fifty to one hundred percent above your price. ("A fortunate few can invest between $15,000 and $20,000. . . .")

(c) Give the actual price as your last figure. ("And then there are those on a limited or fixed budget . . . who can't go over $10,000.")

(d) Then ask, "Which of these categories do you (does your company, family, organization) fit into most comfortably?"

(e) Whichever category they pick, your response is, "What I'm really excited about is this: the model that meets all your needs (that's exactly what you want) only requires an investment of —"

- If they pick the bottom category, finish with, "— which is exactly what you planned to spend."
- If they put themselves in the middle, finish with, "— which is subtantially under what you're prepared to spend."

Before you go on your next presentation with the intention of putting the Triplicate of Choice for Money to work for you, face the fact that it won't work (and you won't even try to use it) unless you have all your figures down pat. If you try to wing this and get your figures mixed up, you'll botch it. Remember this:

To use the triplicate of choice for money, you must practice the figures until you know them perfectly.

You can only use this technique once in each presentation, of course.

Often it's the monthly investment, not the total investment, that's the key money element. If that's how you sell, you can easily adapt the Triplicate of Choice for Money to your selling sequence by saying,

"Many people interested in this service are prepared to invest $120 a month to enjoy its benefits. We have a fortunate few willing to invest between $150 and $200 each month. And then we have those few on a limited or fixed budget who feel they can't go higher than a $100 monthly investment. Which of these categories do you feel most comfortable with?"

Monthly-investment buyers, like cash buyers, usually jump on the middle figure. After they do that, give them the good news: In order to own exactly what they want, they don't have to invest what they expected to invest. The amount of money that's involved is much smaller than that. At this point I've often had clients ask me, "Tom, what can I say?"

I smile and tell them, "I know. Isn't it nice when a good decision is so easy? Now all you need to do is okay it right here."

THE UH-PRICE NON-TECHNIQUE

Some of us go shuffling in there dreading the moment when we have to get down to the hard facts of money. So we uh-price them.

"What's it cost?" the customer asks.

"Well, that one is—uh—it's about—let's see, with tax and freight and the small installation charge we have to make—I'm awfully afraid—uh—it's going to run you right at—well, maybe just a shade under, tuhthzzert. Um, yeah, that's about it."

"What? I didn't catch the price you're quoting me."

"Ten thousand."

"Dollars?"

"Yes, ten thousand dollars, more or less."

"Well, which is it, more—or less? It better be a lot less if you expect me to buy it."

"Uh—let me double check my figures."

While the hapless salesperson frantically adds and subtracts, the buyer sits back and calmly plans his next move to keep him off balance and drive a better bargain.

Never uh-price a possible buyer. Control the money issue by facing it squarely and boldly. The Triplicate of Choice for Money allows you to win every money vote that can be won. Use it. This technique is a reliable workhorse—if you know your figures, adapt the phrases to your offering, and practice them carefully.

13

HANDLING OBJECTIONS

Until you learn how to handle objections, you're not going to approach your potential in sales. Champions have almost an affection for even the peskiest objection because it's concrete. They know they've reached the Klondike and are digging for gold when they start hearing objections. It's when they don't get objections that they're really worried.

Years ago I had a dream that repeated itself several times in a few months. In this dream, I went in to sell my product to a married couple—and they were so helpful! They agreed to everything. No objections. They even helped me fill out the forms. And then the transaction went through quickly and smoothly. Nary a problem in the whole thing.

That was a dream. Such things only happen to salespeople when they're unconscious. I kept on having that dream until I realized that objections aren't sales-killers, they're sales-makers. People who don't object aren't seriously involved. They won't buy because they don't care enough to challenge the price, ask for more proof, or question their need to own what your offering.

MAKE THE HANDLING OF OBJECTIONS AN INTEGRAL AND EXPECTED PART OF YOUR SELLING SEQUENCE.

I hope that you'll highlight this achievement-oriented statement:

Objections are the rungs of the ladder to sales success.

When you climb to the top of that ladder, they own what you're selling. There just isn't any other way to where you want to climb except by grasping and overcoming the objections. If you don't want to get to the top, just don't have any luck with the rungs of success called objections. Unless you can step on them and keep climbing and overcoming them, you'll never become a Champion. But if you decide to overcome objections by learning the material in this book, you'll learn to love objections—because they announce buying intention and point the way to closing the sale.

Love objections?

You may be thinking, "Me love objections? They've been building fires in my stomach."

The reason they've been troublesome is that you haven't gained an understanding of what an objection is, and you haven't learned the fundamentals for handling them.

What is an objection?

It's a statement by your prospect that he wants to know more. Of course, objections don't usually come out sounding like a polite request for additional information. People aren't trying to make it quite that easy for you. They usually are sincerely objecting—they don't realize they're just asking for more information. It's your job to know that, and to know what to do about it.

There are two kinds of objections, minor and major. Please keep this in mind at all times:

Minor objections are defense mechanisms.

People use them to slow things down. They don't mean that they don't want to buy, they just want to mull things over before committing themselves.

If you sell frequently to husband and wife, you've had one of them start to go along with your demonstration and then the other suddenly starts objecting and fighting you. Sometimes the other spouse, the one who's going along, is more surprised than you are. The fighting spouse may only want to catch his or her breath, or make sure that you can answer his minor objections eloquently before things get any thicker.

Of course, not all problems are objections that can and should be overcome. You'll often encounter conditions that prevent the purchase. One of the most common conditions for large purchases, of course, is that they don't have the money and can't qualify for a loan.

WHAT IS A CONDITION?

A condition is a valid reason for not going ahead. It's not an objection to overcome, it's a total block to the sale that you must accept and walk away from. A Champion is quick to recognize conditions. The major aim of qualifying is to determine whether there are any conditions that make the sale impossible, and further attempts to sell pointless. So the Champion, being an expert qualifier, never destroys his enthusiasm by trying to overcome conditions that can't be overcome.

Even a skilled qualifier may occasionally be well into his selling sequence and then encounter what appears to be a condition. When that happens, treat it like an objection. That is, try to break it down. If it doesn't break down, it's a condition, and you'll need to develop the ability to swallow hard and then quickly and courteously disconnect from that prospect who, you've just discovered, can't buy. Some of us have a severe problem here. If we spend time with people and get into our selling sequence with them, we get emotionally involved to the point where we lose our ability to see the difference between an objection that can be overcome and a condition that can't. In this, sales is like poker. Professional poker players are quick to throw in a losing hand, no matter how much they've already bet on it. Average poker players stay in the game and keep on calling bets with hands they know have little chance to win. Instead of accepting a small loss and getting out, they stay in and take a greater loss. As Reinhold

Niebuhr said, "Give us serenity to accept what cannot be changed, courage to change what should be changed, and wisdom to distinguish the one from the other." Have the wisdom—and sometimes it also takes courage—to pleasantly and quickly withdraw from losing situations.

Now let me repeat what an objection is. An objection is a request for more information. Believe me, I won't waste my time objecting to small things unless I'm really considering taking the product or service—I'm the same as most buyers on that point. But understand this: the potential buyer who objects really can't see how your offering will suit his needs. Your job is to use your superior knowledge of what you're selling to show him how it can satisfy his needs. Take a bright highlighting pen and make this point stand out:

If no conditions exist and they don't buy, it's my fault.

It's important to understand and agree with that concept. You represent a fine quality product, or a service that's conducted with skill and integrity. When people own it, they benefit. Let them. Do your job. Help those people enjoy the benefits that only you can bring them. Do you realize how many salespeople won't let their prospects benefit from their offering? These salespeople won't do what has to be done in the way of practice, planning, and performance to permit their prospects to benefit from owning what they sell.

I love the profession of selling. It's been my entire life. I know what a leading part it plays in maintaining our national prosperity and way of life. What I think is sad is the large number of salespeople who damage our profession because they buckle when they hear an objection. These klutzes don't realize that by failing to overcome objections, they not only fail themselves and their families, they also fail their companies, the public, and our nation's future. The prospect came to you in need of the product or service—or you found him in need of it—and if they don't get it, they lose. Everyone else loses too.

As I fly around the country, I talk to people who aren't in the selling profession. When I say that I train salespeople, some of them look at me like I'm doing something wrong. I don't accept any shade of that idea. We have the most honorable profession there is. Selling means helping people benefit and grow. Yet the average salesperson sits and waits. When he finally meets a prospect, the slightest breeze of objection blows him away—and that prospect walks off without the benefits.

I hope you'll decide right now that you'll no longer buckle under and then blow away. Make today the day you take the material in this book (or in my cassettes and videotapes) and start working with all your energy to learn and then shape it to serve your unique requirements. When you've made it yours, you'll love objections like I do because you'll know in your bones that finding and overcoming them is the only way you'll ever get the yes you're looking for. You'll learn to go in hoping to hear the no's you've got to hear before you use your skills and get the yes. Won't you now, as a potential Champion, join me in this conviction?

TWO DONT'S AND ONE DO
THAT EVERY CHAMPION LIVES BY

Here are two things that no Champion ever does, and one thing that all Champions constantly do. Please highlight these three precepts so you can review them quickly and often.

1. Don't argue.

Do you know how many salespeople argue with potential buyers? The prospect voices an objection—meaning that he shows a need for more information—and what does he get? An argument. With anger or sarcasm, or other forms of sales-killing heat and pressure, the salesperson tries to beat the prospect down. Quite often, the salesperson succeeds in winning the argument—and thereby loses all chance of making the sale. Why? Because then the only way the prospect can get even for the way he's been treated is to buy from someone else.

2. Don't attack them when you overcome their objections.

Put space between your prospects and their objections. By this I mean that you must be careful to separate your people from every one of their objections as they come up before you can be sure that, when you shoot at the objection, you don't hit the prospect in a vital spot. Develop sensitivity to how your prospects feel when they voice their objections. You can't reject their objections as being anything less than intelligent and reasonable without striking at their self-esteem. Show concern for saving their face, not determination to prove them wrong. Never allow a prospect to feel that he's in danger of being proven wrong. If you start fighting their feelings, their negative emotions will always take over. You can't make sales by winning logical battles at the cost of losing emotional battles. Objections tell you where their interests lie; this being the case, objections tell you what must be emphasized, eliminated, or changed before they'll buy; which is to say, objections are the feedback you must have if you're going to close them.

3. Do lead them to answer their own objections.

A Champion always tries to maneuver them into answering their own objection because when they say something, it's true. The average salesperson doesn't suspect that this can be done and never tries to do it; the Champion knows that it usually can be done and develops great skill at doing it. Do you know that most prospects will answer their own objections if you'll just work at it, give them time, and lead them to it? After all, deep down they want to go ahead—if you'll just show them how, and guide their faltering footsteps. They wouldn't keep on talking to you if they didn't want what you sell.

Most buyers have certain reflexes they aren't even conscious of that come out as objections. When the secretary says, "We only see vendors on Thursday," or someone coming into a store says, "We're only looking," you're hearing reflex objections. Here's how to overcome these and other types.

THE OBJECTION-HANDLING SYSTEM

1. Hear them out.

Far too many salespeople leap on an objection before the other person has a chance to finish saying it. The prospect barely gets five words out—and already the salesperson is yammering away as though the evil thing will multiply unless it's stomped out faster than now. "I gotta make him wrong quick, or he won't take the product," seems to be their panicky reaction to the first hint on any objection.

Not only does the prospect feel irritated to be interrupted, he also feels pushed. And uneasy. "Why's he jumping on that so fast and so hard?" your prospect will ask himself. "I smell a rat."

And suppose you run south when he hits north, and answer the wrong objection? Maybe even raise one he hadn't thought of? How embarrassing.

2. Feed the objection back.

This is one of the best techniques for getting them to answer their own objection. It works especially well with husband and wife buyers. I've often fed an objection back to the husband, and then sat back while the wife hopped on it and closed him for me.

3. Question the objection.

Ask them to elaborate on their objection. Do it seriously. Avoid any hint of sarcasm, impatience, or contempt. If you really get into the detail of their objection, they'll feel a strong pull toward removing it themselves. Even if that doesn't happen, while the prospect is expounding further on his objection, you have more time to decide what course will best overcome it.

4. Answer the objection.

You might think, "Well, that lets me out." Don't worry—I'm going to show you how. When you've learned all this material and made it yours, you won't tense up or buckle when prospects favor you with objections—you'll just smile to yourself and move forward, confident that you can overcome them.

Have you ever stared at the ceiling in the dark of night thinking about all the objections that prospects could hit you with? Sometimes it seems like they have their own training program to learn every negative that can possibly be raised. Some salespeople strike one objection they can't overcome, and that gives them nightmares. It works on their minds so much that soon they're expecting to hear the objection they dread most from every prospect.

Guess what? Pretty soon that's the one they always get.

Here's how it works. That cruncher objection is on their mind when they go in for every appointment, or walk up to every prospect. They don't know when, or even if, that wipe-out objection will strike—but they can't get it out of their thoughts. So the tension builds until it's too great. Without realizing it, they start dropping little hints that cause the prospect to bring up the objection they dread most.

Is there a single product or service that doesn't have a few soft spots, a few places where it isn't quite as good as something else?

If there is, I've never encountered it.

I feel very confident in telling you that throughout your career everything you sell will have a few features or weaknesses you wish it didn't have. There'll always be something that can turn into a cruncher of an objection if you let it prey on your mind.

Champions study the weak points their offering has, and they learn how to handle the situation. They often do this by admitting the disadvantage and immediately comparing it to an advantage. "Yes, our matrix platform adjusts only forty degrees horizontally, but it provides fifty percent more vertical adjustment than any other machine. That's because our engineering studies prove that. . . ."

5. Confirm the answer.

Don't reply to the objection and then leave it hanging in the air. They may not have understood you. Or maybe they stopped listening before you finally covered the point because they thought of something else. Always allow for the possibility that people who are close to a decision may be a little strange. After you've answered the objection in a way you feel should overcome it, confirm that you have. Ask things like:

- "That clarifies this point entirely, don't you agree?"
- "That's the answer you're looking for, isn't it?"
- "With that question out of the way, we can go ahead, don't you think?"
- "Do you agree with me that we've covered the question you raised, and given you a way to handle it?"
- "Now that's settled entirely, isn't it?"
- "That solves your problem with _____, doesn't it?"

6. Change gears, and immediately go to the next step in your selling sequence.

Once you've confirmed that you've overcome an objection, move on briskly.

To signal that the last step is over, and that you're all now going on to the next step, use body language as you speak. That is, make an appropriate gesture, look or step in a new direction, turn the page on your proposal, shift in your chair—make some small or large physical move. As you do that, introduce the next step with a phrase such as, "By the way. . . ."

Let's review the six steps to handling objections: (1) hear it out, (2) feed it back, (3) question it, (4) answer it, (5) confirm that the answer was accepted, and (6) move on with a gesture and a "By the way."

Make that your standard method for overcoming objections. Learn this material and it'll be better for your energy than any sleeping pills you can buy—no prescription, all the side effects are wonderful, and you'll sleep soundly because you won't fear what bedevils the nights of the average salesperson: objections.

But remember that when I say learn the material, I mean that you must adapt it to your personality, offering, and area, and that you must know it like you know your middle name.

That's the method. Now here are four techniques to break through specific barriers. Incorporate them into your arsenal of objection-busting weapons by writing questions and answers that fit your own situation.

FOUR SHOCK TREATMENTS FOR OBJECTIONS

1. Put the shoe on the prospect's foot.

Use this technique to overcome a direct challenge arising from the prospect's previous experience with your company. Here's how it works. For our example, let's assume that you represent the Dimm Company, who market a high quality line of office copiers. You've just walked in to see Jack Rinehart, a referral from your swap meet. Right away you run into trouble when Mr. Rinehart says, "We had a Dimm Copier two years ago and we had to get rid of it. Too slow. We lost a lot of valuable employee time with your machine."

In this situation, the average salesperson often gets into an argument about whether the Dimm Copier is now as fast as the competition. Such arguments rarely go well. Mr. Rinehart soon says, "Yeah, I hear what you're saying, but I don't want another Dimm around here. Thanks for coming in. Goodbye."

The Champion puts the shoe on the prospect's foot by saying, "Mr. Rinehart, would you for a moment pretend that you're the president of Dimm Copiers, and you've just found out about the problem we had with the reproduction speed of our copiers. What would you do?"

Mr. Rinehart will say something like, "I'd get my engineering department cracking on it, and make them solve the problem in a hurry." By putting him in the shoes of your company's president, you've asked him a question with an obvious answer that strokes his ego, haven't you?

Then you warmly smile and say, "That's exactly what the president of Dimm Copiers did." What can Mr. Rinehart do now but listen to the rest of your presentation?

A common experience in sales, especially when starting a new job, is to take over an established territory. Let's suppose you're doing that.

It doesn't take you long to find out that the person you replaced wasn't promoted for doing a great job. In fact, the opposite happened because he tore the territory down. Now you're picking up the pieces.

As you get around your new area to meet the customers, you start running across a lot of unhappy people. Most of them are now buying your product or service from the competition. When you go in to introduce yourself and say that you're going to be servicing their company from now on, they tell you something like this:

"Listen, we aren't going to do business with your company any more. That last guy was a real loser. Made all kinds of promises he couldn't deliver on, and then he'd never call us back. I've had it. Any company that would put a man like him on the road for them is off our list."

Smile and say, "Sir, please forgive me for what happened in the past before I joined the company."

"Nothing personal, but we've had enough."

"I understand what you're saying. But may I ask you to pretend something with me for just a moment? If you were the president of our company and it came to your attention that one of your salespeople was giving your customers the kind of service he gave you, what would you do?"

"I'd fire him."

Then you smile again and say, "That's what we did—and here I am."

But what if the last representative is now your manager, your boss, or is still with the company in some other capacity?

You smile and say, ". . . If you were the president of our company, and it came to your attention that one of your salespeople was terrible at follow-up even on very important business, but you also knew that this person had some great talents in areas you badly needed help in, how would you handle it?"

You're practically spelling out the answer for him, aren't you?

So he's going to give you a response along these lines: "Well, if he really had talents I needed, I suppose I'd try to put those talents to work where we could keep an eye on him."

Whatever they say about retraining the person in question, you reply, "That's what we did." Don't get into a long explanation. Stop the discussion of the old disasters right there and go with your presentation about the new and exciting things your company now has to offer.

2. Change their base.

Ask a question that highlights major benefits while it dwarfs minor objections.

Here's an example from real estate sales: You've shown the entire home and they like it. But, as you're walking with them down the hall after seeing the three bedrooms in the house, the husband suddenly starts fighting you.

"That last bedroom is too small," he says.

As you feed it back, intensify it to see whether it's more like a condition than an objection. "The third bedroom is too small for a guest room. In other words, it would be like you don't even have a guest bedroom, is that how you'd feel?"

"Well, not completely. But it's sure small."

If the wife doesn't jump in and overcome the objection for you, change his base. "Tell me, Mr. Bjornstad—and this is an important question, sir, because your answer can eliminate this house from consideration—what will you base your decision on, the warmth and liveability of the entire home, or a few inches in the guest room?"

Of course, he's going to pick the warmth and liveability of the entire home. If he doesn't, you better forget that house and find one they will buy.

You're with a prospect who is considering your medical insurance. She says, "Mr. Hopkins, one of my major concerns is that I'd really like to have the insurance company pay the doctor and hospital direct and save me all that hassle."

Your company doesn't handle things that way. So you ask in a cordial way, "Mrs. Wimmer, what will you base your decisions on — the method of payment or the quality of coverage for you and your family?"

She'll say, "The quality of coverage."

Then you eliminate the objection by saying, "Let's discuss the quality of the coverage for your family first, shall we?"

3. Question down.

The prospects walk into your retail store and settle by one of your stereos. When they ask questions, you give your demonstration and learn two things. They are Mr. and Mrs. Tellgren, and they want that stereo. You go through a few closes with no success, and then Mr. Tellgren says, "Thanks for your time. We'll think about it and let you know."

What does "I'll let you know" really mean in cases like this?

It means, "Now that I've found what I want, I'm going to shop around and see if I can buy it any cheaper."

Remember the rule. Always lead them toward answering their own objections.

"We'll look around and get back to you."

"Fine. That's a wise decision. Mr. Tellgren, I'd like to ask you a couple of questions. Were you impressed with the quality of the sound on this model?"

"Oh, yes."

"Is the cabinet the size you're looking for?"

"Well, yeah, it's about right."

"And I think you mentioned that you wanted adequate controls, but not something too elaborate. Does that model fit your needs on this?"

I gently list all the things they were pleased with. As I do this, I work in—very briefly—all the positive things I can: we service everything we sell, we have free delivery and installation, liberal credit terms, whatever. In a few cases, you'll be able to close them by striking a responsive chord with some of the services that you can offer. If not, you'll be able to get down to the final objection which, nine times out of ten, is money. When you get them to agree that the reason they won't buy right now is money, you've isolated your problem. The techniques for coping with this problem are given in chapters 12 and 15.

4. Review their history.

This technique is especially effective if your product or service is something that's bought on a regular, ongoing basis by organizations. You might be selling industrial raw materials, processing services, supply items, generic merchandise. The buying of these products and services often becomes a matter of habit: it's easier to keep on buying the same thing from the same source than it is to cope with change. Many suppliers don't really keep on their toes with their established accounts. Usually they put more value on acquiring new accounts than on keeping old ones, even though the cost of acquiring new accounts almost always far exceeds the cost of keeping old ones. And, of course, many successful suppliers become overly satisfied with their positions, and get careless. When they stop bringing fresh ideas to their established accounts and stop keeping in close personal touch, a gap starts opening up between the best and what they're giving. This means that the supplier isn't helping the customer keep up with change anymore—he's helping the customer fight the losing fight against change. The customer is falling behind and losing profits. The wider the gap grows, the more likely it becomes that someone in the competition will discover it. Then he'll charge in through that gap and capture the customer's business.

If you have established accounts, keep in close personal touch with them, make sure you keep them posted on all new developments in your industry, and stay alert to their best interests. If you're on the prowl to take over some of the competition's accounts, here's an effective way to continue when you hit their resistance to change.

You're selling service, FM radio advertising spots to be exact. Your station is K-WHEE. Red Eye Soap, a major radio advertiser, plays all their spots on K-TOO, a competing station. You're going for the business in a meeting with Jane Mota, Red Eye's advertising manager. (With many products and services, you'd have to ask what they're using now. In this case, you know because you listen to the competitive stations to see who's advertising on them.

"Are you satisfied with K-TOO, Mrs. Mota?"

"Oh, yes. They do a wonderful job for us."

She wants to discourage you so you'll be easier to get rid of. But you have a plan and press on.

"How long have you been using K-TOO?"

"About three years."

"And before K-TOO, did your firm do any radio advertising?"

"Red Eye started on K-ONE in the late sixties, I understand."

"May I ask how long you've been Red-Eye's advertising manager, Mrs. Mota?"

"I've been here five years."

"Then I'd probably be safe in thinking that you had a great deal to do with the switch from K-ONE to K-TOO."

"Yes, you would."

"And you recommended, or made, that switch based on quite a bit of research and analysis, didn't you?"

"Yes, on a tremendous amount of research. We made a detailed market analysis of ten stations. Our studies convinced us that our FM budget would influence more potential buyers on K-TOO than on any other station."

"You were looking for sales potential when you did your study three years ago, weren't you?"

"Certainly."

"And the results have lived up to your expectations?"

"Yes, they have. We're very satisfied."

"Tell me, since you received greater performance by considering, and then making, a change three years ago, why should you deny yourself the opportunity to repeat the process? Your research back then led to greater profits for Red Eye and greater professional prestige for you personally. You did it once, so the possibility must exist that you can do it again, don't you agree?"

"Yes, I have to agree with that; it's a possibility."

"Wonderful. It'll just take me a few moments to explore that possibility—"

She's given you the right to make your entire presentation. The last change worked out well, and she wants to look good to management. So now she has logical and emotional reasons to consider another change.

Isn't that a beautiful technique? What you have to do is adapt it to your offering, and then rehearse a number of variations so that you'll roll it off smoothly no matter what they say. Instead of going back to your manager and saying, "Red Eye's happy with K-TOO and they wouldn't talk to me," you'll deliver the freight. Learn the pattern, write out your approach, and practice it. Then the next time someone says to you, "We're happy with what we're buying now," you'll think to yourself, "You may be using them now, but within the hour, you're going to start getting happily involved with me."

The job of the Champion is to realize that he or she represents the finest product or service available, and then to make sure that everyone who can benefit from it owns it. After you get Mrs. Mota and Red Eye switched to K-WHEE, after you do your thorough job of followup and service, they'll all be delighted that they made the change. And you did it. It never would have happened unless you had adapted and learned the four shock treatments: put the shoe on their foot, question down, change their base, and review their history. Adapt, learn, and use all these techniques and you'll be well on your way to becoming the number one salesperson in your organization. Now that's exciting, isn't it?

14

CLOSING IS
SWEET SUCCESS

It's the winning score, the bottom line, the name of the game, the cutting edge, the point of it all. I've given you lots of techniques for prospecting, meeting people, building a flow of referrals, qualifying, presenting, demonstrating, overcoming objections, and they're all important. But, unless you can close, you're like a football team that can't sustain a drive long enough to score. It's no good if you play your whole game in your own territory and never get across their goal line.

So welcome to the delightful world of closing. If you don't love it now, start falling in love, because that's where the money is. Make no mistake about it, the money isn't anywhere else. When you learn how to use all of these closes, you'll be delighted with the results. You'll be able to get far more people happily involved in your offering than you ever were before.

A Champion is closing most of the time. He's constantly trying test closes, and he'll go into his final closing sequence anytime he sniffs the sweet smell of success. Many a salesman gets so wrapped up in his selling sequence that if the prospect wants it before he's through, he won't let them have it. Some people get sold fast. If you keep talking instead of closing them, you'll unsell them just as fast. After all, they can only buy it once today, so don't try to sell them twice. I've seen it happen. Some salespeople get so excited they can't stop talking when the buyer gives a sign that he's ready. Curb your urge to tell all. Don't be one of those who keep on plowing when it's time to harvest. I've watched salespeople literally grit their teeth as though to say, "You haven't heard it all yet, and by the sun that shines above, you're gonna hear it all before I'll take your order."

More talk just triggers more objections. When they're ready to run with it, shut up and start filling out the form.

Later I'll give you three test closes and twelve major closes. But first, let's study some specific closing tips:

1. ALWAYS HAVE YOUR CLOSING MATERIALS WITH YOU.

Be ready to close anytime and anywhere. Everyone has heard about all the sales that are made on golf courses. Business is also done on tennis courts, in spas and on boats, on jogging trails and at the track—anywhere, in fact, that people play, work, exercise, or relax. Yes, a lot of business is done outside offices and showrooms, and a lot of it soon falls apart. Why? Because the salesperson takes half a week to get his closing materials and the client together after the okay over the bottle of beer. By that time a different wind is blowing and the client has other things on his mind. In a word, he's un-closed. You've got to do it all over again—if you can. The second time around the emotional odds are against you.

When I say, "Have your closing materials with you at all times," I don't mean in your hip pocket on hole nine. Doing business on golf courses and in elegant eateries demands discretion. People hate it if their salad fork loses its chill because you pushed papers at them to approve. When you're selling in social circumstances, it can be tricky to find the right moment, so be ready to make that moment count. A supply of closing materials should take up permanent residence in your attache case, club locker, overnight bag, car trunk—and let's not overlook your office desk. Keep a cache of closing forms and materials in every place you regularly frequent.

2. WHEN DO YOU FLASH THE FORM?

Give careful thought to how and when you'll produce your closing materials. If you go into your full presentation and closing sequence and then reach into your briefcase to pull out the sales agreement or order pad, the prospect sees you do it, sucks in air, and tightens up. While you're flipping forms, he's thinking of ways to escape. Since you must get the forms out of your briefcase before you can write on them, and since doing that at a critical stage of the closing is likely to be unhelpful to the emotional climate, get them out sooner. You don't have to wave them in the air and sing out, "Watch out folks—this is my order pad." You don't need the whole pad. All you need is one form handy in your presentation binder.

3. WORK CLEAN.

Use crisp new forms, not the ones your dog chewed. If you pull out a form that looks like a baby's bib, your prospect will think you haven't made a sale in six months—and he won't want to break your streak.

4. FIND FIGURES WITH FINESSE.

Today's Champions do their selling arithmetic with a pocket calculator, not a pencil. Why? Because buyers believe calculators; they think their numbers must be right. If you're still penciling up the numbers in front of possible buyers, it's time to change. Sure, it feels more down-to-earth and human to scratch away with a pencil stub, but your clients are going to think that you can easily make a very human mistake.

5. MAKE YOUR PROOF LETTERS TALK.

Earlier, we discussed the value of getting proof letters. These are powerful tools to help other people get involved. The important thing to remember here is that the most powerful letters are those from people known to your prospects. The next most powerful are those from people who live nearby and are, therefore, easy for the prospect to check with.

When you have a proof letter from a local happy customer, you have a chance to create an even more powerful closing tool. This is the taped interview that you can play at strategic moments. With the development of the cassette player-recorder, making tapes is easier than making coffee. A portable unit costs less than a tank of gas, and it'll take you a thousand times further. With a cassette player, you can read books while you brush your teeth, drive to your next call, or do anything that requires less than your full attention. Cassette recorder-players are one of the few inventions of this century that really expand the amount of useful time available to you. The true Champion has a cassette player with him most of the time. He listens to good training and inspirational material to reinforce his positive thoughts and the techniques he already knows, and to learn new concepts and techniques. I begin every morning listening to a cassette program because it gives me a good feeling about starting the day. When I drive around in my car, I have a small earphone on that lets me absorb new insights and knowledge from cassettes. Why waste time listening to just music? Fill your mind with the power that is knowledge and you'll reap tremendous rewards.

Get a cassette player for education, and then use its recording capability to create a closing weapon that you can use with devastating effect—the recorded interview.

Let's say that you sell life insurance. One of your best clients is Dave Barkdale, who owns his own company. Dave has been an officer in local service clubs; he's served on civic committees; he's well thought of in the community.

You get on well with him and he was happy to write a proof letter. As you service his account, talk to some of the executives covered by Dave's keyperson insurance plan. After you introduce them on the tape, ask questions to get their feelings about having the additional life insurance for their families that the plan includes. After gathering some of this material, meet with Dave and tell him about the enthusiasm they expressed to you.

"Dave, it's obvious that your insurance program has generated a lot of company spirit among the key people it covers. Do you believe these feelings will have any effect on profits?"

"I think we've already seen results. Of course profits depend on many factors, but there's definitely an improved climate here that I trace directly to the installation of this insurance program."

"I'd like to ask you a favor, Dave. Many companies aren't taking advantage of keyperson insurance the way your firm is, and I really feel that there's a great need for improvement in this area of management. What I'd like to do is ask you some questions about your experience with our insurance and the service I've given your company, and record your feelings on my cassette. But, before asking you to do that, I want to make you some promises."

You've got to make some promises. Usually, what follows will about cover it.

"First of all, I promise that this material will be in my possession only, and it won't be reproduced. Secondly, I'll only play it for executives with companies that have attained a stature similar to yours. That I promise you."

With his agreement, start your machine, ask your questions, and let him talk. You might first say, "I'll just play Johnny Carson for a few minutes."

What does this remark trigger in his mind?

That he's in a relaxed, warm, and personal kind of interview situation. Your recorder should have a pause button so that you can omit silences and interruptions. And, if it doesn't quite go the way you want it to, just press the pause button and tell him, "Beautiful. That's just beautiful. But let me just try a new slant on it." Always encourage them. Keep it light. When you get him moving, you'll be amazed at what a forceful interview he'll give you.

Here's a vital point: End your interview with a strong close. "By the way, what you said about the special service I've given your company puts me on the spot.

"It means that I have to continue giving you and your company—and all my clients—very special service. But that's fine. That's my philosophy for doing business. Thanks, Dave, for your time."

What's exciting is the snowballing effect of cassette interviews. When you work with another executive who's having trouble making the decision, say to him, "Do you know Dave Barkdale? His situation was similar to yours, and I'd like you to hear what he said about our solution."

Then you play the cassette. Your happy client tells what a great job you've done, how happy they are, how they've benefited and increased profits.

And what will your new client want to do after he's happily involved with your product or service?

He'll want to make a tape for you too. It's an ego trip. And he'll want his tape to be better than your first one, so he'll work at it harder and maybe make several until he gets it perfect. It snowballs. By the time you're working with your fourth client, you'll have tapes of epic quality and sales effectiveness.

Some salespeople fight the idea of using this technique because they're afraid to ask — but some of your clients are hams who'll love the idea. If you've never used a cassette recorder-player, don't go for a client interview the first day you own one. Play around with the machine for a few hours and get used to it. Tape some interviews with your friends. Discover for yourself how simple it is and how fine the recordings are that these little portables make. Then write notes for questions that will start your client interviews off strongly. Don't press anyone who's self-conscious. You'll find that many of your clients will be delighted to cooperate with someone who's been a good supplier and a faithful servicer of their needs.

TEST CLOSES

Test closes are special questions. When answered, they show that the prospect has reached a high level of interest, and that they're happy and excited and ready to go further. When you ask a test question, you're looking for an answer that gives you positive stimulus. Here are three test closes:

1. THE ALTERNATE ADVANCE TEST CLOSE.

"Mr. Shealy, which delivery date would be best for you, the first or the fifteenth?"

When he says, "I'd need to have it in my shop by the first," what's happened? He's virtually bought it. Keep on with your closing sequence and you're in.

2. ERRONEOUS CONCLUSION.

A Champion listens all the way through his presentation for anything they say that he can use later for an erroneous conclusion test close. For example, you're in a home selling some kind of furnishings. During your demonstration, the wife tells her husband, "Honey, your mother's coming on the tenth. If we find what we want today, we ought to get it before then."

Many salespeople would ignore that remark, or regard it as an interruption. But the Champion hears it, and he remembers it.

Later, he might smile at the wife and say, "I can see that you're kind of excited about this design. Now, your mother's coming in on the fifth, is she?"

She'll say, "No, on the tenth."

"So about August 8 would be the best delivery date?"

"Yes."

"Let me make a note of that." Zap it on the order form.

You can use the erroneous conclusion test close on color, size—on almost anything. She might say, "Well, against our walnut paneling, I think the ebony would look best."

Later, you use that. "Let's see. You liked the bronze against the walnut paneling."

When she says, "No, I liked the ebony," you respond with, "Let me just make a note of that." Fill the information in on your order pad. If you make a mistake and they correct you, write it down and they own it. It's fun—and there's nothing to it.

3. PORCUPINE.

Here's another technique you already know from previous chapters. It's a terrific test close.

The prospect says, "Does that system come with the multiplex unit on the side?"

Your answer: "Do you want your system to have the multiplex unit on the side?"

When they say yes, they've bought.

Automobiles again. She's walking through your lot looking at colors. All of a sudden, the lady stops and points at a car. "The four-on-the-floor I think I'm interested in, do you have it in that shade of blue?"

This situation occurs thousands of times a day. The average knight of the car lot says, "If we don't have it in Morning-Surf Blue, I can sure call around and get one for you in a big hurry." And what does he have? Zilch.

But you answer, "Bernice, do you want it in Morning-Surf Blue?"

What's she going to say? Bernice has already told you that she's interested in the four-on-the-floor, and she likes that color.

When she says yes, hand her the keys.

HOW TO STEER SAFELY THROUGH THE MOST DANGEROUS CLOSING TIME

What's the most dangerous time in the closing sequence?

When you're busy doing any kind of calculating or writing, and the silence brings on the buyers' anxieties. While you're concentrating on your scribbling, the buyers don't have anything to occupy their minds except fear. This is why the Champion knows his forms so well that he can flash through them while he's talking casually to the clients and keeping them interested. You must have your paperwork routine down to a reflex action that won't soak up all your attention.

Most new salespeople lose their first two or three sales for just one reason: they lack the knowledge and practice to fill out their order form or sales agreement quickly enough. I'm serious. I discovered this in sales management. After that, when I hired a new person, I required that they spend a whole afternoon just filling out our forms. Then they could do it almost without thinking — certainly without concentrating fully on it and letting their prospects get cold feet.

THE CRASH AND BURN CLOSE

Keep the same emotional tone when you adapt all the material in this book to your own product or service. Let me illustrate what I mean with an example based on the porcupine close used as an alternate advance. Here's the salesmaster's version of the close:

Prospect:	Do you have it in blue?
Champion:	Would you like it in blue?
Prospect:	Yes.
Champion:	Let me make a note of that. (And he writes the information on the order form.)

When Mr. Average Salesloser adapts this close to his own product or service, here's what comes out:

Prospect:	Do you have it in blue?
Salesloser:	If I can get it for you in blue, will you buy it?
Prospect:	No, I don't think so. Say, uh, I didn't realize how late it's getting. Just leave your brochure and I'll call you when I have more time. Thanks for coming in.

Salesloser adapted this close like a wrecking ball adapts a brick building. The sentence, *If I can get it for you in blue, will you buy it,* is a say-no question that reverses a powerful positive thrust. What results is another version of the sorry old crash-and-burn. That close will put you on the street quicker than chewing gum with your mouth open.

MOVING TO THE MAJOR CLOSE

When a test close works, move softly but immediately to a major close. Most people, when they finally make up their minds, want it now. Talking about alternatives after they've zeroed in on one thing is playing with dynamite. Don't do it or a lot of sure sales will blow up in your face.

WHAT THE ACTUAL CLOSE IS.

Large numbers of people now at work in our profession (but not necessarily for much longer) don't know what a close is. Even more of our colleagues get confused here, and think their fits of impatience are closes. They only have about two anyway. The first goes like this:

"Well, what do you think?"

If that powerhouse doesn't charge the prospect with buying fever, they wait until the right opportunity comes along to jolt him with this one:

"Well, can I put you down for one?"

Now I ask you, is that closing? More like slamming the door, isn't it?

Let's take a long look at what effective closing technique really is. The first principle, the one you must always keep in mind if you're sincerely dedicated to developing your potential to its fullest, is this:

Closing is the process of helping people make decisions that are good for them.

Unless you base your actions on the understanding with yourself that it has to be good for the client or you won't close, you're trying to build success on false premises. Sooner, rather than later, those falsehoods will destroy everything you've built.

Having the ability to close strongly is, of course, a very good thing for you and your family because it enables you to earn a large income. There's another benefit of equal importance—closers are always in demand. If you know these techniques, you'll never have to use them to close people on bad propositions because you'll always be able to find good propositions to sell. In fact, because of this great skill that you'll then possess, you'll be compelled to find good propositions to close people on, and to avoid working for the companies that peddle wrongness.

It's called **noblesse oblige**. When you're a Champion, you're noble in the true sense of the word. Because you function above the level of the commonplace, you're obliged to have higher ethics. Otherwise, success poisons your spirit and robs you of satisfaction.

There are some highly skilled salespeople who deliberately help people make bad decisions. The top salespeople of this kind, the ones with the ability to manipulate lots of people into making disastrous decisions, are con men. They have to be locked up. A con man will sell anything to anybody, and he doesn't care what happens to them after he does. The con man, of course, is a criminal, and not enough of them are behind bars. The Champion, the professional salesperson, can't be a con man because he or she demands more of life than merely money. The Champion demands the satisfaction of being a positive force in the world, and can't sell anything he knows isn't good for the buyer.

There are a lot of people in this world who really believe that they're going to get ahead faster by caring nothing for others. Unfortunately, some of these people are in sales, and they don't help our reputation. But there's another side to this: overly greedy salespeople make you look great by contrast. Concern for your buyers' welfare is enlightened self-interest. Does it really pay?

I know it does. Lasting success can only be built on a foundation of personal integrity that will support the faith and trust others must have in you.

CLOSE WITH EMPATHY

When I say you must close with empathy, I don't mean that you have any difficulty closing when it's to the prospect's benefit to be closed. Because, unless you have the ability to call for, and frequently get, a positive decision, everybody loses. Your family loses. Your company loses. The national economy loses. But the biggest loser is the client, who didn't get the benefits because you couldn't close.

If you don't develop this skill of calling for and getting a favorable decision that we call closing, it will probably force you out of the profession of selling. At best, you'll be able to stay in it only as an ordertaker. That means, of course, that you'll only earn ordertaker's wages. If you want to earn a professional selling income, make a commitment now to learn how to call for, and get, favorable decisions.

Except for the regular purchases of everyday life, the average person can't make decisions about investing in anything without help. The reason so many people need help in making decisions is that they're afraid of making bad ones. Indecision is one of the great destroyers. It drives a few people crazy, and saps the energy of most of us. The one quality I find in all great human beings is their ability to make decisions. I've seen another quality in all the great people I've known: they don't have to be right all the time. They know that if they're right a small part of the time—and are quick to cut their losses when they're wrong—they'll prosper.

Insecurity causes procrastination, and that leads to indecision. Procrastination is the art of living in your yesterdays, avoiding your todays, and ruining your tomorrows. When you finish this chapter, future Champion, I hope you'll share this belief with me:

People love to buy after they own.

They only have problems with indecision, insecurity and procrastination before they own. That's why the Champion becomes skilled at making people feel that they already own it.

LIKES AND DISLIKES

Many salespeople have a problem with their likes and dislikes. They only sell what they like to the people they like, and make only a fraction of the best income they could achieve. Cater to your own preferences on your own time. During business hours, enthusiastically sell what the customer likes, not what you like; enthusiastically work with all types of people qualified to buy your product or service. By this I don't mean that you should work with vicious or destructive people, but simply that, to reach your full potential, you must expand your comfortable working zone until you can effectively help people with backgrounds and lifestyles that greatly differ from your own. If you can't work with someone because your mental outlook is too narrow, you lose. The prospect doesn't. He'll find someone else to supply his needs and make the money.

CLOSE THROUGH THEIR EYES

Several years ago I attended a huge banquet for real estate agents. Before I gave my talk, the speaker introduced someone in the audience and said, "This man earned twice the national average in residential real estate sales last year —"

The speaker's manner suggested that it was quite an achievement. But it wasn't all that impressive, so everyone craned their necks and looked at the man in puzzlement.

"— and he's totally blind." There was a burst of applause. When that quieted, the speaker said, "I'm sure that many of us are wondering how you got into the top third in sales achievement with that handicap."

"Wait a minute," the blind man replied over a portable microphone, "I don't have a handicap, I have an advantage over every other salesperson in this area. I've never seen a property I've sold, so I have to close my buyers through their eyes. What I'm forced to do, all you sighted people could do—and you'd serve your clients better and make more money if you did."

It was quiet in the hall for a moment while everyone thought that over, and then there was another spontaneous round of applause for this courageous man who could hold his own selling blind, and still offer sage advice to the rest of us.

The point is, you must see the benefits and features and limitations of your product or service from your potential buyer's viewpoint; you must weigh them on his scale of values, not your own; you must close on the benefits that are of value to him.

And you must radiate the conviction that you can satisfy their needs. After you've qualified them and discovered their true motives, you must start radiating confidence that you know how to cope with their requirements. If, instead of that, you radiate a profound doubt about your ability to fill their wants, why do they need you? Buyers need to have a feeling of confidence before they can rationalize the decision they really want to make.

The last time you bought an automobile—did you spend more than you wanted to? If it was a new car, did you go into the showroom with the firm intention of not buying any extras—and drive out loaded with options? If so, you met a professional salesperson who helped you rationalize the decision you really wanted to make.

Aren't you glad when you tilt the seat back, adjust the right hand mirror from the inside, listen to stereophonic sound, and relax in cool air when it's sweltering outside? Of course you are — and the small additional cost on your monthly investment is forgotten.

WHEN DO YOU CLOSE?

There's a certain tenseness, a certain electricity in the air when they're ready. Start your closing sequence:

- When they've been coming along at a certain pace, and suddenly they slow that pace down.
- Or when they suddenly speed that pace up.
- When they've mostly been listening, and suddenly they start asking lots of questions.
- When they give you positive stimulus at the right time. Some people come in and immediately start asking questions about delivery and initial investments before they've settled on a particular model. They know they're safe because you can't close them on the whole store. But if they ask these same questions after you know exactly what they want, it's positive stimulus. So are questions about guarantees and cancellation options. Use a test close after getting positive stimulus.
- When they favor your test close.

WHERE DO YOU CLOSE?

When you know they're ready, don't stand on ceremony. Close anywhere. You may think you've got to haul them up the stairs and down the hall to your office. You don't. Highlight this so you'll remember to make it part of your creed:

I am always ready to close anywhere, anytime.

Most sales are made on the hoods of cars, in restaurants, on the customer's desk, standing in display rooms, on kitchen tables, and in countless other places that are not designed primarily for closing business. For many people, there's a special excitement about executing a decision right now. Most of us feel joy at having the mental strain behind us; we see only the pleasures of ownership ahead. Don't spoil it for your people—and risk having them cool off about buying—by insisting on squishing down in your favorite swivel chair before writing up the sales agreement.

But keep in tune with their feelings. Some people can't handle the idea of approving the paperwork on the run—and if you press them to, they'll pull back, fearful that there are sinister reasons behind your haste. So close where they want to be closed, not where you want to go for that purpose.

THE ANATOMY OF THE CLOSE

Let's cut the close into pieces and see how it goes together.

1. UNDERSTAND WHAT THEY WANT AND NEED.

(a) **Qualify them thoroughly.** Determine their emotional wants, and ability to pay.

(b) **Understand the buyer's motives.** If your buyer tells you, "I just hate that," explore their feelings. Don't simply say, "I don't like it much myself," and go on talking. Find out why they hate that feature so you'll understand their motives in wanting one thing and rejecting another.

2. RECOGNIZE BUYING SIGNS.

People often tell you they want what you're selling by giving you signs instead of saying so. There are two kinds of signs the Champion watches for:

(a) **Verbal.** They ask more questions. They develop a need for more technical data. They talk about things that would happen if they owned your offering. Sometimes, they'll simply start making agreeable sounds all of a sudden.

(b) **Visual.** A smile can be an important buying sign. Their eyes may light up or start twinkling. If your buyers are husband and wife, they may show more affection and consideration for each other after they find the right home, car, appliance, insurance policy, or whatever. Wanting to see it demonstrated again is one of the strongest buying signs. When they say, "Will you go over that one more time," they've almost always bought it.

3. MAKE THE DECISION.

Decide that the best thing for them to do is to buy it. Then lead them through that decision by working on things they like and feel are important. What appeals to you about your offering has no place in the picture—only what's important to them about the purchase does.

4. CLOSE THE SALE WITH CASUAL CONFIDENCE.

You've asked questions and led them to the close. Now casually start writing the order. You'll be amazed at how often that's all it takes. Unless they stop you, they've bought. If your tactics are sound and your timing is right, they won't stop you.

5. DON'T CHANGE WHEN YOU START CLOSING.

Speak warmly and use glamour words as you close. But don't change your tone, manner, or the pace at which you speak when you go into the closing sequence. Be very careful about this. Many salespeople do great until they see their buyers are ready. Then they suddenly change. The warm, friendly style the buyers have become used to vanishes, and a tense manner takes its place.

Every time a prospect freezes up because of this sudden change and walks out without buying, that salesperson is more likely to repeat the same mistake in the next closing situation. Remember this:

If you tense up and change manner when starting to close, the clients will know what's happening and they'll bite you. Your closes must be so thoroughly learned that you use them with relaxed alertness.

6. USE THE PLANNED PAUSE.

Champions use a very simple technique: when they want the client to really listen, they pause and look intently at the other person until they get his full attention.

THE FOURTEEN MOST IMPORTANT WORDS IN THE ART OF CLOSING

Next I'm going to give you a priceless dozen plus two. This is the most powerful pair of sentences that have ever been spoken about the complex, demanding, and enormously well paid art of closing. Please lock these words in your memory and never forget them. If you've skimmed through this book so far and haven't marked anything yet, get your highlighter out now. Here they are:

Whenever you ask a closing question, shut up. The first person to speak loses.

The paramount phrase is *shut up*. That's why J. Douglas Edwards shouts it at his audiences. I was sitting in the front row the first time I heard the fourteen words, all jumpy from the excitement of his seminar, the sleepless nights of studying it, the gallons of coffee I'd put away. When Doug shouted SHUT UP, I dove for cover. My papers flew in every direction. The moment is carved in my memory—along with the words. Those fourteen words have been the most important single element in turning my disastrous sales experience up to that time into the pacemaking success it soon became.

Ask your closing question—then shut up. It sounds simple. Believe me, it isn't. I know. At the time, I had a real problem in that area—and the worst part was that I didn't have a clue as to what I was doing wrong until the moment I originally heard J. Douglas Edwards say those fabulous fourteen words.

The first time I tried asking a closing question and then shutting up, I was prepared for the other people's reaction. I expected them to keep silent. What I hadn't prepared for was the intensity of my own reaction: the silence hit me like a ton of wet sand. Doug Edwards said I would feel the pressure of that silence keenly, but I didn't really think it would affect me much. It did. I sat there that first time with my insides churning, biting the inside of my lip. Finally, the husband said something. They went on to buy—and I never again had as much trouble sweating out the awful silence after asking a closing question.

Why is it so important to shut up and not say a word? Because if you say anything, you relieve the pressure on the prospect to speak first, answer the close, and commit himself to buy. When you ask the closing question at anywhere near the right time, the prospect has to go ahead—or announce that he's asked you to shoot at ducks that aren't there.

Here's how it goes. You've been working with Maggie Thrush, the purchasing agent for a medium-sized company, and you feel that she's ready for the close. So you say, "Mrs. Thrush, we've just about covered everything. Which would be more convenient, delivery on the first or the fifteenth of next month?"

The average salesperson can't wait more than ten seconds after asking a closing question like that. If Mrs. Thrush hasn't answered by then, he'll say something like, "Well, we can talk about that later," and go on talking, unaware that he's just destroyed the closing situation.

And it's not just that one close he's destroyed. All succeeding closing situations—if any more do come up—are doomed to failure. Mrs. Thrush can't be closed because now she knows how to escape this salesperson's closes. She merely has to keep quiet for a few seconds and he'll crack under the pressure. Mrs. Thrush can always keep quiet for a few seconds—almost all undecided buyers can. If you're Champion material, you can sit there with your mouth shut all afternoon if you have to. You'll rarely need to hold on more than thirty seconds. This is something to practice. It takes concentration because if you say anything, or even make much of a gesture, you'll relieve the pressure and blow your chances of closing.

Although having the skill, the courage, and the concentration to sit still and be silent for half a minute is the most vital single skill there is in selling—and despite the fact that this is the easiest thing there is to practice—very few people have done just that. It isn't something you can practice driving down the street though. For it to work, you have to sit in a place you might very well be closing in and concentrate on doing nothing and saying nothing for thirty seconds. I'm very serious when I say, practice that when you're alone. Then it won't be so nerve-wracking when big money rides on how calm and silent you can be in a real closing situation.

YOU WEAR THE SUIT OF LIGHTS

I once saw a bullfight on TV. About three minutes into it, I began to see parallels between the broad aspects of bullfighting and selling. So come with me to the arena, where thousands of people are watching—like all the people you know are watching the progress of your sales career.

A roar goes up as a ton of live beef charges onto the sand. The bull—the client—has entered the arena.

Then the matador comes out in his "suit of lights" and all of a sudden it gets quieter—like when you go in to make your presentation.

Who has the advantage now?

The bull outweighs a dozen matadors and is armed with animal fury and sharp horns. The matador at this point is armed only with a cloth cape and courageous skill. Isn't that the usual sales situation? The client has the absolute power to buy or not buy from you, and you have only your technique and courage.

You can't overpower your client for the same reason the matador can't overpower his—the strength is all on the other side. Like the matador, you must have superior skill to win against the odds you face every time you step out onto the hot sand of the sales arena.

The first thing the matador uses is the cape—to lead the bull and establish moral ascendancy over him. This is what I'm advocating that you do with your prospects. Lead them with questions. Establish a moral ascendancy. Develop a sense in them of your expertise on your offering.

When your prospect snorts, stamps the ground, and then charges at you, do you meet that charge head on? Not unless you want to be carried out on a stretcher. Of course, your wounds won't be visible. You'll walk out on your own two feet. But you'll be hurt in your pocketbook, confidence, and pride.

No, you don't clash heads when your prospect charges into you. Instead, you step aside like a matador and let the prospect run. You listen to his grunts and stompings and watch which way he hooks with his horns like the matador does. And then you work with him, getting closer all the time, leading with questions and more questions.

Tell me more, he says. Tell *me* more, you think. You ask and you answer. You use your cape with exquisite technique and finesse, and in a predetermined sequence gain control of your more powerful opponent.

To hold the crowd's admiration and end the match cleanly, the matador must go in over the bull's horns at exactly the right time and put the tip of his sword through a point the size of a quarter. That's a good description of what the skillful closing of a large and difficult sale is. Both in bullfighting and in sales, the time of greatest danger comes at the close of the performance, and the matador's final thrust is much like your final close. For the unskilled, the unpracticed, the unprepared, the close in selling is like the matador's estocada over the horns of a fighting bull. In both cases, it's all or nothing—the only things that count are knowledge, technique, and courage.

I often think about my introduction to many of the techniques in this book. As I sat there in Doug's seminar that first morning, I was mentally challenging the material. In fact, I think I was spending more energy fighting it than trying to learn it. Suddenly I caught a glimpse of what knowing these techniques could mean—a sort of future-flash. During the next few moments I made a conscious and highly emotional decision to throw away my fears and give it all I had. Five days later I came out of that training with confidence in my heart and determination in my soul. For about two months I applied everything I could remember or pull out of a quick review of my notebooks. Before the training, I hadn't even been making gasoline money; after the training I started making ends meet. That was a tremendous improvement percentagewise. But I wasn't satisfied to merely get by—I wanted to fly high.

I sat down one evening and went over every word of my notes on Doug's seminar. What an amazing experience that was. I could hardly believe how much I'd overlooked and failed to grasp—and how much I'd forgotten after just sixty days. Only then did I realize that I'd only sampled what this material could do for me. I had learned several valuable tricks, but I hadn't really mastered the entire range of techniques. And my adaptation of the material to my product, personality, and area was but a shadow of what it could be.

But I had felt its power.

So I went back to work on my notebooks, and hammered at that material. I mastered every concept, adapted every technique, and practiced every skill until I felt in my bones that it was all mine. Suddenly it *was* me—and I was it. And then my income started shooting up. It doubled, doubled again—and kept on growing. Before long I set the goal of $100,000 a year—something I hadn't even thought of achieving a few months before. In those days that was considered to be a monumental income for a salesperson.

When I had really mastered the techniques I'm giving you in this book, I found it wasn't difficult to achieve that level the first time. Then I discovered something. Making that much money the second time is rather easy; once you've done it, once you know you can, it's not hard at all. Now, many years later, after having trained thousands of Champions who earn incomes that are top level in their company's sales forces, I've had the opportunity to ask many great salespeople how they close.

One question I've asked many times: How many closes do you try before you succeed?

Among the great ones, it averages out at about five closes. That is, the great ones usually close after their fifth attempt. You can immediately see from this extremely important bit of information that if the great ones have to use five closes to succeed, you're not going to get very far in sales if you only know two closes—or none. If they have more reasons for not going ahead than you have techniques for helping them go ahead, they aren't going ahead. It's that simple.

Learn these closes conceptually. Then learn them word for word. Adapt them to your needs. Then learn your adaptations word for word. You're probably fighting the idea of doing all this work. I know. I fought it too, at first. But just remember that there's an alternative to learning and growing and paying the full price of switching to success—you can try to stay just as you are. Good luck—the world is rapidly changing all around you.

15

TWELVE POWER CLOSES FOR ASPIRING CHAMPIONS

Every time you master one of these closes, you'll increase your sales by at least ten percent. You may double your sales with each close that you master. You may even do better than that.

One or two of these techniques may not apply to your operation. Most of them will. Adapt every one that you possibly can, and then practice your adaptations until you can use them with conviction, warmth, and flair while planning your next move in another pocket of your mind.

Suppose you can only use ten of these closes, and each one of them, on the average, increases your sales by only ten percent. That means you've doubled your volume and, probably, more than doubled your net income after expenses. If you don't do at least this well, you haven't mastered these closes.

Now let's get at them:

1. THE BASIC ORAL CLOSE.

This is used primarily for industrial, commercial, and governmental sales. When you've defined the needs you can fill, ask this question:

"By the way, what purchase order number will be assigned to this requisition?"

When they tell you they don't know, smile and say, "Why don't we find out?"

In most of these situations—industrial, commercial, and governmental sales—you haven't made the sale until you get "the P.O. number." So start hunting for that number at the first reasonable moment.

2. THE BASIC WRITTEN CLOSE.
(THE "LET ME MAKE A NOTE OF THAT" CLOSE.)

This is an effective close if you use an order form. Walk in with a leather binder for a letter or legal size ruled pad. Have an order form there under a cardboard separator to protect it. This allows you to flip to it instantly when the time is right. My favorite way to work with this close is to answer a question of theirs with one of my own.

Prospect:	"Does it come in walnut?"
Champion:	"Would you like it in walnut?"
Prospect:	"Yes, that's the color I'd prefer."
Champion:	"Let me make a note of that."

Then write that bit of information on your order form.

Prospect:	"What are you doing? I'm not ready to give you an order."
Champion:	"Mrs. Palmer, I organize my thoughts and keep every-thing in the proper perspective. I do that on the paper-work so I don't forget anything." (If it suits your product or service, add: "particularly anything that could cost you time or money.")

Then roll on to the next close. Go into every closing sequence by asking a reflex question. A reflex question, you'll remember, is any question they can answer without thinking.

Champion:	"Mary, do you have a middle initial?"
Prospect:	"It's 'H.' "

For a corporate executive, a good reflex question is to ask for his company's complete name and correct address. If he hands you his card and lets you copy that information on your order form, he's bought what you're selling.

Let's run this close through an industrial situation. You sell machinery, and Mr. Zale is your prospect.

Mr. Zale:	"Yes, we'd need the heavy-duty gear box."
Champion:	"Let me make a note of that."
Mr. Zale:	"Are you putting that on your order form? You're getting ahead of yourself. I haven't decided to buy it yet."

I'm repeating the twenty-one words that the Champion says next because they're the heart of this close. Read them again. Highlight them. Memorize them. And use them to advance on the close.

Champion:	"Mr. Zale, I organize my thoughts and keep everything in proper perspective. I do that on the paperwork so I don't forget anything."
Mr. Zale:	"You're probably wasting your time. At this point, the odds are against me buying from your company."
Champion:	"Oh, I know that. But I just don't like to risk forgetting anything — particularly anything that might cost you time or money."
Mr. Zale:	"Well, I guess I can't quarrel with that."

Perhaps you think you'd be better off making your notes on the legal pad so you could save yourself the hassle. If you decide to do that, you've also decided to demote yourself from salesperson to ordertaker. Let them stop you. It helps, not hurts, to have them understand that you're a strong seller who's there to do a job, not a pencil nibbler who doesn't know how to make things move.

Keep filling out that order form. By the time you've gone through your entire presentation, it's going to be almost entirely filled out. In many cases, the forward motion you've developed by completing your order form will be enough to get it approved. It becomes the easiest thing for the prospect to do. Once your pen touches your order form, your run for home starts. If they get used to having you make notes on the order form, you're halfway there. If you can make a note of the exact model they want, you've turned the last corner for home. The problem with most salespeople is that they won't start writing during the sales interview. They just exercise their vocal cords.

3. THE BENJAMIN FRANKLIN BALANCE SHEET CLOSE.

When I was involved in the high intensity five-day seminar with J. Douglas Edwards, we had a contest in the form of an examination on the last day. I wanted to win that contest. So I sat up, studied late, and got by on about two hours of sleep a night. The item that won the contest for me was the Ben Franklin Balance Sheet Close.

Salespeople frequently tell me that they've heard of this close. When they say that, I ask, "Do you use it?"

Almost always they say no. This never ceases to amaze me because I paid for the farm with this one. It's one of the most magnificent closes that have ever come into the selling profession. Maybe I shouldn't be amazed, because I fought it at first—but I did try it. Not only did I try it, I made it work and I still use it. Let me tell you about the first time.

The buyer looked at me and said, "I just can't make the decision now."

I thought, "I've just spent five days learning a lot of techniques. The Ben Franklin seems like the best one for this situation—why not try it? I can't see any other way to close him."

I excused myself, left the room, got my workbook, made sure I had it cold, and went back in. Then I went through the Ben Franklin step by step—and they approved the agreement. That was one of my first big successes with the material, and after that I used the Ben Franklin Close every chance I got. I couldn't even guess at how much money I made with it.

You may worry that clients have heard the Ben Franklin before. Don't. I'll show you how to handle that situation in a moment. Always remember this: if you've qualified them, if they need your offering, if you know what you're selling and if you're strong in your tactics, they can fight you, but they can't win. You'll win—you'll sell them.

By the way, I really do depend on this technique for arriving at many decisions in my private and business life. That's true of many people. You may at any time find yourself working with a client who makes use of it as a regular part of his decision-reaching process. Here's the Ben Franklin Balance Sheet Close:

(a) Validate it with good old Ben.

If you went to elementary school in the U.S., you'll remember studying Benjamin Franklin's life and epic achievements. On his way to eternal fame, he made thousands of wise decisions. This close is based on the actual way he arrived at decisions, and much of its persuasiveness comes from our respect for his name. Introduce it by invoking his name.

(b) Learn the exact words.

Do that first, and then let your adaptation come naturally. Here are the words:

"As you know, sir, we Americans have long considered Benjamin Franklin one of our wisest men. Whenever old Ben found himself in a situation such as you're in today, he felt pretty much as you do about it. If it was the right thing, he wanted to be sure and do it. If it was the wrong thing, he wanted to be sure and avoid it. Isn't that about the way you feel, too?

"Here's what old Ben used to do. He'd take a sheet of plain paper and draw a line down the middle. On this side he wrote *yes*, and under that he'd list all the reasons favoring the decision. Then, under *no*, he'd list all the reasons against the decision. When he was through, he simply counted the columns and his decision was made for him.

"Why don't we try it and see what happens? Let's see how many reasons we can think of that favor your decision today."

Take a piece of paper and start listing all the benefits you've discovered that appeal to them, that is, all the selling points that you and the prospect have agreed on. When the two of you have written down all the yeses, here's what you say:

"Now let's see how many reasons you can think of against it." And you let the prospect handle this part of it on his own. It's no part of your business to help him list negatives. When that's completed, move forward with:

"Now let's count them." (Do it out loud.) "One, two, three . . . twenty-four. That's twenty-four on the *yes* side. And on the *no* side we have, one, two, three, four, five. Twenty-four yeses and five noes. Well, the wise decision is pretty obvious, isn't it, sir?"

Don't hesitate more than a split second here. Go right into a reflexive closing question:

"By the way, what is your full name?"

If they give it to you now, they own your product or service.

Here's the Ben Franklin close as done in a corporation executive's office:

". . . so I feel that adding the JLG Lift to your facility might be a wise decision, don't you?"

Frank replies, "Well, Tom, this is a pretty expensive investment here. I don't know—it's not that I have any trouble making decisions —"

"I'm sure not. You make decisions on this level all day long, of course."

Frank mutters absently, "Yeah."

I can see that he really doesn't want to bite the bullet. He's impressed with the JLG lift. He needs it. The numbers work out. He knows his company will profit greatly by having this lift—but he's hoping for a way out of committing himself. In other words, he's behaving like a typical buyer. So I wheel up my Ben Franklin gun:

"Could it possibly be, Frank, that one of the problems is that you haven't had a chance to weigh the facts involved?"

"Yes," Frank says. "I think that I haven't really gotten down to the nub of this thing yet."

"Well, a decision is only as good as the facts, isn't that right?"

"I believe that's true," Frank says.

"You know, it's interesting—a while back I was reminded of a man we Americans have long considered one of our wisest men—Benjamin Franklin."

"Oh, Tommy—you're not going to pull the old Ben Franklin close on me, are you?" Frank laughs out loud. "I used to be in insurance. I heard about that one in a seminar a long time ago."

That doesn't bother me because I know it's likely to happen once in a while. I go along with it. "You know what's amazing?"

"What's that?" Frank says, still chuckling.

"When I first heard about the technique, I thought, 'I don't know.' Let me ask you this, did you try it? Did you use it selling insurance?"

"Oh, no," Frank says. "I never used it." (It actually doesn't matter much whether he did or not. My purpose here is to relieve tension and then lead him on through the close. If he has experiences with this technique to relate, fine. If not, it's still fine. In either case, I'm going to move ahead.)

"It's a funny thing," I tell Frank. "I decided to try Ben's system not only in my business life, but I started doing it on personal questions—and pretty soon I had my whole family using it to solve all sorts of problems. Amazing. We started making some excellent decisions. Do you remember how it goes?"

"I remember—you draw a line and you put the yeses on one side, and the noes on the other."

"Right. On this side you list all the reasons favoring the decision, and on the other side, all those that weigh against the decision."

"Yeah, right," Frank says.

The important thing here is to keep going with the flow of the conversation, rather than to try to stick rigidly with a set of words you've learned like a parrot. When you've mastered the material, you can wander on both sides of the path and still get where you're going.

I continue with, "Ben Franklin said if it's the right thing to do, he wanted to be sure he knew about it so he could go ahead. And if it was the wrong thing, he wanted to be sure to avoid it. Isn't that more or less what you're going to do now? Analyze the decision and get down to the nub of it, as you put it?"

Frank shrugs. "Yeah, that's what it boils down to."

"So you're going to list all the reasons favoring the decision on one side, and all those against the decision on the other side. Then you'd do as old Ben would do: add the columns up and the decision is made for you."

"Well, I'd like to think my method of analysis is a bit more sophisticated than that."

"I'm sure it is. But if the reasons for and against are sound, a count of them would certainly point the way toward the right decision, wouldn't it?"

"Well, I suppose so."

"We both know the Ben Franklin method. It's logical. It's simple. Emotionally, at this point, I think we ought to try it. May we?"

"Well —" Frank lets it hang.

"We've got the time, haven't we? A couple of minutes —"

"Yeah, okay."

"Let's start it off here. Let's think of the reasons favoring the decision," I say. "We agreed originally that if one person in the basket could operate the whole vehicle and eliminate the need for the second operator, you'd realize a large savings in labor cost. Isn't that right?"

"Yes it is," Frank says.

"And I sent a man out for one purpose only, you'll remember, to measure all your doors. So we know that the JLG can get to every part of your facility."

"Right—it fits through all our doors," Frank says.

"I made sure of every one of them."

"All right—that's an important point."

"The biggest problem that a lot of hydraulic equipment has—I know you're aware of this—is in the seals. The hydraulic seals. That's why the JLG has the finest heavy-duty seals that are available."

"No leaking?" Frank asks.

"No, none."

"All right."

"The JLG is far more agile. It can go into smaller spaces and get the work done."

"Okay."

"And it's got a smaller turning radius."

"Yeah, that's a factor. We've got some narrow squeezes at the end of aisles."

"Multiple uses in maintenance," is my next yes point. "For maintaining your facility—how many uses do you have for that lift? The eighty-foot boom if you wanted it, the twenty-foot—the JLG has outstanding versatility, don't you agree?"

"All right. Put it down."

"Local servicing is available. Now that'll cut out a lot of downtime, and you know how much it costs to have a machine sitting there waiting for parts."

"Yeah, that's true," Frank says.

"We were looking at the tax benefits. We felt that a least might be better that purchase because of the tax savings, and of course keeping the cash flow —"

"Okay."

"If you decide to build the warehouse, Frank, you won't have to worry about not having the finest crane equipment. We've got them. It's not like we give you the lift and say, 'Goodbye.' No way. We stick with you. Let me think, can you come up with any others, Frank?"

"Well, your lift has higher maximum load capabilities than the others."

"Okay, we'll put that down. Now Frank, how many reasons can you now come up with on the negative side?"

Frank thinks for a moment and then says, "Well, okay, number one, this is not planned in our current budget. And what about our present equipment? I'd want to do something with it because I know how the guys in the plant are—if the JLG was busy, they'd just wait for it instead of using the old klunker we've got now. So I'd have to get rid of it—sell it or trade it in."

"Those are both valid points, Frank. When you're right, you're right. Okay, I've got them. Any others?"

After a pause, it's apparent that Frank isn't coming up with any more objections. As you can see, both his points are really money. I don't want to get into that right at this moment, so I say, "Why don't we just add them up?"

I count out loud and announce the results: nine yeses and two noes. "Frank, don't you really think that the answer is rather obvious?"

I expect to wait through a long silence now. The key thought here is, **shut my mouth**. Frank doesn't disappoint me. There isn't a sound in the room for some time while Frank thinks this over. At last he speaks, "I'll tell you something, Tom. I'm the kind of a guy who just has to think it over."

Could you pick up off this cold printed page how nicely and warmly this technique was delivered? That's how techniques should all be handled: in a relaxed and alert, friendly and respectful, confident and competent manner.

4. THE SHARP ANGLE CLOSE.

This carries the porcupine technique (discussed earlier) to a higher level of effectiveness. Instead of merely answering a question with a question as in the standard porcupine, answer with one that, if they reply the way their original question indicates they will, they've bought it.

In this example of sharp-angling, you're still leading Mr. Zale toward buying a batch mixer.

Mr. Zale:	"If we decided to go with your product, we'd have to take delivery by June 15. Could you handle that?" (Most salespeople would be tempted to jump in, say yes, and have nothing. Note how a professional takes advantage of this opportunity.)
Champion:	"If I could guarantee delivery by June 15, are you prepared to approve the paperwork today?"

The Champion, of course, now remains silent until Mr. Zale answers. In order to use the sharp-angle close, you first have to maneuver them into making a demand or expressing a desire that you can meet. There are many demands or desires (that is, needs) that you can sharp-angle besides delivery. Getting an order in before a price increase takes effect is a powerful one. Credit terms, installation assistance, and color choice are others. Almost any benefit that people want can be sharp-angled.

Favorable delivery is the benefit that's easiest to sharp-angle in most sales organizations because it's the most predictable. And, because it's a universal situation, the delivery question lends itself to further detailing of the sharp-angling idea. Bear in mind that the principles suggested are easily applied to whatever benefit you can most effectively sharp-angle to sell your product or service.

Sharp-angling involves two pivotal points: (a) you must know what benefits you can deliver, and (b) you have to know how to pan the gold from that information. We've already shown you how to handle (b). Now let's talk about (a). Using the information is the easy part; getting it is about ninety-nine percent of the battle. I want to emphasize this point:

> **A Champion develops superior sources for sharp-angling information because he understands what a powerful closing lever that information is.**

I'm going to continue to talk about sharp-angling information as though it was the same thing as delivery information, but again I remind you that other benefits may provide you with better sharp-angling tools than being able to offer favorable delivery.

One of the reasons why Champions outsell average salespeople five to one (or more) is that they know five times as much about what their company can deliver—and when—than the average salesperson does.

How do they get this information?

The answer, of course, depends on the product and the company. Many losers in the sales department tend to make enemies in the production department and on the shipping dock. The Champion makes friends in both places. He knows they crave recognition just like other folks do. He isn't above sending thank-you notes to people in the organization who help him in the normal course of business. Nor is he insensitive to the fact that shipping dock and production people are on fixed incomes; that many of them would welcome an occasional lunch, dinner, or beer after work. Avoid big-shotting them. You can't make friends playing Hot Stuff Harry.

The Champion builds his information network on the standard delivery data put out through channels. He doesn't fight the system, he helps it function effectively by working with it and adding to it from his own connections and sources.

5. THE SECONDARY QUESTION CLOSE.

When used at the right moment with the right people, this close can snap shut like a bear trap.

Here's the technique: Pose the major decision with a question, and without pausing add another question that is an alternate advance involvement question. That's a mouthful, so I'll give you an example that'll make it clear. You're walking around the plant with the head man at Frankly Better Products, a manufacturing operation. Frank is pondering whether to buy a JLG Lift from you. Sensing that the moment is right for the Secondary Question Close, you say,

"As I see it, Frank, the only decision we have to make today is how soon you'll start enjoying the increased profits the JLG Lift will make for you—by the way, are you going to use it in your main plant or your new warehouse?"

Let's try this SQC technique on a service you're selling.

"As I see it, Frank, the only decision we have to make today is how soon you'll start enjoying the increased profits that a happier staff will make for you—by the way, are you going to pipe the music into your offices and warehouse only, or to the entire plant?"

You can easily adapt this format to any product or service. The major decision is introduced with these words:

"As I see it, the only decision we have to make today is how soon. . . ."

The major decision is then followed, without pause, by the secondary question that you introduce with these words:

"By the way."

To use the Secondary Question Close successfully, you must:

(a) State the major decision in terms of a benefit to the client:
"The only decision . . . is how soon you'll start enjoying (the benefit)."
Never pose the major decision in negative terms: ". . . how soon you'll stop losing money. . . ." Of, even worse yet, in aggressive terms that are thinly disguised by an attempt at humor: ". . . how soon you'll get on the ball and start saving money by ordering from me."

(b) Avoid any pause between posing the major decision and asking the secondary question.

(c) State the secondary question in terms of an alternate advance involvement question.
Let's review that. An alternate advance is any question that indicates a choice of answers, all of which confirm that they're going ahead. An involvement question is one that requires them to make ownership decisions.

Now, you don't really care whether Frank uses your JLG Lift in the plant or the warehouse, do you? But when he thinks about where he'll use it, he's thinking about some of the choices he'll have when he owns your product. So that one sentence is both an alternate advance and an involvement question, isn't it? That gives it double-barreled sales power.

(d) Prepare your complete close in advance.
It requires some effort to create a secondary question for your offering that packs as much selling force into so few words as the example above does. That effort will be repaid many times over. I doubt that there is any other sales activity that can make you more money in less time than developing an effective Secondary Question Close. When you've worked out your complete close, memorize the words until you can roll them off effortlessly. Losers wing it, winners prepare.

(e) Use the casual format given here.

The introductory phrases not only keep this close organized in your mind so that you'll have no trouble adapting it to the different situation you'll encounter with each different client, these phrases also help you deliver the close properly. Delivery is so important that I'm going to emphasize it below:

(f) Deliver the close in a relaxed and alert manner.
Practice this close so that you can say it clearly and casually. Otherwise your art will be obvious—and unlikely to succeed.

The purpose of all this, of course, is to get Frank to answer something like, "Well, I guess we better assign it to the new warehouse because they'll use it all the time. We'll only be using it in the main plant once or twice a shift." When Frank says that, he's bought.

The casual approach is the cornerstone of sales success. By casual, I don't mean careless. You must cultivate an alert but nonchalant attitude that people feel comfortable with. Learn to be relaxed without seeming impertinent or inefficient; learn to be alert without seeming nosy or officious. In a word, be competent.

Watching Colombo on TV makes me think of what the professional salesperson should aim for. Colombo doesn't threaten anybody. He drives a beat-up old car, wears a wrinkled old raincoat. When he walks up, the suspect thinks, "This clown is trying to trap me? Impossible." So the suspect lets his guard down because he doesn't feel there's anything to worry about. Then Colombo starts asking the right questions and the suspect feels a little tightness run up along his spine. Colombo senses his tension and changes the subject. Colombo is a great interruptor. "By the way," he says, and takes off on a new tangent. Once the tension has eased a bit, he goes right back in. You've probably watched him walk away from a suspect six times. Each time, the suspect thinks it's all over. He's done. He's in the clear. Nothing to worry about. Then Colombo comes back. This is very professional.

In sales we do much the same thing. We ask questions, not to threaten, to get next-step information. We ask the questions in a warm and nice way. If we see that we're threatening the other person, that we're building tension, we back off. When the pressure is off, we try again.

You must learn many closes because you have to know more ways to get *yes* than they know ways to say *no*. If you don't outgun them here, you're dead. This book would be worth a million dollars to you if I could give you one close that would work every time. There'll never be one close that will work every time. If one close worked even a quarter of the time, so many people would jump on it that overuse would ruin it within days.

All Champions are multi-closers. This is just difficult enough to keep the uninspired majority from paying the price for this entree to sales and financial success. But you don't need a towering intellect to become a multi-closer, all you need is the determination to organize your time so that you learn several closes thoroughly. It's really that basic. I'm always amazed at how few salespeople will pay this price—a ridiculously low one in comparison to other professions—for becoming skilled enough to earn a professional's income in their chosen field. Maybe the reason is that no one makes them do it. This has a tendency to fool us into overlooking the fact that in sales, it's the sharp scissors of competition that cuts away the incompetent. Ours is a free field. This means that you're free to succeed, and you're free to fail. As you hang out your shingle and tell the world you're a professional salesperson, dedicate yourself to mastering your art: invest the time and effort that's required to:

Learn multiple closes.

Let's say that I just used the Ben Franklin balance sheet close and the client hit me with, "I'll think it over."

If I can't handle that, I'm in trouble—I'm not going to make that sale that day. This means that I probably won't ever make it. Now is always more certain than later.

BRIDGING

How do you get across the creek that runs between a close that didn't work and the next one you want to try? You build a bridge. Here's how:

(a) Apologize.

Especially if you feel you've pressed a little too hard, back off with a quick apology. I used to say, "I'm sorry. I just got carried away. I didn't mean to move so rapidly." What you're really doing is apologizing to yourself for not making the close. Don't worry about it. All it means is you get a chance to practice another of your many closes.

In this situation, one of our Champions says, "I didn't mean to push you." He is sincere in apologizing because a Champion doesn't push—he pulls. That is, he pulls by leading with questions.

(b) Summarize the benefits they've already agreed to, using tie-downs.

Play it safe, and aim for minor agreements only now.

- "I know there are still a lot of questions in your mind, but this model is the size you wanted, isn't it?"
- "I wouldn't be here if you didn't have a need, would I?"
- "You wouldn't let me in your office if you weren't interested, would you?"
- "So all I'm trying to say is that the JLG Lift seems to meet your needs, doesn't it?"

(c) Ask a lead-in question.

Complete your bridging to the next closing sequence by asking a lead-in question. I used to say it this way: "I know I went through that rather rapidly, but those are the things we've discussed thus far, and we've really agreed on them, haven't we?"

Now you're set for your next close. If you keep using this technique to roll into your next close, eventually they will own what you're there to sell them.

Why?

Because you know more closes than they know objections. Won't that be an exciting change?

It will if you've been losing because your prospects all just naturally react with more negatives than you have positives. But is it fun when you know more ways to get them to say yep than they know ways to say nix. That's when you're the champ.

6. THE HIGHER AUTHORITY CLOSE.

This is devastating—if you know it thoroughly and set it up right. Again, I'm going to use an example to show in detail exactly how a technique works. You may be selling carpet cleaning service to homemakers, group insurance to companies, or works of art to collectors. Whatever it is that you offer, the principles in this example apply. All you need do is adapt the wording to your own product or service.

The higher authority must be exactly that—a person respected by and known to the prospect. He doesn't have to know your higher authority personally; all that's necessary is that the prospect knows of the authority's existence and position. If you're selling agricultural machinery, you'll want a prominent farmer; if you're selling furnishings or home services, you'll want a civic or social leader in your community; if you're selling industrial equipment, you'll want to use a decision-maker at a large and growing company as your higher authority.

Here are the steps for using this close successfully:

(a) Select your Higher Authority Figure.

You should constantly be on the lookout for more higher authority figures. For now, let's work on the idea of using one. In this example, you're a sales-record-smasher for Brawnybead Welding Equipment Corporation.

The number two steel fabricator in your area, Finekrax Inc., is a happy client of yours in the person of Mark Cade, its production manager. You've given first class service, thank you notes, the whole bundle—and, of course, your Brawnybead machines are doing a great job at Finekrax Inc.

Mark Cade is an ideal higher authority figure for any of the smaller steel fabricators in your entire territory.

(b) Recruit your Higher Authority Figure.

On one of your visits to Finekrax after they've had a dozen of your Brawnybead machines long enough to be experienced with them, you ask Mark Cade if he'd be willing to share his knowledge of your machines with other steel fabricators. Mark agrees to do that for you because you've done a solid sales and service job for him on a good product, and you've assured him that you'll only call when you need help with prospects operating on his general level. In other words, you promise not to bother him if you're trying to sell one small welder to a fix-it shop.

(c) Set your Higher Authority Figure up for the specific sales situation.

You're out to replace all the outdated welders at Slagfild Iron Works with your new high speed Brawnybeads. Slagfild is number four in your territory, and Tony Alioto is the decision-maker there. While planning your appointment with Tony, you decide that you'll need the Higher Authority Figure close, so you call Mark Cade and determine that he'll be available to take a phone call while you're with Tony Alioto. With Mark set up, you complete your plans for a powerful presentation to Tony at Slagfild.

(d) Set your prospect up for the Higher Authority Figure Close.

You know that Tony will have the same concerns about the reliability of your Brawnybead welders that Mark Cade had.

Will the innovations that make the Brawnybead superior stand up under actual shop working conditions?

Is your service department really as good as you say it is?

In planning your presentation, you expect Tony to have specific technical questions. A simple demonstration is pointless; Tony knows your machine will make two pieces of metal stick together.

So you recognize that the primary purpose of your interview with Tony Alioto is to isolate the specific technical and other reservations that he has about your equipment and company. Once you've clarified these questions in his mind, and you and he have agreed that these are all the reasons that cause him to question the wisdom of installing your equipment now, you're ready to throw the close. It's vital to make that list of reasons specific, and to get agreement that they are all the reservations Tony has. Write them out on a piece of paper. As soon as you come to this point, reach for the phone on Tony's desk.

"You know Mark Cade, don't you?"

"Runs the shop at Finekrax, doesn't he?"

"That's right. He's one of our clients." Then make the call.

When Mark Cade is on the phone, tell him, "I'm here at Slagfild with Tony Alioto and he has some questions about the Brawnyweld." Then hand Tony the phone and let him take it from there. He has the list of his questions in front of him so nothing will be missed.

(e) Close after the call.

Once Mark Cade has discussed the technicalities and reassured Tony that the Brawnybead is performing well in his larger shop, Tony's objections aren't there anymore. When the phone conversation ends, you're in a position to ask "By the way, what delivery date is most convenient, the first or the fifteenth?"

If something happens and Mark Cade isn't available even though you set it up with him — after all, his job comes first — you probably won't be able to close that day. Set yourself up for a recontact at a specific time, and leave the higher authority's phone number with the prospect so that Tony can call Mark on his own. Take a copy of Tony's objections with you so you'll be able to get back quickly at the start of the recontact to where you left off.

Some salespeople turn away from the Higher Authority Close because they feel that all competitors hate each other and won't cooperate. There are exceptions but as a general rule, the people in companies operating in the same field are friendly. They respect each other and have many reasons to cooperate, not the least of which is the possibility that they may be looking for a job at another company in their industry sometime. If you do happen to run into one of the few cases of bad blood between competitors, simply back off — but don't assume there's trouble in advance. The truth is that most people in business are too busy to waste energy hating the competition. And it's a big ego boost to be a higher authority.

This is a powerful close. I know because the sales representatives of Tom Hopkins/Champions Unlimited have taken this technique from our sales training videotapes and used it to boost sales production. (They use all the others too—with great results.) Our people in the Champions Unlimited sales organization are always on the lookout for more higher authorities to use in their own selling activities. Don't settle for just one because you can wear out any higher authority with overuse. Every happy client is a potential higher authority for some other prospects. Keep that in mind as you work with your customers—it's another spur to give that extra bit of service with a smile.

THE CASE HISTORY APPROACH

Doctors keep a running record of every patient's condition. Why? Because they're professionals, and they know they can't remember all the important details about every patient.

You can't remember all the important details about every client either. Keep a case history, and when the sale is made, use it to summarize that case history with a brief memo that tells you what benefits they bought, what major objections they raised, how you overcame them, and any special circumstances or problems you ran into that might come up again with another prospect.

Keep your memos to yourself brief. Create a simple form, or use the outline format. Then make it a weekly habit to study your growing file of case histories and successful sales reports.

You'll soon find that your case history file is worth its weight in gold. Writing this data down and summarizing it will focus your attention on the key elements that make sales. It'll highlight strengths and weaknesses faster, so you can exploit the first and correct the second; it'll help you spot subtle trends quicker; it'll show you where your prospecting efforts will pay off best.

7. THE SIMILAR SITUATION CLOSE.

When you find yourself working with a prospect who has an objection or problem similar to one you've already overcome, you can tell your new prospect about the previous situation. That's what the average salesperson does.

The Champion has the facts documented in his case history file. When he pulls a memo out of his attache case that shows how another company solved the same problem, the prospect is impressed—and convinced.

For example, you're working with the Zap Corporation, and you know they can increase profits by using the JLG Lift you're selling. But it's not in the budget, and they're putting you off until next year. In your case history file, you have the record of the Yip Company, who put off buying the JLG Lift for a year and paid fourteen percent more for it. Not only that, Yip Company lost $36,000 in profits by not having the JLG Lift that year. You have the figures, and they'll prove to be solid ammunition for blowing the budget door open at Zap Corporation.

Seasonal backlog patterns may help you in the similar situation close. Wup Industries ordered the JLG Lift in the first quarter, your peak sales season, and had to wait four months for delivery. It's all in your case histories. Now, in November, you can offer Zap Corporation three week delivery—but time is running short. You can close on the fact that they must act now to get quick delivery.

8. THE MY-DEAR-OLD-MOTHER CLOSE.

This is a cute one. In the right situation, it'll really shake the apples out of the tree. To use it, you have to talk to someone's mother—your own if possible, someone else's if not—in which case you say, "A dear old mother who means a great deal to me. . . ."

You first ask mother to repeat some advice she probably gave you years ago that you've forgotten. So ask her, "Mom, would you tell me, word for word, that *silence means consent*?" After she's told you that, mind your mother. (It's absolutely essential to go through these steps by talking to your mother—or someone's mother—before you use this technique. Unless you demand honesty of yourself, you can't project a convincing image of integrity.) Here's how you use mother's advice:

Let's go back to J. Douglas Edwards' statement: "Whenever you ask a closing question, shut up. The first person who speaks, loses."

That's very sound advice. Between ninety and ninety-five percent of the time, if you go against it and speak first, you'll lose. So don't go against it until you've risen far above the average and can start going for that last five or ten percent, until you've learned when the tension hurts the close instead of making it, until you've learned a way to break the tension and still close. That's where dear old mother comes in. If you've been wondering what she's done for you lately, here's your answer.

This technique can be your salvation when you find yourself involved in a series of silences as you roll from close to close with the same prospect.

If you have a clever way to break tension, pressure turns into humor. Explosive laughter sometimes. Lots of people can handle pressure, but laughter will pop them wide open.

So when the pressure has been on for several seconds after your last close and it's getting heavy in the room, suddenly grin from ear to ear and say, "My dear old mother said, 'Silence means consent.' Was she right?"

He'll usually laugh, and laughing is just like talking—it means you've won—you're closing. It's a minor technique that's only for the special situations where your intuition tells you it's right. It breaks the tension and it works.

But don't use it until you've talked to mother.

9. THE "I'LL THINK IT OVER" CLOSE.

There must be some guy running all over the country giving seminars on how to put off buying decisions because all prospects know these techniques.

"I'll think it over."
"We want to sleep on it."
"We don't jump into things."
"Let us mull this thing over."
"Leave your stuff and we'll run it through our grinder."
"Why don't you come back tomorrow (next week, after the holidays) and we'll let you know."

When you hear any of that stuff after you've learned this close, you'll think, "I own this one." They expect you to say okay and leave, because that's what the average salesperson does. If you do that, will they think it over?

In a word, no. As soon as you leave, new problems will come up. The prospect will forget about your proposition.

Then suddenly it's tomorrow, next week, or after the holidays. You come back and ask, "Did you run my proposal through your think machine like you said you would?"

He doesn't want to tell you the truth because he would have to say something like, "No, I haven't had time to give it a second thought. We're exactly where we were when you were here last." If he says that, he sounds inefficient. So what does he say?

"Yes, we gave your proposal very careful consideration, and I'm sorry but we're not going on it now. We'll keep your proposal on file, and if anything changes, I'll call you."

What can you do? Nothing. You're dead — because you shot yourself.

Here's what the Champion does when they play the old I'll-think-it-over number:

(a) Agree with them.

"That's fine, Harry. Obviously, you wouldn't take your time thinking it over unless you were seriously interested, would you?"

What will they say? "Oh, we're interested. You bet. We're going to think it over."

It helps to give them a brave little smile and act defeated as you ask that question. It's as though you're thinking, "Okay, they've won. What can I say?"

(b) Confirm the fact that they're going to think it over.

"Since you're that interested, may I assume that you'll give it very careful consideration?" Speak the last three words slowly, with just a touch of emphasis.

What will they say? Because you're acting like you're leaving, you're letting go, they'll say yes.

(c) Make them squeak.

"Harry, you're not telling me this just to get rid of me, are you?" You have to act like you're licked at this point.

They'll answer something like this, "Oh, no. You're the greatest. And the little model? I love it. My kids love it."

(d) Clarify and twist harder.

"Just to clarify my thinking, what is it that you wanted to think over *is it the integrity of my company?*" Notice how I ran those two separate sentences together. More about this later.

What'll they say? "No, your company is great."

"Is it my personal integrity?"

"Oh, no, we think you're the greatest," Harry says.

"Is it the lift's capability to handle your loads?"

"No, no. We agreed on that. It'll handle it."

"Is it the agility of the lift?"

"No, that's fine."

"Is it? Is is? Is it?" Every time they say no, they're in essence saying yes, aren't they?

This technique allows you to summarize the benefits that you're offering them, and to do it with subtlety and finesse. Don't argue. Don't tell them. Ask.

What do you ask them about?

You ask them about every benefit or feature your prospect wants that you can supply.

"Is it the speed of the lift?" you ask.

"No. As a matter of fact, I think the speed of your lift is a real plus."

Ask questions that'll cause them to tell you how good your product or service is. There's no better way to convince them of its merits.

What will people do when you've learned this technique and are working it effectively on them? They'll say to themselves, "I know what he's doing." So what will they grab?

One of the objections. Once they grab one, what do you have?

The final objection.

Now, if they were going along with you at all, what should you normally come up on last?

The money.

"Is it the investment that's involved in purchasing the JLG Lift?"

What'll they usually say? "Well, we don't put out that kind of money without really doing a lot of considering."

"So the problem really is money, isn't that right?"

"Yeah, that's it."

So what have I accomplished? Quite a lot. I've broken through the think-it-over-and-forget-it routine. Now I'm down to the real objection, which is money.

That's nothing new, is it? Money is the major objection we have to face on every, or nearly every sale, isn't it?

The problem with think-it-over is that it's too big of an objection. It's a whole colony of ghosts, and there's nothing to grab onto. Smoke those ghosts out as we've done above, get down to the final objection, and then you'll be able to use the six steps for closing on a final objection that we've already given you.

But, please, be careful when they give you the old think-it-over routine. Don't say to yourself, "Okay, it's really the dollars," and put all your money on one roll of the dice by going straight for, "Is it the money?"

Why not?

If you ask them that first, they'll say, "No, it's not the money; we just want to think about the whole proposition."

That answer rubs you right off the board. Where can you lead them to from this point? Now you'll have to make them own up to lying before they can admit it's the money. Since you're almost certain that money really is their final objection, all you can do now is go away—or stay awhile and chase yourself around in circles with pointless "Is it—?" questions. Your only hope is to eventually lead them back to the money, and then close on that final objection. In this situation, it almost takes a miracle for that to happen.

This close, like the others, works only if you follow the steps and use it right. Shortcuts cut your throat.

There's a critical instant in this close that comes when you say, "Just to clarify my thinking, what is it that you wanted to think over is it my company's integrity?" Remember that a pause between *over* and *is* will often be pure disaster. Don't turn this most important element of the close into two sentences: ". . . what is it that you wanted to think over? Is it my company's integrity?" Don't pause or even raise your tone to indicate a question after the word *over*.

Why is this important? Because if you pause, they'll say, "I want to think over the whole proposition." That turns your canoe over—all you can do then is swim for shore.

(e) Confirm that it's the money.

You've got to make sure that you're not dancing with phantoms anymore. There's no point in trying to close on the money problem if they aren't sure they'd buy it even if it's a wise money decision for them. What do they care what it costs if they don't want it?

When it seems to be down to money, you're very near paydirt if you handle it right—so handle it right. Ask them if there's anything else they're unsure of except the money. Confirm that you're at the final barrier before busting through it with our next close.

10. THE REDUCTION TO THE RIDICULOUS CLOSE.

Have you ever heard, "It's higher than we wanted to go?" I have—nine million times. And I never sold much until I learned how to overcome this objection in its several forms.

We salespeople tend to look at the total investment when we're hit with the it-costs-too-much objection. That's big trouble. Go for the difference instead. For example, you're selling high-speed office copiers. The total investment required is $10,000.

The first step is to find out how much too much it is. When they express the idea that it costs too much, say in a warm and pleasant way, "Today, it seems most things do. Can you tell me about how much too much you feel it is?"

Let's suppose that the prospect says he's only budgeted $8,000 for the copier. The money problem isn't $10,000, is it? They never expected to get your product or service for nothing. No, the money problem in this case is only $2,000. That's where you start, on the difference, on the smaller amount. Once you determine what the difference is, stop talking about total investment. In reality, that's not what they're having trouble with, do you agree?

Let's work through our example on high-speed copiers. Your prospect is Ruby Wellman. She's interested in the model that involves a total investment of $10,000. Ruby budgeted only $8,000. Here we go.

"So really, we're talking about $2,000, aren't we, Ruby? All right. My thought here is that we should be careful to put this into proper perspective. Here."

Hand her your pocket calculator. "Let's just say that, hypothetically, you own the Superpow copier. Do you think you'd keep it for five years?"

"That's about right," Ruby says.

"Okay, divide $2,000 by 5 years and we get $400 a year, don't we? Now, your company would use the Superpow about 50 weeks a year, wouldn't they? If you'll take $400 and divide it by 50—we get $8.00, don't we?"

Of course, the figures you'll actually be working with won't round out so neatly—that's why you ask the prospect to figure them on your calculator. Bear in mind that having them use your calculator is in essence a minor close of physical involvement.

We continue: "I understand that there's a lot of weekend work in this office, a lot of overtime, so I think it might be reasonable to say that the copier would be in use 7 days a week. Okay? Would you please divide $8.00 by 7? And we get?"

Ruby says, "$1.14."

You smile and say, "Do you think we should let $1.14 a day stand between your company and the profits, the increased production, and the expanded capabilities that the Superpow will bring you?"

"Well, I don't know."

"Ruby, may I ask what the lowest-paid entry-type job in this office is, and roughly how much it pays?"

"The coffee girls get about $3.50. That's about the bottom."

"About $3.50. So the $1.14 a day that we're talking about will buy twenty minutes work from your lowest paid helper."

"Well, if you put it that way, yes."

"Ruby, let me ask you one more thing. Won't this high-speed machine with all its sophisticated capabilities and timesaving features—all the benefits we talked about—won't this machine make more profit for your company in a whole day than a coffee girl can in twenty minutes?"

"Yes, I think it will."

"Then we've agreed, haven't we? By the way, which delivery date would best suit your time schedule—the first, or the fifteenth?"

Are you thinking something like, "Wow, I couldn't do that."
Why not?

I think I'm safe in saying that money is an objection you're going to
encounter frequently as long as you're in sales. That being so, can you reach
your full potential without learning how to cope with it?

Of course not. So adapt this technique to your offering, work out the
bugs with a friend, memorize every word, get the numbers down pat, and
USE IT. Your sales results will show a startling difference.

If you really have a hangup with any of these closes, decide that it's
okay to fail with them, but it's not okay to avoid learning and using them.
Make it your goal to use each one of them ten times—and of course to give
each time the best shot you're capable of when you do it. If you decide not to
try, you've failed completely, you're batting zero, you're going nowhere.
But if you try each close ten times, you'll have some success. Try each one
ten more times and you'll have a lot of success. Try each one a third set of ten
times and you'll be flying high, eating lobster, and ordering custom-made
clothes.

If you've qualified them and they need the benefits, you have the right
to reduce their final objection to the ridiculous, don't you? Of course you do.
Isn't it ridiculous for them to let such an insignificant sum stand in the way
of their enjoyment of the benefits they want? And wouldn't it be ridiculous
for you to ignore this powerful technique for helping them have what they
need?

Ignore the time periods that don't apply to what you're doing. When
you walk into a presentation, you probably won't know what the difference
is that you'll be reducing with that particular client—but you will know the
time period, won't you? If you're selling office machines, you'll try for five
years; if you're selling elevators to hotels, you'll go for forty years.

Make knowing the figures easy for yourself: use one key number. If you
represent Superpow Copiers, all you need to remember is fifty-seven cents,
because that's what $1,000 reduces to over a five-year period.

If they hit you with a difference of $2,000, you simply double fifty-seven
cents in your head and come up with a dollar fourteen. Before they can
calculate the answer, you know what it should be and, if they've made a
mistake, you can lead them through it again smoothly to eliminate the error
instead of retreating in confusion.

Suppose they hit you with a difference of only $300, and the only
number you have memorized is that same old $ .57? Here's the quick and
ready way to figure it. Round the $ .57 out to 60 cents. Since 100 is a tenth of
1,000, a tenth of 60 cents will be the reduction for $100. That's 6 cents.
Multiply 6 cents by 3 and you get 18 cents. It'll cost them just 18 cents a day
over their budget to own the benefits they want.

Now let's suppose that you're selling elevators using the 40-year
period. A thousand dollar difference amounts to only 7 cents a day. What's
exciting is that a million dollar difference costs them less than $72 a day on
the 40-year line. (Just move the figure in the $10,000 column two decimal
points to the right to get the rounded number for $1,000,000.

Know your figures. They're fantastic.

Let me give you a cautionary note on the reduction close: you must know the figures. With a pocket calculator you can easily work out a table like the one below for your product or service.

TABLE OF AMOUNTS
REDUCED TO THE RIDICULOUS
(COST PER DAY)
(Based on 50 week year, 7 day week.)

PERIOD	AMOUNT REDUCED		
	$100	$1,000	$10,000
3 years	10 cents	95 cents	$ 9.52
5 years	6 cents	57 cents	$ 5.71
10 years	3 cents	29 cents	$ 2.86
25 years	1 cent	11 cents	$ 1.14
40 years	—	7 cents	71 cents

11. THE NEGATIVE CLOSE.

The concept of negative selling is very simple: If you express doubt in your prospect's ability to do something, he'll tend to do it just to prove that you're wrong.

This potent technique can be used to sell almost anything, but one of the best situations for it occurs when your prospect has to qualify for financing in order to make the purchase. Even though he hasn't definitely decided on buying yet, you set this close up by creating a doubt in his mind about whether he'll actually be able to make the purchase. As in most aspects of selling, good timing is vital here. Unless you delay creating that doubt until two things have happened, you'll lose the prospect every time. Here are the two essential foundation stones for the negative close:

(a) Your prospect must have warmed up to a specific product or service that you're selling.

(b) Your prospect must be aware of you as a distinct personality.

If nothing you can offer him excites his interest, he'll simply walk away if you express doubt. And if you're nothing more than a blur to him, that is, if he hasn't focused on you as a living, breathing, human being, he won't know or care whether you doubt him. How long it takes to get such a reaction varies widely. Salespeople who dress with conservative good taste often achieve this effect instantly. When your prospect starts talking with you rather than at you, you know you've got the necessary reaction.

When you have that, and your prospect has warmed up to something specific that you can sell him, start setting up the close. Here's what you say:

"You know, one of the biggest problems we have in providing (name your product or service) to people is getting them qualified. And we have amazing things happen. Just the other day I had someone with an income of (name a yearly figure that qualifies for the purchase in question) and they looked good as gold to me. But when we applied for the financing, we were told no. My people were horrified. They told me that their credit was good, but it didn't make any difference. You run into some pretty weird things once in a while."

After laying that groundwork, continue with your presentation until you're ready to start closing. By this time they should be quite warm for the product. They haven't said, "We'll take it," but you know they want it. Like most buyers, they can't make up their minds without help. In the next step, you say:

"By the way, are you sure you could qualify for this model if you wanted it? Maybe you better not get too interested right at this moment. Let's not let your wife get her hopes too high; let's not let you get your hopes too high. Before we go any further, we better find out whether you could have it if you did want it."

What will go through his mind now? He's going to start proving to you that he can qualify. Here's how you wind it up:

"I'll tell you what let's do. Let's fill out the application. Once I get this filled out, I can tell you pretty well what chance we have of qualifying."

Now you fill out the form you use to apply for customer credit or loans. If you understand how to qualify, before you've asked five questions you'll know whether it'll go or not. You still fill the form out completely—if the buyer qualifies. After you've got that done, you sit there staring at the paperwork for a moment. Then take out a writing pad and start marking figures on it. Work in dead silence. Don't even look at the buyer. After at least three minutes, during which time only the sound of your pencil scratching on the paper can be heard, sit back and say, "Yup, I think we can get it done." Then turn the form around and ask him to "okay it here."

Out of relief that he qualified, he'll do it. When he does it, you've made the sale.

This tactic of doubting the prospect's ability to do something can be an effective last-ditch close in situations where no qualifying is done. For example, let's suppose that you're selling to a tax-supported agency or a large business. In these cases, what you express doubt about is whether the person you're talking to has the authority to place an order.

You'll have to work very carefully in this area or you'll make an enemy instead of a sale, especially if the other person really doesn't have much power. But if everything else fails and you're convinced that you don't have anything to lose, start asking questions about committees and boards. Talk about how nobody can make a move anymore because of all the red tape. Do this with verve and you'll frequently walk out with an order you'd given up on.

The third area where negative closing works often and well is with cash buyers who have chips on their shoulders. A good many of them never part with much of their money except to show some salesperson how important they are. Give them that pleasure—they're willing to pay for it.

12. THE PUPPYDOG CLOSE.

If you can—and will—use this one, it'll send you cruising around the world in the best cabin on the ship. The puppydog is something of a paradox because it's the most powerful closing sequence known for many products and services, yet in reality it eliminates the need to close. So it flies in the face of everything I've been telling you about closing. Don't worry about that. It works. The buyers close themselves. All you have to do is be sure that you use it on the right people. And you have to be selling a top quality product or service. If you've got that going for you, stand back and collect the money.

It also takes nerve to use the puppydog, and the willingness to be different. You'll remember that in chapter 5 we talked about giving up what you've got in order to get what you want. There's no better place to start doing it than with the puppydog. However, if you're the newest salesperson in the office, you may have to wait a while before management will let you do it. Find out. Tell them you'll guarantee the credit.

Their response may be, "Guarantee it with what?" That means you're moving too fast. For your own good, wait until you've used the other closes to make a place for yourself among the top third in sales production in your office. That achievement will give you enough leverage to get your use of the puppydog okayed. Then use the puppydog right and it'll propel you into the elite five percent who make the really big money in sales.

Here's how this close works. You sell your product or service just like it was a puppydog. How do you sell a cuddly little puppy?

You let them take it home with them.

Then what happens? That puppy puts its wet nose against their cheek. It stares at them with its big soft eyes. It whimpers when they leave. The kids adore him—and suddenly there's no way they'll let you take their puppy away from them. It's really that simple with top quality products and services supplied by companies that are dedicated to giving their customers satisfaction.

Selling machinery is a far cry from selling puppies—or is it? Before you answer that question, let me tell you about someone I know who manufactured metal specialties. One day a salesman for a very expensive metalworking machine came to my friend's office. The machine was a big one, so the salesman of course didn't have it with him. He had brochures, specifications, samples of the work the machine had done, and he also had a good idea of how to sell it. Here's what happened.

The salesman's machine was faster and more versatile, and it worked to closer tolerances, than anything my friend had ever owned. It also cost ten times as much as he'd ever spent for a single piece of equipment. So he wasn't about to buy it. My friend was the kind of manager who bought nothing but used machinery. He had the work to justify the new machine, and he could stretch to pay for it. That means he really couldn't afford not to own one, doesn't it? My friend didn't see it that way. He told me later that he never really considered buying it then. Regardless of how good that machine was or how profitable it would be to own it, the cost was more than he could handle at that time from the emotional, not the financial, standpoint. Buyers are often gripped by that mood, aren't they?

The machinery salesman said, "Tell you what. I don't want you to have this machine unless we both know it's right for your shop. If you can make room for it, I'll put one in. Try it on your work for a while. It won't cost you a dime."

"How long can I keep it?" my friend asked, already thinking about a couple of production runs he could knock out on the new machine. If it would do everything the salesman claimed it would, my friend knew he'd save quite a bit in labor cost.

"Well," the salesman said, "It'll take you two or three weeks to really see what it can do for you, won't it? What do you say we put it in for a month?"

When the machine arrived, my friend put it to work immediately. Within four days, it had run all the jobs he knew were ready. Quality was up and costs were down. But now the gleaming new machine was standing idle. My friend looked at it and decided that he was going to have to get along without it. The thing was just too expensive. At about that time, the salesman phoned.

"Is the machine working okay?"

"Yes it is."

"Do you have any questions or need any further instruction on using it?"

"No," my friend said, and braced himself for the close. He didn't get one. The salesman said he was glad it was going all right and got off the phone.

The next day, my friend went out into his shop and noticed that the new machine was chomping out parts. His shop foreman was doing a small job that my friend hadn't thought about using it on. He went over and watched for a few minutes. All through the next week he noticed that the new machine was often in use. Like the salesman said, it was fast and versatile.

My friend's factory is a noisy place. The workers wear hearing protectors. It's always grimy and often hot as well. Not the sort of place where you'd expect people to fall in love with a puppydog in the form of a big, clanking machine that chews up metal. But that's what came to pass. When my friend mentioned that the new machine would be going back soon, his foreman started giving him what seemed like an endless list of reasons why they had to have it. The other workers joined in, and pretty soon my friend heard himself say, "Well, I'll think about it."

When the salesman dropped by to see him after a month, my friend had a purchase order for the machine ready. He wasn't about to lose his shop's puppydog.

You'll find five more power closes in chapter 22.

16

A CLUTCH OF MONEYGRABBERS

The product or service that you sell, and the location you work in, are less important than your techniques, your time planning, and your determination to do the most productive thing possible at every given moment to organize, plan, prepare, learn and practice new techniques, and to put all these good things to work. If you make all these habits of the Champion your habits, you'll become a Champion. You'll have the prestige, the money, the recognition, and the self-acceptance that all Champions have. Many of us want to find reasons why we can't do this. When we hear of a salesperson who's earning a six-figure income, we have a tendency to say, "I'll bet he sells million-dollar products."

But the truth is, that's rarely the case. There just aren't that many buyers for million-dollar goodies. Most of the big earners in sales are selling everyday things: insurance, automobiles, residential real estate, and a host of other products and services that are not unusually costly. Of course, they're not selling bean bags and corn candy at the five and dime either.

Regardless of the price of your product, you can use the secrets of the super-Champions. I'm talking now about the great ones who earn in a good week what the average worker earns in a year. Now let's talk about eight systems that the great ones use to turn little dollars into big dollars.

TURN LITTLE DOLLARS INTO BIG DOLLARS

The super-Champions, and most of the top producers, combine all the techniques given in this book to build a base of referrals into an ongoing operation that continues to generate its own momentum. The average salesperson has a hard time getting referrals from the people he sells; the super-Champion often gets referrals after a short phone conversation with people he's never seen. The super-Champion paid the price to acquire his skills, and he has the confidence to use them to the fullest possible extent. "Nothing succeeds like success," Alexandre Dumas wrote over a hundred years ago, and the words were never truer than they are today. To succeed, gather the skills and knowledge that are the tools of success. Then use them.

Having done that, you'll be ready for eight systems to magnify the values you work with.

● **Multiplying money** is moneyclutching System 1.

The people you involve in your product are surrounded by other people who have the same aspirations, interests, and financial capabilities. Each person you sell can be multiplied by the number of his associates who are prospects for your offering.

The average family has two and a half automobiles, but the average automobile salesman stops when he sells them one car. Why? Because he's organized to work only with the people who come into his showroom. The concept that every buyer is a referral base for more sales is foreign to him. Yet the Champion works with his buyers and multiplies the one sale by a factor of two—three—five—sometimes ten or more over a period of time.

Leasing is another business with explosive potential for multiplying effects. From one car leased to an individual you go to several cars leased to associates of that person, and then on to friends of each of the associates. And somewhere in this you hit a fleet lease because you give service, keep thinking big, and ask the right questions. Highlight this thought:

If they'll take one, they or their friends will always take more.

You've got to do the job, of course. You have to work with them, make sure they're happy with the service, and handle any problems quickly. So highlight this idea also:

Work with every buyer as though that person represents a thousand referrals.

Let's think about this for a moment. Suppose you make only one small sale this week. However, you give them fine service and obtain four pre-qualified leads from that buyer.

On week 2, you work with those four pre-qualified leads and sell the number you should sell, fifty percent. So you pick up two sales. You also get four leads from each of your new buyers. During the following week 3, you work with your eight leads, sell half of them, and ring up four sales.

Please take a pencil to paper and work this out for yourself because we're covering something now that's of paramount importance to you.

When all this happens, let's say that you're working in a home appliance store. A terrific new product has just come out, a kitchen blender priced at $79.95. You make ten percent—$8.00—on each blender you sell. There's something about that blender that makes you decide to give it a good solid push.

Here's how your results look after three weeks:

WEEK	SALES	LEADS	EARNINGS
1	1	0	$ 8.00
2	2	4	16.00
3	4	8	32.00

Not very impressive is it? You've pushed that dang blender hard for three weeks—and all you've made is a measly $56.00.

Now here's what I'd like you to do. Take your pencil and work out what would happen if you doubled the sales of the blender for ten weeks, getting four leads from each sale, two of which you sell the following week. In other words, extend the table above a full ten weeks. It'll only take you a minute.

You'll probably go to your pocket calculator to check the figures because they're surprising. Rather than give you all the answers here and spoil your fun, I'll just tell you one thing. If you could actually do that with the blender for ten weeks, and then hold your sales at that level for a full year, your income would be one-fifth of a million dollars. ($200,704.00 to be exact, assuming that you take three weeks off.)

Isn't that exciting?

Of course, it isn't realistic to plan on selling that many units of the same appliance out of one retail store. But you could have a good thing going on several different appliances, including some priced at ten times what our blender goes out the door for.

This example illustrates the enormous multiplying effect of the referral. Use this concept. Why be satisfied to let a buyer — and his thousand possible connections — walk out with only one of your products? Probe a little. Among his friends and relatives and fellow workers there are bound to be several people who need the benefits you're purveying.

During my last year in sales before I went into training, my business was ninety-nine percent referrals. It wasn't just the service I gave — I used this concept. The only time I prospected, I was showing other people how to do it. Now, what did the referral nature of my business allow me to do? Spend every bit of my selling time working with people who trusted me. About all I did was qualify and close.

If you're new, of course you can't start right out working with referrals — you have to wait until you make your first sale. Most new salespeople are so concerned with making each sale that they don't open their minds to the tremendous number of opportunities that just one sale can create for them.

- **Add-on** is System 2.

The second system for expanding volume involves using your imagination. Keep thinking of ways to add-on accessories and additional products, and of ways to find different uses for your product or service with the same customer. Always keep this question in the front of your mind:

How can I add-on to what my clientele already has?

If you're selling companies and you get one of your products into the shipping department of a firm, are you satisfied? Or will you service that shipping department and work with them to give you a referral to their accounting department, or production department? Of course, it depends on your product or service, but I keep hearing about salespeople who go in with a piece of equipment that many different departments of a company could use. They sell one department and forget about the rest of that firm.

There's a fundamental rule for add-on sales that I recommend you highlight:

Never go for the add-on sale until you've completely closed the original sale.

If I walk into your appliance store looking for a vacuum cleaner, I don't want to discuss the fantastic new blender you're all excited about until I've satisfied my need to suck up dirt. Once that's off my mind, you have a chance to arouse my blending urges. But don't even mention blending until I own the best vacuum cleaner you can close me on.

The person handling my insurance is one of the best salespeople in the country. He never mentions what he's planning to do for me until he actually finishes doing something for me now. Then, a moment after the close, he starts setting me up for what's going to happen in the future.

What's fun and exciting is that when people like and trust you, you can do that. The last time I wrapped up some added coverage with my insurance representative, he smiled and said, "I'll see you again soon."

The ink wasn't dry on my check—a fat one—yet. I stared at him for a second and then said, "I don't want to see you again soon."

He laughed and said, "What? Are you going to quit growing?"

And I had to laugh with him, because of course I intend to keep on working hard, growing—and increasing my need for more of his insurance. As I reach my expanding goals and set new ones, I help him reach his present goals—and set new and higher ones. Isn't that the kind of upward spiral you want to develop with your clients? You can do it with add-ons that you work on after you've solved each client's problem.

J. Douglas Edwards and I are close friends and next door neighbors in Scottsdale. We frequently swap stories that people tell us at our separate seminars. Doug came back from a speaking tour in Canada one day and told me, "A young man in Toronto said, 'I've become a multi-millionaire since the last time I heard your program, and it's all because of one sentence in your speech.'"

Now that's heady stuff to a speaker. It's the hope of hearing exciting success stories—though rarely as spectacular as this—that keeps Doug and I climbing on planes. "From that one sentence?" I asked, somewhat wistfully. "What was it?" His answer is the name of the next and my favorite system for turning small change into big money:

● **"Sell them in bunches, like bananas"** is System 3.

Here's what the young man, Ed Dardon, did with the concept he discovered in Toronto at Doug's seminar. A few weeks later, Ed went out to see a referral. The man had a problem, of course. He was a member of a real estate syndicate that had built a magnificent apartment complex. The problem came when they completed the project and set their rents to earn a return on their investment. They had priced themselves out of the market; their project was just too magnificent. So it sat vacant. Taxes and expenses were mounting up, and nothing was coming in to service those costs and the mortgages.

Ed Dardon opened his mind and came up with a plan. Then he met with the entire syndicate and outlined his program. Condominiums are very popular today, but at that time they weren't well known. Ed convinced the syndicate that the only profitable way out of their predicament was to convert the apartments to condominiums and sell out.

Speed was essential. Ed trained a small, capable sales force around the concept of selling them in bunches, like bananas. He packaged the condominiums by the threes, fours, and fives—and often they sold two or three bunches to one investor. The people who bought weren't intent on getting immediate cash flow because of the tax advantages.

Along with his sales organization, Ed also set up a management company to handle the rental details for the new owners. Both companies were profitable and grew rapidly. Ed's success at turning a financial fiasco into a profitable venture for the original developers brought him a flood of new opportunities. Not only was the word out that Ed was someone special, the trade magazines hailed his achievements throughout Canada. In less time than he'd spent in high school, Ed Dardon became a multi-millionaire.

Keep looking for opportunities to sell them in bunches, like bananas. And keep this thought in the front of your mind:

- **Every time you hit pay dirt, dig all the way through the mountain.** That's System 4.

Sell one bank, and you know how to sell them all. If one boat catches more fish with your net, you can sell one to every tuna clipper in the harbor. Are you bothered about how you'll make doing an all-out job of preparing to sell one customer pay off? Stop worrying. Start planning how to use the new knowledge you'll gain. Sell everybody in that same business or interest group. In other words, look on each prospect as if he were a member of a specialized group that you're now going to learn how to sell—because that's exactly what he is.

Now, if you use the same plan to sell bunches of things to bunches of people, how are you going to spend all the money you'll earn?

- **Use your business cards to reach people you've never met.** This money earner is System 5.

When we're new in sales, many of us give out a thousand cards. Then we stop doing it because we've got enough business to get by on. We don't realize how much of that business came from the cards.

When I was in real estate sales, I sent one of my cards along every time I paid a bill. Someone had to be opening all those envelopes, I thought. One day a woman called me and said, "Mr. Hopkins, you don't know me, but my husband and I want to buy a bigger house, and we'd like to talk to you about it."

After telling her that I'd be delighted to work with them, I asked, "How did you get my name?"

"I handle your account at the gas company," she said, "and I've got about two dozen of your cards in my desk."

The fee I earned for satisfying that lady's real estate needs paid for more business cards than I could use in a hundred years—and that's only one instance. Unless you sell special things to limited groups, miss no opportunity to put your business card in the hands of anyone you come in contact with, however remotely or briefly.

• **Be a walking ad for yourself.** Put System 6 to work for you whenever you go out in public during the workday. Do it with class—carry a plastic writing pad binder that's imprinted with an attention-catching message. The next time you're in a restaurant at lunch time waiting to be seated, look at the crowd waiting with you. How many of them need what you sell?

Rather than stand there fidgeting every day from now on, relax, look amiable, and casually hold your binder where it can be seen. Have WE STRETCH DOLLARS or some other teaser slogan imprinted on it. Your company's name, if it's well known or tells what you sell, may be your most effective binder imprint.

A Champion knows that people will read his binder advertisement and start conversations. Often they'll say something like, "Oh, you're with _____" as they read his company's name.

Every time this happens, the Champion smiles and says, while handing them his card, "Yes, I am, and obviously you wouldn't have asked unless you had some needs." Another thing the Champion knows is that these chance encounters often lead to lucrative business that he wouldn't otherwise get.

• **Learn how to recoup on the recontact route** and take advantage of moneyclutching System 7.

Whether we like it or not, recontacts are an essential part of many selling sequences. The need for recontact arises when, after you've demonstrated your product or presented your service, they aren't ready to make the decision. In many cases, their reasons are valid and can't be overcome. They ask you to leave your figures and brochure, and say they'll look at them and let you know. In chapter 15's Close 9, I gave you a technique for overcoming many of these delaying causes, but you'll always encounter some situations that can only be won by recontact at a later date. If recontacts are a common occurrence with you, study how to raise your score on closing them. I've broken the process down into steps.

1. **Prepare the way in the prior meeting.** Don't hard-sell yourself out of any chance to work with them again. And avoid committing yourself to phoning for an appointment for the second meeting; it's too easy for them to have a secretary tell you to call back next year. In most cases you can simply go in and see the person on a recontact even though you had to make an appointment for the first meeting.

2. **When you walk in on your recontact.** Smile, greet them, repeat your name and company if there's any possibility they don't remember it and, again, unless they make the move, don't push for a handshake.

3. **Begin with a summary of benefits.** The average salesperson doesn't

do this. Instead, he starts off with a say-no question that immediately kills the sale. Then he spends the rest of his time with the client trying desperately to breathe life back into the corpse. How does he kill the sale?

By asking something like, "Well, did you decide?" Charging straight in for the decision, without first renewing the agreements reached during the last meeting, almost guarantees a turndown.

The professional never asks a say-no question, and takes another tack entirely. Let's suppose that a week ago I demonstrated a piano to Mrs. Kellens. Ordinarily, I'd want both husband and wife present at the demonstration, but in this case it was clear that Mr. Kellens wouldn't be available, so I went ahead with the wife only. Now I'm recontacting, and the first thing I do is get back to where we were.

"Mrs. Kellens, I thought I'd reiterate what we've already talked about. As we agreed, the piano you liked best, the Singsweet, would fit nicely in that corner, wouldn't it?

"And we also agreed that the tone and quality of the Singsweet, even though it's not our largest or most costly piano, is more than sufficient for your needs, didn't we?" Mrs. Kellens says yes to both these propositions because she's already agreed to them in our previous meeting. I go on.

"And we agreed that one of the most exciting things about having this piano in your home is that your children would then be able to take advantage of the five years of piano lessons you and your husband have already invested in."

I give her a chance to say something positive about that and then continue: "And we also thought they would bring their friends home more often if you have a piano. You said you want to have your children home more often didn't you?"

She has to agree with all this because it's what she told me herself. Of course, when she did that, I recognized the vital importance of these emotional buying triggers, and tried to etch them in my brain. (Many Champions don't trust their memory here. If they need a recontact, they jot down all the prospect's reasons for buying as soon as they walk out of the first meeting. Then they can review them before the recontact and be sure of not overlooking any.)

Not until I've reviewed all the benefits she expects from the purchase of the piano, not until I've brought all those emotions back into play, do I get to whatever held up the purchase at the last meeting. But I still don't ask for a decision. Instead, I focus on the emotional barrier.

"I really feel that the only thing we didn't adequately discuss and agree on was whether you husband would be as excited with the investment you want to make in your children as you are, isn't that right?"

What have I done? Brought her back to the emotional state she was in after the demonstration. When I walked in on the recontact, if they'd definitely decided to buy the piano, she would have interrupted to tell me so. Mrs. Kellens expected me to say something like, "Well, I'm back. Did you talk to Mr. Kellens? What did he say about buying the Singsweet?" Then she planned to answer:

"I'm afraid he said no. I'm sorry—I really tried—but I guess we'll have to wait another year."

She and the children want and need my Singsweet. They can afford it. It's my job to help her get that piano, not make it easy for her to get rid of me. So instead of leading her into saying, "Sorry. Goodbye," I lead her through the emotional reasons why she wants the piano. If I can keep her talking and emoting about having the piano for her children and their friends, she's going to think of a way to get it. Tell yourself, "I'm not taking up space on this earth to be a sponge for negative feelings; my purpose is to help people own benefits."

Here's a popular line with salespeople who enjoy no great success selling in the corporate situation: "Well, I'm back. Did you think about my proposition?" What answer do they almost always get to that brilliant query?

"Yes. No." ("Yes, we thought about it. No, we don't want it.") One chop and the salesperson is dead. But he asked for it.

In the business situation, as in the personal situation, you have to do a benefit summary of what you've already agreed to when you go back on a recontact. You have to restore the climate of benefit-consciousness that you had at the last meeting. When recontacts are the rule rather than the exception, the Champion plays the game with an ace up his sleeve. He deliberately leaves a benefit out of his original presentation, so that when he comes back for the recontact, he can say something like this after doing the benefit summary:

"Mr. Selvan, when we were together last, we discussed how your corporation would benefit from the higher rate of production our Chompslick will give you. I think I overlooked mentioning something during our last meeting that I believe is critical to your decision. I know that we're over the budget figure with our present proposal, but I'd like you to keep this in mind. With the Chompslick, you're not locked into even its high production rate. We can supply a robot feed mechanism that will increase production up to eighty percent."

After dropping that gem, you go into your closing sequence.

• Our last system **works like wings, costs almost nothing, and isn't used much**. Yet it's one of the greatest moneygrabbers around. System 8 is the most powerful method I know about for obligating people to boost your sales potential. For some reason that I've never been able to understand, few salespeople will use this technique. Maybe I shouldn't be surprised. After all, only about five percent of us are using all the techniques we could to make more money and do our job better. And only about five percent of salespeople are using this simple technique regularly. Maybe it's not direct enough—or maybe it just requires alertness and a little effort.

What are the two most important words in the English language for our profession of selling? Not gimmie, gimmie. The words are *Thank you*. That's right, thank you. I found this out years ago when I started writing thank you notes to everyone I could. The results were amazing. Let me give you one example. When I cashed my first sizable check in sales, I went right out and bought a suit because I needed clothes desperately. During the next few days that suit got a lot of wear. Then it had a collision with a gob of oil. When

I rushed my suit to the cleaners, the owner of the shop rushed it out in time for my next appointment. So I wrote him a thank you note that he taped on the front of his cash register along with my business card. Three days later I got a call from another customer of his who'd seen my note. That call led to a large sale. Besides putting a chunk of money in my pocket, that incident taught me a lesson.

Thank people. Do it in writing. And do it right away.

Spoken thanks are nice, they're necessary to courtesy, and sometimes they're the only thanks you can give someone. But spoken thanks rarely bring in referrals. For that, you need to write a thank you note.

Don't think that my note to the dry cleaning establishment was the only time this technique has worked. I get letters all the time from Champions who have taken my advice and made thank you notes part of their selling sequence. One of our trainees, obviously a Champion, wrote: "Tom, at the supermarket, the woman checking out my order said, 'Aren't you in real estate?' I said I was, we talked for a moment, and I gave her my card. Then I got to thinking about it, so I found out her address and sent her a thank you note for taking my card. Two weeks later she called me up. Her brother-in-law and sister wanted a house. Because I sent her a thank you note, I was able to get that couple happily involved in owning a home."

What a powerful tool. Why aren't you using it every day?

Maybe your answer to that question is that you can't think of anyone to thank — everyone you do business with just does what's necessary, and no thanks are called for.

Thank them anyway. If you're starting out and have no clientele, send a thank you note to almost everyone you meet. Bear in mind that this is a broadcast technique. Send lots of messages and some of them will get through. Beam them in the right direction. If you sell insurance or real estate and almost everyone is a potential client for you, send thank you notes to the manager of the neighborhood ice cream parlour and everybody else you get the slightest attention from. If your product is diesel trucks, be more selective. No matter what you sell, always carry a set of 3 x 5 cards for the express purpose of fueling your thank you note machine. Suppose you're out prospecting by cold calling on company offices. In one of them, while waiting to see someone, you happen to meet and have a brief but cordial chat with an executive from another company than the one you're calling on.

When he goes back to his office, he won't remember much about meeting you, and in a few days he will have forgotten all about you. But what if you send him a thank you note that very day? For what? For the pleasant chat you had with him. If you can learn his name and company affiliation during your chance meeting, you can look the rest of the address up later.

The next day, what will his secretary give him to read first? Your thank you note. Do you realize how few they get? She'll walk into his office and say, "We sure got a nice thank you note this morning. Has he ever been here? I don't remember him."

"Oh, yeah, I remember this fellow. Nice guy. I just met him." How you work from that point depends on the situation. Even if the company this executive works for doesn't use your product or service, he very likely is acquainted with the executives of many companies that do. Selling is not an isolated function done in a vacuum—it's the thread our society's fabric is woven from. None of us can foresee or understand all the complex relationships within a community that influence who buys what from whom. But we can be sure that the more people who like and trust us the more success we'll have in sales.

What a powerful technique thank you notes are. Use them constantly and heavily to keep expanding the list of people who know, like, and trust you—the list of people who will buy from you or give you referrals any time they can.

Here are some of the times you should never miss sending thank you notes:

CONTACTS.
Any time you meet someone and there's any discussion of your product or service, send them a thank you.

RECONTACT.
Mail them a thank you note for seeing you after every visit.

CLIENT AFTER DEMONSTRATION.
Every time one of your established clients allows you to demonstrate something new, send him a thank you note.

CLIENT AFTER PURCHASE.
"Just a note to thank you again for . . . and to let you know that I'm available to help if there's any way I can be of service." Generally it's better to avoid suggesting that they may have problems by using that word, but make it clear that you're available if needed. And then, of course, be fast and energetic in solving every problem that does arise. Shortsighted salespeople make themselves scarce when their clients have problems. These are the kind of people who keep moving from company to company because they never can build up a clientele. The Champion has a completely different attitude toward product or service problems. He knows that if everything goes with perfect smoothness, the client will have trouble remembering him. He's in, out, and that's the end of it. But if there's a problem and it's handled promptly and well, that client remembers. The best source of referrals is the client you've solved problems for.

CLIENT AFTER REFERRAL.
Whether you make the sale or not, a written thank you to the people who referred you is essential. You may want to take them to dinner—or send them out to dinner at your expense.

FOR EFFORTS ABOVE AND BEYOND THE CALL OF DUTY.
Remember anyone in any industry who does something nice for you. For example, do you ever take clients out to lunch or dinner? Would you like

the maitre'd to treat you with special attention when you walk in with clients? Then send him a thank you note. Tell him how happy you were with his service, and how you look forward to bringing anyone you can to his restaurant. You'll find that you get treated beautifully when you make reservations and go in there after he gets your note.

How would you like to be the only person who never has to wait for his car when it's in the shop for maintenance? The next time you take your car in, write a note to the service manager afterwards: "Dear Chet, thank you for getting my car out so fast yesterday. I really appreciate it. I'm going to send you all the business I can. Sincerely." Send a copy to the owner of the business.

TO PEOPLE YOU DON'T SELL.

Why not send them a thank you note? After all they did give you the courtesy of hearing your presentation. Now people are going to be asking them how they like the new item they bought from the competition. What if they don't like what they bought, or if the competition hasn't done a good job on service and followup? They may regret their decision and tell their friends to check with you before buying. That's called a referral, and this is the best kind: from someone who owns your competition's latest model and now says your item is better. Yes, send thank you notes to the people who don't buy from you. And keep in touch with them. The odds are that the person who sold them won't—or he'll change jobs and leave an orphan who'll get lost in the shuffle at the competing company. Keep that foreign orphan posted on new developments and, when the itch cycle makes a full turn, you'll be in a perfect position to recapture the business. By then the price and feature factors that caused them to buy from the competition will probably have changed.

The thank you note that kicks off this whole process runs something like this: "Thank you for letting me show you (whatever). I enjoyed meeting you, and I appreciate being considered. We couldn't get together on your needs this time, but I hope that when you think of (your general line), you'll remember me.

Please let me know if there's any way that I can be of service. Cordially."

I carry 3 x 5 cards with me today—as I have for many years—and I travel with the materials needed to send thank you notes. I average between five and ten thank you notes every single day to the Champions I meet, to the people who attend our seminars, to business owners who invest in our video training systems, and to a variety of other people.

Start now. If you don't have a supply of 3 x 5 cards and stationery suitable for thank you notes and letters, don't pass an office supply or drugstore without going in and buying them. This one concept can deliver results that will amaze you.

Ten thank you notes a day is 3,650 a year and 36,500 in a decade. Some Champions tell me they get ten sales from every hundred thank you notes. You'll certainly get more than one from every hundred. Multiply your average income per sale by 36 to see the minimum extra income this one technique will generate for you in the next twelve months. I think you'll decide it's a winner.

All it takes is three minutes and a stamp for each note. Use the time you'd otherwise spend staring at the wall waiting to see someone. Start doing it today because the results don't reach you overnight. And, like all successful methods of coping with life's opportunities, consistency counts. Ten thank you notes a day is three hundred a month. That's enough to give you a tremendous boost in the length of a single season.

17

HOW TO PERSPIRE LESS AND PROFIT MORE FROM PAPERWORK

To most salespeople, paperwork is like oil to the Arabs—messy and troublesome stuff they have no use for—but unless they keep it moving, there's no money. Ask any sales manager about paperwork. Although the top third of his sales force generates several times the volume that the bottom third does, he'll tell you that he has more trouble with the bottom third's paperwork. Why? Because the people in the top third are too busy to answer avoidable questions about their paperwork. So they do it right the first time.

No single quality separates him from the average performer more than the ability the Champion has of doing things right the first time. As an exasperated sales manager once said, "Why is there always enough time to do it over, but never enough time to do it right in the first place?"

Of course, the answer is that do-it-over time has to be taken from time that could be used to generate more business. In sales, as in every area of life, there's no such thing as useless time; there's only time that's used—and time that's wasted. And nothing wastes more of it faster than turning in orders whose meaning people have to guess at.

The first rule for fast paperworking is to be clear. Learn to print fast and clearly, or learn to type. The Champion doesn't risk enraging his customers with costly delays or mistakes caused by carelessly written orders; he double checks everything relating to orders for accuracy and clarity.

But once we step away from the actual processing of orders, we get into areas where a different set of imperatives apply. Now your company is using paperwork to:

(1) Control you.

(2) Furnish information the government demands.

(3) Gather information for production and marketing decisions.

Let's talk about these three classes of paperwork.

1. INFORMATION TO CONTROL YOU WITH.

Most of the salespeople in most sales forces are, by definition, average. This means that almost all sales departments set up their paperwork with the average salesperson in mind. In other words, because **the average salesperson doesn't motivate himself**, the company is forced to motivate him.

Think about that. With rare exceptions, all managers find themselves faced with these two realities:

(a) Less than 20% of the salespeople form a group that produces more than 60% of the total volume—and this group requires little urging to do the job.

(b) More than 80% of the salespeople form another group that produces less than 40% of total volume—if the pressure is kept on. If the pressure slackens, this group's production falls even further.

If you want to get rid of a lot of pettifogging paperwork in a hurry, prove to your sales manager that you're moving rapidly into the (a) group and that you're a self-starter. He'll love it.

2. INFORMATION REQUIRED BY THE GOVERNMENT.

The Champion gets this kind of information in promptly. He knows the company has to have it (or thinks they do, which is the same thing) and he also knows that it takes less time to get it over with than it does to cope with repeated reminders.

3. INFORMATION YOUR COMPANY NEEDS FOR MARKETING AND PRODUCTION CONTROL.

Here again the Champion cooperates with enthusiasm. He realizes that his chosen company's future is no better than the marketing and production decisions they make that are partly based on what he reports. Most companies look to their sales forces for two vital functions: sales and information gathering. Because of the crucial nature of both categories, no company is stronger than its sales force.

The road to ruin is paved with good intentions. In school, were you ever given thirty days to complete an assignment that you knew could be done in a few hours of sustained effort? Did you knock it right out and get it off your mind? No. If you thought about it at all after three days, the comforting knowledge that you still had twenty-seven days removed any possibility that you'd give it even an odd hour's effort yet. Then two weeks are suddenly gone, and you began to feel some twinges. You see the big F looming up in front of you. Failure. More days slip by. The F keeps getting bigger in your mind. You suffer more pain and anxiety. Finally, two days before—or the last night before—the due date, you sat down and whipped the assignment out. And then you felt a great sense of relief. You probably said, "Why didn't I save myself all that cold sweat and get it done a month ago?"

The Champion prefers the hot sweat of work to the cold sweat of worry—so much so that before long, he has plenty of time to work up the best sweat of all, the one you get playing hard when you've got your life together, your work and goals on schedule, and your bank account in good shape.

Being on time is a habit. Being late is a habit. You can set your mental clock on time, or ten minutes late. You can set your paperwork clock on

time, or three reminders late. And you can change any habit like this that
you want to change. All you have to do is concentrate on doing your new
habit instead of your old habit for twenty-one days.

This means that you do your new habit for twenty-one days without
missing a stroke. If you slide back once, start all over. If you really want the
new habit—and aren't sabotaging your own efforts with little voices complaining inside your head—you can own any habit you choose in just three
weeks.

Here are some rules for handling paperwork fast:

(1) **If it's clear that it has to be done sometime, do it now.** The quickest way
you can handle any paper is to finalize it the first time you see it.

(2) **If it doesn't have to be done, trash it now.**

(3) **Develop a double standard of accuracy for paperwork.** If big bucks are
involved, give it your best (order form and sales agreement) grade of
accuracy. If big bucks are not involved, give it your fast estimate grade of
attention.

A Champion realizes that he must operate like an independent company. The nature of the sales profession is that you are really in business for
yourself. In fact, many salespeople have more freedom than most small
business owners do. But, because we in sales have so much latitude to do
things when, where, and how we want to, many of us don't discipline
ourselves. You can earn twice as much money in half the time if you'll just
discipline yourself to charge into your job, get on top of it, and then stay on
top. To do that, you have to tear into getting yourself organized—you can't
dink around with this.

Why is organization so important?

It saves time, and all we have is time. Organization prevents future
problems. It is the basis for building referrals. If you're organized, you won't
forget the small details you promised to handle for the client. If you say,
"Sure, Mr. Boehm, when we deliver, I'll be there to make certain that the
installation goes right," you better be organized. Otherwise, you won't be
there. Then Mr. Boehm will start looking for little things to give you trouble
about, things you could have brushed over if you had done what you said
you'd do. You made promises to get the order that you could have kept, but
didn't. So he wants to get even. And now Mr. Boehm won't believe anything that you tell him. Why should he? You've already demonstrated what
your word is worth.

Your company may supply you with a highly organized follow-up
system or tickler file. These are great because they're designed for what
you're doing. But you have to pay the price for using them by doing the
paperwork that's required to keep them up. There's rarely a better place for
some of your non-prime selling time than keeping up your follow-up and
tickler files—and pulling out calls to make at the times your file tells you are
most likely to develop sales.

I like to keep organizational tools simple. Inexpensive 3 x 5 card files are terrific. You need four different ones:

(1) CLIENT-BUYER FILE.
Break this file into three sections:

(a) Hot. These are the people who have the need, are qualified to buy, and are sincerely interested in making a decision soon.

When buyers are truly interested, they'll make a decision within seven days. Now that doesn't mean they'll purchase *your* product within seven days, but they'll purchase *a* product within seven days. A Champion tries to work with between three and five highly motivated buyers at all times. Some of you have a large stack of all your leads—and you call none of them. The average salesperson has a rubber band for his prospects and when his attitude is down, what doesn't come off? That rubber band.

Then, when he starts feeling good again, he starts calling all his people. Guess what? They've already bought — and his enthusiasm dives back into the garbage can.

(b) Medium. The second division in your client-buyer file is for the people who are apparently qualified, have the need, but are not yet highly motivated.

Perhaps they're waiting for some future event to heat their medium needs up to a hot need. Think back to the itch cycle. If you're working with a thirty-month cycle, a buyer is medium a year after purchase, medium-to-hot two years after purchase, and hot when his old item is two years and four months old.

(c) Cold. In the third section of your buyer-client file, keep all the leads you get from any source that you don't immediately classify as hot or medium.

These are the people who were just looking, who walked in, or called in from ads or signs, and seem to have a mild or future need for what you sell.

Keep in mind that few people call on ads, or come in when they see a store or sign, unless they have a definite interest in the product or service that's offered. Very few people spend their days wandering around looking at products and discussing services they have no need for and couldn't buy if they did. The average salesperson is far too quick to dismiss lukewarm people as being unworthy of any effort at all.

A Champion goes through his client-buyer file every three days, spotting the best opportunities that day for adding heat. Every time one of his *hot* buyers approves the paperwork, he finds a *medium* to put on the front burner.

And, all year long, he keeps in touch with everyone in the cold section. Depending on the itch cycle of what he's selling and the individuals involved, he's in touch once every ninety days, once a month, once a week— in any case, often enough to make sure that when their bread rises he'll be there to pop it in the oven.

Most people want everything that's new—but the average salesperson isn't organized to take advantage of this fact. When his company comes up with something new, the Champion knows exactly what to do. He works through his medium file, telling everyone about the new product or concept, knowing that it will turn some of those mediums into hots. And then he works through his cold file and turns some of the colds into mediums.

(2) SWAP MEET FILE.

Leads from this source should be in a separate file because they're likely to become hot at any moment. Also, you should coordinate your sales activity on them with other members of your swap meet, and report your progress on each lead to the swapper who gave it to you.

(3) ITCH CYCLE FILE.

Any stationery store will have sets of 12 monthly file guides for 3 x 5 cards. Fill out a card for each client when they buy, or when you encounter them in your search for orphans, and put that card behind the appropriate month's guide. On the first of each month, pull all the cards behind that guide and you'll have a fistful of hot buyers to work with.

(4) REFERRAL FILE.

Here's where you put the names you gather from buyers with the card referral system. (See chapter 7.) Contact each of these people as quickly as you can and classify them as hot, medium, or cold prospects.

In addition to the 3 x 5 files above, you need a simple system for maintaining records of income tax deductions and expenses. The government wants a diary or log book type of record that you keep up on a daily basis—so do it. It's merely a matter of habit, and it'll save an enormous amount of strain when the tax deadline arrives. It'll also save you money, because missing receipts and unrecorded expenses are money thrown away.

The average new salesperson thinks, "I don't have time to keep records now. I'll wait until I have some sales income and then I'll worry about deductions." The next time you think about it, you get a very sick feeling because you've made lots of money, you've lost hundreds of dollars of receipts for deductible expenses—and Uncle has his hand out. File your receipts and jot down your expenses as you go, and take advantage of all the legal tax breaks you can. Tax competence is part of sales competence. Operate like a company because you are a company unto yourself.

One last word about paperwork. If you want to grow with the company you're now working for, don't fight its paperwork. Go with its flow, or you'll stifle your chances there. Business lives and breathes with paper; people who can't push their share of it along can't rise far.

I've often heard people say, "I should've had that promotion. I was next in line."

I ask them, "Have you been operating like a business? Do your superiors know you are? Have you shown them that your capabilities are growing larger than the job you now have?"

Seniority isn't given much weight when promotions are handed out. Fortunately. Few business managers will hesitate to pick ability over seniority any time they have a clear choice. And what is ability?

It's largely a matter of having your work and your resources organized so that you can perform with maximum effectiveness. Doing this requires that you use your time to best advantage, which leads us to the subject of the next chapter.

18
FORTUNE BUILDING STARTS WITH TIME PLANNING

Salespeople who turn in average performances rarely plan their time. Almost all Champions and top producers plan their time. Therefore, to increase your sales and your income, you must plan your time.

I think you'll agree with the statement above—but will you plan your time?

The odds are that you won't, because you have the strange idea that time planning is a difficult and complex task.

It isn't. In fact, it's one of the easiest things in the world, one that starts paying immediate dividends. To start, list the things you must do tomorrow on a piece of paper, and then mark them in order of importance. If you'll do that at the same stage of your routine every night between the time you get home and go to bed, you'll increase your efficiency and your income by at least twenty percent. You may even double your efficiency by this simple means. Far too many of us spend our entire days dashing about doing the next thing that grabs our attention. We keep so busy that we overlook the most important moneymaking opportunities that we could just as well be working at instead.

If you've never planned your time, start with this simple but highly effective method. Make it your firm habit, every evening, to sit down for a few minutes at the same time and list all the things you must do tomorrow to make the most of that day. Then number them in order of importance. Many highly successful people use this, and only this, system for controlling their time.

Next—and you can start on my next recommendation the same evening as you do the above habit—tear into getting yourself organized. Sit down and list all the things you can do and learn to make yourself more effective, and work out a schedule for getting these things done or learned in the shortest possible time. The sooner you clear that list, the sooner your income will start shooting up, right? So don't wait. Start tonight.

None of the top Champions, the ones earning tremendous incomes, will go to sleep before they've written down the most important things they must do tomorrow. No matter what's going on, they first jot down in their planning notebook what they've got to do the next day in order to keep their great incomes flowing. Let me tell you what will happen if and when you start writing down each night the most important things you must do tomorrow.

Your subconscious mind will work on your list all night, without disturbing your sleep, because it wants to help you solve your problems and achieve your goals. But your subconscious mind can't help unless you tune it in to what's going to happen next. That's what listing the things you have to do the next day does: it cocks the hammer on the power of your subconscious mind. The very best time to do this is shortly before you go to sleep. When morning comes, you'll find that your mind fired some accurate shots in the night, and now you have fresh ideas up front in your conscious mind about how to handle the things on your must-do-list better.

Give this process several days to start flowing. Nothing helps it more than going over your list in a quiet room, and seeing yourself involved with the most difficult part of each thing you have on your list. Equally important—and be careful never to omit this phase—see yourself happily enjoying the fact that you've successfully accomplished each of your goals for tomorrow. Make these sessions brief and upbeat. Don't concentrate on fear and dread of what you *have to do* tomorrow. If you try that, your subconscious mind may solve these problems by figuring out ways to make you forget or otherwise avoid meeting what it sees as painful experiences. Turn the primitive, powerful, never-sleeping subconscious part of your brain onto helping you achieve your goals by visualizing yourself confidently brushing aside an occasional setback, but succeeding most of the time.

Establish a follow-up system. There are many excellent time planners on the market that take your yearly plan down to a monthly plan, then to a weekly plan, and finally to a daily plan. These devices can do much of the organizing work for you.

Here are some things that should appear on your daily work plan, your list of important things to do tomorrow:

(1) LEAVE THE OFFICE.

How many games would a professional ball club win if they never left the locker room? There are an awful lot of salespeople who lose a lot of games (sales) because they don't leave the locker room (office) often enough. The business, in the form of people who buy, is in the larger world outside the walls of your office. Go. Go often. And go early.

(2) SCHEDULED APPOINTMENTS.

At the time you make one, you probably think there's no possibility that you'll forget it. But as you start to hit harder, you'll start missing appointments unless you write them down—all of them—in a notebook that you keep with you.

(3) RESEARCH.

Ours is a changing world; yours is a changing business. Whenever there's a new product, or a new development in your service, you must sit down and research it, analyze its effect, and regain your competence to explain your offering adequately to potential buyers.

(4) FAMILY.

Many of us salespeople take care of everybody else, and the last people we plan for are the ones who are most important to us: our families. Don't lose what you've got while you climb the ladder of success. When you should do something with your family, write that in your planner and put it on your list of important things you're going to do the next day.

(5) PHYSICAL HEALTH.
Champions keep themselves in shape for three reasons:

(a) they don't want to be the richest person in the hospital,
(b) they know they're more effective when they feel good,
(c) the point of the whole exercise is to get more out of life, and they can't do that, no matter how much money they make, if they lose their health in the process. So schedule your exercise program along with your business appointments. This is definitely one of your most important daily (or thrice-weekly) activities. You don't have to become a fitness nut. But at the other extreme is the unfit nut, whose neglected body destroys his energy, enthusiasm, and zest for living. Somewhere between these two extremes, according to your interests, is where you should aim to place yourself.

(6) EMOTIONAL HEALTH.
Schedule personal rewards and, when you've earned them, never miss taking them. Don't try to cheat yourself here. The concept of personal rewards is vital to maintaining a strong sense of purpose. Without a strong sense of purpose, you can't maintain a strong drive to succeed. Your personal rewards may take the form of recreational activities, high quality possessions, upward social movement, charitable or spiritual activity—or quite the opposite. Many varieties of acceptable personal rewards await you, and can make all the effort worthwhile. Schedule frequent recreational activity to reward yourself. Don't give it up except for clear and compelling reasons and, if you do, compensate yourself. Unless you adequately reward yourself, the entire concept of personal reward will cease to have meaning for you—with disastrous effect on your will to win.

And schedule some of your time, money, and effort into something larger than yourself to build your sense of strength and personal worth. Nothing clears our minds for greater achievement more than doing something to make the world a better place because we are here.

(7) PROSPECTING.
If you don't schedule prospecting, if you don't put down the exact hours and days that you'll do it, what's the last thing you'll do?

Prospect.

And what's the first thing that'll dump your sales volume into the cellar?

Not prospecting.

Keep your income growing; schedule a daily stint of prospecting.

Here's an allocation of time for most effective sales work:

Preparing to prospect: Spend only five percent of your time getting ready to prospect, and ninety-five percent of the time allocated for prospecting actually on that phone. (Many beginners spend half their time getting ready and a few spend all their time getting ready). Prepare and practice your lines the night before. Remember, there's no substitute for on-the-job training, and the only way you can get that in prospecting is by dialing a number and talking to a possible buyer.

Prospecting. When you're new, if you'll spend seventy-five percent of your time prospecting, you'll soon be in the top group in your company's sales force.

Preparing for appointments. You should be so well organized that you need spend only eight percent of your time getting ready to make top quality presentations or demonstrations.

Presenting. Between five and ten percent of your time should be spent actually in front of customers. Don't hang around. Get in and get out. Your customers will have more respect for you if you move things along. As you get more organized and experienced, and are working more with referrals, you'll be able to spend more time actually selling. The elite of our profession have secretarial, clerical, and technical help for the express purpose of allowing them to spend nearly all their time planning and presenting.

Merchandising and servicing. Five percent. Keep in mind that these starting percentages will change as your sales operation matures. Your initial prospecting will develop leads, then sales, then referrals. You'll start making money—and you'll prospect less because you'll be working with referrals more.

On the first day of every month, sit down with your planning/appointment book and write down everything you want to do that month. Write down any family or social event that you're committed to.

Note all the company meetings that you should attend. Be mature, responsible, and realistic. Unless you support your company, your company can't support you. Be part of the team. Be part of the solution, not part of the problem; be on time for meetings. And use your time there to help the company build a greater future for itself—which means for you.

Enter all the educational programs you're getting involved with.

Then pull that month's itchers from your Itch Cycle File, call all of them, and schedule appointments. Next, go through your other files of leads and schedule more appointments.

As soon as you complete this work, you can see how much time you have available for the month. Work out a schedule for prospecting that will develop as many more leads as you can handle, and go to it. Isn't that simple? Your whole month is planned out for maximum efficiency and sales performance just by following those few easy steps.

Never allow yourself to think that planning your hours, days, and months is a baffling, frustrating, and impossible task. Take it one step at a time and it will go beautifully. Let me tell you why I'm so sure by relating an event that has had a tremendous impact on me ever since it happened a number of years ago. After I started doing some good in sales, I had a thought. Why not get some ideas from people who are more successful than I am? I began going to lots of seminars. At one, I heard a man whose introduction impressed me more than his speech did. He was earning $400,000 a year as the president of a major conglomerate.

I decided that I could learn something of great value from this man, so I set out to get an appointment for lunch with him. That took two months. When I was finally sitting across from him, I said, "I'm here for a very sincere reason. I want you to tell me how you've become so successful." I was twenty-one years old then.

He chuckled, and started talking. After about ten minutes, I think he realized that I really was sincere. I said, "Tell me what I have to do."

Here's how he answered me. "Tom, all my adult life I've lived by a saying, and it's made all the difference. If you live by this saying too, I don't see how you can fail to be extremely successful."

That was a pretty heavy statement. I grabbed a napkin and got ready to write.

He went on, "If I give it to you and you really live by it, there'll be days when you'll hate me."

"I don't care. Give it to me."

He did, and I wrote these words:

I must do the most productive thing possible at every given moment.

For years, those words hung by my desk. Today I can state that I too have spent all my mature years living by that saying, and it's made all the difference. And I can also tell you that, if you will live by that saying, I don't see how you can fail to be extremely successful. Let me also add the same caution that the president of the conglomerate did all those years ago, "If you really live by this saying, there'll be days when you'll hate me." But I also know that there'll soon be stretches of time when you'll bless me for giving you that saying—if you live by it.

Is sitting in the office jawing with other salespeople productive? Of course not. If you'll start doing the most productive thing possible at every given moment, you'll not only become a Champion and enjoy a high income, you'll also become a finer, happier, person. Let's understand each other here. The most productive thing that you can do at every given moment is not always something aimed directly at making money. The most productive thing you can do during many given moments is to be with your family, relaxing, playing, and rewiring your dynamo. Rest and recreation are essential parts of the productive rhythm. It's not productive to run a machine until it overheats and breaks down, it's simply stupid. The same applies to your own brain, body, and set of drives. It's also stupid to rest from goofing off, or to take a vacation from doing nothing.

19

HOW TO SELL YOUR WAY OUT OF A SLUMP

Our premise here is that you've learned the techniques in the previous chapters, you've put them to work and made some money, and now you find yourself in a slump.

What's the biggest obstacle to getting out of a slump?

Knowing why you're in it in the first place.

Where do you start looking for the knowledge?

By asking yourself this question:

Am I happy?

Any genuine response to the question, when reduced to the basics, will drop into one of these categories:

- "I'm miserable all the time."
- "I'm happy all the time."
- "I'm miserable some of the time, and happy some of the time."

A lot of people don't want to face this question. They'll try to avoid it by saying, "I'm not miserable, and I'm not what you'd call happy either. I'm just so-so all the time."

I won't buy that. If that's your reaction, you're doing what most people do: faking yourself out, sticking to the mediocre center, avoiding reality. If you're not enjoying your life, if you're not pursuing your goals and opportunities with joy in your heart, if you're not reaching out for more of the good things you're capable of winning, you're not merely unhappy—you're miserable. The opposite of happy is *unhappy* but I'm calling it *miserable* because the importance of this idea demands all the impact I can give it. Every person who can't say he's happy is missing the greatest thing life has to offer and that, I'm convinced, is genuine misery.

You won't get over having sales slumps unless you get over having misery problems. Why? Because every time you get rolling the miseries reach up and pull you off the wagon. That is, the miseries will do that until you learn how to conquer them.

More people are successful part of the time than are successful all of the time. Average performance is often made up of a good month offset by a bad month. If you're blaming this on how the marketplace acts, on how the planets line up, on how your luck breaks or whatever, you're hiding from reality. If you're in a slump now, you have a better record that you've slumped from. This means you've proven you can sell well. In reality, doesn't this also mean that you've proven your slumping problem is your attitude?

Say yes. Until you've admitted to yourself that your attitude is responsible for your slump, you're not ready to get well.

We're all part of the greater community of humankind, and we all need help constantly to achieve our full potential. But there's one basic fact that you must accept and act on if outside help is to make any lasting difference in your life: you must internalize that outside knowledge with your own energy, determination and discipline, and then you must put your new skills and wisdom to work with your own energy, determination, and discipline. Whether you get that outside help from a book, a seminar, a cassette tape, a personal interview in a professional's office — it's all the same in that respect: unless you make it work, it won't work.

Are you ready to make it work?

Great. Let's start by studying how you really feel about the question, *Am I happy?* We'll discuss each of these broad categories in turn.

"I'm miserable all the time."

If this is your answer, I feel for you. I've been there. Twice. I know you need help, just as I did, before you can shake the miseries, get effective, and go on to greater things.

My first case of continuous misery occurred years ago when I started in outside sales and was a washout because I didn't know anything about selling. The only cure for that kind of misery is to learn how to do what you have to do to be a success—and then to go out and do it. I did. My non-success misery vanished. Then a new kind of mental anguish started developing in its place.

After I finished my first year of success, I thought I was more miserable than ever. This was my second bout with continuous misery. It was different, of course, from the empty-wallet kind of pain I'd felt before. Now my family had the things they needed. I had the buyable things I needed. But money doesn't buy happiness—it can only give you the means to find it. My new misery was the high-pressure kind created by doing a large volume of business with the wrong attitude for doing that kind of volume. After suffering with my new pains and anxieties for several months, I realized something that's had a profound influence on my life ever since:

> **Being miserable is a habit; being happy is a habit;**
> **and the choice is yours.**

If you gave the second reply to the happiness question, the next paragraph contains a note of caution that's worthy of your most careful consideration.

"I'm happy all the time."

Some people really are that way. Nothing bothers them, not even the things that should bother them. Carried to the extreme, this makes for another kind of dangerous person. When tragedy strikes nearby, we should feel grief. Then we should express that grief so that we can come to terms with it and go on reaching for our full potential. Anyone who can't do that should get professional help.

There are other times when we should feel unhappy—for a few minutes. When chance plays a particularly bad card, when something you could have prevented shatters your hopes for a sale, when a well-laid plan fails for reasons beyond your control, you certainly shouldn't be happy when you discover the disaster. Neither should you be smashed. But this kind of thing can't bother you more than a few minutes, can it? You've made the Champion's Five Attitudes Toward Rejection and Failure part of your personality, haven't you?

Your mind is probably racing ahead to the last answer to the happiness question.

"I'm miserable some of the time and happy some of the time."
That's the best of the three answers, but it still isn't good enough for you. A Champion says, "I know that some trouble and grief are part of life, so I'm miserable for brief periods when I should be, and I'm happy the rest of the time."

Understand and act on the knowledge that you must meet and overcome your problems yourself—not necessarily alone, but by and within yourself. Get all the help you can so long as the help you accept brings you nearer your goals. Always be alert for any yearning on your part to form the habit of being miserable.

In other words, don't be a neggie.

What's that?

A neggie is a negative person who wins by losing. He or she feeds on trouble, illness, and fear. If nothing is happening at the moment to justify the misery they've trained themselves to need, they invent something—or replay some past misery.

What's the opposite of being a neggie?

Being a successful, happy, and growing person.

You can be the opposite of a neggie by making it your habit to be happy except when there's a clear and present need for you to be sad for a while. Then be sad. Wash away your sorrow. Don't be afraid to cry. If your inhibitions won't let you do it in public, cry in private. Express your sorrow and get rid of it. Whether it's deep grief at a personal tragedy or the superficial but keenly felt remorse for a business matter not handled well, you must give vent to your feelings of grief or disappointment. Then turn resolutely back to your usual happy state.

This is one of the most valuable habits you can cultivate: **Change what you want to change. Accept what you can't hope to change. Be stubbornly happy no matter what, once you've rid yourself of the latest negative feelings that have a necessary part to play in your life.**

When I made my breakthrough and started handling a large volume of real estate sales, my problems multiplied with frightening speed. To most people, buying or selling their latest house is the largest transaction they've ever had to cope with. This creates pressure. Any quirks they have are exaggerated. A touch of greediness can run wild and blind them to their own best interests. Since most real estate transactions take weeks or months to complete, there's plenty of time for lots of things to change or go wrong. With the volume I was handling, for weeks at a time hairy problems hit me every time I showed my face at the office. Many days I didn't want to go in; I wanted to drive past the office and hide. The top producers in most fields have similar experiences.

When the urge to escape came close to overwhelming me, I'd pull into a public park and spend a few minutes staring at the trees and grass. Then I'd have a calm talk with myself. Champions believe in talking to themselves. But they don't do it in bars, they do it in quiet places where they won't be distracted—or *un*happily involved.

After getting my emotions under control, I'd drive to the office. Bear in mind that everyone there had been taking messages for me from people who were crackling with anger or anxiety. And, since I frequently called in, they knew that I had already heard about most of the problems.

When I walked through the office door, I'd start pumping out the good cheer. Strolling down the aisle between the desks, beaming smiles right and left, I'd say, "Good morning. How are you? Isn't this going to be a beautiful day for sales?"

The confirmed neggies would put their heads down and pretend they were too busy to notice me. The semi-negative types would grimace trying to smile. I could almost hear them all thinking, "Here he is, up to his eyeballs in problems—and he's got the gall to keep on grinning. I hate him!"

Do yourself a favor when you have a personal or business problem, when you have an ailment, when you've taken a jolt from the school of hard knocks: *don't tell anyone.* Twenty percent don't care, and eighty percent are glad to hear about it.

Don't give them the satisfaction. The only pleasure trouble can give you is keeping it to yourself—at least you know something that no one else around the office knows. If any rumor about your problem leaks out, play it down. Then change the subject to something positive as fast as you can. Humor is always positive. Any business problem is fair game for humor. Drive misery away with a laugh. It works. Misery loves company and losers love losers. When you're down you don't need sympathy, you need success. You attract what you are in both people and events. Happiness loves company too, and winners also love winners.

Another thing about losers: they love to talk about losing, about problems, about why it can't be done. The next time someone in your office has a disaster, notice how people react to it. The losers will hurry over to get the whole story in all its grimy detail. Then they'll tell a few sad tales of their own, and before you know it a royal banquet of bad news is in full swing.

Winners handle someone else's trouble differently. With silence. Or they may offer a few quick words of encouragement. There's none of the loving analysis of catastrophe that losers insist on.

When someone has a great success, the same split between winners and losers shows up. This time it's the winners who are crowding around ing to hear every detail, and perhaps share a success story or two of their own. Now it's the losers who are too busy to talk to you.

Have you ever gone into an emotional slump? A financial slump? A performance slump? Of course you have. Slumping is normal for anyone who hasn't trained himself to prevent slumps. I spent three months studying how to cure slumping, and I'm convinced that there is only one way. It's an old idea that goes under many names. This is the one I like best.

THE GOYA FORMULA

Using this formula is very easy—it only seems hard at the time. Here it is in it's entirety:

> *G. O. Y. A.*
> *Get off your backside;*
> *Get out into the field,*
> *And go to work.*

That's really all there is to it except for making yourself do it. This can be hard when your chin is on the floor and you're ready to give up on the whole world. I've been there too. But the amazing thing is, it's always easy to G.O.Y.A. Do I really think it's easy?

Yes. All you have to do is start—take the first small step—and after that it's all downhill. If you can just get yourself to start you'll be all right.

So far I've sounded like I always knew exactly how to unslump. Not so. I started off in real estate with the naive idea that if I could only get a few transactions into escrow, all my troubles would be over. A few of the old hands—not negative people, realists—had told me that making the sale is just half the battle, that closing the transaction is often the most frustrating and difficult half of an opportunity to serve a client.

I didn't believe that until suddenly I had six last-half battles going on at once, and none of them were going well. At the time I had a sales manager I was mad at almost constantly because he wasn't interested in hearing why it couldn't be done. I despised him for making me work so hard—until the end of the year when I realized how much money he'd led me to make.

One day three of my sales cancelled out bang, bang, bang. Other transactions were in trouble. As if that wasn't enough, some of my clients were being nasty about wanting their homes sold fast. I went into my manager's office with the top blown off my danger zone.

He looked up and asked, "What's wrong?"

"What's right?" I said. "Selling is for the birds. Every buyer I meet is a liar. The sellers are stealing my socks without even taking my shoes off. Then they call up complaining and insult my ancestry. I've had it. Take this business and flush it."

Murph smiled at me and said, "Tom, it sounds like you're down."

"What are you, a psychic? Certainly I'm down. I never get anything in this business except what's already been eaten."

"Do you know what you really need?" my manager said, "You need to get away."

That's the first thing we always want to do when things get tough, isn't it? I hadn't expected him to say that. I thought he was going to tell me to charge back in there and confront my problems. So I said, "I think you're right; I do need to get away."

"Let's go for a ride," he said.

"That's a good idea." Tom Murphy had a beautiful car with a splendid stereo and no phone. I thought I'd enjoy a drive with my manager. We jumped in his car and drove about three miles from the office. Suddenly Murphy pulled over to the curb and stopped. Then he looked at me and said, "Get out."

"What?"

"Your attitude is bad, and there's only one way out. GOYA. Get out of this car and knock doors back to the office."

The last thing you want to do when you're down is the one thing that you have to do to get yourself up. GOYA. You get lucky when you go out and meet people. But I didn't know that then. After using every descriptive phrase I could think of, I got out of the car and started walking back to the office. I passed a few houses. Then I decided to knock on a door or two so I could tell Murph his system didn't work.

But of course when the first door opened, I couldn't blame my troubles on the lady who answered. I had to play my role. We talked, and I felt just a little bit better when I went on. By the time I got back to the office, I had picked up three very qualified leads and I felt good. I had worked myself out of my slump.

When you get down, it's because you've drifted away from the basics. You've stopped doing what you know you should be doing. It's strange how quickly salespeople can retire to executive administration. One good month does it—until reality hits in the form of a slump in sales. Then they start feeling guilty. That makes them tense. The tension causes them to get upset over things that have little or no real importance. The only problem is that they're coasting, not working. And, of course, they don't want to face up to that fact.

When you want to pull yourself up, get off your backside, go back to the basics, and do what you know you should do. It works every time. As soon as you start doing that, you start winning again. You see the money coming in. And you start ignoring minor annoyances and feeling good about yourself once more.

However, no matter how good your attitude is, no matter how resolutely you confront your difficulties, there will be days when things do not go right. On these days, a second problem will hit you before you can put the first one on the shelf, and then a third problem will slam into you. And another. And then it seems like there's no end to them.

Expect to have a few rough days in your selling career and you won't be disappointed. Just don't forget, while you're having one of those days, that if you'll keep on working, the tough period will pass and the good days will come back.

Are you a worry machine? Some people keep thinking, "Will I make it? Can I pay my bills?"

Stop worrying. Make up your mind that you won't worry anymore. When you've finished making your plans, think of something pleasant. Remember that planning creates success but worry kills. Spend your worry time relaxing. If you can't relax, spend the time training yourself to be more competent. If you're tempted to worry during business hours, stop, get a grip on yourself, and decide what is the most productive thing that you can do at that moment. Then do it. If you'll do these things, you'll soon have no need to worry about money because you'll be making more than ever. Don't worry yourself out of sales; work yourself into a successful career instead.

"What if —?" When you're afraid that something terrible may happen, sit down and accept that it will happen. Then outline all the things you can do to prevent it from happening. List those things in order of importance, and get busy doing them. If you'll follow that practice, none of your favorite nightmare what-ifs will ever come to pass.

If you're new in sales, realize that your work will soon become fun. Whether you're a physician or a salesperson, using skills confidently is fun. That's why the first of the ten steps in the GOYA system for unslumping starts with this one.

1. Become highly skilled at what you do. If you haven't perfected your knowledge and skill to the highest level you're capable of, how can you say that you're slumping? You don't need to get out of a slump in this case, all you need do is practice, drill, and rehearse. Get out of the unskilled mass of salespeople, and join the highly skilled elite who are impervious to slumps.

2. Burn the past daily. We're all tempted to dwell on the past, to make up lists of wilted hopes that all start with "If only —" Every time you feel this temptation, say to yourself, "That's dead and I've buried it. I can't change it, so now I'm going to think about something I can turn to my advantage." If you'll make that a habit, you'll start molding your future, you'll start making progress toward your goals, and you'll feel the special joy that comes only from being in control of your life.

3. Live in this moment. You can't live in your tomorrows. You can't live in your yesterdays. If you try to do either, the only thing you'll succeed in doing is ruining all your todays. Never forget that life is always this minute's consciousness. Whether you're ten or a hundred years old, today could be the last day. Your inventory might be counted tonight. So why be overly serious about the future? Enjoy this moment. You'll never have more than one moment at a time to enjoy.

4. Plan your future instead of worrying about it. Once you've made your plan, give it a solid shot all day every working day—and then enjoy your free time. If you don't want to plan for success and happiness, what right do you have to worry about non-success and unhappiness? If you're not planning where you want to be, what reason or excuse do you have for worrying about being nowhere? The biggest wasters of their own resources are the people who don't know who they want to be or where they want to go. Study how you want to have your life evolve. Then plan how you'll make it all happen. Schedule the time you'll work at creating what's success for you, and also schedule the time you'll devote to renewing your energy, rewarding yourself,' and enriching your sense of self worth. Then be sure you never allow worry to intrude on your moments of renewal, reward, and enrichment.

5. Don't demand fairness from life. "That's not fair" is one of the most idiotic statements in the English language.

"She's getting the best leads from the manager—that's not fair."

"They didn't call me back—that's not fair."

"He got the business because they went to college together—that's not fair."

Forget fair. Our world was not designed to be fair. If you demand it, and use that unanswered demand to excuse a lack of drive, you'll be miserable. You have to survive—if you're going to—in a world where there'll always be people above you and people below you in every facet of life you can name.

One of our Champions that I'm proudest of is Chuck Hill. Chuck will always have to use crutches when he walks because he had polio when he was two. That isn't fair. But Chuck doesn't sit around complaining how unfair polio is; he spends his time thinking about, and doing, everything he can do. And it turns out that what he can do is a whole lot. He's a leading salesperson in his office, a true Champion who's making a Champion's income and enjoying the good things it buys. At least once a week Check is out on the street canvassing—on crutches. If you're not out there prospecting as much as you should, what's your excuse? Imagine telling it to Chuck.

The first time I noticed him was in one of my real estate seminars. When we came to the part about prospecting door-to-door I remember thinking, "I wonder if he can make it." He made it, all right. Chuck Hill simply would not be denied.

Once in a while we should stop and be thankful for what we don't have. Some people out there are doing great in spite of heavier burdens than you carry. And, of course, there are also people out there with lighter burdens than you carry, and some of them have turned their lives into one long whine. That's the saddest story. Compared to one of those, Chuck Hill's story is a joy. And he's a greater joy to be with than any whiner I've ever met. People are amazing. Most of us are convinced that our problems are greater than anyone else's. They aren't—unless you're the guy in the iron lungh who can only move his eyebrows. So quit asking for fairness and stop letting your limitations depress you. Take what you've got and get what you want with it. If that means not paying the price for success, be happy with unsuccess. You were born to be happy, but no one else can make you happy for long. Only you can do that. Being happy is a personal responsibility; it's a duty you can't delegate. The only way you can keep happiness is to accept that reality.

6. Don't be guilty. If you're tempted to do something that will make you feel guilty, don't do it. However, if you decide to do it, also decide to enjoy it and forget the guilt. You need to be hardnosed about this. Push all the people back who'd love to drop a load of guilt on you for doing the normal things you have every right to do if you so choose.

7. Commit to high performance, and accept the consequences of that commitment. You can't be everywhere at once, and you'll have to learn how to say *no*. The best way is to say it straight out in a kindly tone: "No, I'm sorry, I can't fit that in. But thanks, anyway."

When you commit to high performance, you automatically put heavy pressure on your time and energy. We all have a tendency to keep on saying yes to our family, our customers, our boss, our friends, our associates. This means that the only person we say no to is ourselves. When you wind up having zero time for yourself, you're on a collision course with a crisis of will. When the crunch comes, you'll find yourself overwhelmed by demands. You won't have the willpower to meet those demands because you've failed to make it worthwhile to yourself to put out the great effort that's required. Take care of number one or you'll wind up not taking care of anyone.

8. Work on procrastination. Notice that I said *work on it*. You'll never overcome procrastination entirely because it's part of human nature to let a few things slide once in a while. And sometimes, when it's used with care, procrastination is a useful tactic. Many things respond best to no treatment at all, and a lot of pesky problems will disappear if we ignore them.

I suffer from procrastination occasionally. Sometimes I fly half the night to get to my next seminar, and then the next morning I don't want to learn the program I must learn. But I live by three words:

DO IT NOW.

Try them for 21 days and you'll start a whole new power pattern that will open up new vistas of opportunity for your future.

9. Keep your sense of humor growing. Our world is a riot of yuks. You can make it a habit to spot them and squeeze chuckles out of every possible situation. Or you can make it your habit to grind your teeth all day long except when you're licking your chops over bad news. Quick-to-laugh people get there faster and they get there fresher because they get more help along the way. Some people have difficulty building their sense of humor due to something held over in their personality from childhood. This is one of the easiest problems to solve that a person can have but, like any other, you have to work at this problem to solve it. Make sure you never miss a funny movie. Select TV programs for humor. Read things that make you laugh. Bookstores and libraries have large volumes of jokes and funny stories. Memorize one every day. Make friends with people who like to laugh, listen to their stories, and tell a few of your own. If you're Chief Iron Mouth you can't change overnight—but you can make a start tonight. Every morning and every night, tell yourself that you have a great sense of humor and it's getting better all the time. Also tell yourself that you love to laugh. Try this for three weeks and you'll own a wonderful new habit that'll put you on a highway running to financial success and greater happiness.

   10. Learn to love growth, change, and life. The truly successful person knows that growth, change, and life are interwoven; they are inseparable; they are one. Reader, friend, Champion-to-be, the methods in this book make whatever future you're willing to order yours for the taking. With these ideas and techniques you can write a check payable in your own effort for your chosen future—and be sure it will arrive. Accept this idea. Have complete faith in it. And, most important of all, act on it. You can have whatever future you're willing to GOYA for.

20

THE MOST NECESSARY
SKILL OF ALL

For years I've been asked: How did you get it all together and do all you've done?

I don't believe people ask in idle curiosity. I think they have the same reason that compelled me when I was twenty-one to ask much the same question of an extremely successful corporate executive: a sincere desire to learn how to make my own dreams come true.

The average human being has the ability to achieve almost anything. Lack of basic capability is rarely the problem—we all have great reserves of untapped power. The problem is almost always in finding out what you want. Before we go any further, let me define how I'm using the word *want* here. I'm not talking about mere wishes now, I'm talking about wants that gnaw at you.

Maybe you think you don't have any gnawing wants. If you think that, you're wrong. You have the wants. But they're bottled up where you can't get at them. Your early experiences and training poured them in and pounded the cork home. And there they sit, building pressure for their next destructive burst of envy and vindictiveness. They may leak out as blind resistance to change, stubborn refusal to put out extra effort, and instant insistence that all your problems are caused by others. Instead of trying to bottle your true wants, learn to understand them. From such understanding springs the knowledge of how to use this vital force to power your drive for greater things. Your drive has to come from this source: there is no other that works for long.

It's often the fear of failure that makes us bottle up our wants. But failure isn't the worst possible result. Not trying is. If you try you can succeed; if you won't try you have already failed. Do you suffer from this fear? Then decide in advance that you've failed—and after that go out and give it the best try you're capable of.

Lots of us are willing to risk failure but we still don't exert ourselves. We don't see any reason to. Why? Because we wouldn't do anything very exciting or satisfying with success if we could win it. If that's your problem, you need to give it a lot of attention. Finding the answer will take deep thinking. Widen your horizons, seek out new friends and activities, and search for unthought of rewards that will make success worth its price to you. The pivot point here is finding what will motivate your own unique personality. Many of us are so blinded by what society and other people think we should want that we can't hear our own cries for help. Getting in touch with your true self must be your first priority.

If you really want something, that want will make a difference in your life. You'll work to satisfy that want. You'll sacrifice pleasures for it. You'll even be willing to change and grow for it. In fact, you'll deliberately change yourself and grow so that you can have what you really want. But you won't do any of these things for mere wishes. That's why you must put what you think you want on paper. Then look at your goals, written there in black and white, and commit to them. You're not done yet. It's no good to write pages of goals down somewhere and then go on about your old routine as though nothing had happened.

Every day, look at each goal. Think whether you're doing what has to be done, whether you're paying the price that has to be paid. It doesn't matter at this point whether or not you already possess all the abilities and resources you must have if you're to achieve your goal—those you can pick up along the way. But you won't start without having the desire. The first step is to commit to the goal **in writing**. The great majority of people never once in their lives will take this simple first step on the journey to achievement. For this reason alone, they'll never take the last step that brings them what they wish for. Apathy stifles more careers than inability ever does.

In recent years we've heard quite a bit about people who can't find themselves. Confusion about identity keeps millions of people operating far below their potential, and helps pay the rent for the nation's psychoanalysts. Some people really need professional help in this area. Most of us would do better to bury the past and concentrate on getting in touch with what we really want from the future.

Since you can't unleash your creativity or accelerate your growth until you commit yourself to a goal, any positive goal is better than no goal at all. You'll probably make many false starts before you discover the course that'll keep you happily involved for the rest of your life. That's wonderful. All the time that you're committed to written goals, you're growing rapidly. You're experiencing much. Striving on the field, you're learning a ton for every pound the apathetic person learns sitting in the bleachers of life. Every moment that you're playing the great game of living to the fullest, you're charging toward an understanding of your best potential, of what your finest destiny is. Allowing ourselves to bury our lives in apathy is the greatest crime—and we commit it by not committing ourselves to goals that are real to us.

You can achieve almost any goal you have the courage to set—but sometimes it takes a painful experience to light the way.

That was so in my case. When I was seventeen years old I broke my father's heart. He had saved enough from a very average income to send me to college to become an attorney; ninety days later I was home telling him that I had quit college—and for the first time I saw him cry. With tears in his eyes he said, "Son, I'm always going to love you even though you'll never amount to anything."

That was my first motivational speech.

When I walked out of that room, I was burning with something not everyone has the chance to feel. I didn't just want to succeed—I had to succeed.

But I couldn't see how to do it. I became a bridge deck specialist and carried steel up construction ramps for eighteen months—and all the time my father's words were eating at me. I had a wage job that led nowhere except to old age.

I went into sales—and the wages stopped. I earned nothing because that's what I knew about my profession. Then, just as I was going under for the third time in sales, the man came by and sold me on the Edwards training seminar. I went, I learned the closes and techniques, I lost no time putting them to work. Soon after that, I started tasting the sweet fruits of success for the first time.

Some time later, I told the management of the company where I worked that my goal was to meet personally with Mr. Edwards. They arranged it for me. When the day came, I told him, "Mr. Edwards, my goal is to someday take your place and someday be able to train people as well as you trained me."

That all came to pass because I set goals to make it happen. Committing to the goal was the essential element. You can't rise unless you set goals that make you stretch.

Start with short-term goals. My first goal in sales—beyond making enough to eat and cover my back—was to buy a new car. Autos make great starting goals but, unfortunately, they often become the end goal. There's more to life than rolling around town in an expensive car. A lot of average salespeople set average goals, achieve them, and then fade into a state of suspended animation. Like a bear in winter, they go to ground and live off their fat. The true Champion keeps setting new goals whenever he achieves old ones. Achieved goals are like yesterday's newspapers: useful only for lining bird cages.

In this most necessary of all skills, effective goal setting, some rules must be followed if the system is to work. Here they are:

1. **If it's not in writing, it's not a goal.** An unwritten want is a wish, a dream, a never-happen. The day you put your goal in writing is the day it becomes a commitment that will change your life.

2. **If it's not specific, it's not a goal.** As I found out carrying steel on my shoulder, broad desires and lofty aims have no effect. Merely wanting to be somebody, or having the determination to make it big, isn't enough. Until you translate your vague wishes into concrete goals and plans, you aren't going to make much progress.

3. **"Goals must be believable."** Now I'm quoting Doug Edwards on one of the most vital aspects of successful goal setting. If you don't believe that you can achieve a goal, you won't pay the price for it.

4. **An effective goal is an exciting challenge.** If your goal doesn't push you beyond where you've been before—if it doesn't demand your best and a bit more you didn't realize you had in you—it isn't going to change your ways and elevate your lifestyle.

5. **Goals must be adjusted to new information.** Set your goals quickly, and adjust them later if you've aimed too high or too low. Many of the goals that have the greatest positive influence on our lives are those we set in unfamiliar territory. As we learn more about the realities, we adjust our goals down if they become unbelievable, or up if they lose their challenge because they're too easy. But we don't put off setting goals until we know more.

6. **Dynamic goals guide our choices.** We live in a world that constantly threatens to overwhelm us with alternatives. If you want something badly enough, you'll turn off the TV to get it. If your goals are set up right, they'll instantly show you the right way to go on most decisions.

7. **Don't set short term goals for more than ninety days.** After you've worked with short-term goals for half a year, you may find that a shorter or longer period works better for you. Ninety days is the period that works for me. If I set a short-term goal that takes more than ninety days to achieve, I tend to lose interest in it.

8. **Maintain a balance between long-term and short-term goals.** Your wants for clothes, cars, savings accounts, vacations, and all sorts of material possessions make great short-term goals that put excitement and frequent gratification into your goals program. If your goals are all long-term, you'll have difficulty keeping your performance up because all your payoffs are hidden in the fog of the future.

9. **Include your loved ones in your goals.** You'll be amazed at how hard you can work when your kids know that they get a bite of the larger pie if you reach your goal. When their goals are intimately involved with your goals, they'll buck you up when you need encouragement.

10. **Set goals in all areas of your life.** They aren't just for making money. Set goals for health, for exercise, for sports, in your personal life, and in your family and spiritual life. This is a system that works with astonishing power *if it's used*. It's simply too valuable to reserve only for your career objectives.

11. **Your goals must harmonize.** If they fight each other, you lose. Whenever you detect a conflict, set priorities that will eliminate the conflict. Use your goals program to get rid of frustration, not to create it.

12. **Review your goals regularly.** Remember that your long-term goals can only be achieved if they are the culmination of your short-term goals, and that your new goals will rise out of the old ones you've realized. In the future, you'll set short-term aims that are far beyond your present capacity—and you'll achieve them with the skill, confidence, and resources you've won achieving your present goals.

13. **Set vivid goals.** Excitement is the basic ingredient of successful goal-setting. You won't stretch for the ho-hums of life, will you?

My first flight was from California to Arizona to make one of my early speeches. Since then I've made hundreds of flights I can't remember, but I'll never forget that one. Perhaps you can remember your first flight. Were you white-knuckled? I was.

Just before we took off, I looked out of the window. Sitting on the runway nearby was a beautiful little plane. I asked the man sitting next to us about it.

"That's a corporate jet," he said.

"What a neat little number," I said, taking out my goals notebook. In it I wrote "Ten year goal—Jet."

It's surprising—no, it's amazing—how goals work if you put them in writing and concentrate on them for a few moments every morning or evening. I'll never forget when the jet arrived—ten years later to the day. I had just completed a program with a large audience in Baton Rouge. As soon as I walked off the stage, I hurried out to the airfield in time to see a beautiful little plane come in and land.

The Captain welcomed me aboard and off we went. "This is it," I thought, "Ten years and I've arrived."

14. **Don't chisel your goals in granite.** A lot of people put off setting goals every time they think about it because they're afraid. Remember that you aren't swearing on oath that'll cause your ears to fall off if you decide to change a goal later. I'll never forget the first time we refueled the jet. The pilot came back and handed me a bill for $882.00.

I said, "This is for the month?"

It wasn't for the month.

That long-term goal turned out to be a $30,000 a month item, which is why we only had it sixty days. What had once been a vivid and compelling goal, on realization turned out to be just another toy—and a ridiculously expensive one at that for my kind of activity. It had no place in my new aspirations. There are times when we have to change goals to conform to our growing awareness of what's really important in our lives. Your goal-setting and goal-achieving program is a lifelong commitment to growth. That growth will take unexpected turns, and your future holds achievements that you haven't yet thought about.

15. **Reach out into the future.** The whole idea of setting goals is to plan your life rather than to go on bumbling along, muddling through, taking it as it comes. Begin by setting twenty-year goals.

First, list the personal achievements you want to accomplish. Who and what do you want to be in twenty years? What do you want to own? Where, and in what kind of housing, do you want to live? Again, you're working with goals that can be changed. What are the status symbols you've always dreamed of? What do you want for your family? If you don't know what you want, how can you get it?

Start thinking about the net worth you want to have twenty years down the road. Start watching your equity position now and get ready for the future. It only happens when you start writing down goals, working with them, and causing your mind to reach out. Take a hard look at the future and at yourself. Say, "That's the person I want to be in twenty years, and I'm willing and eager to pay the price to become that person."

Once you have your twenty-year goals sketched out, cut them in half and there are your ten-year goals.

Halve them again and you've got your five-year goals. Do it one more time and your thirty-month goals appear before your eyes.

Then set up your next-twelve-months' goals. Work on this one carefully. Then break your one-year schedule of goals down to months, weeks, and finally to goals for tomorrow and for each day of the coming week.

16. **Have a set of goals for every day, and review results every night.** You may be thinking, "This will take a lot of time. Will it be worth it?"

Is making a success of your life worth a little trouble? But let's be honest—it's not the trouble that's bothering you, it's the idea of submitting to any form of discipline, even self-imposed discipline. Think that through before you turn away from this idea, because if you're not willing to accept your own discipline, you're not going to accomplish two percent of what you could—and you're going to miss out on ninety-eight percent of the good things you could have.

17. **Train yourself to crave your goals.** Spend time (odd moments when you're driving, waiting, and so on) visualizing yourself possessing what you've set your goals for. The more ardently you desire your goals, the more ready you'll be to pay the price you must pay to get them.

18. **Set activity goals, not production goals.** How many people will you see today? How many demonstrations will you give? How many rejections will you go looking for? If all your goals are production goals, you're setting yourself up for a slump. A few lost sales, a change in competitive conditions, and you're hopelessly behind, you're feeling guilty, and you don't want to even think about the system. But if your daily and weekly goals are based on activity (on the number of prospecting calls to be made, the number of presentations to be given, and so on) you'll keep on meeting your goals during problem periods. Because you're active, you'll adjust to the new conditions faster and sell yourself out of the slump before it can get you down.

19. **Understand luck, and make it work for you.** Do you know that the really successful people, the big winners, the ones who are achieving their goals, all believe that they understand luck? It's really very simple. You begin by always expecting good things to happen. You don't rely on having good luck, you expect it. This means that you prepare carefully, keep lots of things going, and stay alert for Lady Luck's whispers. You never expect trouble — you plan ways to prevent it. Do you know that some people have been proven to be accident-prone? And why are they? Because they spend so much time thinking about getting hurt that their subconscious minds get confused, and act like that's what they want to have happen.

The winners understand that good luck is a manufactured article. So they think in terms of good things happening to them and make themselves good-luck-prone. Always make your subconscious mind work for you.

20. **Start now.** Give goal setting two hours of concentrated thought today. Then set aside ten minutes a day for the next twenty-one days to review and revise your goals. After that, two minutes a day, plus one hour a week, will keep you flying toward the immensely greater and richer future that the goal-setting system will deliver if you follow these rules. Go to it. You'll have a terrific year if you have 365 fulfilling days in which you achieve your daily goals. And on into the future, as one terrific year follows another. What an exciting prospect! And it'll all be yours if you'll just start setting your goals **now.**

21
HOW TO SELL TO THE MOST IMPORTANT PEOPLE YOU KNOW

Now that you're rapidly becoming a professional salesperson who's earning a professional's income, your inner private self is changing just as your outer public self is changing. Adjustments will be required in many areas of your life. As this happens, you may discover that the more you achieve outside your home, the less you achieve inside your family or within your circle of friends. If this seems to be happening, maybe it's because you haven't been making full use of your new sales skills. They aren't only for work. Don't turn them off when you head for home—turn them on.

At this point in your life, you may be single. You may be living where you have few relatives or friends. If you're not satisfied with your social situation, use salesmanship to improve it. With a little thought, a little ingenuity, most of the techniques in the previous chapters can be adapted to the after-hours scene. There they can do wonders in helping you achieve your private-life objectives.

In order to be a master of the art of selling, you must be able to sell effectively to the most important people in the world—your friends and loved ones.

Sell them what?

On whatever you believe is best for them. On achieving their own goals. On leading happy, fulfilled lives. On keeping pace with you—or on accepting and respecting themselves as they are.

You may think it's enough to bring home a professional's income, that your responsibilities are over when you've worked long and hard. If you have loved ones, this cannot be the case. You and your devoted concern are irreplaceable in your family. If your swiftly rising career allows you less time with your loved ones or friends than you'd like, make every minute you do have with them count. *I must do the most productive thing possible at every given moment* applies with great force to your private life. The most productive thing at some moments is holding your small child and teaching him how to overcome fear; at others, it's saying to someone special, "I'll always love you." For an infinity of reasons such as these, this last chapter is devoted to how you can apply the principles in this book to enhancing your home life.

Let's clarify exactly what we're talking about. After you internalize and reinforce the attitudes and techniques in the preceding chapters, you'll automatically use them now and then with your loved ones. But it's one thing to use them catch-as-catch-can in the daily rush of living; it's another thing entirely to put these powerful techniques to work as part of a plan to solve family problems and achieve family goals. We're concerned here with the deliberate use of your new sales skills in this most important area of your life.

While you've been growing fast professionally and personally, your spouse may have continued to amble along at his or her usual pace. Maybe that's fine with you. If it isn't, start now to bridge the gulf that's opening between you and your mate. Later may be too late.

There are basically only three ways that you can cope with this situation successfully: (1) you can slow down, (2) your spouse can speed up, (3) you can both accept that you'll be growing at different speeds and be happy about it. Only the first alternative is completely within your control—probably the least attractive of the three to you. The other two can't work unless your mate participates willingly. Making this happen often calls for highly skilled sales work: discovery questions, minor closes, leading questions, top-notch objection-handling, major closes—not to mention lots of thought and the giving of much approval and encouragement.

If your spouse feels threatened by the new person you're becoming, have empathy. Be patient. Bear in mind that you can't dictate other people's feelings—but you can relieve their anxieties as to how you feel about them.

Early in this book we discussed the value of learning what benefits your prospects really want before you try to sell them a specific product or service. This same step is equally valuable to the creation of an atmosphere in which every member of your family will expand in accomplishment and confidence. As you've learned here, there are no limits to your growth except the limits that you impose on yourself. Those limits, of course, are your willingness to pay the price of achievement. Do you want to fasten additional limits on your children by dictating what achievements they should pursue?

Never lose sight of these facts: you can't live someone else's life; you can't control someone else's emotions; you can't pay the price for someone else's achievements. Much as we love our children and our friends, each of them is a separate individual with goals, preferences, limitations, and opportunities that differ from our own. As my father and I discovered after he guided me toward becoming an attorney, success wears many different suits. Your children can't achieve your goals for you. Neither can your friends. You can only help them all achieve their goals for themselves.

The preceding chapters are loaded with techniques and concepts that can help you lead your family toward achieving whatever goals you and they want. I'll briefly recap a few of these ideas.

Tie-downs. Use them when talking with your family to reinforce the positive things you want to have happen, and to discourage the negative things you don't want to have happen. Leading people is largely the business of getting them to realize, and then to agree, that what you propose is best for them.

Alternate Advance. This technique is a real beauty in home use. Compare these two ways of handling the same situation:

(1) **Wife:** "Honey, do you want to go out to dinner tonight?"

Husband: "No. I want to eat here."

   Wife: "You never take me out. I work too—or have you forgotten?" And they're off to another argument brought on by a say-no question.

(2) **Wife:** "Honey, would you like to have dinner at The Blue Bucket, or would you rather eat at Smokey Jo's?"

Husband: "Let's go to The Blue Bucket." When an alternate advance will get what you want, why ask a say-no?

Porcupine. This technique is a real workhorse for clarifying domestic issues and avoiding unwise family decisions. Very often, your best answer to a question around the house is another question that's also an alternate advance toward what you want to achieve.

Involvement Questions. When you want to invest time and money in something for the both of you, excite your spouse about the project with involvement questions. When you want to encourage your children to achieve, ask them involvement questions about the goal that's under consideration.

Discovery questions and leading questions. Intense listening is the key to discovering what your prospects really want. Intense listening to your loved ones is just as important if you're serious about strengthening your relationships with them. In many cases, an unruly child simply wants to know that his feelings of frustration, anger, or disappointment are understood by his parent. Acknowledging the distress is often all that a wise mother or father has to do to relieve his child's feelings and restore calm. It may take more. But how can you know unless you ask discovery questions and then listen intensely to the answers? When you know precisely what the problem is—but not before—you're fully competent to lead your child in the way you want him to go.

In chapter 6 we talked about catching change on the move as you work with prospects. This is also a key concept for influencing your family. Probably the easiest and most effective way that you can have a long-lasting good effect on your loved ones is to encourage them to pay the price to achieve goals they've found for themselves. The first few steps beyond mere wishing are the hardest. Miss no opportunity to motivate your loved ones to act instead of watch when it's within their ability. The more they do today, the more they can and will accomplish tomorrow.

Many of us have been taught that we should always go with the logical choice, that relying on our emotions is somehow bad. Logic and careful analysis are supposedly the only ways to make decisions; intuition and the emotions must be left out. This destructive idea ignores reality. In the real world, we rarely have the complete facts when we have to make a decision. We're forced to fall back on our emotions and intuition. This makes us worry and feel guilty. Avoid this by guiding your children toward striking a balance between logic and emotion in decision making.

The do-nothing twins, apathy and inertia, thrive on the denial of emotional involvement. When we foster the belief that emotions are dangerous, we create frustrations that often paralyze our children's efforts. Whenever your loved ones want to do something positive, encourage them if you possibly can. Discover what rewards will motivate them and go with the best you can afford. Arouse their emotions to help them achieve their goal, and teach them how to use their emotions to psyche themselves up. Success is a habit. There's no better one that you can pass on to them.

Use go-ahead terms on your family instead of rejection words. By developing positive communication within your family, you'll discover the rejection words that wound and defeat your spouse and children. Every time you spot one of these discouraging words, think of a go-ahead term to replace it, and use that from then on. Finding and saying go-ahead things instead of rejection things will have a wonderful effect on your family's happiness and ability to cope with problems, to achieve goals, and to be happy. You'll get a bonus for doing this. It's great training for your professional sales work; you can't fail to profit from becoming more sensitive to other people's feelings and needs.

I haven't recounted all the ways that this book's concepts and techniques can help you attain a richer and more fulfilling lifestyle for your family. Reread it with that idea in mind and you'll find new insights every time you do so. You can become a Champion of sales, a Champion parent or friend, and a Champion wife or husband. It's all yours. All you have to do is pay the price and you can have your finest goals.

22
FIVE MORE POWER CLOSES
FOR ASPIRING CHAMPIONS

What is the greatest and most widespread urge that all buyers share? The feeling that they must say *no*. As you develop your skills further, and rise from above-average to a Champion's level, it's imperative that you realize the absolute truth of these two statements:

All buyers feel and act on the urge to say no at first. With rare exceptions, every buyer-contact you make during your entire sales career will begin with that person being committed to rejecting whatever you're proposing.

Before you can approach a Champion's performance, you must understand and be comfortable with those two realities. Make no mistake here; all Champions are very comfortable with the two facts given above. They know that the say-no-first habits of all buyers are their only source of job security, and their only guarantee that successful sales work will continue to offer great rewards. If you want to be a Champion, get comfortable with those two ideas.

In other words, the noes that buyers flip out so easily are the raw material of your trade. Without their inevitability, you have no economic function to perform: brochures and videotapes could do it all. When those noes come to you they are like rough stones to a diamond cutter. To fashion the most valuable gems from those rough stones, that is, the largest possible sales from your buyers' noes, you must work with a diamond cutter's precision.

Now you've been forewarned. Now you know that you'll have noes to contend with every day of your sales career. Now you're aware of the enormous value they have for you. So throw yourself into learning how to convert those predictable negatives into equally predictable positives. What this book is all about, and what your sales career is all about, comes down to converting noes into yeses—am I right?

Another very important truth is contained in these approximate figures: fifty percent of your sales will result from closes that handle major objections; forty percent will come about because of your ability to overcome procrastination; ten percent will be gained through your ability to alter outright rejection. Your exact percentages will vary a little, but they'll still emphasize the necessity for using multiple closing techniques. Please keep this fact constantly in mind as you prepare for and work with selling situations: the world's highest-paid salespeople make most of their sales on the fifth major closing attempt.

When their first major close fails they move smoothly into a bridging sequence, taking as much time as is necessary to prepare the way for taking another carefully aimed shot at the target. Then they play their second major close. It also fails. Without feeling any dismay or loss of enthusiasm, they move easily into another thoroughly practiced bridging sequence. When the timing seems right, the world's highest-paid salespeople run off their third major close, which fails as quickly as the first two did. So they instantly and warmly go into another completely different phraseology to set up their next attempt to cinch the sale.

Sensing another closing opportunity a short time later, they pump in their fourth close. It too fails—and they confidently use another transition phraseology to prepare the way for yet another try. At the next propitious moment, they fire off their fifth major close and, even though they've failed four times in a row, they aren't discouraged, tense, or desperate as they do so—and this time it works. They close the sale, as they expected to, on their fifth major closing attempt.

Remember that we are speaking here of qualified buyers who need and can afford the product or service in question. Do the world's highest-paid salespeople quit if they fail to close after their fifth try?

You know the answer to that one, don't you? Superchampions have more closes than the space shuttle has tiles. The world's highest-paid salespeople never stop practicing, improving, and adding to their closes. They also have plenty of bridging sequences rehearsed so a few discouraging words won't derail their train as it rolls confidently from one close to another. Nothing will do more to raise your sales performance than having a battery of proven closes at your disposal that you've practiced until their use is completely reflexive.

Here's the formula for multiple closing:

First, present your close, If it is rejected, apologize warmly, and begin building your foundation for the next closing attempt. Two examples:

"I'm sorry. Please don't feel that I'm pushing you. I'm not. But I am sincerely excited about this opportunity for you, so what do you feel I haven't made clear?"

"Forgive me—I didn't mean to seem overly-aggressive. However, all indicators point to this being a wise decision for you, so please tell me what areas I haven't fully satisfied you about."

Multiple closes must be separated by bridging sequences or they won't be effective. Practice your separating speeches until you find yourself swinging into them automatically—reflexively—every time you get a no to your latest closing attempt. What is a bridging sequence? It's any rehearsed patter that lets you cross over the river of their latest *no* and keep on traveling down the road to the sale. Top level salespeople give bridging sequences the attention and preparation they deserve, knowing that their next close won't be any better than the bridging sequence they use to lead into it.

A good bridging sequence is one that you feel comfortable with, one that comes naturally to you—after you've carefully thought it out and rehearsed it. Many fine ones begin by acknowledging what the prospect has just said. Making a quick apology for pressing too hard often clears the air. Some excellent bridging sequences move quickly into changing the emotional climate. Others review a benefit that you've confirmed is important to the prospect you're selling to, or ask the prospect to name the most important benefits he or she sees in your offering.

When you're meeting in the prospect's office and you need to bridge from a no to your next closing attempt, avoid bringing up subjects that are completely unrelated to the business at hand. Average salespeople often respond to a *no* by changing the subject, thus taking the prospect completely off the hook. Sometimes they comment on a recent event in the news, tell a joke, or relate a personal anecdote. Do that with busy buyers and you'll discover that you've wound up the interview and bridged yourself right out the door. Practice, drill, and rehearse to handle the noes smoothly and to avoid dismissing yourself. Chitchat makes a safe bridge only when your meeting is under circumstances that prevent its abrupt termination, such as presenting your proposal over lunch or discussing it while riding with your client to a demonstration.

Now let's get into some more closes, powerful ones that will do the job for you. You can't know too many. New closes are constantly coming along, and you'll develop some of your own as you become a Champion salesperson. After you've mastered the twelve power closes in chapter 15, put these five extra bullets in your bandoleer. Any one of them might be the only shot that can knock over the rhinoceros you'll be hunting tomorrow.

1. THE "NO" CLOSE

Have you ever had a prospect give you a flat "No!" without another word to soften it? Sooner or later you will. Think about this in advance so that hard *no* won't be unnerving when it slams into you. More often, you'll hear it softened somewhat like this: "Everything seems fine, and yes, it's true, we do need your product (or service), but I just have to say *no*." For these occasions, learn this powerhouse close of the super pro. For maximum effectiveness, learn it word for word.

"Mr. Billings, there are many salespeople representing many products and they all have good and persuasive reasons for you to invest in their products or services, haven't they?

"And you, Mr. Billings, can say *no* to any or all of them, can't you? My position as a (name your product or service) professional is quite different. You see, my experience representing (your company's name) has taught me an overwhelming truth: No one say say *no* to me—they can only say *no* to themselves or their company.

"How can I accept that kind of a *no?*—Tell me, Mr. Billings, if you were me, would you let Mr. Billings say *no* to anything that is so important to his . . .?" (End this statement with the word or phrase that has the greatest emotional power to describe the benefits you're there to sell. Use such terms as: *life, health, happiness, loved ones, family, security, future profits, business, success, competitive survival, financial growth, career advancement, personal achievement.)*

2. THE "IT ISN'T IN THE BUDGET" CLOSE

Here's one that must be in the repertoire of every salesperson calling on companies, institutions, or governmental agencies during these times of tight money. It's designed to be used when you're working with the president or owner of a business, or with an upper management executive of a large company or institution. When you're told that your product or service isn't in the budget, respond in a cordial manner with these words:

"Of course it isn't. That's why I contacted you in the first place."

Don't pause here. But how you proceed depends on whether you're selling to a profit-seeking company or a non-profit organization. Let's look at the commercial and industrial application first.

Continuation for use with companies: "I'm fully aware that every well-managed business firm controls its money with a carefully-planned budget. Am I also right in assuming that the chief executive of a productive, trend-setting company such as yours uses that budget as a guideline, not as an inflexible anchor?

"So you, as the chief executive, retain for yourself the right to flex that budget in the interest of your company's financial present and competitive future, isn't that right?

"What we have been discussing is a system that will give (name the buyer's company) an immediate and continuing competitive edge. Tell me, Mr. Chamberlain, under these conditions will your budget flex—or is it an anchor?"

Continuation for non-profit institutions and governmental agencies: "I'm fully aware that every well-managed institution controls its money with a carefully-planned budget. I'm also fully aware that your office (agency, institution, district) is very responsive to the public's rapidly-changing needs. Isn't it true that you have this reputation?"

After the response, go on with, "This means that you, as the chief executive of such an effective organization, must be using the budget more as a guideline for expenditures than as an inflexible anchor. How else could your public be gaining the benefits of new developments and new technologies as quickly as they are gaining them through your facilities now?

"So you, as the chief executive, retain for yourself the right to flex the budget to allow your organization to carry out its responsibilities in the most efficient manner possible.

"What we have been discussing is a system that will give immediate and continuing cost savings (gains in attendance, increases in visitor security and comfort—whatever your benefits are). Tell me, Mrs. Spencer, under these conditions, will your budget flex—or is it an anchor?"

3. THE PERSONAL INFLATION CLOSE

The greatest problem—and opportunity—facing most of us today is inflation. Inflation has been called the Robin Hood of the 80's, but it robs the ignorant and gives to the well-informed. As a Superchampion, you'll realize that inflation can and must be used as a motivation for buying in today's decision-making process. Learn and use this close if you're active in personal sales:

"The most critical decisions we have to make today are money decisions, aren't they? We no longer have the luxury of deciding between three possibilities—to save, spend, or invest. Today, because of inflation, we can no longer decide to just save it, and I'm sure you know why, don't you?"

(Pause for response.)

"That's right! As economic factors increase inflation, every dollar we have saved is worth less than it was when we earned it, isn't that true?"

(Pause for response.)

"Today, we must make whatever money we have left after meeting our daily expenses *do something positive* for us. And isn't it true that we only have two choices? We can find ourselves an investment that will provide a return greater than the inflation rate—rather tough if we aren't wealthy, isn't it? Or we can use the money to improve our standard of living.

"Now, we've found that you really want (name your product or service). Tell me, are you—or are you not—entitled to a reward for all the work you've been doing?"

(Pause for response.)

"Right again. The next question is, will you take that reward, or will you let inflation have it?"

4. THE BUSINESS INFLATION CLOSE

If you're in the commercial or industrial selling field, add this close to your trouble-shooting kit.

"Along with the government's bureaucratic regulation, inflation is one of our major business concerns, isn't it?"

(Pause for response.)

"Then tell me, is this a problem that's unique to your business?"

(Pause for response.)

"Then am I correct in assuming that all of your competitors are faced with this same inflation problem?"

(Pause for response.)

"Would this statement be wrong? When your entire industry is fighting the same problem, some companies will cope better with that problem than the others will."

(Pause for response.)

"That's right! Now, hasn't my entire objective been to provide you with a method of gaining a competitive edge? And gaining edges— gaining any edge, large or small—is the only way you'll make this company do a better job than the rest of the industry, isn't that right?"

5. THE STATE OF THE ECONOMY CLOSE

Far too many people today are living in a state of fear. In fact, the care and feeding of fear is one of this period's fastest-growing industries. Some people are determined optimists, others are equally determined pessimists, but most of the public swings back and forth. Without question, the news media's soothsayer-of-doom attitude has immobilized much of the decision-making power that thousands of influential people have.

With the vast majority of people who vacillate between fear and enthusiasm by the hour—or even by the minute—you can break that decision-making power loose. This close is designed to do that. However, it won't reach a confirmed pessimist—but they're in the minority and you can't sell them anything except bullets and bad news anyway.

Here's the close for everyone in the middle: (Confirmed optimists also like to hear this one.)

"Yes, I know that the media is constantly selling everyone on fear during this recession and inflationary period—and that fear itself is creating a deeper recession, don't you agree?

"Tell me if you have ever had the media explain this truth: a great percentage of today's giant corporations, of today's outstanding marketeers, and of today's foremost salespeople, gained their original momentum during a periods of economic upset. That original momentum then carried them to greatness. Yes, while others were saying *no* to everything, these great ones learned the *yes* habit. Did you realize this truth?"

(Pause for response.)

"It seems to boil down to this: *No* has always been the first two letters of *no*thing. I don't like what nothing implies. Would I be right in assuming that you don't like the meaning of *no* either?"

INDEX

Mr. Hopkins conducts sales training seminars and motivational programs internationally. When time is available, he also accepts a limited number of personal speaking engagements.

A complete sales training program entitled "How to Master the Art of Selling Anything" is also available for both individual and company use on audio cassettes and on video tape.

For information on Tom Hopkins sales training seminars, video tape training programs, and personal-use audio cassette albums, call or write:

Tom Hopkins Champions Unlimited
P.O. Box 1969
Scottsdale, Arizona 85252
(602) 949-0786

BESTSELLERS TO HELP YOU
GET TO THE TOP

WORKING WARDROBE   *large format paperback*
by Janet Wallach   *(J37-253, $8.95, U.S.A.)*
                                            (J37-277, $10.75, Canada)

Affordable clothes that work for you! At last! Here is an easy way to
build the wardrobe you want and need. In *Working Wardrobe* noted
designer and fashion director Janet Wallach introduces her Capsule
Concept. It's a simple formula that will help you make over 40 different
outfits from just twelve pieces of clothing.

Learn how to coordinate colors, fabrics, shapes; mix and match jackets,
skirts, blouses, sweaters, dresses; build upon and organize what you
already own; add flexibility to your wardrobe for both day and night;
adapt the Capsule Concept to your personal life-style; revitalize your
image; select styles that fit your taste and figure; and buy all-season,
natural fibers for year-round efficiency. *Working Wardrobe* is your key
to looking better, feeling more confident, and moving up in social and
business life.

DRESS FOR SUCCESS
by John T. Molloy   *(K30-511, $3.95)*

The # 1 book to make you look like a million so you can *make* a million
will: make it easier for many men to sell everything better; open doors
to the executive suite to men for whom they are now closed; make the
right wardrobe less expensive; give women a simple, sensible guide to
buying men's clothing; and teach men how women like them to dress.

THE WOMAN'S DRESS FOR SUCCESS BOOK
by John T. Molloy   *large format paperback*
                                            (K37-171, $5.95)

Here Mr. Molloy reveals to you advice his clients pay a minimum of
$800 a day to learn, such as: what to wear to get that promotion; how to
compare quality and price to get the best buy; how to avoid fashion
industry rip-offs; when and where to wear a suit, dress or pants; what
shoes to wear and what accessories bring the most success; and even
what to wear to attract that "certain" man.

FOR YOUR CAREER
FROM WARNER BOOKS

OVERCOMING THE FEAR OF SUCCESS *(K97-998, $5.95, U.S.A.)*
by Martha Friedman *(K37-336, $6.95, Canada)*

• Are you always late, no matter how hard you try to be on time?

• Are you a perfectionist?

• Do you procrastinate?

• Do you fear intimacy or closeness?

If you said yes to any of these questions, chances are you have a fear of success. Psychotherapist Martha Friedman tells us in plain language how we unconsciously sabotage our chances for success, how to recognize and overcome our hidden fears, and how to discover true fulfillment in love, work, and play.

INC. YOURSELF
How to Profit by Setting Up
Your Own Corporation *large format paperback*
Judith H. McQuown *(K97-817, $5.95)*

In easy-to-understand terms, Judith H. McQuown, an expert in the field of money management, explains the dollars-and-cents advantages of incorporating yourself:

• Getting "free" life and disability insurance

• Setting up your own tax-sheltered pension and profit-sharing plans

• Obtaining greater benefits than you get through the Keogh plan

• Generating legitimate "cashless" tax deductions

• Incorporate without a lawyer.